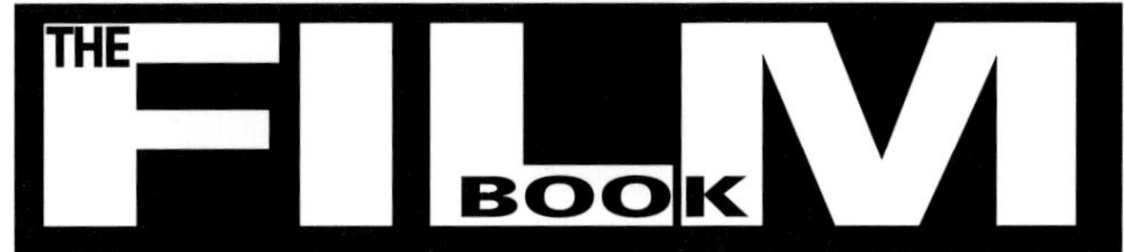
THE FILM BOOK

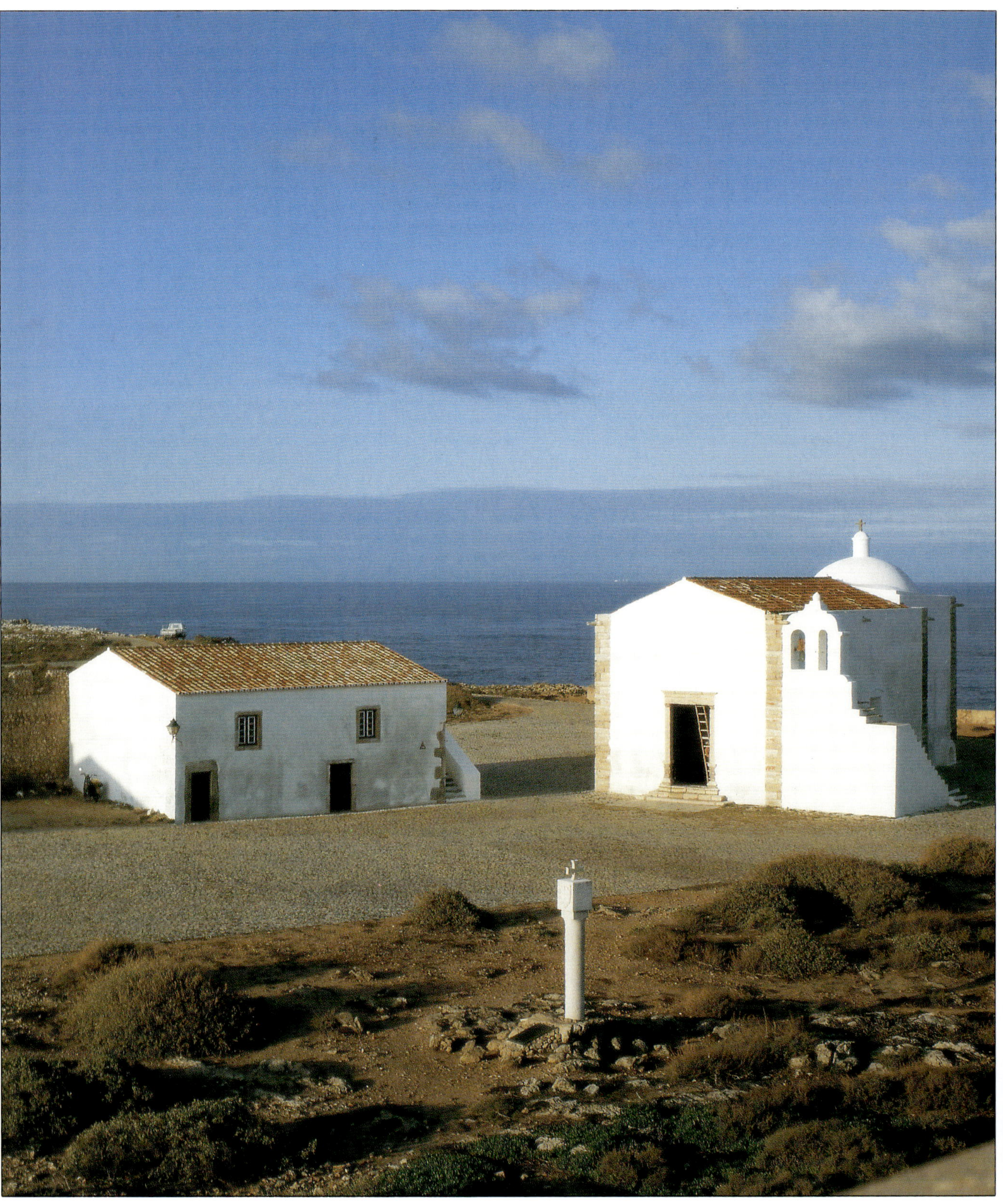

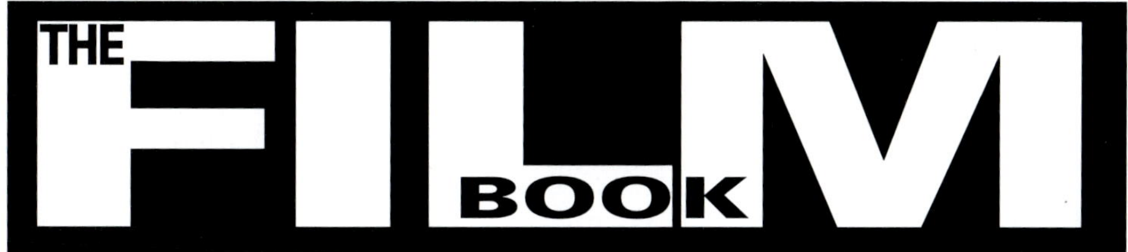

CHOOSING AND USING COLOUR AND BLACK & WHITE FILM

ROGER HICKS AND FRANCES SCHULTZ

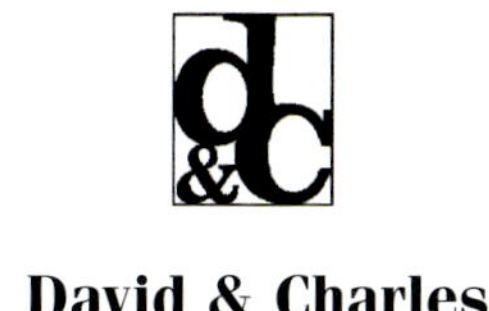

David & Charles

For Terry Harper

A DAVID & CHARLES BOOK

First published 1994

A catalogue record for this book is available from the British Library.

ISBN 0 7153 0150 0

Designed and typeset by Les Dominey Design Company
on an Apple Macintosh
and printed in Singapore
by C S Graphics
for David & Charles
Brunel House Newton Abbot Devon

(Previous page) ***Fortalize, Sagres, Portugal***
Ektachrome 64/Linhof ST IV

CONTENTS

ACKNOWLEDGEMENTS

It is impossible to acknowledge all the debts which one acquires in the course of researching a book like this – and even when one wants to make the acknowledgements, it is not always possible to find the right person's business card!

We would like to thank all those manufacturers who kindly made equipment, film, information and advice available, especially Stevie Robinson and Tony Johnson at Ilford; Pat Wallace and Charlie Yiannoulu at Polaroid; Sarah Estall from Konica; Fuji Film; Tim Goldsmith at Paterson Photax (importers of Meopta enlargers and manufacturers of Paterson chemistry and Photax lighting, among other things); John Purkis at CZ Instruments (importers of the superb Sigma line of lenses); John Dickens of Pentax UK Ltd, and Belinda Lawson at Lawson Dodd, their PR agency; Marti Salzman at Saunders; Harutada Shimoda of the Toho Machine Company, manufacturer of the Toho ultra-lightweight 4x5in camera; Michael Ash of theBottomline, and the Press Department of Doskocil, both manufacturers of camera cases; Bryan at Bryan Cowley Photographic of Canterbury; Veronica Cass Weiss, for Veronica Cass photo-colouring materials; our lab, Thomas Neile Ltd of Whitstable; everyone at Henry's in Margate; Winston G. Yonan of SlideScribe, makers of the LabelBase slide-filing system; Del and Tony at Del's Camera in Santa Barbara; Len Welford, at The Bell; Colin Glanfield, for help and advice beyond measure, and for the picture on page 132; Frances's father, Artie Schultz, for the pictures on page 55, 62 and 123; Linda and Greg Tresize; Malcolm Glanfield; Lewis Lang; Ed Balian; and Bob Shell. It was a great comfort to know that when we didn't know the answer, we could generally telephone someone who did – though if there are mistakes, they are ours and not theirs.

Royal Sea Bathing Hospital, Margate

The chief advantage of Polaroid 35mm films – this was shot on ISO 40 Polachrome – is not really their rapid processing. Rather, it is their unique colour signature. The colours have a 1950s quality, rather reminiscent of the old Viewmaster slides, those miniature stereo viewers which were popular in the 1940s and 1950s. That strange photomechanical blue in the sky, and the very even, flat contrast of the whole image, combine to give a distinctly vintage effect. We chose this image as the first in the book in order to show how changing your film can often have at least as much effect on your photography as changing your cameras or lenses. The camera in this case was a Nikon F, with a 15mm f/2.8 Sigma lens. The (hand-held) exposure was about 1/125 at f/4 in afternoon sunlight. The Royal Sea Bathing Hospital was founded in 1791 for the 'scrofulous poor' of London; doctors could do little for anyone in those days, and sea bathing was the fad of the time. It now dispenses conventional allopathic medicine. (RWH)

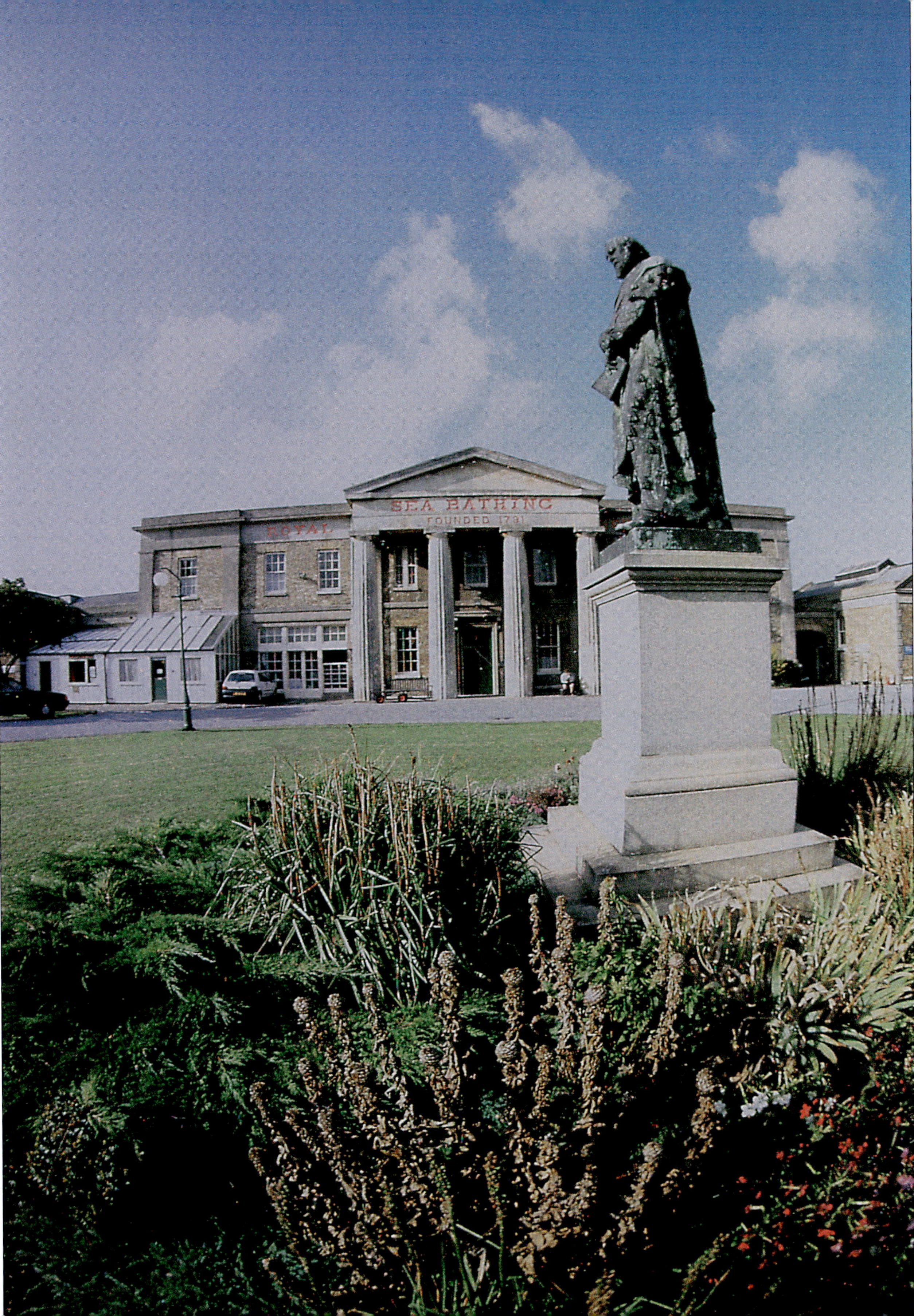
ROYAL
SEA BATHING
FOUNDED 1791

1 CHANGE YOUR FILM AND CHANGE YOUR LIFE?

Most photographers pay far more attention to cameras and lenses, and even to tripods and accessories, than they do to film. Hardware is glamorous, exciting, and expensive. Film, on the other hand, is... well... just film. Everyone knows in a general sort of way that films have improved over the years, but few people really pay very much attention to the improvements. They choose a film that they are happy with (or they may buy on price alone), and they go right on using it, sometimes for years on end. They dream of a new super-zoom, or maybe an ultra-fast 300mm lens for sport, but they don't fantasise about what a new film could do for their photography.

Anyone who takes more than a minimum of pictures will, however, spend far more on film in the course of a photographic lifetime than they ever spend on equipment. If you can afford it, there is much pleasure to be gained from the latest, the best or the most exotic cameras and lenses available; but ultimately there is only one reason for owning all those cameras and lenses, and that is to take pictures. If you don't take pictures, you are not a photographer. You may be a camera collector, or an historian, or even (perish the thought!) someone who regards cameras as an investment; but until you put a roll of film in at least one of your cameras, and press the button, you ain't a photographer.

Given the cost and importance of film, therefore, we really ought to pay more attention to it; and when we do, we find that there is a lot more to it than we thought. There is the question of film speed, of course; and then there is sharpness; and grain; and contrast; and exposure latitude; and (for colour films) saturation and colour balance. These and many other terms are bandied about, often by people who are not entirely sure what they mean, and we shall look at all of them in more detail in the next chapter; but for now, let's ask a philosophical question: is there some sort of 'universal' film, or does every single one of the different films on the market have its own special advantages and disadvantages? Strangely enough, even professionals do not agree on this.

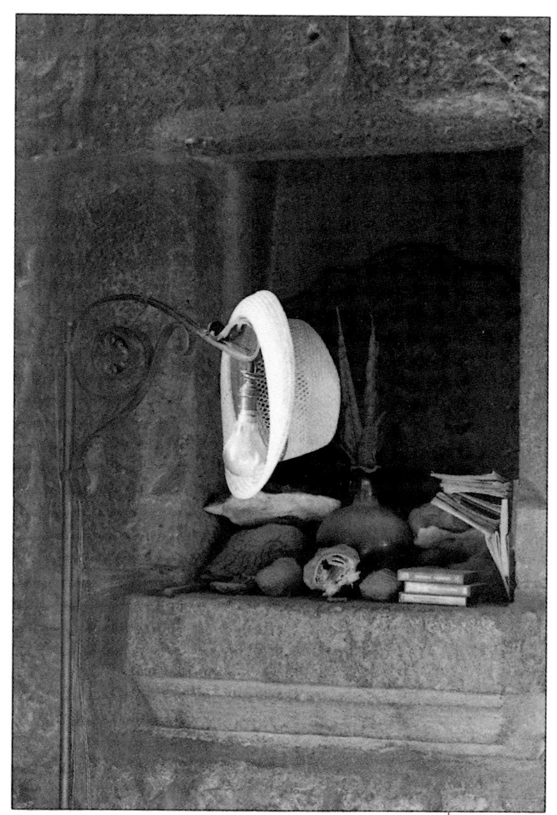

Panama hat, Auberge St Hubert
Often, we find that a subject will only 'work' in one medium or the other, black and white or colour, but this was a time when we wanted to try both. Roger shot it in colour (page 11), while Frances used Ilford XP-2 for this shot because of its extremely long tonal range: she wanted to hold as much detail as possible, even in the deepest shadow. While some of this detail may not show in reproduction, it is certainly there in the original print. Exposure was 1 second at f/16, rating the film very close to its nominal 400 speed. The alternative to XP-2 would have been a conventional film, but preferably down-rated to half its ISO speed and with reduced development in order to get the contrast range right. This was taken with the same lens as the colour picture on page 11, and another Nikon F body. (FES)

THE 'UNIVERSAL' FILM

In its purest form, the 'universal film' argument says that you can use a single film for everything – prints, slides, colour or black and white. Believe it or not, this is just about possible. A good colour negative film can be used to make colour prints (obviously); it can be duplicated onto slides; and with the aid of panchromatic black and white printing papers, it can be used to make black and white prints. It can be scanned electronically and transferred to video disk, or turned into a four-colour separation for photomechanical reproduction. It is also far more tolerant of incorrect exposure than colour slide film, and arguably a little more tolerant than most black and white films.

The trouble is, any 'universal' film is inclined to be a jack of all trades, and master of none. Making slides from negatives is not particularly difficult, but it requires a slide-duplicating set-up, and there is always the inevitable degradation that is inherent in making a copy: the sharpness of a second-generation copy (a slide made from a negative) can never be as great as a camera original. Printing black and whites from colour negatives is possible, but you have nothing like the opportunities for contrast control or subtlety of tone which you would have if you were printing using more conventional materials. The technology of putting slides onto video disks was explored long before anyone considered making everyone's snapshots available that way. Even where it might seem that colour negative film was the only logical choice – for making colour prints – there are many photographers who feel that the very finest prints are made direct from slides.

To cap it all, for a given film speed, colour negative films are almost invariably the least sharp films available. Black and white films will always be sharper than colour films, because their structure is very much simpler and the emulsion layers are very much thinner, but for reasons which are not entirely clear, slide films also seem to be sharper than negative films. This may be because most professionals use rollfilm or large-format cameras when they shoot colour negative, so there is not the pressure on the manufacturers to develop reasonably fast, fine-grain films. When it comes to slide film, on the other hand, many professionals do shoot colour slide films in 35mm, so the competition to deliver the sharpest films for professional use is intense.

Despite all this, there is one professional area in which colour print films are currently treated as more or less 'universal', and that is in newspaper photography. The reason that newspaper photographers can get away with it is because the reproduction quality in newspapers is generally so awful; but as colour negative films improve, other publishers and printers may also start to use them more.

Colour Negative Film and Electronic Imaging

One way in which colour negative film may well become the 'universal' medium of the future is as a capture medium for electronic imaging. At the moment, and for years to come, electronic cameras are likely to remain very expensive, and to deliver significantly poorer quality than conventional film cameras. Even if new imaging sensors were developed which could rival conventional films – and at the moment, conventional films can hold thousands or even millions of

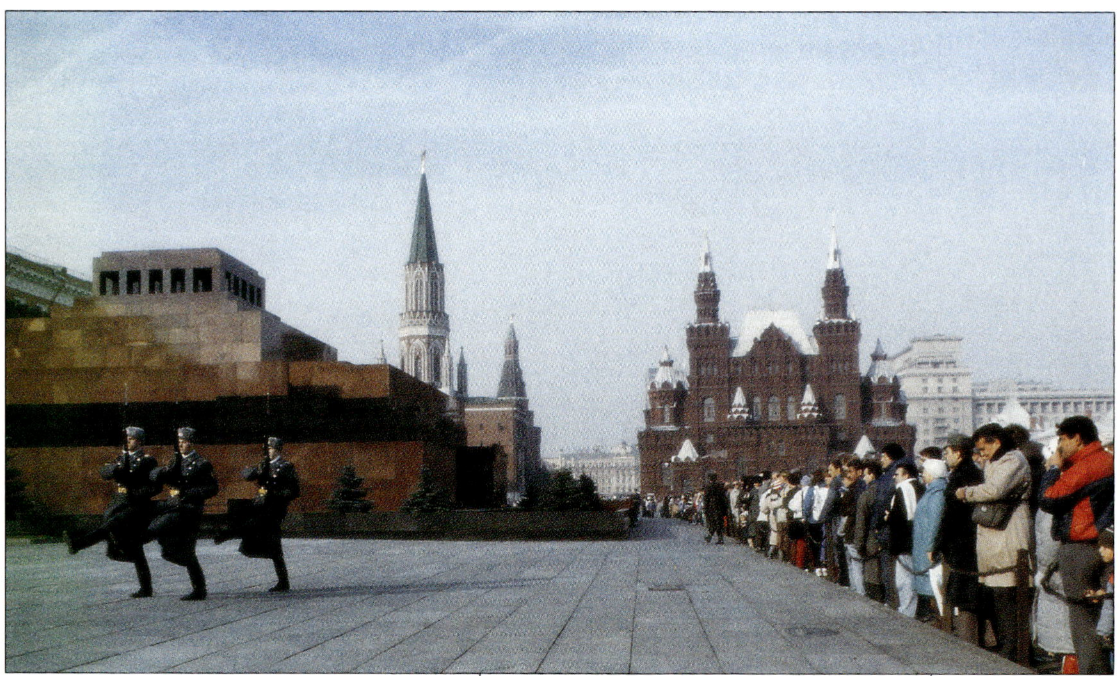

times as much information as electronic imaging media – then electronic cameras would still remain highly battery dependent as well as more expensive (and bulkier) than traditional cameras.

Once the film is processed, though, it becomes a different story. It no longer matters if the equipment is bulky and electrically powered: you can stand it in the corner, and plug it into the wall. If you can scan the image into some form of image manipulation machine, you can do an immense amount with it. Your output can be in the form of a colour print; or a video disk; or a colour transparency; or even a very high-quality black and white print. Because you are scanning a camera original, the losses involved in making your second-generation images are (or can be) very small indeed.

It is however a matter of conjecture as to when all this will come to pass. At the time of writing, you would need to spend over half a million pounds – a million dollars, say – in order to get a top-flight scanner, image manipulation station, and output equipment. Even then, the results would be no better than you would get with any good 35mm camera from the 1960s, or from rollfilm or large-format cameras of considerably earlier vintage. It is safe to assume that traditional photography will be with us for a long time yet.

'SEMI-UNIVERSAL' FILMS

Falling back from the 'universal film' argument, you can make a rather stronger case for 'semi-universal' films: for choosing one film each from the three main groups of colour negative (colour print), colour slide, and black and white. For many photographers, a

Lenin's tomb

'Gritty' is an adjective that many people use of Moscow, and this picture of the changing of the guard at Lenin's tomb uses the grain of Scotch/3M ISO 1000 film as a metaphor for that 'grittiness'. Also, the desaturated colours of this particular film seem to echo the pervading greyness and dullness of so much of the city. This is of course only one way to represent the place, which also contains much beauty: compare this with the picture on page 23, where the glowing blue and gleaming gold of the onion domes inside the Kremlin are captured on a bright, saturated film. It is not so much that the camera can lie: it is more that it can deliver different versions of the truth. The film that the photographer uses, and the way that he or she chooses to expose it, is an important factor in determining which version of the truth is presented. (RWH: probably shot on a Leica M2 with a 90mm f/2 Summicron, exposure details forgotten)

Panama hat, Auberge St Hubert

This 'found' still life in an old coaching inn in Burgundy is somehow very Gallic. While it would have been possible to shoot it hand-held with a fast film, the low light level in the bar would have necessitated a wide aperture and very shallow depth of field. It therefore seemed a better idea to use a tripod, and to stop down well. This in turn meant that there was no great disadvantage in using a slow film, in this case Fuji 100: the actual exposure was around 1 second at f/8 or f/11. The colours were so subtle that a higher-saturation film (such as Velvia) might well have meant that it would not have been possible to hold both highlight and shadow detail. Neither of us would have hesitated to use Agfa 1000, but the camera was loaded with the slower film, so Roger (who took the shot) used what was in there. The faster film would have created a picture which was different, but in no way inferior, and the extra depth of field would have been welcome: it would have been possible to stop down to f/16, and still have used a faster shutter speed. (RWH: Nikon F, Sigma 70-210mm f/2.8 APO, probably at about 105mm)

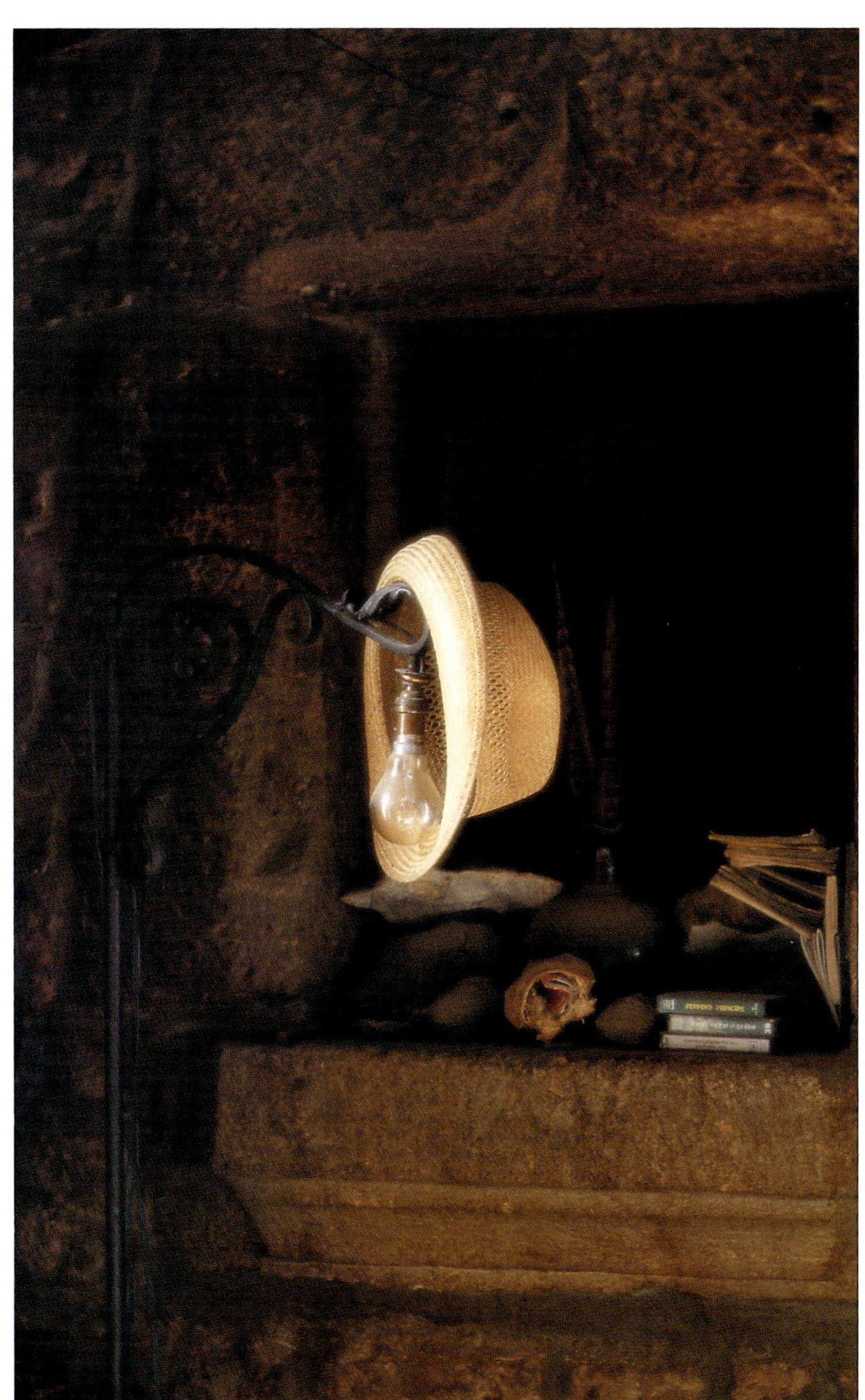

single example of each type of film can meet all or nearly all of their requirements.

There are several advantages to adopting this approach. It greatly simplifies film-buying, for a start. It means that you get to know each film very well, so that you can predict how it will work in different (and difficult) conditions: low overall lighting levels, different colours of light, varying degrees of contrast, and so forth. It means that you can monitor processing carefully, because you know what the film is capable of delivering: you will know whether a problem is an exposure error, a processing error, or some other problem such as poorly stored film.

There are however a couple of drawbacks. The first is that while a film may be adequate for a given task, it is not necessarily the best for the job. You might well do better to use a different film, which is more suited to a particular combination of light and subject and working conditions. The other drawback with sticking to one favourite film is that you may remain unaware of the potential of other films. This is one of the main purposes of this book, to point out just what you might be missing.

The 'Universal' Colour Print Film

For the vast majority of photographers, an ISO 200 or even ISO 400 colour print film will deliver all the print quality they ever need. From a 35mm original, it will deliver very acceptable prints up to the typical 4x6in or 5x7in maximum size that most labs deliver as a develop-and-print package; 10x15cm or 13x18cm, say. Only if you want larger pictures than this, and if you want minimum grain, do you need to

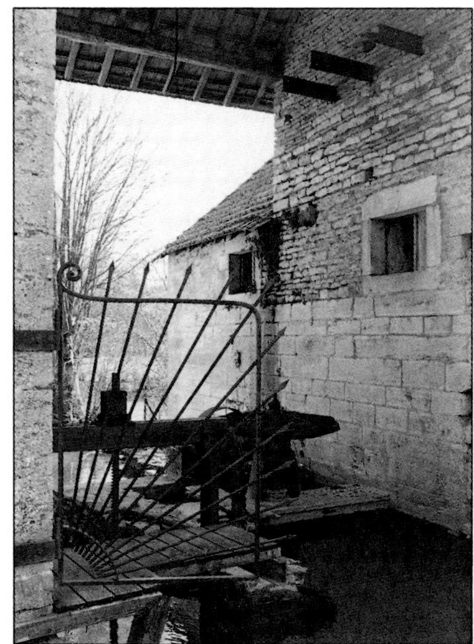

Mill-race

This disused mill-race is a good illustration of how black and white film can capture a tonal range which would be impossible in colour. You can almost feel those textures, which are what give the picture its mood. They also convey the age of the disused mill. In colour, only a small part of the picture could have been correctly exposed, and even then the glaring white sky would have dominated the composition. Here, it is unimportant. As usual when faced with a long tonal range, Frances used Ilford XP-2, rating it at about EI 200 in order to get finer grain and as insurance against under-exposure in the darkest parts of the image. The exposure reading was taken with an incident-light meter. A spot meter would have been better, but the only spot meter we have is Russian and we have not fully worked out how to use it yet! (FES)

use anything slower. Faster films, on the other hand, are detectably grainier even at modest enlargement sizes, have less saturated colours, and are significantly more expensive.

The 'Universal' Slide Film

For sheer versatility, ISO 100 slide materials are hard to beat. Which manufacturer's film you choose is up to you, but they all offer a useful combination of reasonable speed, good sharpness, colour saturation and contrast. Slower films are often too contrasty for use in direct sunlight, while faster films are grainier and (once again) more expensive.

Again, ISO 100 films are not the only possible choice. Another strong contender for 'universal' status is Kodachrome 64. True, it is somewhat slower than an ISO 100 film, but it is a flexible and forgiving film with superb sharpness, excellent gradation and contrast, and a tremendous resistance to bad storage.

***Millpond and weir in* La France profonde**

'La France profonde' – 'deep France', as the French themselves call it – is one of our favourite places for taking pictures. We rode past this village on our motorcycle, but turned back when we saw from the main road the potential that it had for picture-taking. As far as we can remember, this was shot with Frances's favourite lens, her 35mm f/2.8 PC-Nikkor shift lens on a Nikon F, and it was a hand-held shot. In order to take it, she was right on the edge of a slippery grass bank, with Roger holding on to her belt to stop her falling in. The extra speed of an ISO 400 film (this was XP-2) was very welcome, because even though it was a bright day, it was useful to be able to stop down to f/11 in the interests of depth of field, and it was possible to do this even with a shutter speed of $^{1}/_{500}$ *second. No doubt Delta 100 could have delivered better quality, but we prefer not to shoot at even* $^{1}/_{125}$ *second hand-held, especially when we have just been scrambling over poor surfaces. If we had had the Benbo tripod with us, when we could have cantilevered the arm out to the position needed, it would have been a different story. As it was, we had only our travelling tripod, a lightweight Manfrotto/Bogen. (FES)*

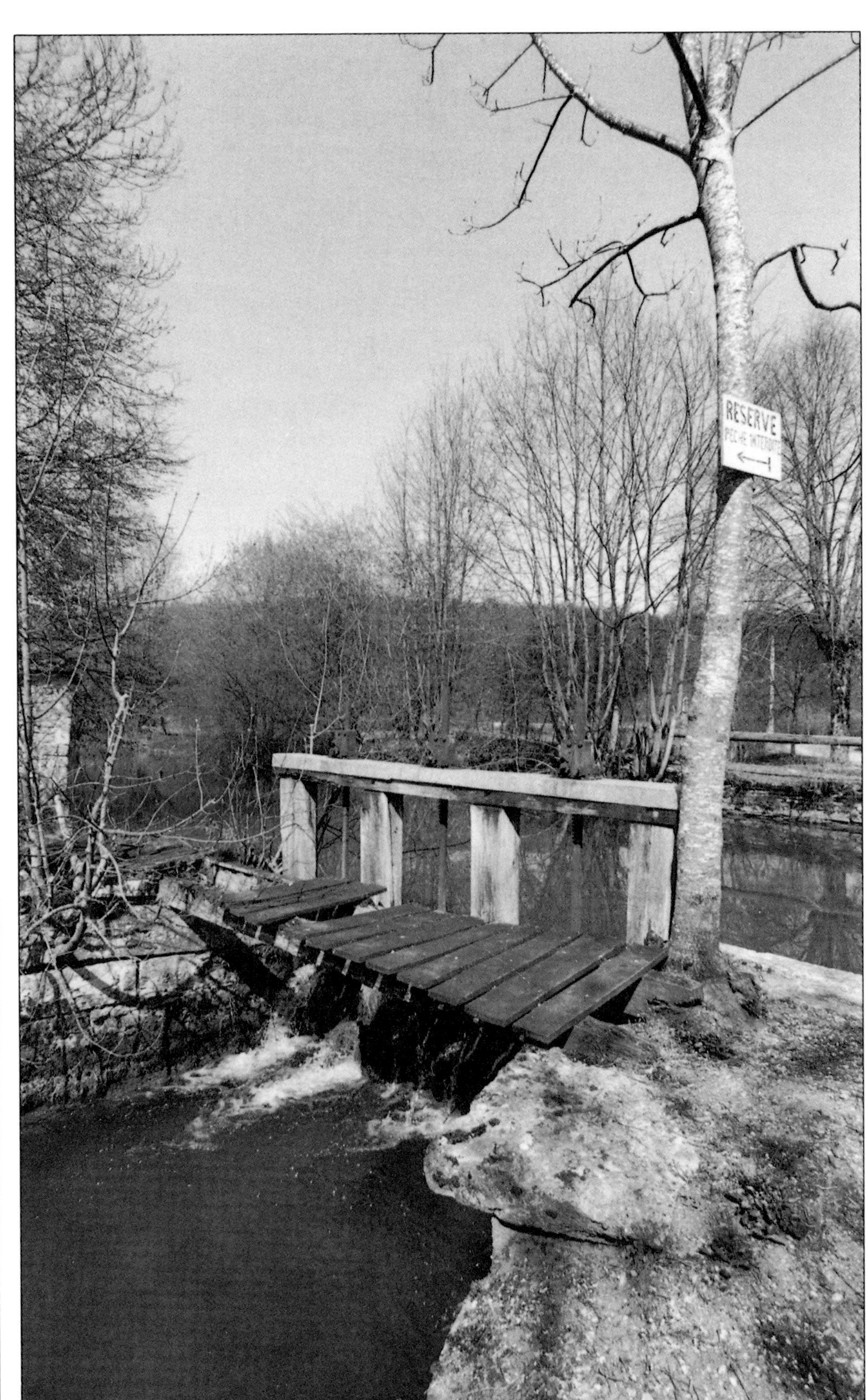

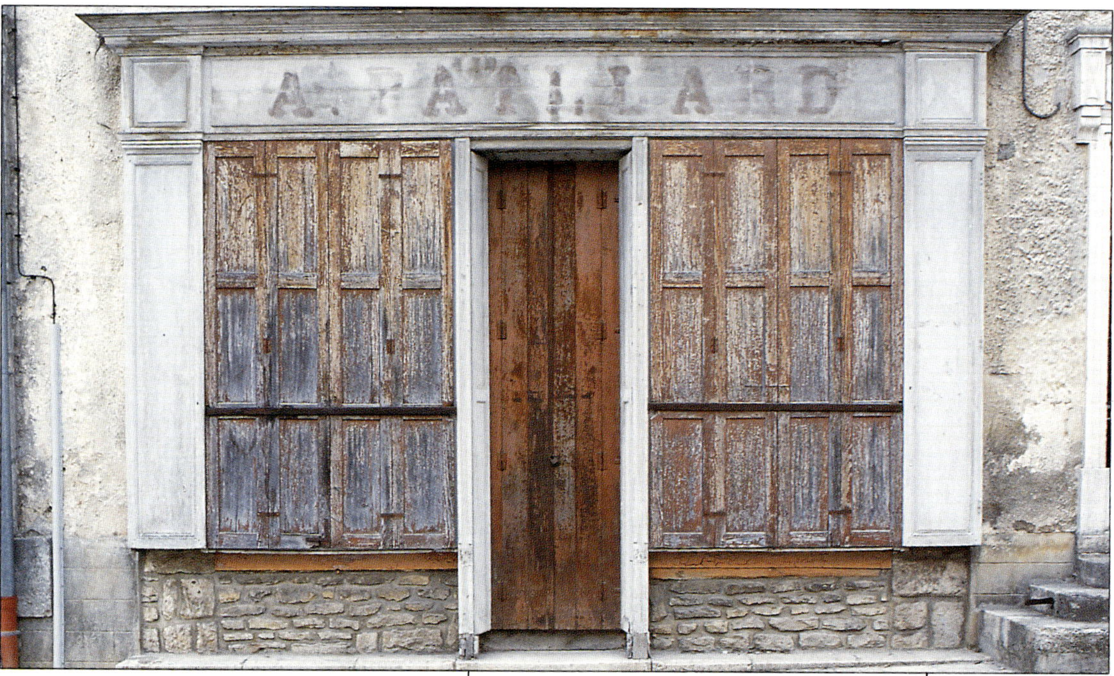

The 'Universal' Black and White Film

Modern fast black and white films – ISO 400 – are so good that for most people they can be treated as 'universal'. This is especially true of Ilford's chromogenic range, launched as XP-1 and then improved and refined as XP-2. These films, which use an adaptation of colour film technology (hence 'chromogenic') are incredibly tolerant of over- and under-exposure, and they are quickly and easily processed by any lab that can handle conventional colour print film. They offer excellent quality. Alternatively, if you prefer to process your films yourself, the 'old technology' ISO 400 films like Ilford HP5 Plus are still admirably tolerant of over- and under-exposure, and can be processed in virtually any developer. 'New technology' films like Delta 400 offer better quality under ideal conditions, but are more demanding when it comes to both exposure and processing.

Until recently, ISO 125 films were commonly described as 'universal', but now the only reason to use them is if you want the ultimate in quality: you then .have to put up with slightly more critical exposure requirements and (of course) less speed. They can however be cheaper than the faster films.

THE 'PALETTE' APPROACH

The opposite of the 'semi-universal' approach is what you might call the 'palette' approach. Each film, the follower of this system maintains, has its own virtues and drawbacks. At its most extreme, there are those who will load a particular film just for one shot. They maintain that they are not 'wasting' the rest of the roll: they are getting *precisely* the results which they

Door, France

French politicians refer to the 'desertification' of rural France, where populations are declining and more and more houses stand empty. In fact, this shop in Burgundy is apparently still in service, but many French home-owners and businessmen are inclined to be very economical with paint. The light was already failing when Roger shot this picture, hand-held at something like 1/60 second at f/1.9 on a 28mm Vivitar Series One lens. He bracketed the exposures, but this one seemed best to express the fadedness of so many French villages. It was ISO 100 film (Fuji RDP), which bears out the claims made elsewhere in the book that you can use ISO 100 films for just about anything. A faster film would have been grainier, which would have detracted from the cool dullness of the picture, and a slower film would have been excessively risky to hand-hold as well as possibly exaggerating the intensity of the colours. (RWH)

Loch Torridon

The traditional advice to a press photographer was 'f/8 and be there'. There are certainly times when it is more important to be there than to worry too much about your film or equipment. The weather was bad as we were driving across the far north of Scotland, well above Inverness, and we had pretty much given up any hope of taking pictures. Light levels were low, and mist often restricted visibility to a few yards. When we saw this through the window of the car, we stopped and shot fast, using a Nikon F loaded with Kodachrome 64 and relying on the speed of our 50mm f/1.2 Nikkor to enable us to focus. Unless you have an autofocus camera, fast lenses are of course much easier to focus than slow ones, and if you use fast lenses, you can use slower film. We both shot pictures, and this is one of the ones that Frances took. Maybe it could have benefited from more depth of field, but the weather was so bad (and getting worse) that we did not want to take the time to set up a tripod and stop down to allow the use of a longer shutter speed and a smaller aperture. Also, because we almost invariably used Kodachrome 64 in those days, we were able to visualise pretty well what the picture would look like on film: this is one of the arguments against a 'palette' approach. With a faster film of (say) ISO 400, especially in those days, it might have been impossible to get quite the same effect, even if we could have pre-visualised it. (FES)

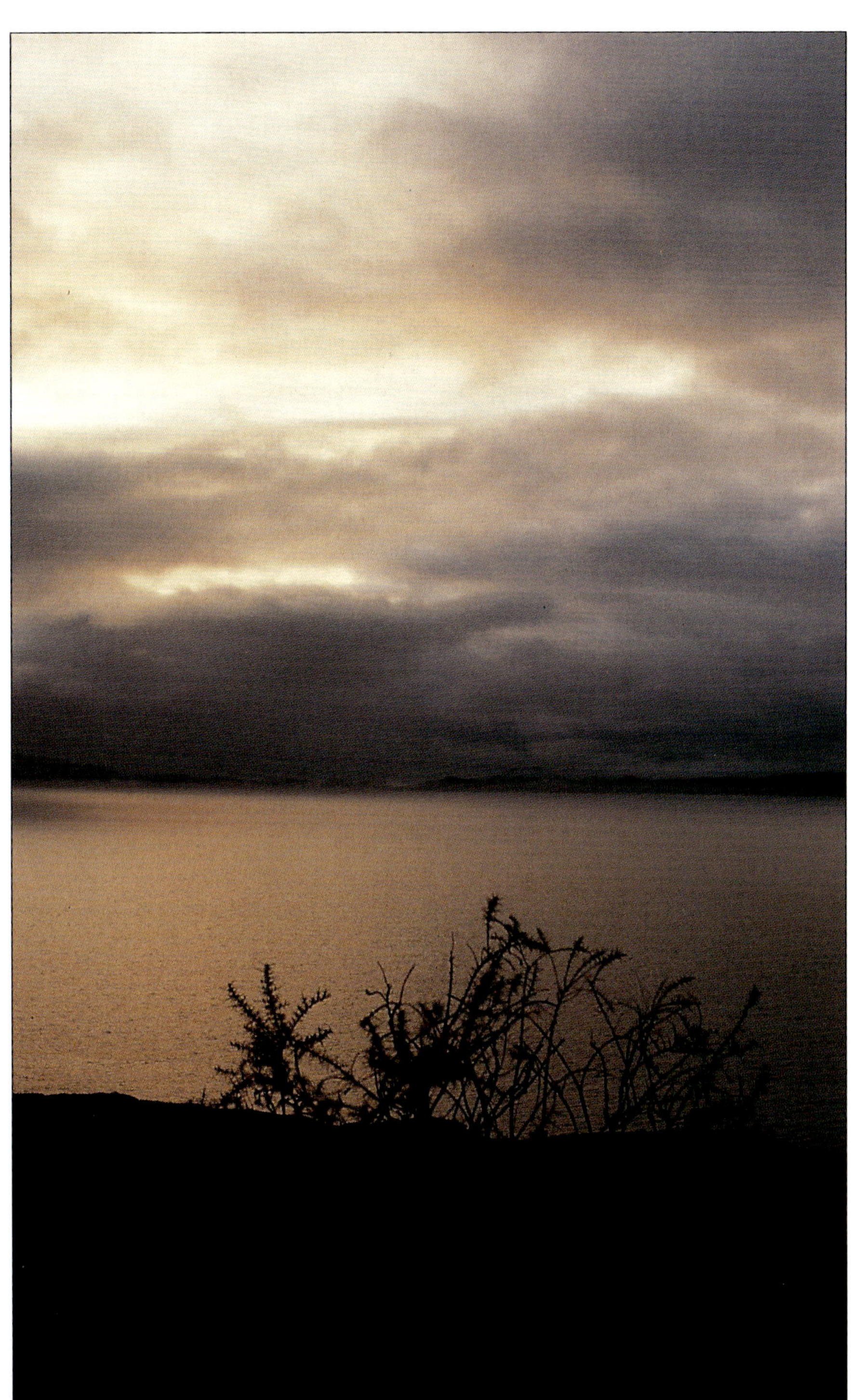

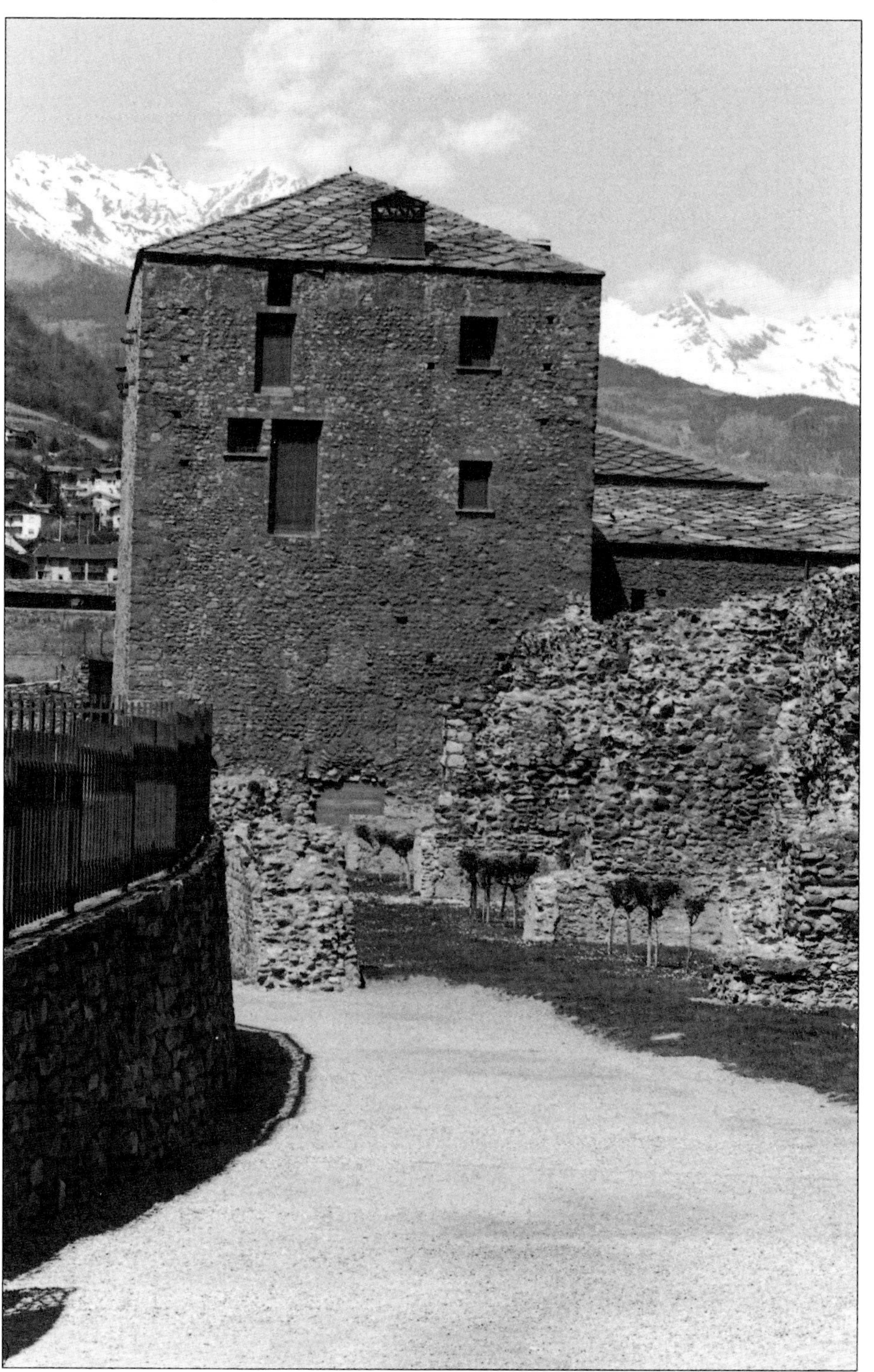

Tour de Fromage, Aosta

This ancient tower in Aosta is known as the 'Tour de Fromage' or 'Cheese Tower' for no very clear reason. It attracted Frances because of the range of subjects – the Roman wall, the tower itself, the characteristic slate roofs of the Val d'Aoste, the Alps in the background – and the composition, which is basically triangular: the dark mass of the tower, flanked by dark walls. Triangular compositions are always solid and enduring, which seemed to sum up the subject matter rather well. The principal reason for including it in this book, is to make the point that the main aim of the photographer is to make pictures. The professional must make the pictures the client wants, but the amateur can take pictures to please herself or himself. Frances was very much shooting as an amateur when she took this, because it is not necessarily a very saleable picture. We just like it. (FES)

Child in pushchair *(right)*

Black and white had at least two advantages here. One was that it suited the rather old-fashioned pushchair, which was built somewhat along the lines of the Brooklyn Bridge, and which contrasted well with the child riding in it. The other was its timelessness. When you are using colour, it is hard not to take a snapshot, but with black and white, there is a feeling of making a record. Yet a third advantage was that by reducing the background to tones, and removing the element of colour, it concentrated attention on the foreground. Unfortunately, we do not know the parents of the child; but if it was anyone we knew, we would give them a picture for posterity. This photograph will still be substantially unchanged when this little boy is an old man. The film was Ilford Delta 400; the camera was a Nikon F; and the lens was a 90mm f/2.5 Vivitar Series One macro. Exposure was probably 1/250 at f/5.6. (FES)

Smashed-up motorcycle

We had been in Italy half an hour. We stopped at a traffic jam; the girl behind us didn't. The damage to the motorcycle was over £1000 – close to $2000 – though fortunately we were not badly hurt. Although we had colour print and colour slide film with us, we decided to shoot the damage on black and white for a number of reasons. First, it meant that we could conveniently make larger prints, which would show the damage more clearly. Second, black and white has a more formal, legalistic feel to it. As the pictures were to be used to try to help us get money out of an Italian insurance company, this was important. Third (to be cynical) the bike was rather dirty and ratty-looking: Roger had not polished the exhaust pipes for a while, so there were rust spots on them, and the final drive casing was oil-stained. This is less clear in a black and white picture than it would have been in colour. Film was Ilford XP-2; the camera was a Nikon F with a 90mm f/2.5 Vivitar Series One macro lens. (RWH)

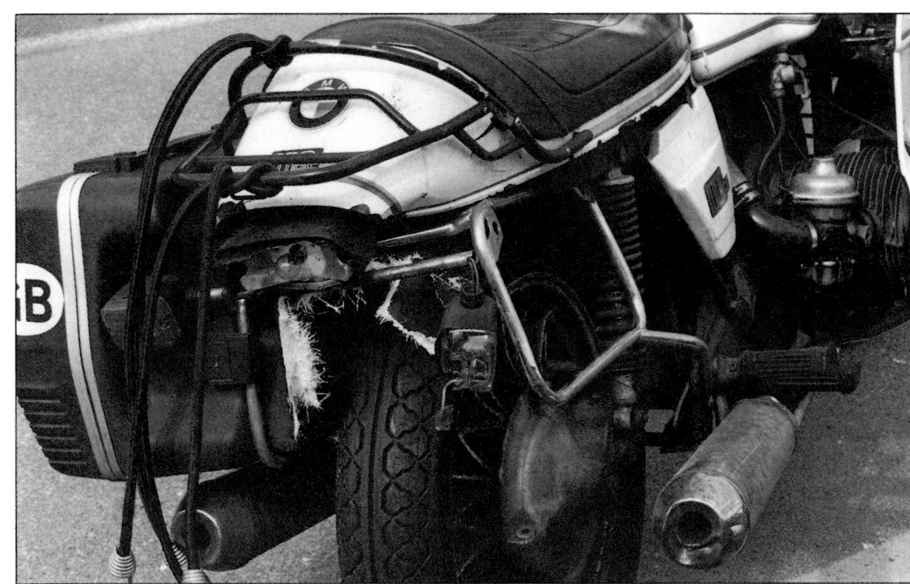

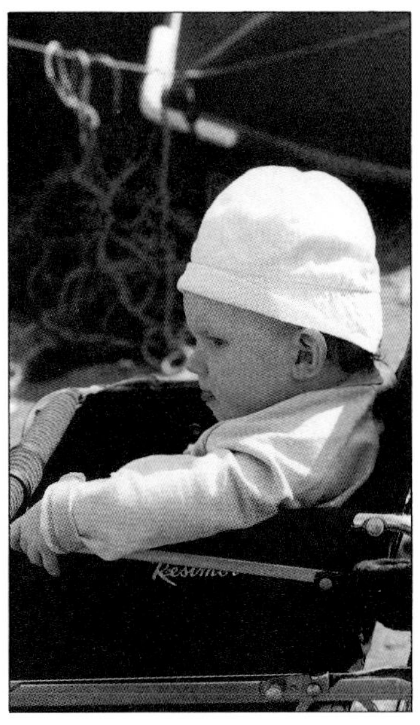

want from a particular combination of film and subject. While it is hard to argue with them, most of us are either unable to afford to change our films like this, or simply cannot bring ourselves to do so.

The approach which we adopt is something between the 'semi-universal' approach and the 'palette' approach. In colour, for example, we shoot almost exclusively slide films. The greatest percentage of our shots are probably on ISO 100, for the reasons given above, but we also use ISO 50 when we want higher saturation and finer grain; Kodachrome 64, when we are on an extended trip in the tropics or in warm weather anywhere, because the Kodachrome family is far more resistant to heat than any other type of colour film; Agfa 1000, for astonishing quality from such a fast film, albeit at a stiff price; and 3M/Scotch ISO 1000 film for dreamy, grainy, romantic images. At the time of writing, we used mostly Fuji 100 (RDP) and Fuji 50 (RFP), but we have also cheerfully used Agfa and Kodak in the past, and we might yet switch again. From time to time we also use different makers' films in order to get different effects: Konica, for example, has quite a different 'feel' to Fuji or Kodak or Agfa.

In black and white, we have been through rather more changes. At one time, we used only two films. One was Agfa Dia-Direct, a slow, direct-reversal black and white film which gave (and still gives) extraordinary sharpness and a stunning gradation. The other was Ilford HP-5, which we developed either in Microphen (for speed) or Perceptol (for fine grain). The rated speeds in those two developers were EI 650 and EI 320 respectively: when you depart from ISO film speeds, which are scientifically determined by the International Standards Organisation, it is no longer correct to refer to ISO speeds. The term then is EI, for Exposure Index.

When we moved to the United

States in 1987, we found that Dia-Direct was not available there. Also, for convenience in processing as much as for anything else, we tried XP-1 and then XP-2. The results were so good that for several years this was our 'semi-universal' black and white film, and it remains our film of choice for reportage to this day. When we need real speed, we supplement XP-2 with T-Max P3200, normally rated at EI 1600.

Then, when Ilford Delta 100 came out, we added that to our 'palette' of black and white. In our experience, there was at the time of writing no other film on the market which even came near it for grain and gradation: 35mm shots looked as if they were taken on a Hasselblad or other leading medium-format camera. As with colour, we do use other black and white films, but not very many or very often.

Specialist Films

There are also all kinds of specialist films, some of which we use habitually, some of which we use occasionally, and some of which we know about only from casual experiment or from friends. For example, we habitually use Kodak SO-366 duplicating film for making slide duplicates,using a Bowens Illumitran electronic-flash slide copier. On the other hand, Kodak Technical Pan Film is something which we have never cared to try, but which some people swear is the finest black and white film available. Inevitably, we are biased towards the film which we use; but we have tried in these pages to give a fair assessment of the advantages and drawbacks of these different specialised products.

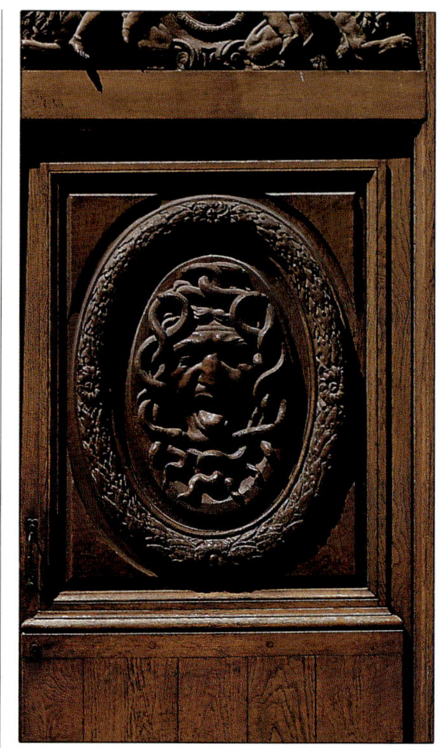

Carved panel on wood door

This is roughly contemporaneous with the picture of Mandi Fisher opposite, but the film quality is infinitely better: this is Kodachrome 64. Earlier 'fast' Kodachrome – the Kodachrome-X of unfond memory – was awful film, with colours which went all over the place, but by the 1970s Kodak had definitely got it right. Even so, today's Kodachromes are probably even better than they were then and, like almost all modern colour films, they are far more fade-resistant than they used to be. An interesting feature of Kodachrome is its superb dye-fastness under dark storage conditions, though under projection conditions a modern Ektachrome will fade less quickly. The camera was probably a Pentax SV with a 55mm f/1.8 Super-Takumar. (RWH)

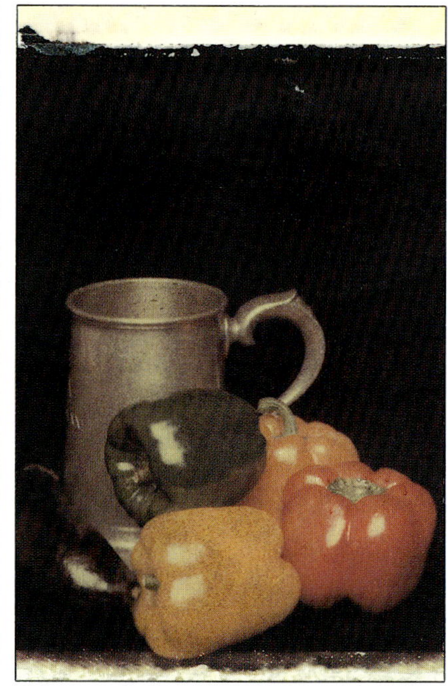

Image transfer, fruit

This was one of our first attempts at image transfer, a technique described at greater length in Chapter 9. It uses the old 'peel-apart' style of Polaroid film, but instead of leaving the film to develop normally, you peel it apart and transfer the image onto a sheet of drawing paper. It is an unpredictable technique, and you can spend quite a lot on film while you are learning how it works, but it gives a particular image quality which is quite unobtainable in any other way – a true film technique, rather than the usual sort of equipment technique. The more you play with different types of film, the likelier you are to find that you can often accomplish more by changing your film than you can by changing your equipment. (RWH/FES)

Mandi Fisher

It would be almost impossible to find a film this bad today though lousy processing could help. This is a (mercifully) long-forgotten 'own brand' film from one of the discounters of the early 1970s, which Roger processed himself in the manufacturers' own proprietary chemistry. The film speed was only ISO 50, but the grain is spectacular and the maximum blacks are not very maximum. Roger was twenty-three years old when he shot this, temporarily working as a teacher, and very broke: he just could not afford to use Kodachrome very often. As a general rule, it is always better to have even a bad picture, rather than no picture at all, but a good picture is better still! The camera was probably a pre-war Leica rangefinder with a 50mm f/3.5 Elmar, though it might have been a Pentax SV with a 55mm f/1.8 Super-Takumar. (RWH)

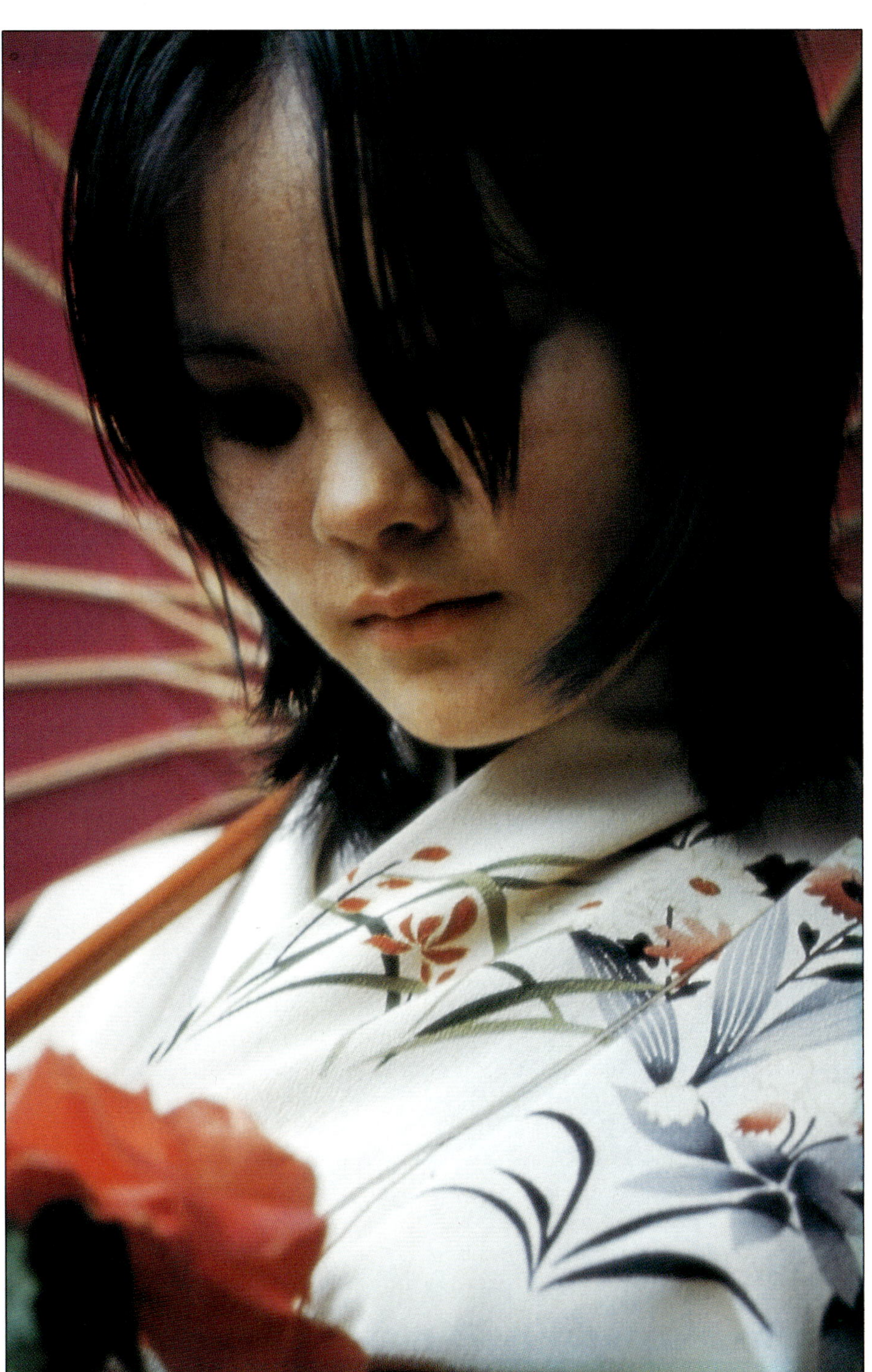

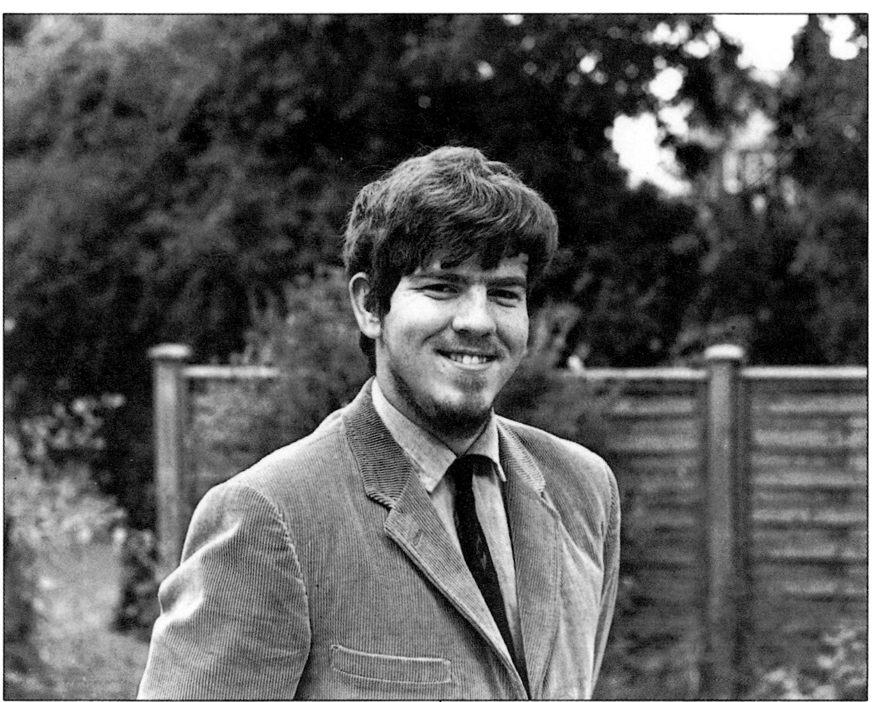

Roger Hicks, about 1970

Looking back at one's old negatives is always deceptive, because so much changes. Not only have films improved, but the photographer also tends to improve with practice! In those days, Roger was much inclined to over-develop his films, which builds both grain and contrast, and he was also inclined to use out-of-date film stock: he 'won' four 200ft cans of Ilford FP3 which were outdated when he got them in 1967, and we suspect that this is from the last of that batch. It was probably developed in home-compounded D19b, which gave contrasty negatives in any case. Also, of course, remembering details from almost a quarter of a century ago is not easy: Roger cannot even remember whether this was shot by his brother or by his girlfriend, Dail Hussell, though it would obviously have been very important to him at the time. The bottom line, though, is that although it required a very low contrast grade – about 0 on the Meograde head, using Ilford Multigrade paper – it still printed very acceptably. The grain is however quite large, certainly much larger than you would expect from even a maltreated ISO 125 film today, though this may not be clear in reproduction. The camera was almost certainly a Pentax SV of about 1964 vintage, which Roger's father bought for him when he was 16; the lens would be the 55mm f/1.8 Super-Takumar, the only one he owned at the time.

CHOOSING THE BEST FILMS

It might seem that by laying our cards on the table, and explaining which films we use, we have to some extent removed the point of the book. This is not actually the case.

It is not our intention to give a blow-by-blow account of each and every different film on the market, for several reasons. One is that if we did, the book would go out of date so rapidly that there would be little reason to buy it. Another is that there is no such thing as a 'best' film: too much depends on what sort of photographer you are, what sort of pictures you want to take, and what you want to do with them afterwards. A third reason is that the film market is constantly changing.

An example makes this clear. Years ago, Ektachrome 64 was so blue that many photographers would not use it at all, and others habitually put a yellow or warming filter on to bring the colour within sight of where they wanted it. Agfa, on the other hand, delivered superb colour – but at the expense of far coarser grain than the Kodak equivalents. You therefore had the choice of good colour and poor grain, or good grain and poor colour. Today, both manufacturers' films – which have always been among the best available – are incomparably better in every way, and the choice between them is made on much subtler bases, principally on personal preferences and (it must be said) on availability.

Or, for another example, Ilford's Delta 100 (which was launched when this book was in the planning stages) completely revolutionised the market for medium-speed films. It might be that another manufacturer could

Market scenes, Gran Canaria
Almost everywhere we go, we photograph the marketplaces if we possibly can. By seeing what is on sale, and how it is sold, and who is buying, and what the prices are, you can learn an enormous amount about any society. Inevitably, some of your pictures are going to be grab shots, so it is a good idea to choose a film with as wide a latitude as possible. These two pictures were shot on Ilford XP-2, one in extremely contrasty light and the other in very flat, well-shaded light, and both worked well – though the picture of the palm-frond brooms would have benefited greatly from a tripod and (better still) Ilford Delta 100. If you are shooting this sort of scene in colour, then a wide-latitude colour print film such as Konica's excellent ISO 400 material would be the best bet. You might also care to try using a grey-graduated 'system' filter for shots which include a lot of sky: they are a bit of a nuisance to use, and you have to be careful if the effect is not to look too unnatural, but they are a (relatively) easy way of keeping the foreground exposure correct while still retaining a deep blue sky instead of a washed-out white one. A grey grad will cause most metering systems to under-expose slightly, so you might care to re-rate ISO 400 film at EI 200. The only graduated filters we ever use are grey-grads, because most others look so horribly unnatural: pink dawns and tobacco sunsets work sometimes, but mostly they look very contrived. (Marketplace FES; brooms RWH)

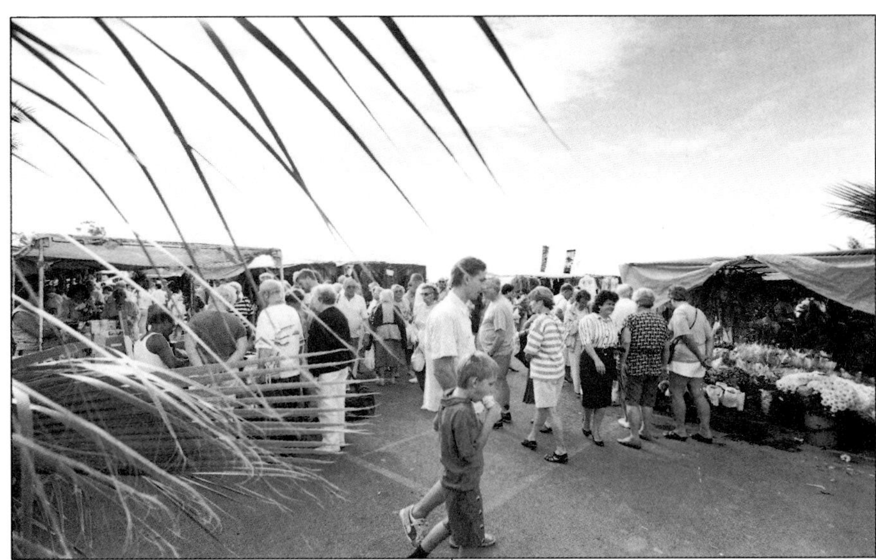

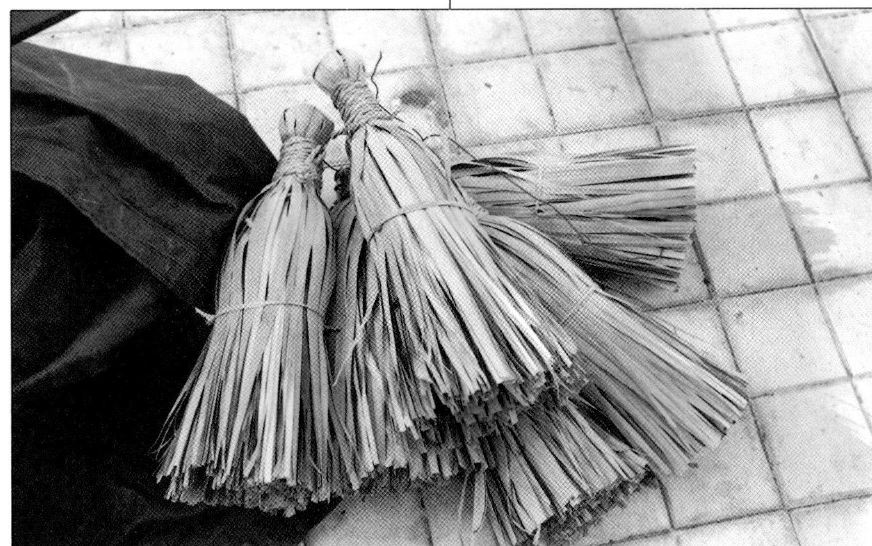

develop something as good, or better, tomorrow – but Delta 100 certainly shook up the market-place.

The Luck of the Draw?

One last factor which influences film choice is that some people seem to 'get on' with some films, and others do not. The most extreme and inexplicable example, at least among commonly available films, must be Kodak T-Max 100. We know many photographers who swear that this is the finest film they have ever used, and the quality of their results bears this out: they produce prints with exquisite detail and gradation. We also know roughly equal numbers of photographers who damn it utterly, saying it is the worst film Kodak has ever produced, and that there is no excuse for its existence. Why?

Who knows? It does not seem to be anything to do with skill, or persistence, or the quality of the water used to make up the processing solutions, or anything else, quantifiable or unquantifiable. It is just that some people get on with it, and some don't. We are actually fairly indifferent to it: it is all right, but we would far rather use Ilford's Delta 100. There are others who would say the exact opposite. What we have tried to do in this book, therefore, is to give guidelines which will help you to decide how to choose film, rather than telling you which film

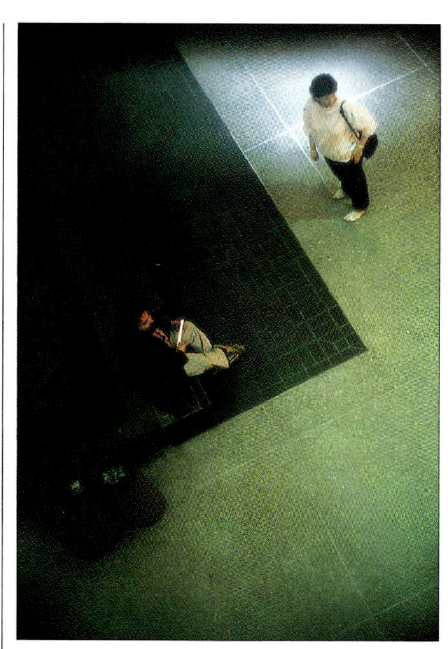

Mall Scene

Under the right (or wrong) conditions, one film can mimic another. This is a very slow film, Fuji 50 (RFP), exposed by a mixture of daylight and fluorescent light. Slow colour films are almost invariably less tolerant of mixed lighting sources than fast ones, and in this case the effect of the mixed lighting and the various textures in the subject is to create an apparent graininess reminiscent of a much faster film. This is however one of those subjects where the composition is more important than the choice of film. The awkwardly jutting dark area from the upper left begins the mood of alienation; the harsh lighting contrasts accentuate it (and slow films are always harsher than fast ones); while the separateness of the two characters completes it. If they were looking at each other, it would have a completely different mood; if they were looking in different directions, it would be different again; but both looking in the same direction, it sums up the way in which we can be physically quite close yet spiritually and mentally very distant from one another. (RWH)

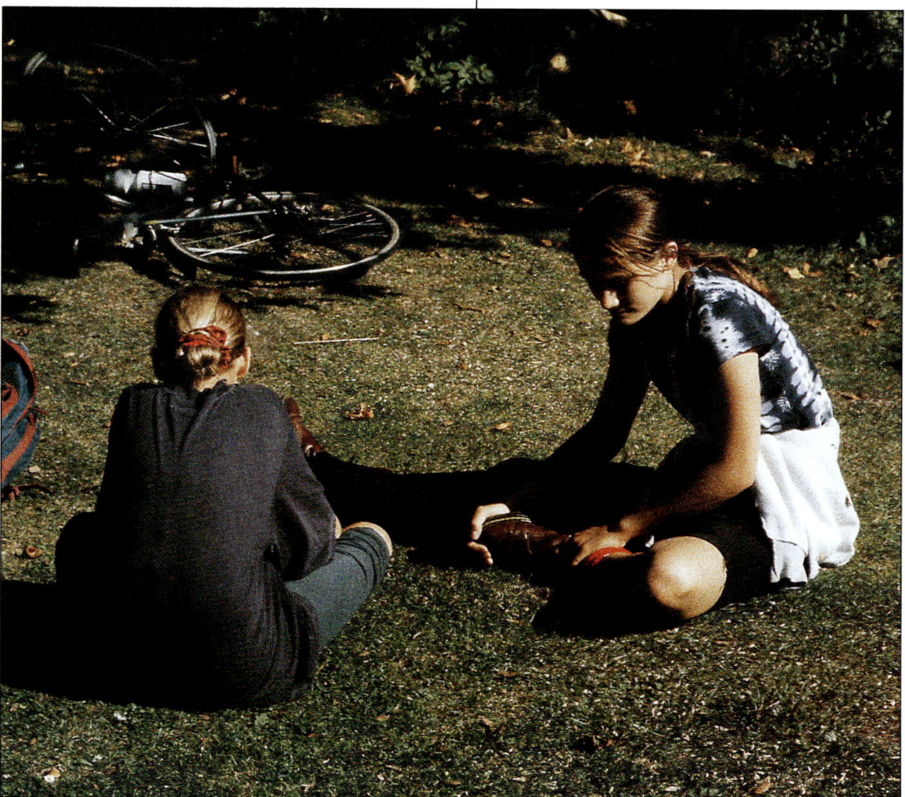

Cyclists, Sandwich, Kent

This is a very undistinguished picture, but it demonstrates two things. One is how much films have improved over the years: this was shot on Agfa 1000 RS film, and the grain and gradation are not really inferior to the off-brand film that was used for the picture of Mandi Fisher on page 19, while the maximum black is very much better – but the film is 20 times faster! The other thing it shows is how you really can use ISO 1000 film even on sunny days. The exposure here was 1/1000 at f/16 (using the 'sunny f/16 rule'), which was the fastest speed the camera could offer and the next-to-smallest aperture on the lens, a Vivitar Series One 35-85mm f/2.8 Varifocal. This was the end of the film: it is always worth making experiments like this with the last few frames, rather than just winding them off and wasting them. An extra half-stop of exposure might have been beneficial, but this film is extraordinarily contrasty for such a fast film and the highlights might have burned out unacceptably. (RWH)

The 'Ivan Velicki' Bell Tower

The Russian authorities seemed amazingly mellow about letting us inside the Kremlin with tripods and all sorts of focal lengths from 17mm to 800mm, even in the early days of glasnost – this was about 1990. This is, however, very much a matter of luck: a couple of days later, we were forced to deposit the tripods in a sort of 'left luggage' before we were allowed in. If you contrast this with the picture on page 10, you can see how a photographer can change his or her story by careful choice of film and weather conditions. The majesty and richness of the churches inside the Kremlin walls are very different from the grittiness of the changing of the guard in Red Square, outside the walls less than a couple of hundred metres away. (RWH: Nikon F, 35mm f/2.8 PC-Nikkor, ISO 50 film [Fuji RFP], Gibran tripod)

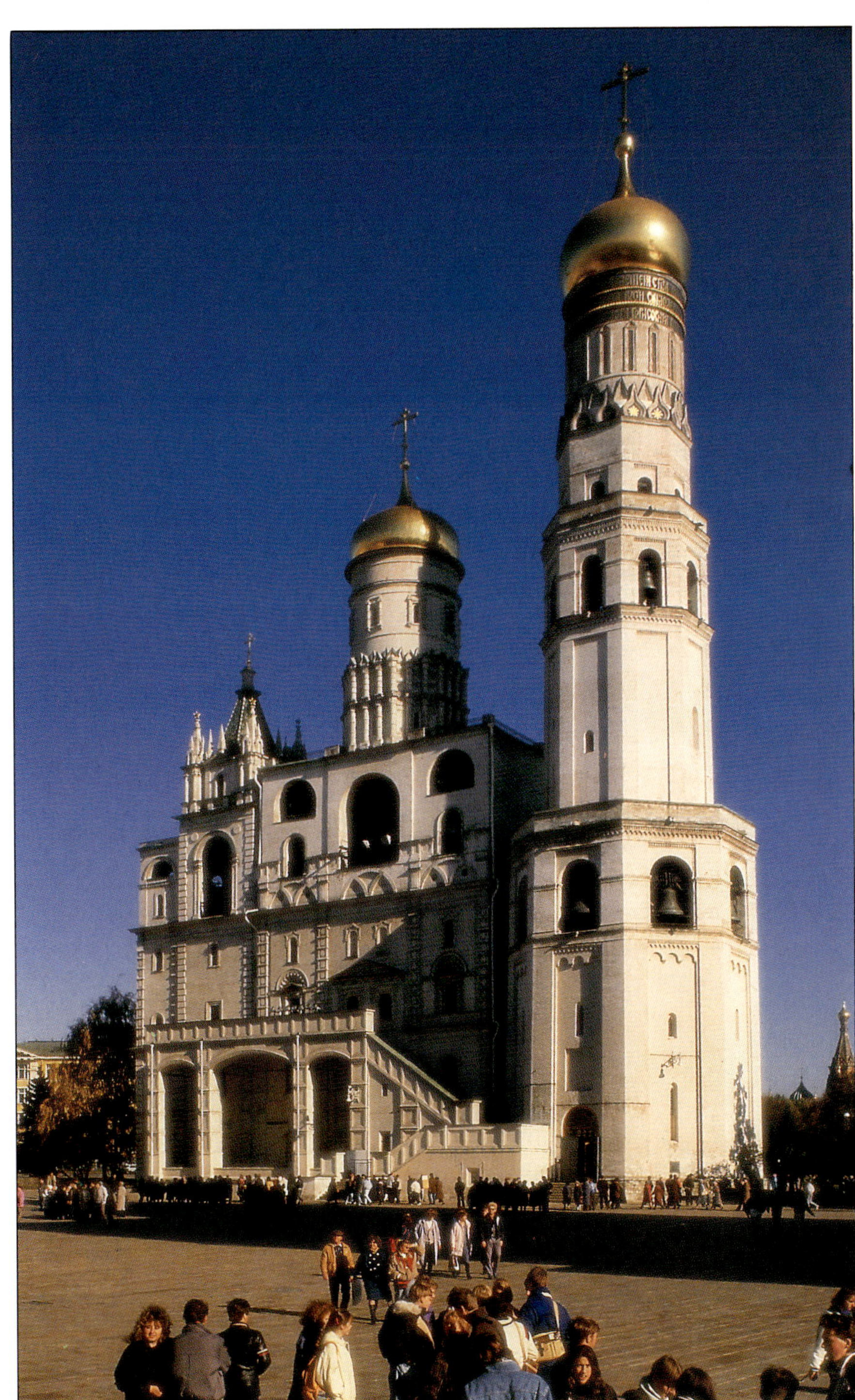

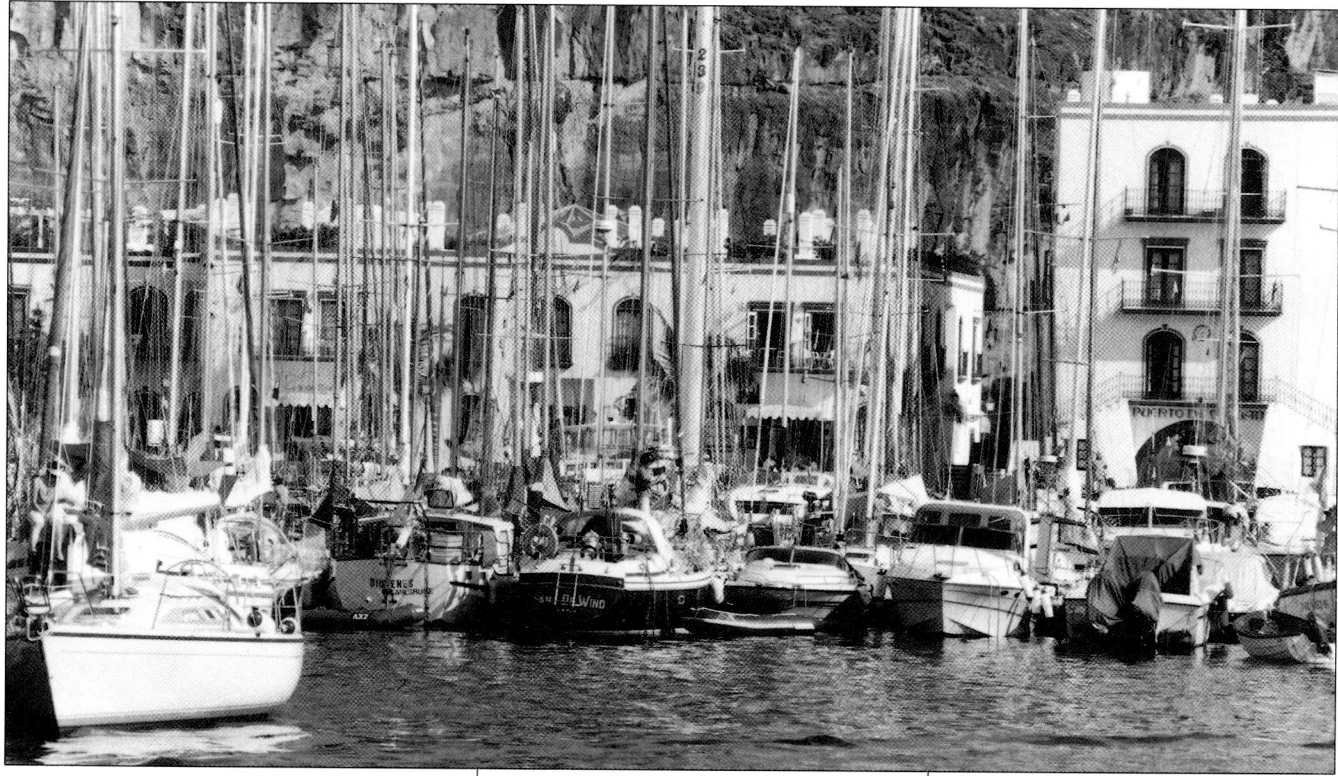

to choose – and once you have chosen it, we tell you how (in our experience) you can get the best out of *any* film, regardless of who made it. Maybe there is a degree of alchemy, or even real magic, in photography: how you feel about your film will influence the results you get from it.

THE PICTURES YOU THROW AWAY

Regardless of what film you use, you should always throw some of your pictures away. Throw out the technical failures, obviously, and either throw away or at least separate the duplicates and near-duplicates. A sports photographer or natural history photographer may well shoot 'for the percentages', and use only one-tenth or less of his or her exposures; a landscape photographer should have a considerably higher success rate, but even so there will be failures, and they should be thrown away. By all means pore over them yourself, trying to work out what went wrong, but do not inflict them on other people.

Your reputation does not rest, after all, on the pictures that you take; it rests on the pictures that other people see. It also rests on how you present them, and on how you edit them. A few pictures, in the right sequence, can make you look very good indeed. Too many pictures, thrust under someone's nose in no particular order or projected haphazardly on the screen, will simply cause people to find excuses for escaping your company.

Boats, Gran Canaria

The sun was very low in the sky when Frances took this picture, and light levels were falling fast, so she used a tripod. The camera was a Nikon F with a 35-85mm f/2.8 Vivitar Series One varifocal lens, set to maybe 65mm (we do not record these details – and nor does anyone else we know). The exposure, again from memory, was about 1/30 at f/8, on Ilford Delta 100 rated at ISO 100. Although it would have been better to stop down to f/11, for more depth of field and maximum sharpness, it was not feasible to use a slower shutter speed, or the movement of the boats on the water would have become too obvious. A faster film, such as Delta 400, would have allowed f/11 and 1/60 second, but it would have lost the superb gradation and resolution which is the essence of this shot. (FES)

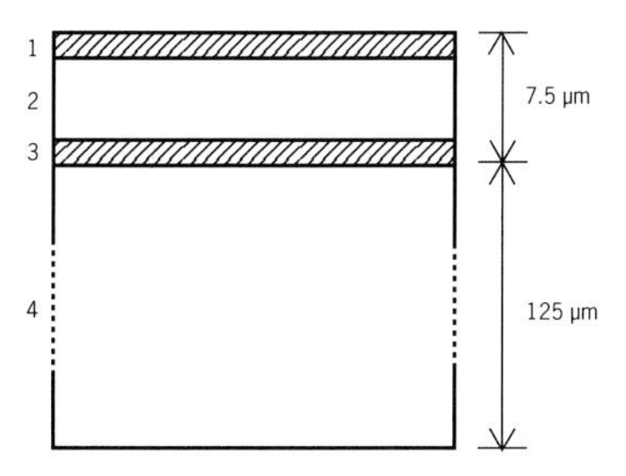

Cross-section of black and white film
Even the simplest black and white films typically have three gelatine layers on top of the film base. The lowest is a thin layer of near-opaque gelatine which reduces halation. The colour disappears during processing. The next, and thickest, layer is the emulsion itself. The top layer is the gelatine 'supercoat' which resists abrasion and (in the case of large-format films and some sheet films) provides a 'tooth' for retouching with a pencil. Some films may have two emulsions, a fast one on top and a slower one underneath: the slow emulsion helps to extend the latitude of the film, allowing it to record highlight detail when the fast emulsion is overexposed. It is also quite common for there to be another gelatine layer on the back of the film. This further suppresses halation and helps to resist curling when the film is drying.

Anti-halation backing *(far right)*
When a ray of light strikes a film, part of it penetrates into the film and is scattered by it. If there is no anti-halation layer, the light then passes through the film support and is reflected from the back of the support, to reappear as a halo around bright areas and also as a general degradation of the image. An anti-halation layer means that very little light is reflected at the anti-halation layer; still less light passes through to the back of the support; and virtually no light is reflected from the back of the support to the emulsion. Some films also use a grey support to absorb light which might otherwise cause halation, but this is not very satisfactory on its own.

2 TERMS AND CONDITIONS

Setting aside the existential question of whether there can ever be 'universal' films or not, there are a number of characteristics of films which can be discussed more or less objectively. The first and most basic is their structure.

STRUCTURE

At its simplest, a film consists of a support and a light-sensitive coating. Today, the support is almost always flexible plastic, but in the past it has been glass, paper (still used in Polaroids), silver-plated copper (Daguerreotypes), and even pewter (Niepce's original pictures).

Likewise, the light-sensitive coating today is almost always gelatine based, though in the past it has been based on gun-cotton (the Collodion or wet-plate process), silver halides formed on polished metal (Daguerre again), and bitumen of Judaea (Niepce again). The so-called 'emulsion' of a modern film really is not an emulsion in strict scientific terms – it is actually a suspension of light-sensitive silver salts – but the term 'emulsion' is so well established that it would be foolish not to use it.

The Emulsion

The emulsion is an unbelievable cocktail of chemicals, which interact in ways that are not fully understood even today. Somehow, different dyes affect the sensitivity of the silver salts, but the strangest story is that the sensitivity of a film can be affected by the diet of the cows from whose hooves, skins and bones the gelatine is made! Film manufacturers have to test their gelatine carefully, and mix gelatines from different sources, in order to make a reasonably consistent product. The process of manufacturing films involves many stages of mixing, shredding, re-mixing, cooking and 'ripening', and there is not much point in going into it here.

Multi-layer Films

In practice, any modern film has many layers. Even the simplest black and white film is likely to have three layers on top of the support: an anti-halation layer, the emulsion itself, and then an anti-abrasion supercoating.

The anti-halation layer is to stop light which passes through the emulsion from going on through the support as well, after which part of it would be reflected back into the emulsion, thereby causing halos to appear around bright light sources – hence the name 'anti-halation'. The supercoat protects the emulsion itself from mechanical damage. Some movie films apparently do not have this coating, or have a supercoating that is nothing like as tough as the ones on a still camera film, which is why respooled movie film (which is

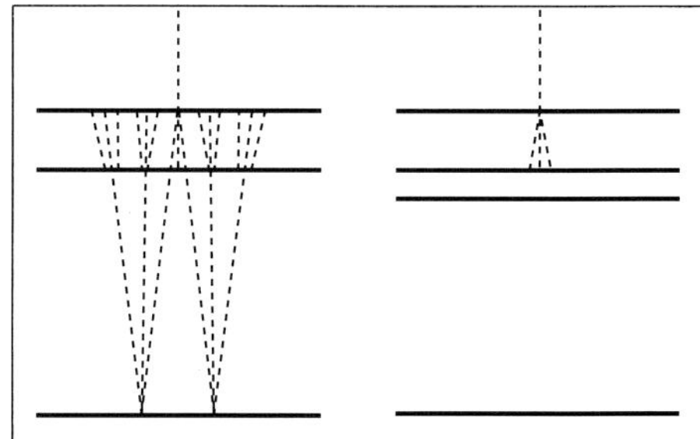

sometimes advertised as a 'universal' film) may be a bad risk in still cameras. On rollfilm and large-format films, the supercoating also provides a 'tooth' to allow pencil retouching of the negative.

In addition to these layers, there

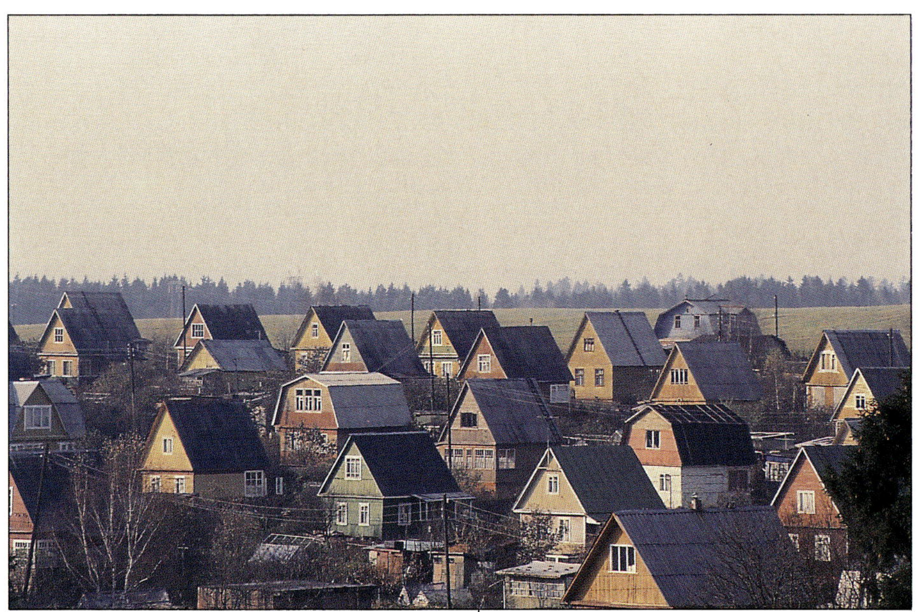

Dachas outside Moscow
If you are using a very long lens, and shooting over a long distance, even the slightest atmospheric haze will be greatly accentuated. This was taken with a 600mm lens, on the road from Moscow to Zagorsk. It is very much a matter of personal taste whether you prefer to use a high-contrast, high-saturation film such as Velvia, or (as Roger did here) a more conventional-contrast film. We believe that in 35mm, where the degradation of detail is much greater than it would be with rollfilm, it would look unnatural in a picture like this to have bright colours and poor definition. On the other hand, when (later on the same trip) we spent some time in St Petersburg, we would very much have liked some Velvia to 'spike up' the colours, because the weather was dull and overcast for most of the time we were there. Yet another consideration is that if you are using very long, slow lenses like the 600mm f/8 'cat' (with an effective speed of nearer f/11), you really need to use a fast film if you are to avoid camera shake, even on a tripod. According to some tests, mirror-induced vibration in SLRs is worst in the 1/30 to 1/125 range. (RWH)

may be an extra gelatine coating on the back of the support, partly as an anti-halation layer (it absorbs any remaining light which might otherwise be reflected back) and partly as an anti-curl layer to counteract the natural tendency of wet films to curl.

Then, the emulsion itself may be coated in two or more layers. At one time, it was quite common for medium-speed films to have both a fast emulsion and a slow emulsion, to allow maximum exposure latitude (page 36), and today there are still many fast films which have a fast upper emulsion and a slower emulsion between it and the anti-halation layer.

Colour Films

A colour film must have at least three emulsions stacked one on top of the other, sensitised in turn to blue, green and red light. In practice, many films have two emulsions for each colour. Between these, there are filter layers and interlayers, and on top there will usually be an ultra-violet filter layer. There may also be an adsorption layer, so the whole sandwich may consist of more than a dozen layers, plus the support! When you consider that the total thickness of all these coating layers together may be 25µm or less (25 microns – a micron or micro-metre is 1/1000 of a millimetre, or about 1/25 of 1/1000 of an inch), you can see that coating technology is an exacting undertaking.

Emulsion Thickness

The reason why the emulsions are made so thin is that a thick emulsion inevitably scatters light and leads to less sharpness. This is why slow, sharp films are sometimes touted as 'thin-emulsion' films, and it is why modern films are very much sharper than old ones: they are simply thinner. It is also why black and white films are sharper than colour films: the coating thickness of Agfa

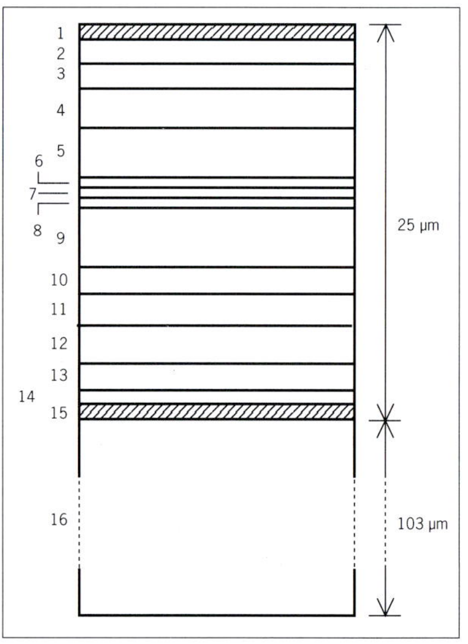

Graffiti

Most graffiti is (are?) just plain boring, but every now and then you see something which is either particularly witty or particularly well-executed. Because it was a sunny day, and Frances was just going for a walk along the beach with a friend, she automatically chose ISO 100 slide film. This would not be too contrasty for photographing people (which ISO 50 film might well have been), but it would still give bright, punchy colours if under-exposed slightly, as here. This picture would not have worked quite so well in black and white. The contrast of the grass above the grey wall really 'lifts' the picture. (FES)

Cross-section of colour film (left)

It is almost unbelievable that the total combined thickness of the fifteen gelatine layers in this typical colour slide film (Agfa 50RS) is a mere 25µm – 25/1000 of a millimetre. Starting at the layer furthest from the film base, they are: (1) protective supercoating; (2) active interlayer; (3) UV filter layer; (4) fast blue-sensitive emulsion; (5) slow blue-sensitive emulsion; (6) gelatine interlayer; (7) yellow filter layer; (8) active interlayer; (9) fast green-sensitive emulsion; (10) slow green-sensitive emulsion; (11) gelatine interlayer incorporating red filter layer and active interlayer; (12) fast red-sensitive emulsion; (13) slow red-sensitive emulsion; (14) gelatine interlayer; (15) anti-halation layer. The film base is 130µm thick, about five times all the gelatine layers put together. With three emulsions stacked on top of each other, this is called an 'integral tripack'. Once processed, it filters out all the colours which are not needed from white light shining through it. This is why it is called 'subtractive'. If the dye precursors are added during processing, it is 'non-substantive', but if they are already in the emulsion, they are called 'substantive'. All subtractive integral tripacks except Kodachrome are substantive.

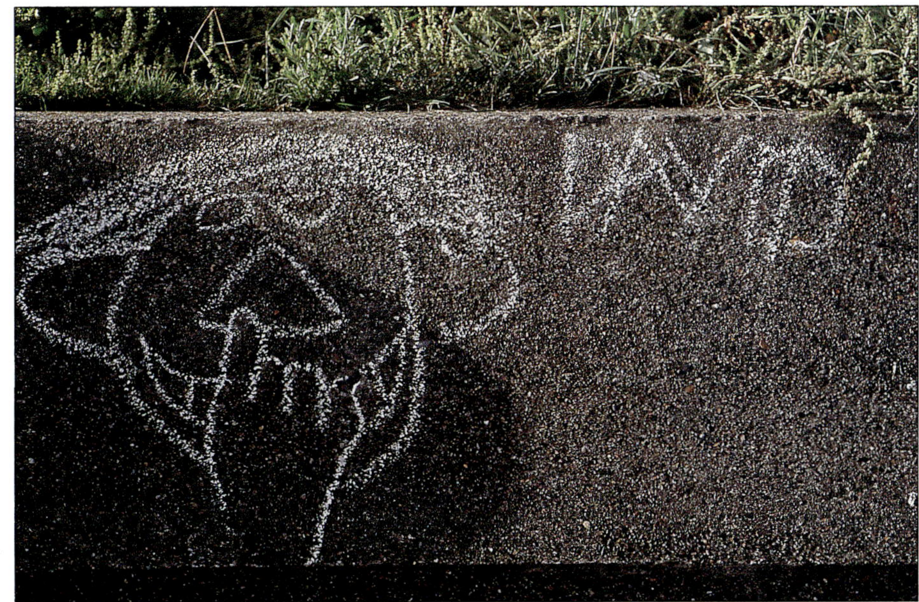

Dia-Direct is 7µm, about a quarter of the thickness of a typical medium-speed, medium-quality colour slide film.

SPEED

Film speed is nothing more nor less than a measure of how much light you need to get onto the film in order to get an image. A slow film requires a lot of light, and a fast film requires less.

The slowest films designed for general use are ISO 25, and the fastest are ISO 1600 or more. This represents a speed range of 1:64, an enormous difference, though it would be more accurate to say that the vast majority of films which are actually used every day range from ISO 100 to ISO 400, a range of only 4:1. It is quite easy to see why most films fall in the ISO 100 to 400 range, though, and it is also easy to see why there are both faster and slower films. It is a matter of general usefulness: being fast enough for all but the poorest lighting, while not being inconveniently fast for bright daylight.

The 'Sunny f/16' Rule

A surprising fact about film speeds is that you can always judge the exposure on a sunny day by a very simple rule of thumb. At f/16, the shutter speed will be one over the ISO speed of the film in use. In other words, an ISO 100 film will require a shutter speed of 1/100 second, an ISO 200 film will require a shutter speed of 1/200 second, and so forth. At the limits, an ISO 25 film will require 1/25 second, and an ISO 1600 film will require 1/1600 second. If the camera's shutter cannot match those precise speeds, you can either approximate, or adjust the aperture instead.

With very fast films, you are obviously limited to high shutter speeds and small apertures. This is not really a problem at ISO 400, except on those relatively rare occasions when you want

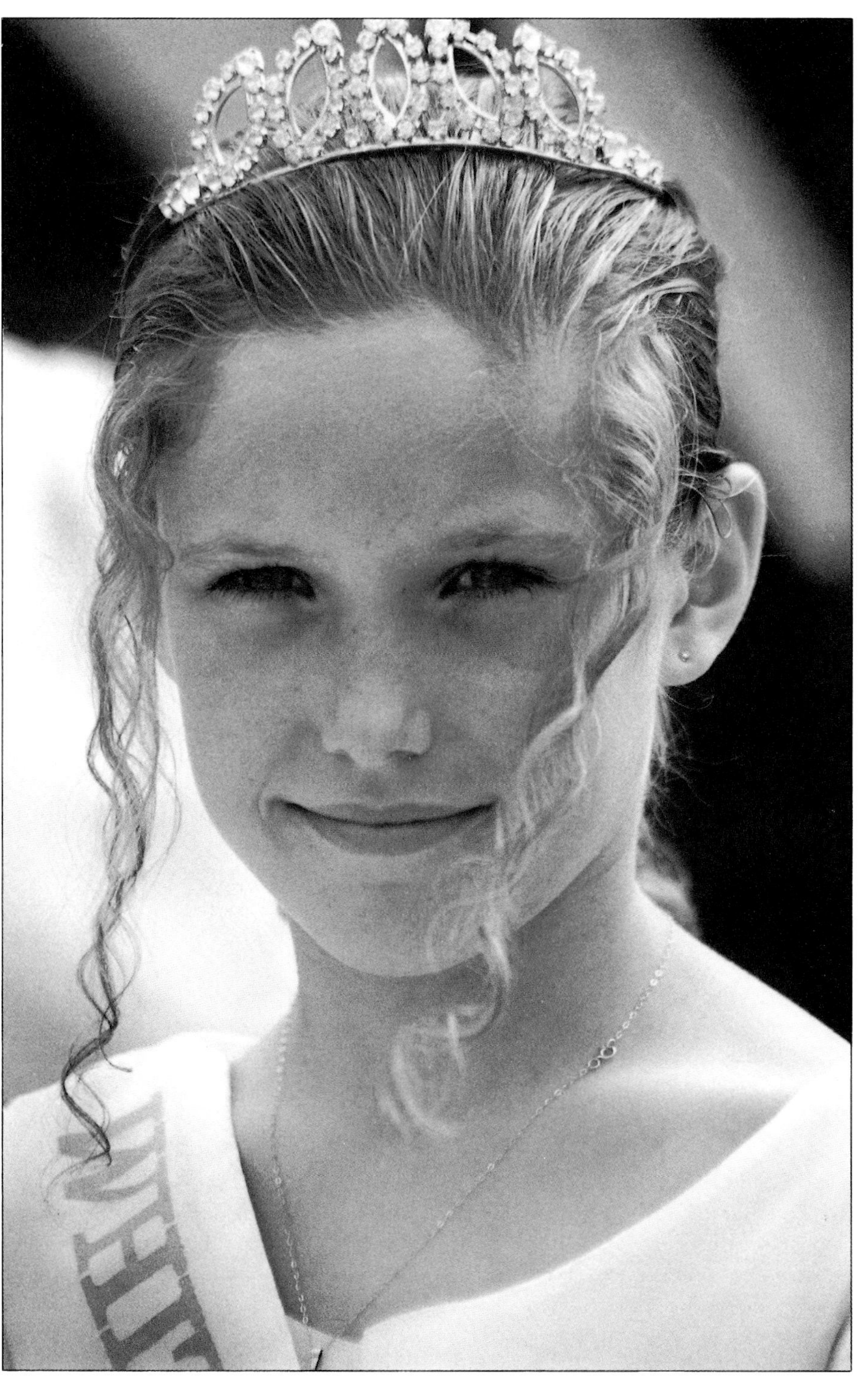

Miss Whitstable

Fast film might not look like the likeliest choice for a shot like this – until you know how it was shot. In the part of Kent where we live, carnivals or village parades are commonplace. They mostly take place in late summer and early autumn, and historically they are pre-Christian harvest festivals. Each town and village has its own carnival queens, and they and their 'courts' (typically two princesses) ride on floats; the symbolism is obvious. Roger wanted to take head-and-shoulders pictures of these girls, some of whom are very pretty, without the surroundings of the floats. The obvious choice was the superb Sigma 300mm f/2.8, because it meant he could take the pictures without aggressively pushing and shoving his way to the front, and without pushing his camera into the girls' faces. In order to counter camera shake when hand-holding such a long lens, a very short shutter speed was essential: 1/500 or (preferably) 1/1000 second. With Ilford Delta 400, the film used here, it was feasible to shoot at anything from f/5.6 to 'f/2.8 and a half' (f/3.4 or so) under the lighting conditions which obtained. In a 6x blow-up (6 x 9in , 144 x 216mm) the grain is barely detectable in the original print, and it will almost certainly be invisible in reproduction. Even more speed would have been useful, as it would have allowed more depth of field, but it would have led to more grain than is really desirable. (RWH)

Royal Pavilion, Brighton

The Royal Pavilion at Brighton is one of the most unexpected pieces of architecture in England – which is saying something. Its Indo-Saracenic style looks more like a Maharajah's palace than many Maharajahs' palaces. Frances photographed it on Ilford Pan F Plus purely for this book; Pan F was not a film she had previously used much, so she deliberately set herself the task of shooting two rolls of it out of doors. This is an excellent way to learn about films you have not tried before: buy a roll or two, and resolve to expose the lot in a single day. Although we both find that Pan F is too harsh for most out-of-doors subjects, it was just about perfect for the Royal Pavilion. It turned the afternoon light in a slightly faded British holiday resort into the hard, bright light of India. As soon as it did this, all the other parts of the scene also became Indian: the ornate white-painted railings against the shadows on the left, and the rather ugly railings along the sides of the paths carved through what was once lawn, now that the old Maharajah no longer walks on the grass with his friends, and hoi polloi wander in the grounds. All that is missing is an ox-pulled lawnmower, and a few gardeners in loin-cloths and puggarees. The camera was a Nikon F, and the lens was a 35mm f/2.8 PC-Nikkor, hand held for an exposure of about 1/125 at f/8. (FES)

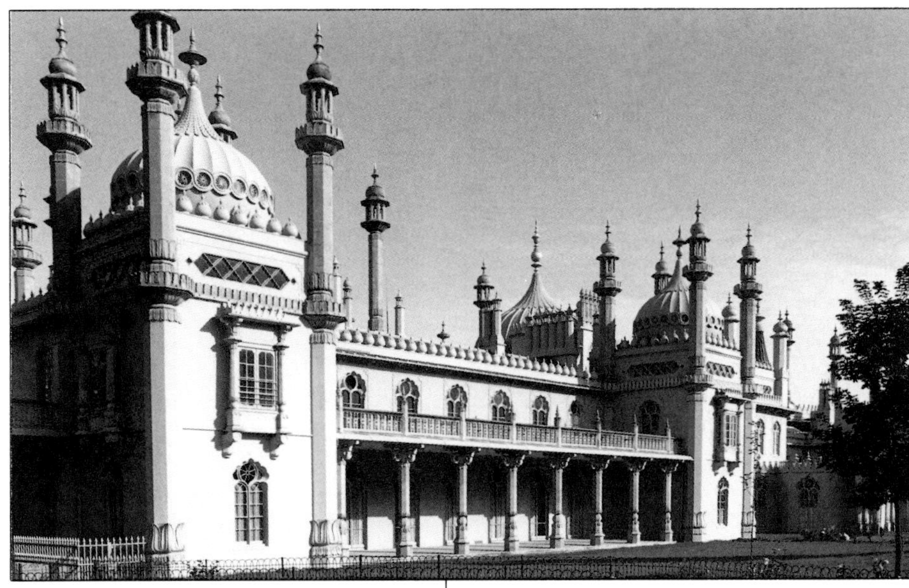

to use wide apertures to throw the background out of focus. With *really* fast films, though, the camera may not be able to give exposures short enough. There are still many cameras with fastest shutter speeds of 1/1000, and compacts may be limited to 1/500 or even 1/250. It is true that there are other cameras with top speeds of 1/2000, 1/4000 and even 1/8000, but not everyone can afford them, even if they wanted them.

With a top speed of (say) 1/500, and a lens which stops down only to f/16 (which is the normal limit), anything more than ISO 400 on a sunny day is going to result in over-exposure. While over-exposure is not a great problem with colour negative films, and modest over-exposure is acceptable with conventional black and white films, you are at a severe disadvantage if you try to use slide films of ISO 1000 or above. With many of our cameras and lenses, 1/1000 at f/16 is the limit, so we simply cannot use faster films on a sunny day – even if we were not worried about the significantly higher prices of some very fast films.

Running out of Light

At the other extreme, an unduly slow film may well mean that you risk camera shake: that is, you cannot hold the camera steady for the duration of the exposure. It may not matter on a sunny day, when even an ISO 25 film can be exposed at about 1/250 at f/5.6, but light levels do not have to fall very far for you to encounter problems with depth of field, or camera shake, or both. If you are using a tripod, longer exposures should not matter too much, but there are all kinds of occasion when you do not want to use a tripod.

This is why most films are in the ISO 100 to ISO 400 range. While an excess of light is rarely a problem – it is the price of the film which is more of a deterrent, in many cases – a lack of it frequently is. Unless you want to use flash, therefore, there are limits to how slow a film you will want to use. From

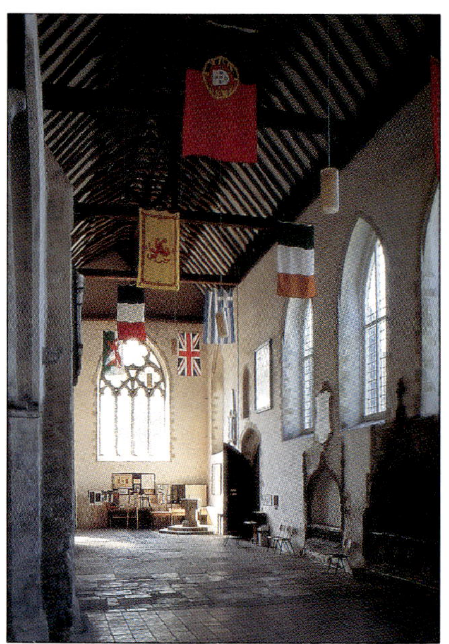

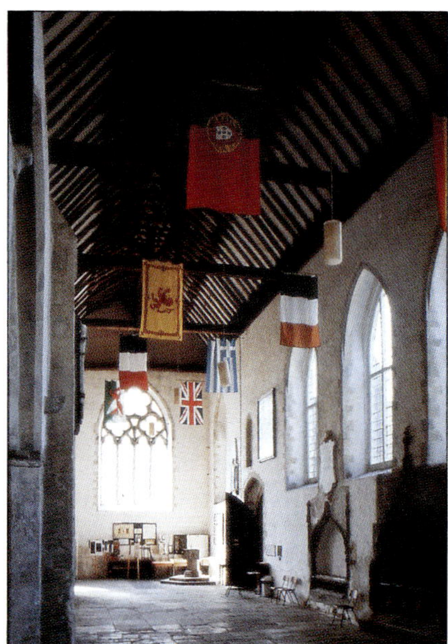

Interior, disused church, Sandwich

We very rarely run 'side by side' tests of films except when we need to illustrate a particular point: normally, we would try to use the right film for the right subject. Sometimes, of course, we do not have the right film with us, or we have just loaded a roll of something different into the camera, so we shoot on the wrong film anyway! These two pictures were shot specifically for this book, and they show that while modern ultra-fast films are extremely good, slower films are even better. Fast films are grainier; less sharp; less saturated; less contrasty; and somewhat more prone to flare than slower films. In this case, the fast film (Agfa 1000 RS) was also around twice the price of the slow film (Fuji 50 RFP) – not a decisive factor, but certainly significant. We therefore use super-speed films only where we really need the speed, or where we actually want the image quality that we get from the fast film rather than from the slow one. Where we need the speed, we use the sharpest, most saturated films we can get (at the time of writing, Agfa 1000 was our favourite, rated at its full speed), but if we want the grain and the lack of detail, we are equally likely to use Scotch/3M ISO 1000, typically with an 81-series warming filter and rated at about EI 650. The cameras in both of these shots were tripod-mounted Nikon Fs, and the lens used for both shots was a 35mm f/2.8 PC-Nikkor used at about f/11. Exposures were about 1/2 second and 1/30 second. (RWH)

years of experience, we can assure you that except in the most extreme low-light conditions, you can just about get away with ISO 100 and an ultra-fast lens (f/1.2 or f/1.4), or with ISO 400 and a normal f/1.8 or f/2 lens. You will only need fast lenses *and* fast film in very poor light, or when you also need to stop down for depth of field or to use a fast shutter speed to 'freeze' action.

Going Outside the ISO 100 to ISO 400 Range

There are of course perfectly good reasons for using films slower than ISO 100 or faster than ISO 400, and we shall illustrate them in this book. The point is, though, that only professionals and rich amateurs are likely to use film quickly enough to justify loading whole rolls of these speeds: most people will compromise instead. If you want the ultimate in fine grain and sharpness, you must however switch to a slower film, and if you need to take pictures in poor light, you switch to a faster film.

Most of the time you will not need to do this, but you must be prepared to do so if you feel that it will give you a very much better picture. For example, the last time we shot the Moscow State Circus we used film that was too slow. Our pictures were not very good. If we were shooting it again (as we hope to do), we would almost certainly use ISO 1000 film. It is downright stupid not to use the right film for a rare opportunity like that, even if it is expensive and even if you do not finish the last roll.

Colour Sensitivity, Speed and Reciprocity

The speed of a film can also be affected by the lighting under which it is exposed, and by the duration of the exposure. The first is a matter of colour sensitivity, and the latter a matter of reciprocity.

Historically, many black and white films were designed to be exposed by

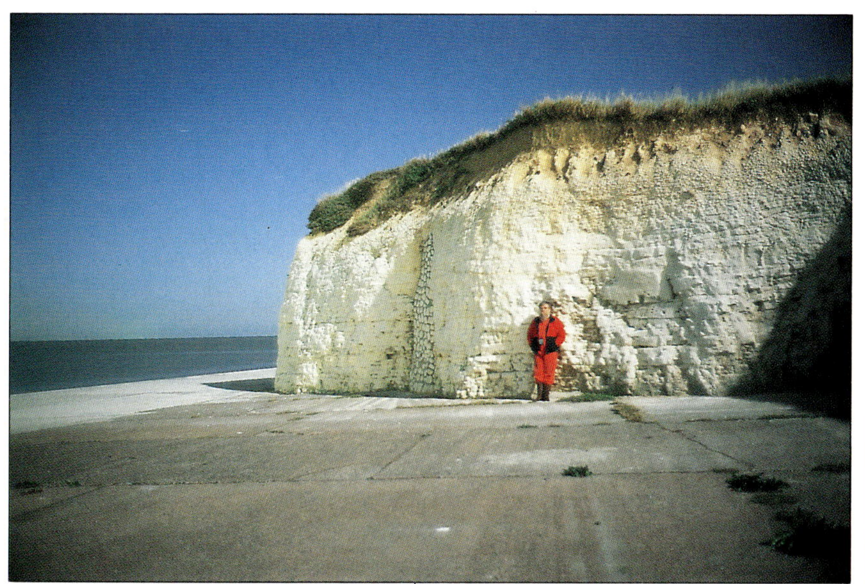

White cliffs by moonlight

The light of the full moon is said to be one millionth as bright as the light of the sun, but of much the same colour; and this picture pretty much confirms it. It was shot on Fuji 100 film, with no filter, using an exposure of six minutes at f/1.4. Exposure was determined by applying a factor of one million to the 'sunny f/16' rule: with ISO 100 film, exposure would be 1/100 second at f/16 in bright sunlight, so in bright moonlight it should be 10,000 seconds at f/16 or 78 seconds at f/1.4. Applying a 'rule of thumb' reciprocity correction of at least one stop, this meant 156 seconds at f/1.4, rounded up to three minutes and bracketed at six minutes. In practice, six minutes was a little too long and five minutes would have been better – but it is still a fascinating tribute to the versatility of modern films. With Agfa 1000 film, the exposure would be cut from five minutes to 30 seconds, though once again one would need to bracket to cover reciprocity failure. We have plans to try landscape photography by moonlight on ISO 1000 film, with four minutes at f/4 using medium-format cameras. (FES)

daylight, which has a great deal more blue light in it than artificial light. If you tried to expose these films by artificial light, their effective speed would typically drop by half. Today this is very rare, because most films have what is known as 'extended red sensitivity', which gives them the same speed in artificial light as in daylight.

Reciprocity failure, on the other hand, is harder to ignore. It is something you have to worry about when you want to use much longer, or much shorter, exposures than the film was designed for. 'Reciprocity' is the technical name for the relationship between aperture and exposure time. Normally, you can compensate for one by adjusting the other: open up one stop, halve the shutter speed, or vice versa. Outside a film's designed exposure range, however, this reciprocity relationship breaks down.

For example, a typical daylight colour slide film is designed to be exposed between 1/2 second and 1/1000 second. If you want to give a very long exposure, several seconds or even minutes, you will almost certainly have to increase the exposure as compared with what you would expect. For example, a 10 second exposure might call for an extra half stop, so you would need to open up the lens by that amount. It might also call for modest filtration, with a weak blue or yellow or red filter: the precise filtration will depend on the film, and can only be determined by getting hold of the manufacturer's information sheets. You can often ignore the filtration – we have given exposures of several minutes without any very adverse effects – but the increase in exposure is another matter. Again, it varies from film to film, but a good rule of thumb is 50 to 100 per cent at 10 seconds, and 100 to 200 per cent at one minute. Polaroid films (Chapter 10) are particularly prone to reciprocity failure.

At the other extreme, you might not think that problems with ultra-short exposures would be something most people would encounter – though the 1/8000 top speed of some cameras can lead to reciprocity failure problems with some films. The real problem is that you can quite easily run into exposures as short as 1/30,000 second if you are using automatic electronic flash at close range: check the instruction book of your flash-gun if you do not believe us. Once again, you need to give extra exposure (typically half a stop, though it may be as much as a stop) and you may need to add weak filtration.

True Speed and Shadow Detail

If you are not concerned about shadow detail, you can rate films at a very much higher effective speed than the manufacturer's ISO rating would indicate. In particular, if you are only interested in getting recognisable Caucasian faces (as is the case in some kinds of surveillance photography, or some kinds of reportage), you can cheerfully set your meter to two, three or even four stops faster than the ISO speed. For an ISO 400 film, this implies an EI of anything from 1600 to 6400. This is without making any changes to processing, as described in Chapter 3. Whenever anyone makes dramatic claims for 'push' processing, always check to see how much shadow detail they have.

Nominal, Actual and Effective Speeds

The nominal or box ISO speed of a film may or may not be the actual ISO speed, and that in turn may not be the best speed at which to rate the film. Speed variations are most critical in slide films, where tolerances for amateur films are held to a third of a stop: this is the minimum variation which actually matters for most purposes. This means, though, that an ISO 100 film can be anything from ISO 80 (a third of a stop slow) to ISO 125 (a third of a stop fast). If you were very unlucky, you could in theory buy two boxes of film, one of which was a third of a stop fast and one of which was a third of a stop slow, so you would have a clearly visible two-thirds of a stop difference between apparently identically exposed films. There are however several ways around this.

The cheapest is to use films with the same batch number. The batch number is stamped on the side of the box, and all films with the same batch number will have the same emulsion. This is how professionals used to work in the days before 'professional' films. They would buy large quantities of film at a time, often several hundred rolls, test them carefully, and then expose (and sometimes filter) them accordingly.

Today, 'professional' films do some of this work for you. Either they print the true speed on the information slip which comes with the film, or (increasingly) they simply down-rate all out-of-spec film to 'amateur' status, so that all 'professional' film has the same actual speed as its nominal speed. This is how Professional Kodachrome works, for example. In general, you only need the extra consistency of 'professional' colour films if you are shooting similar subjects under

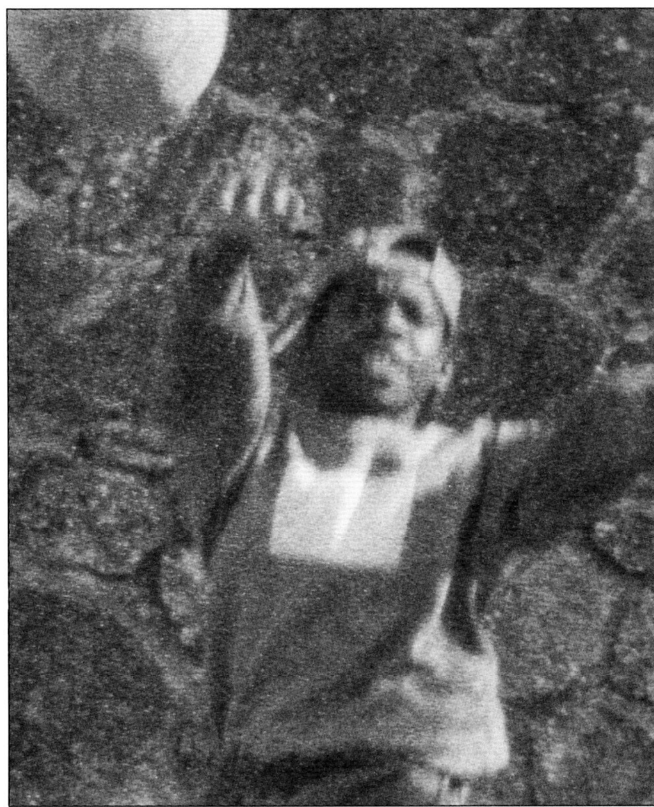

Grain

Most modern films are so grain-free that they have to be enlarged very considerably in order to see the grain structure. An exception is Polaroid's instant-process PolaPan, which reveals quite impressive grain even at 5x enlargement. As noted in the text, the term 'grain' is strictly a misnomer, as the individual grains of silver in an image are too small to see: what you are actually seeing is clumps of grain or (in the case of colour films) clumps of dye-clouds. You do not need to go back very far to see very much grainier pictures; and if you go back to the 1930s, when the Leica and the Contax were popularising 35mm photography, even medium-speed films had grain like this. It is because of this vintage grain structure that so many advertising photographers use 35mm PolaPan.

Interior, Cravens House, Chattanooga

One of the most delightful things about the United States National Parks Service is that there are almost no restrictions on photography – a welcome contrast to the custodians of beautiful places in many other countries, such as Britain's National Trust, which tries to ban photography. You can even set up a tripod if they are not too busy (it is only common courtesy to ask), and then you can stop right down and produce sharp 'set-piece' pictures like this one. We chose Ilford XP-2 principally for its long tonal range: we actually rated it at about EI 100 for this shot, over-exposing two stops in order to get the finest possible grain and plenty of detail in the shadows. The exposure was about one second at f/16. In printing, Frances had to burn in the upper part of the room by about a stop, using a lower contrast grade in order to build density without making the manipulation look too harsh or obvious. The Cravens House in its present two-storey form does not date from the Civil War: it was rebuilt on the foundations of the earlier one-storey building, which was destroyed in the Battle of Chattanooga. (RWH)

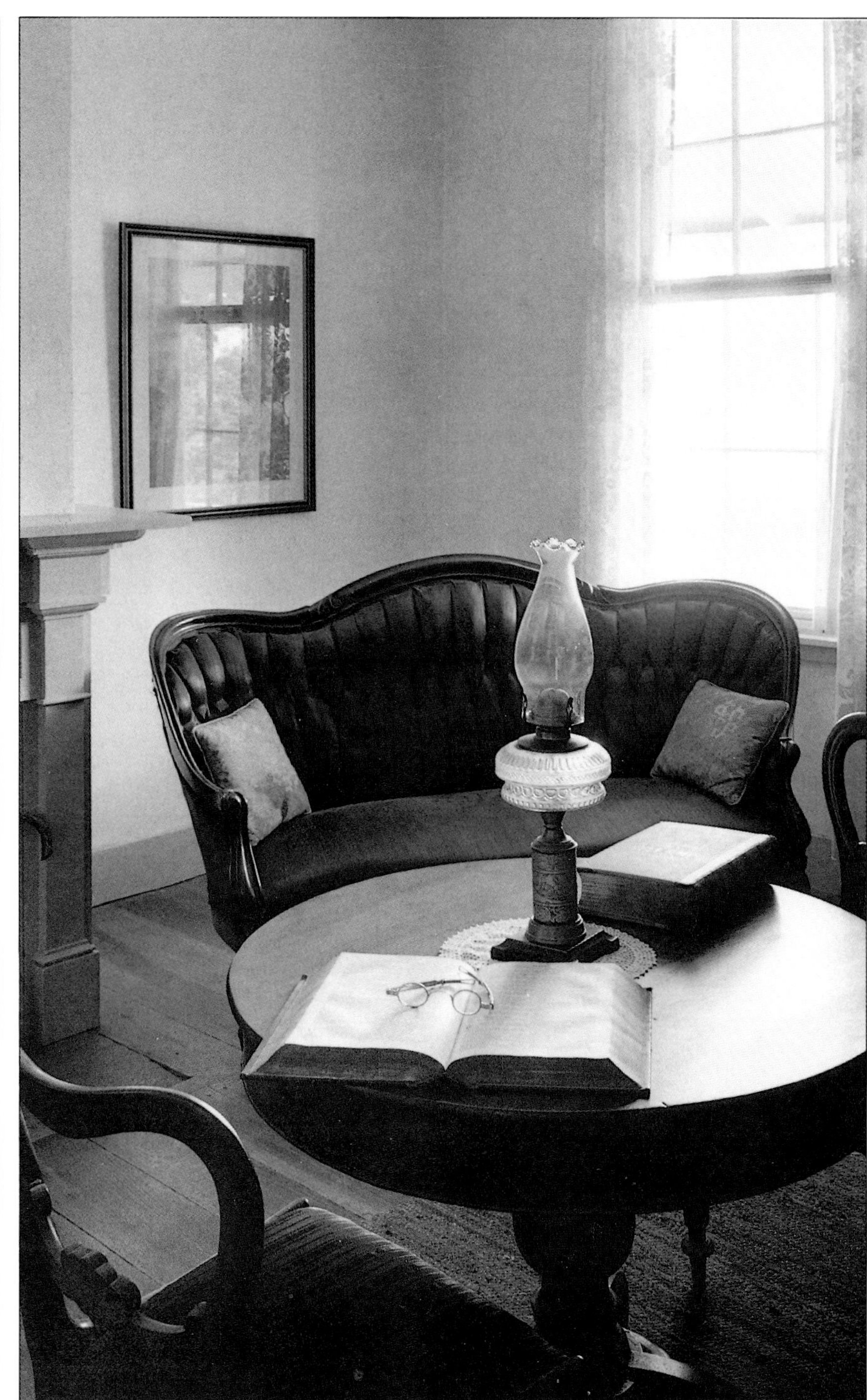

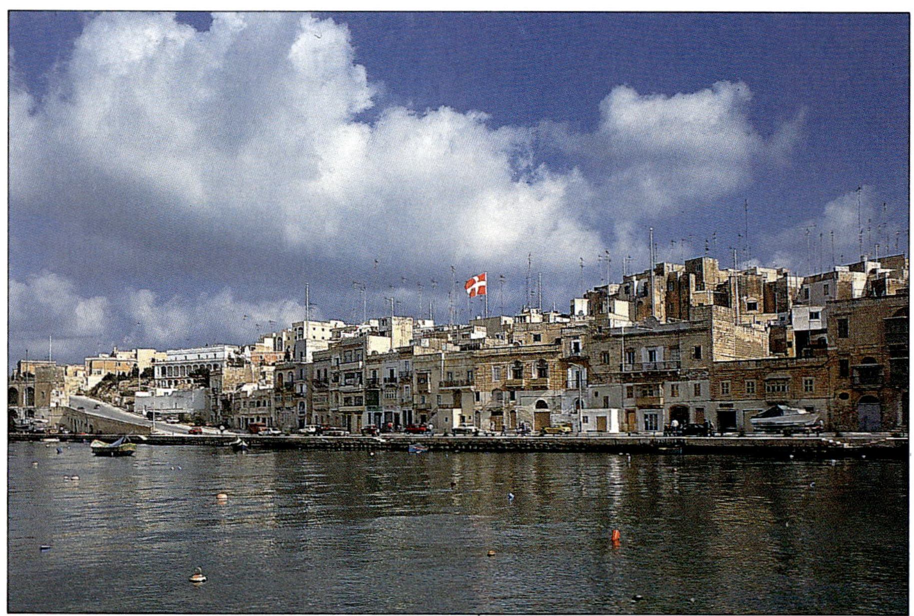

Senglea

The principal requirements of a picture like this are sharpness and fine grain. There is a great deal going on, and this invites the viewer into the picture. In truth, nothing that is happening is very exciting, but for most people the location is sufficiently exotic to excite their curiosity – this is Malta, where in 1565 the armies of the Grand Turque were decisively repulsed and Christendom was saved. There is plenty of clear, bright Mediterranean light, and depth of field is not really a problem, because there is nothing of real interest in the foreground. Even with ISO 50 film, a hand-held exposure of 1/250 at f/8 produces excellent results. The limiting factor is lens sharpness, and Roger has no recollection of which lens he used; but it seems to have been sharp enough. Our standard films in Malta were normal-contrast ISO 50 and ISO 100 colour slide materials, Fuji RFP and RDP, because the light is contrasty enough already. (RWH)

controlled lighting, ie in the studio. For most kinds of location shooting, of different subjects under varying lighting conditions, you are extremely unlikely to see the difference.

Finally, the effective speed at which you choose to rate the film will depend on your cameras and lenses; your meter and metering techniques; and the purpose for which you want the pictures. The most extreme example of variation from ISO speeds is Agfa's black and white slide film, Dia-Direct, which used to be rated at ISO 32 and is now rated at ISO 12. Both figures are irrelevant – or to be more accurate, they straddle the effective film speed, which is (and always was) EI 20 or 25.

With slide films, if you are shooting for reproduction, it is quite common to under-expose slightly (by about a third of a stop) in order to get a little extra density and more saturated colours. If you are shooting for projection, on the other hand, the exposure should be slightly greater. Thus, many people would rate Kodachrome 64 at EI 50 for reproduction, but at its full ISO 64 for projection. There are also some slide films which many photographers agree do not match their nominal ISO speed: it is quite common, for example, to rate Velvia (ISO 50) at EI 32. This does not mean that Fuji are 'cheating' in any way: it just means that exposure requirements in the real world are slightly different from those in the rather artificial world of ISO film-speed determination.

As for black and white print films, it used to be the case that a very modest amount of over-exposure – a third of a stop, or half a stop – improved shadow detail significantly, and gave better overall gradation. This meant rating an ISO 100 film at EI 80 or thereabouts. Today, fewer and fewer films seem to need this over-exposure, and most should be rated at their nominal ISO speed.

Girl burying brother

This is a good example of a picture which is a very successful snapshot, but which would be a commercial failure: the piece of plastic embedded in the sand on the left is very obtrusive. In fact, the picture was shot merely to test a rangefinder camera that we bought for $15 (under £10) at a photo-show in 1991, an old Konica IIIS dating probably from the early 1960s. The best film for testing a camera is always a slow colour slide film: in this case, ISO 50 Fuji RFP. Because of the limited exposure latitude of the film, deficiencies in shutter speed or metering will be shown up mercilessly (as are defects in the auto-diaphragm, in an SLR) and the sharpness of the lens and accuracy of the focusing system are tested equally mercilessly by the extreme sharpness of the film. You can see that the camera scores astonishingly highly on all counts, especially given the price and the age, and you can also see that the film is barely suited to the subject. Even with the strong 'fill' provided by the sand, which helps to flatten the contrast range, the boy's cheek and the girl's legs are almost burned out. This is why we normally switch to ISO 100 film such as Fuji's RDP for pictures where flesh tones are important. (RWH)

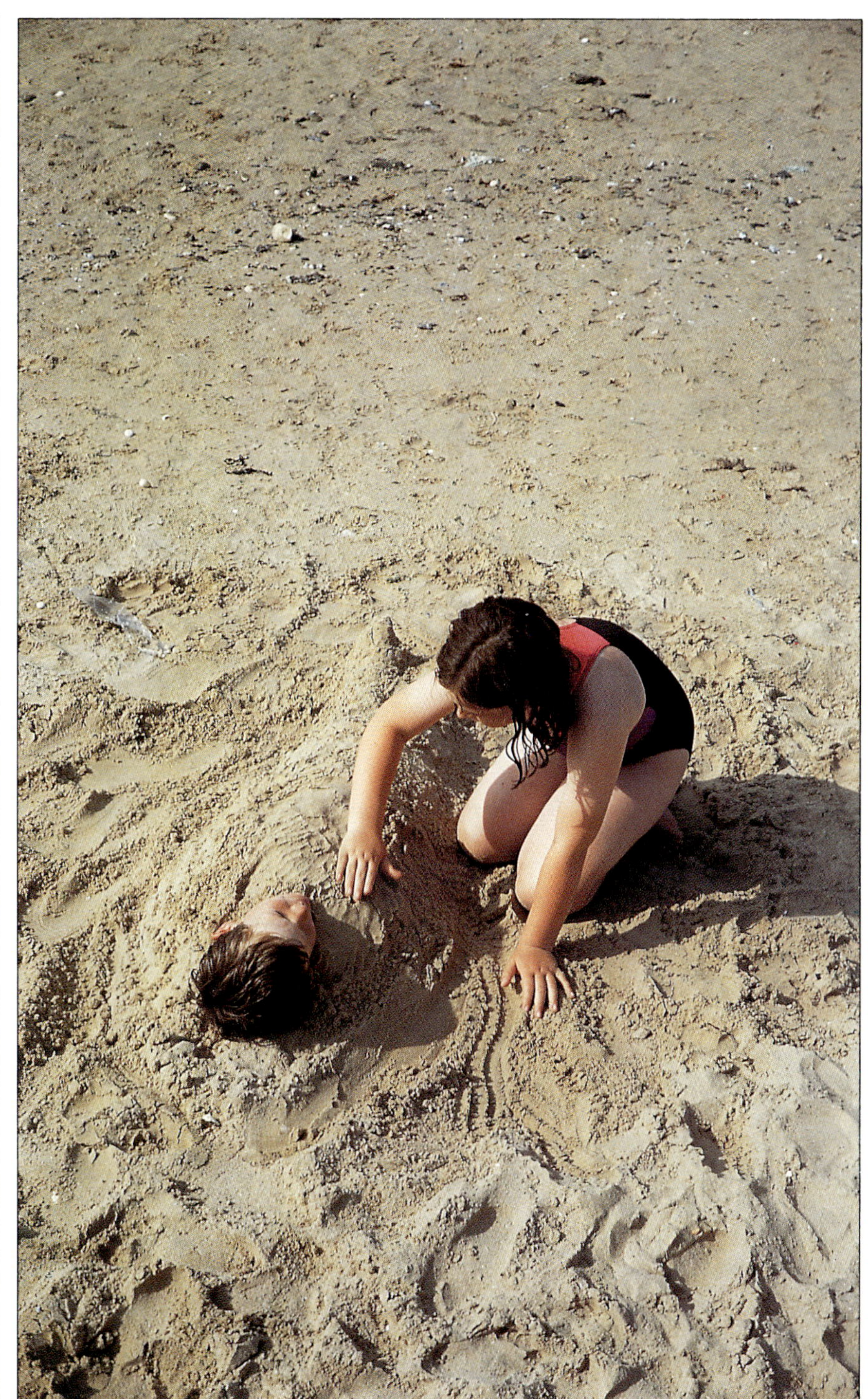

LATITUDE

Latitude is a film's tolerance for over- and under-exposure. As a general rule, slow films have less latitude than faster ones, though at a given speed latitude will depend on the type of film (negative or slide) and to a lesser extent on the manufacturer's cleverness.

The most tolerant films are colour negative films, and Ilford XP-2, which uses the same technology as colour negative films. They can only stand a small amount of under-exposure, maybe one stop, and only then at the expense of significantly increased grain and (in the case of colour films) thin, greenish shadows. They can however stand an enormous amount of over-exposure. One stop of over-exposure is actually beneficial, resulting in tighter grain and better colours, which is why many professionals rate these films at less than the manufacturers' recommended speeds. Some labs may object, and you may have to send the negatives back for reprints, but if they tell you that the negatives are too dense to print, they are lying. If you can see the detail in the negative, they can print it. A further stop of over-exposure will result in a still denser negative, of course, and the practical limit is three stops; but given that this is equivalent to rating an ISO 400 film at EI 50, this is serious over-exposure.

Conventional black and white films are next in the tolerance stakes, but a lot depends on your expectations. For the very best results, a conventional black and white film of any speed must be exposed at something very close to its optimum exposure index. Even so, a fast film should be quite tolerant: anything up to a couple of stops of

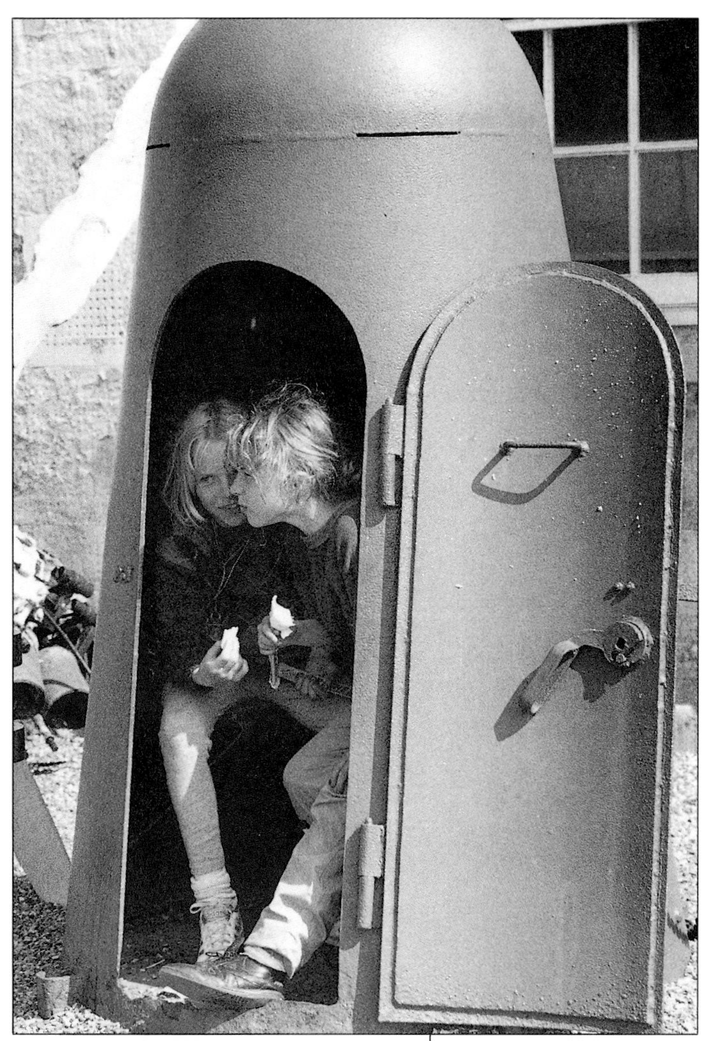

Children in diving bell

This old diving bell is outside Ramsgate Museum, and Frances photographed it using Delta 400. There would have been plenty of light to use a slower film – the exposure was something like 1/500 second at f/8 to f/11 – but the faster film had several advantages. One was its tonal range: a slower film would have been more contrasty, and with this picture you obviously need to see into the shadows. Another was its latitude, though the latitude of XP-2 is even greater. A third was the extra depth of field and freedom from camera shake compared with a slower film. Shaky hands run in Frances's family, and if she is not using a tripod, she likes to use a rather faster shutter speed than most people would consider necessary. This was shot with a 90mm lens on a Nikon F, and using ISO 400 instead of ISO 100 allowed her to use one stop smaller aperture and one step faster on the shutter-speed dial. We use Delta 400 whenever we want a combination of speed and quality. For really demanding reportage we prefer XP-2, and for ultimate quality Delta 100 wins; but this film is an impressive compromise between speed, latitude and image quality. (FES)

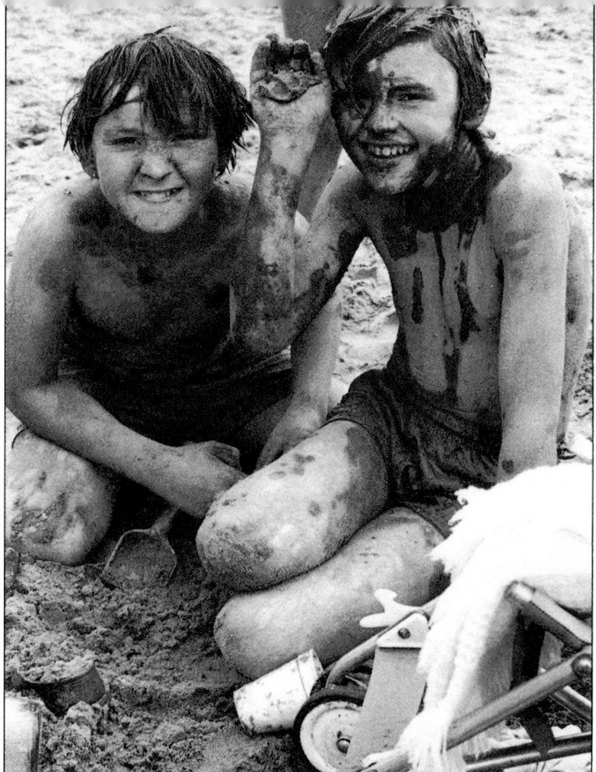

Children, Weston-super-Mare

As described in the text, subject matter can quite often disguise grain. Sand, and sandy skin, conceal grain almost perfectly: only when you look at the pushchair on the right do you see how even grainless metal 'reads' as if it were textured. This was taken many years ago on Ilford's old (pre-Plus) HP5, probably rated at EI 650 and developed in Microphen. The great advantage of that combination was its enormous latitude. Roger's technique in those days (long before we met) was to take periodic readings with a Weston Master meter, then adjust the exposure for individual shots on the basis of experience. It is not clear why the shawl on the pushchair is so burned out. The first possibility is that the whole shot is over-exposed, in over-compensation for the fact that the children were in shadow. The second is that the film is over-developed (something Roger often did, in those days). The third, which is probably a contributing factor in any case, is simply that in the 1960s and 1970s, films were not as good as they are today. (RWH)

over-exposure, or a stop of under-exposure, is likely to prove acceptable for most purposes. Slower films are less tolerant, and with the very slowest films (ISO 25 to ISO 50) even half a stop of under-exposure or one stop of over-exposure will result in significantly harder-to-print negatives.

Least tolerant of all are reversal (slide) films. Slower films (ISO 100 and below) can normally tolerate at most one stop of over-exposure, and half a stop of under-exposure. Faster films are more tolerant, and ISO 1000 films may provide acceptable results with as much as two stops of over-exposure and one stop under-exposure; but you would be rash to rely on it.

GRAIN

It is possible to tie oneself in all kinds of linguistic knots here, with 'grain', 'granularity' and 'graininess' all having different and carefully defined meanings. From the point of view of the practical photographer, though, we can subsume them all under the heading of 'grain'.

Grain is what you see when a subject which should be smooth and featureless – a blue sky, say, or the polished metal of a car – has a detectable speckled pattern in it. Strictly, you are not seeing 'grain' at all, but clumps of grain; but this is not a very useful distinction. With colour film, you are not even seeing clumps of grain: rather, you are seeing clumps of dye clouds. Again, this is not a useful distinction. It is included only as a nod to the pedants.

Grain is much more obvious in some subjects than others. It is most obvious, as already intimated, when the subject should be absolutely smooth and free of texture. It is least obvious in those pictures where we can read the grain of the film as being the texture of the subject. A shingle beach, or an animal's pelt, or even the texture of a human face, can 'hide' a great deal of grain.

For some unknown reason, it also seems that some kinds of grain are much more acceptable than others. You can look at two prints, side by side, and see that there really is not much difference in the grain size, but that somehow the grain in one picture is significantly more obtrusive than in the other. If you compare Ilford's two ISO 400 non-chromogenic films, HP5 Plus and Delta 400, the grain is simply less obtrusive in the Delta, though it really does not look very much smaller.

Grain and Speed

Other things being equal, grain and speed are intimately related: the faster the film is, the grainier it will be. But other things are not strictly equal. New grain technologies mean that fast films can be made finer and finer grained; or alternatively, that fine-grained films can be made faster and faster. The net result is that at the time of writing, there were effectively three separate 'families' of grain.

Leading the pack are the state-of-the-art films, things like Ilford's Delta 100 in black and white or Kodak's Lumière and Panther in colour slide or Konica's Impresa in colour print. All have grain which is (to an old-fashioned photographer) quite miraculously fine. Then, in second place, are the so-called 'old-technology' films from the major manufacturers such as Kodak, Ilford, Agfa, Fuji and so forth. Then, lagging quite a long way behind these, there are the genuinely old-technology films from places like China: still of surprisingly good quality, but clearly in another league.

Grain and Format

Fine grain only matters, of course, if two conditions are met. The first is that the picture is going to be enlarged to the point where the grain would become visible, and the second is that the photographer cares about this.

If you are using 35mm, and you care about grain, you have to use slow, fine-grain films. But if you are using medium format, or (better still) large format, there is very little likelihood that the grain will be detectable in any but the largest blow-ups, unless you use quite fast films. Even with a more than averagely grainy ISO 400 film, grain starts to become detectable at about a 4x or 5x blow-up, and it becomes obtrusive at 6x or 8x. With a 6x7cm Linhof negative (actual dimensions 56x72mm), a 4x blow-up is 224x288mm, or 8.8x11.3in; close enough to an A4 page. With the typical ISO 160 colour

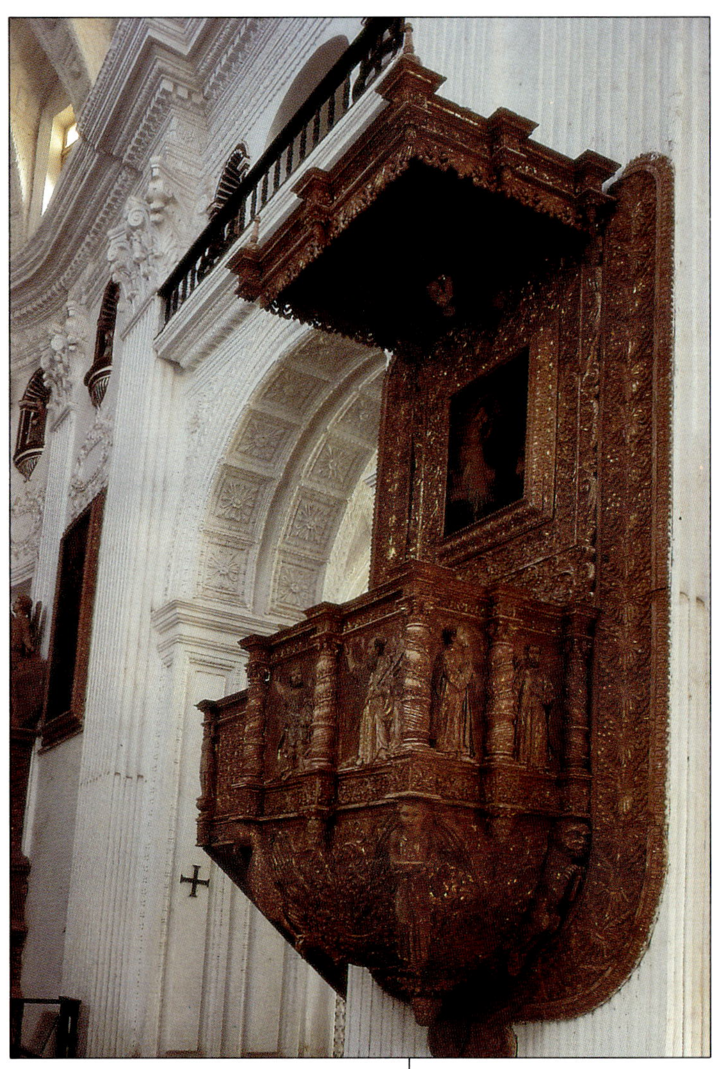

Pulpit, Goa Vieja

Goa Vieja – Old Goa – is an extraordinary collection of vast churches in the formerly Portuguese enclave on the west coast of India. Surprisingly few visitors go there: most of them are more interested in the beaches a few miles away. It is however a magical place. Only a slow film, in this case Kodachrome 64, could do justice to the wealth of detail in this church, and a degree of under-exposure (about half a stop to one stop) has held a great deal of detail in the white-painted mouldings and carvings in the background, without losing anything in the pulpit itself. As explained elsewhere, Kodachrome is our standard choice for travelling in hot weather, because of its resistance to colour-shifts even when it cannot be stored under ideal conditions. The camera was tripod mounted: as far as we recall, it was a Leica M4-P with a 90mm f/2 Summicron, stopped well down for depth of field, so the exposure would have been something like 1/4 second at f/11. A shift lens would have been nice, but the only one we own is the 35mm f/2.8. (RWH)

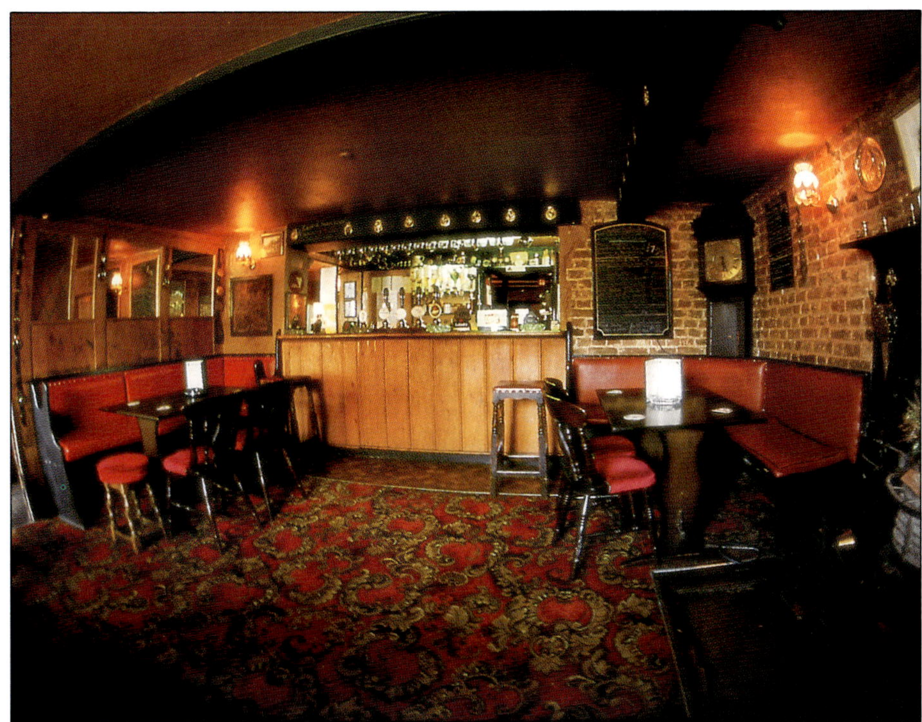

The Bell Inn, St Nicholas at Wade

This is an experimental shot using a full-frame fish-eye, the Sigma 15mm f/2.8. There is a slight loss of sharpness – you cannot quite read the menu on the blackboard as easily as you would wish – but this is nothing to do with the lens or the film. Rather, it is because this was a hand-held shot at a full half second, with the lens at full aperture. Roger braced his elbows on the table, but even so, a half-second hand-held shot is a remarkable trick. He could get away with it, of course, because of the extreme angle of coverage of the lens. The trouble is, the loss of sharpness is all the more irritating because both the lens and the ISO 50 film (Fuji RFP) could do very much better. The picture would be much more acceptable if he had used a faster, grainier film which would have obscured the lack of ultimate sharpness. Alternatively, mounting the camera on a tripod would have allowed him to stop down a little – which improves almost any lens – and to give whatever exposure was needed, without the risk of camera shake. As with a number of other experimental pictures in this book, this one was the result of using up the last three or four frames of a film. Very often, you can learn a great deal about your equipment, your film and your personal abilities by just trying something for yourself, rather than by looking for the answer in a book or magazine. (RWH)

negative film used for weddings and portraits, even a 6x blow-up appears substantially grain-free. This corresponds to 336x432mm, or approximately 13x17 in. It suddenly becomes very clear why high-street photographers use medium-format cameras instead of 35mm!

SHARPNESS

Even if two films are about equally grainy, one can still appear much sharper than the other. There are several reasons for this, but the two most important are the fact that grain and sharpness are not quite the same thing, and the way that sometimes, grain can actually make a picture look sharper.

One of the main factors governing sharpness is emulsion thickness. In a thick emulsion, light scatters more than in a thin one, and it is therefore impossible for a fine line to be reproduced as finely as in the thinner emulsion. Once again, reducing emulsion thickness is one of the great goals of the modern film designer, and this is why even the 'old technology' films from the major manufacturers – such venerable offerings as Tri-X – are still sharper than they used to be. Thick emulsion is also one of the main reasons why genuinely old-technology films from the more backward countries are less sharp than their equivalents from the major modern manufacturers.

The paradoxical effect of grain making pictures appear sharper can occur when you have big but 'crisp' grain – the sort of thing you get if you process a fast film in paper developer, for instance. Because the grain itself is sharp, you can fail to notice that the actual detail, the thing that the picture is supposed to be about, is really quite soft. Grain can conceal more than just lack of film sharpness, too: soft lenses, poor focus and camera shake are also less obvious. Given that large, crisp grain also has a great deal of immediacy, because we automatically associate it with news pictures, this can be a useful trick to remember!

As with graininess, sharpness is very much dependent on format. If you are using 35mm cameras, and blowing the pictures up more than about 8x, lens sharpness is more of a limiting factor than anything else, even with the very finest-grained films. In fact, although films like Orwo 25 (black and white) or Ektar 25 (colour print) are detectably sharper than (say) T-Max 100, you will only see the difference if you are using the finest lenses under ideal conditions and blowing the images up a long way. You might as well use the faster films.

If you are using medium format, there is absolutely no need to use the slower films: even genuinely old-technology films in the ISO 80 to 125 range will deliver more than adequate sharpness. Once again, you are looking at 6x to 8x blow-ups before film sharpness even becomes an issue. By the time you are using 4x5in originals, *any* film is fine: XP-2, rated at EI 200, will give you superb results, with no grain and no sharpness problems, even if you make enlargements several feet square.

Acutance

A special consideration of sharpness is edge sharpness or acutance. This is most easily explained graphically, as in the drawing on the right.

During development, developer by-products increase the density of the dark area, and decrease the density of the light area, just where they meet. The result is that resolution of bar targets (or of fine detail of any kind) is greatly improved, though it makes little or no difference to anything else. Some developers are specifically formulated for high acutance.

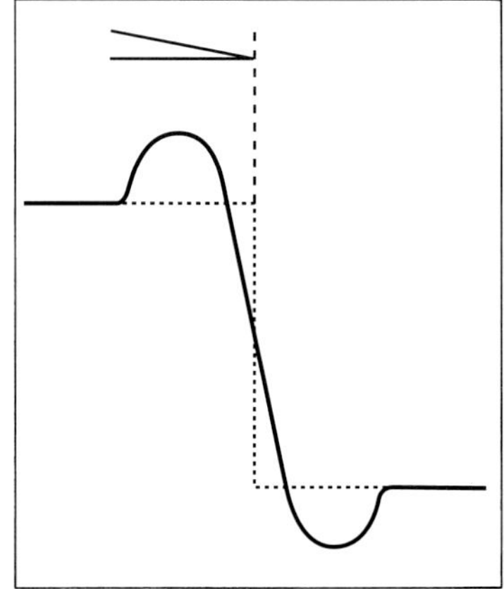

Acutance

The way that acutance or edge sharpness is tested is by laying a knife-edge on the film and exposing the film. If the film were perfect, the exposed area would be black and the unexposed area would be clear; but of course no film is perfect, so there is always a grey transition area, caused mostly by diffusion or scattering of the light by the emulsion. Some film/developer combinations compensate for this grey transition area by creating an area of unusually low density just before the transition, and unusually high density just after it. The distances in question are usually measured in microns (millionths of a millimetre), so the edge effects do not show up as lines.

CONTRAST

A contrasty film is generally trickier to handle than a less contrasty one. Unless your exposure and development are spot-on, you will tend to lose either highlight or shadow detail, or both. Highlights will 'burn out' to a featureless white, and shadows will 'block up' to a featureless black. This is equally true of both black and white and colour films. Kodak's Technical Pan film (black and white) is notoriously contrasty, and its *aficionados* use all sorts of trick developers and careful variations in development timing to tame it. Again, Fuji's Velvia gives stunning colours under the right conditions; but try to use it out of doors, on a sunny day, and be prepared for inky shadows even where you do not want them.

On the other hand, a contrasty film under the right conditions has the power to 'punch up' a dull image to an almost miraculous extent. We normally only use contrasty films in the studio, where we can control the lighting, but there are a few situations in which we also use them out of doors. At an air day, for example, Velvia has far more 'punch' even than its same-speed stablemate Fuji 50 (RFP). This can be

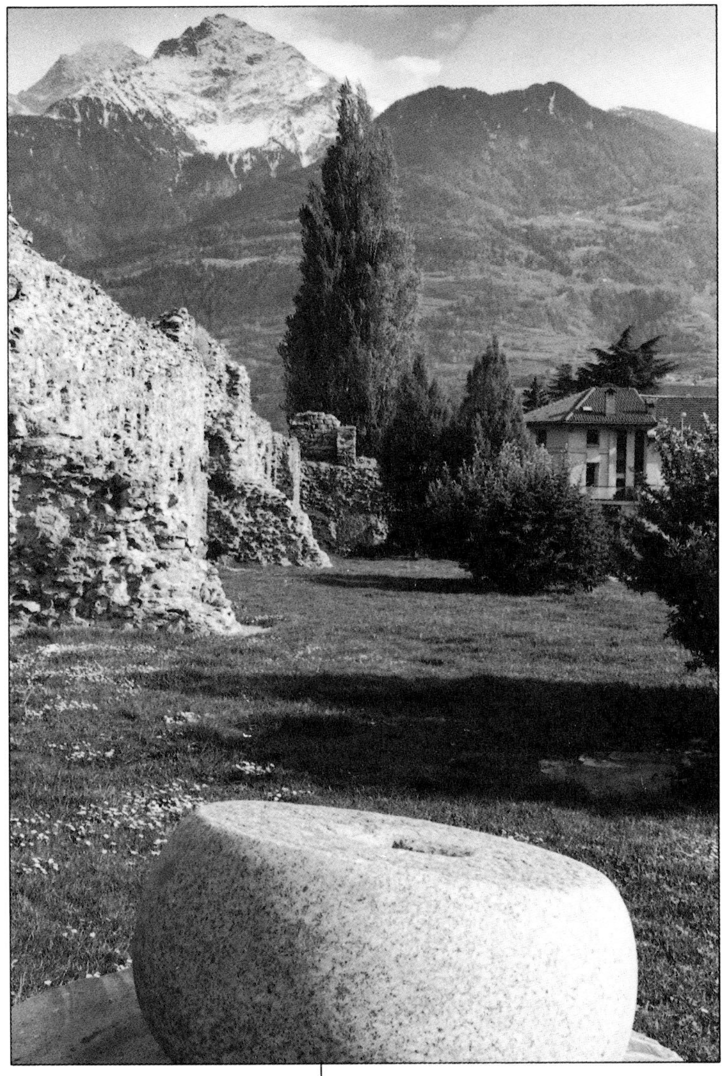

Aosta
The walls on the left are Roman; the mountains in the background are the Alps. We are not sure what the stone in the foreground is: it looks to us like a rather fat millstone. This is the kind of picture where acutance or edge sharpness counts for a lot.
It will not show very much in reproduction, but there are many places where in the original print there are sharp contrasts between light and dark.
There is the speckling in the stone; the individual blades of grass, some sunlit and others not; the mountains against the sky; the stones of the wall; and the tiles on the roof of the house. Acutance makes all this kind of detail stand out, without reducing the print to 'soot and whitewash' contrast. The camera (Nikon F) was on a Manfrotto/Bogen tripod with a Kennett Engineering ball and socket head, and the lens was the 35mm f/2.8 PC-Nikkor, stopped well down for depth of field – probably to f/16, which implies a shutter speed on Ilford Delta 400 of 1/125 or 1/250, given that it was late in the day. (RWH)

very useful, because all too often air-day pictures are flat and hazy.

A special application of low-contrast films, on the other hand, is for portraiture and (especially) for weddings. A traditional wedding is a very high-contrast affair, with the bride in white and the groom in dark clothes, and you have to hold detail in both the dress and the faces. There are several films designed especially for this sort of application, mostly ISO 160 rollfilms which are the mainstay of the high street professional. This is another reason, along with his use of medium-format cameras, why his results are so much better than most amateurs'. This is all the more true if the amateurs are using ultra-slow films in their search for fine grain, which they get at the expense of altogether unacceptable contrast and saturation, at least for this application.

Contrast and Speed

As with grain and speed, there is a clear general relationship between contrast and speed. For the most part, slow films are more contrasty than fast ones. Once more, different manufacturers seem able to tame contrast to differing degrees, so (as usual) things are not quite equal.

Different people find that different films suit their particular subjects or ways of working, but it has to be said that one of the strongest arguments for medium-speed films of any vintage has always been their gradation. They have a sort of 'sparkle' which is the ideal compromise between the subtle, long tonal range and subdued colour of a fast film, and the excessive contrast and indeed garishness of many of the newer slow films.

Gradation

'Gradation' is not quite the same thing as contrast, but it is not entirely different either. It is one of those things which you recognise when you see it, and it seems to be a synthesis of the inherent contrast of the film and the skill of the person using it – especially, in a black and white print, the skill of the printer. It might best be defined as making the most of a film by means of perfect exposure, which is something to which we shall return in Chapter 5.

It is also worth noting that some photographers reckon that they got their very best gradation from long-obsolete thick-emulsion films, with plenty of silver in the emulsion – rather like the current 'silver-rich' premium printing papers such as Ilford Galerie. Because of the emulsion thickness, sharpness was nothing remarkable, and grain was not too impressive either; but gradation was first class. Having looked at old prints made from (for example) Ilford FP3, we can see what they mean. But we would still argue that the very best modern films are as good.

Lens Contrast

We should not leave the subject of contrast without raising the question of lens contrast. With any lens, a proportion of the light does not pass through, but is reflected back at each glass/air interface. It is then bounced around inside the lens. Some of this unfocused, non-image-forming light falls upon the film, where it inevitably reduces contrast.

In the days of fast, uncoated lenses – the late 1930s to late 1940s and even early 1950s – the amount of light which behaved in this way could be impressive. The old Leitz Summarit had seven glasses in five groups: a total of ten air/glass interfaces. Reflection at each interface was about 5 per cent (95 per cent transmission). This meant that total transmission of image-forming light was only 0.95^{10}, or just under 60 per cent. Some of this light was reflected out of the front of the lens, but some ended up on the film, resulting in an overall flattening of contrast. In the early days of Kodachrome, which was a ferociously contrasty and very slow film (ASA 8), this was actually an advantage, as it got the contrast down to reasonable levels and also gave the impression of a slightly higher film speed, thereby compensating for the alarming light losses. This scale of contrast loss explains why Zeiss preferred to arrange the seven glasses of their f/1.5 Sonnar in three groups: the resolution was not as good, but the contrast was significantly better, with about 78 per cent transmission, so the lens looked sharper.

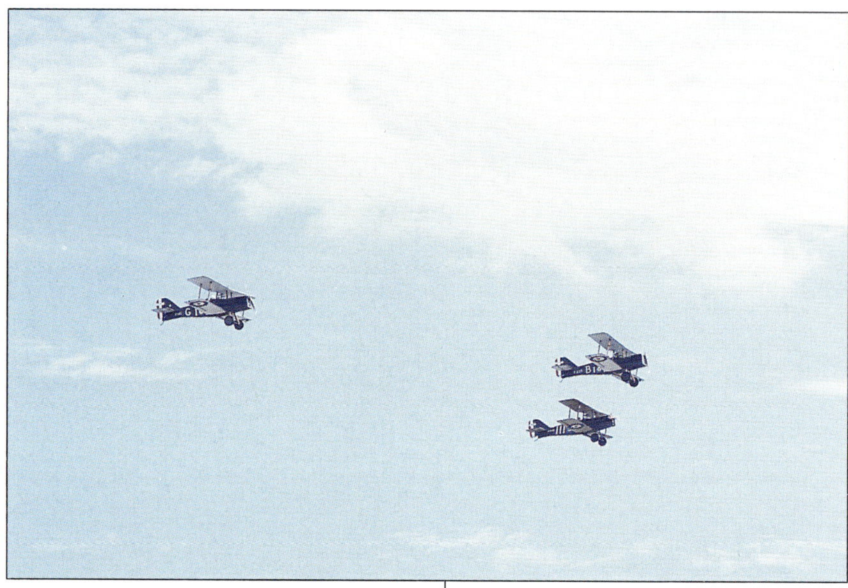

Manston Air Day

There are some circumstances in which any film you use will have to be a compromise, because you may want to take two pictures a few seconds apart where under ideal conditions, you would want to use two different films. For instance, the picture of the World War 1 replica biplanes would arguably have profited from the use of a film with a higher colour saturation, but the picture of the parachutists would not; it is colourful enough, and contrasty enough, already. Also, it is disputable whether a more contrasty film really would have improved the picture of the biplanes, because the desaturated colours are somewhat reminiscent of a chromolithograph, as well as metaphorically echoing the 'faded memories' of what its combatants believed was the War to End Wars. On looking at the pictures, it is hard to escape the conclusion that we did use the wrong film – ISO 100 instead of ISO 50 – but we are still not convinced that a high-saturation film would have been better than a more traditional type, though a number of our friends reckon that high saturation is where it's at on air days. Also, a slower film would have meant that it was impossible to use quite such action-stopping shutter speeds. It is interesting to note that with the exposure used, probably 1/1000 at f/4 or thereabouts (depth of field was not really a problem), the slow-revving airscrews of these fighters are almost sharp. The camera was either a Nikon F or a Nikkormat FTN, and the lens was probably a 200mm f/3 Vivitar Series One. The very best air-day shots are normally taken air-to-air, rather than ground-to-air, which is why it is so hard to equal some of the pictures you see in magazines. (Both RWH)

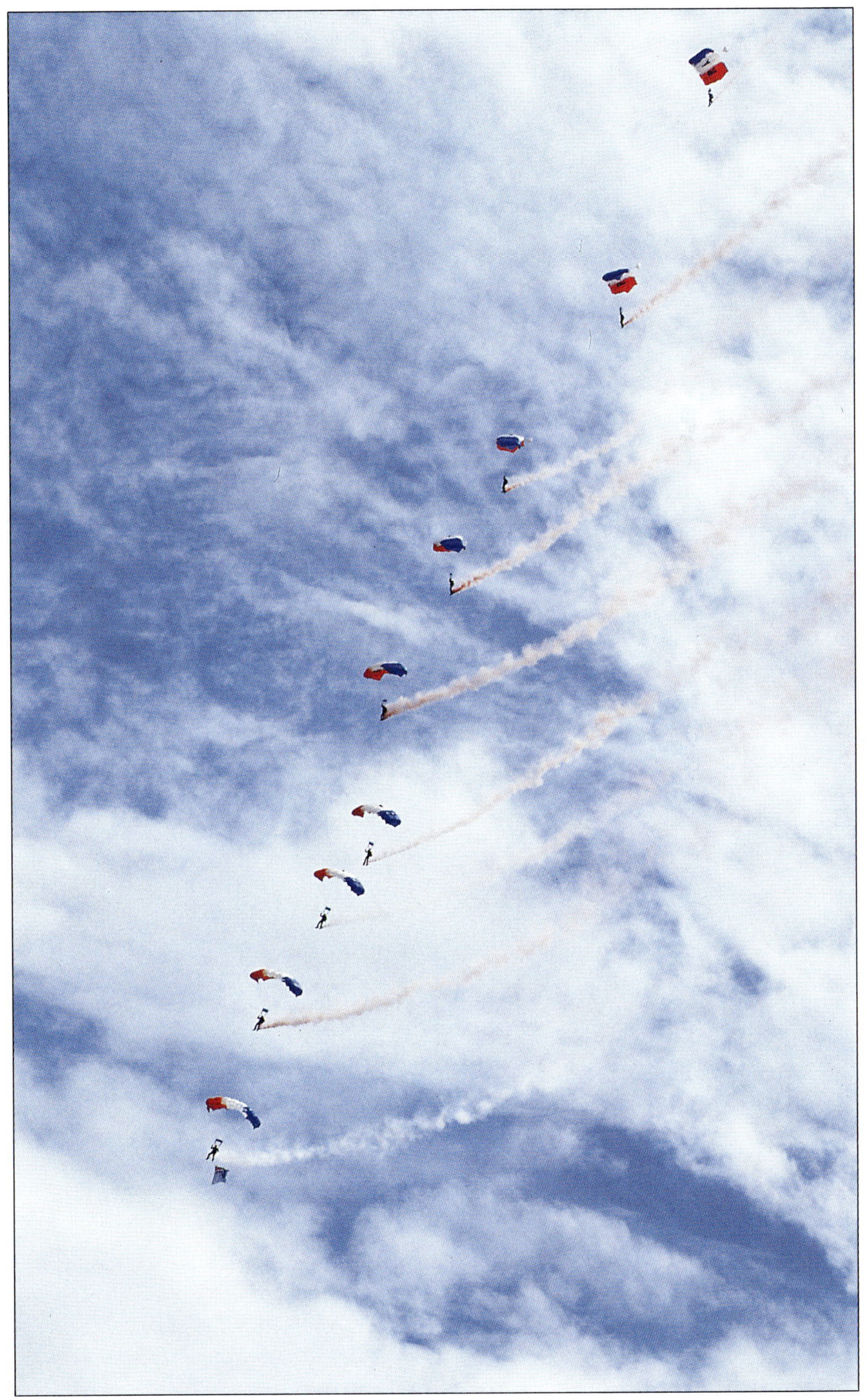

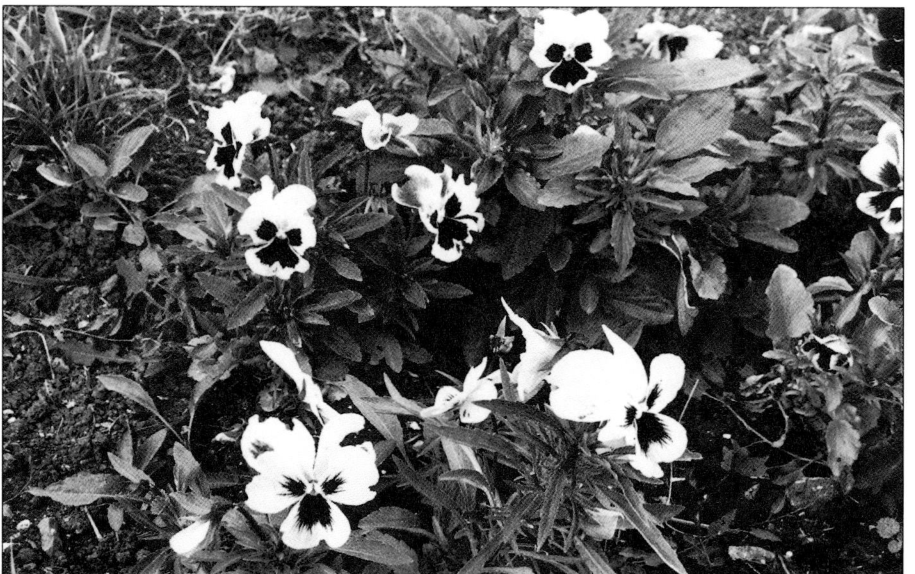

Pansies
Most people (including Roger) cannot understand why Frances likes shooting flowers in black and white, but the attraction lies in the contrast between the flowers and the foliage, and in the textures of the foliage itself: and once she points it out, you can see that there is a sort of richness in black and white photographs of plants. This shot is technically interesting, though, in that it was shot on Ilford HP5 Plus rated at EI 3200 – just as was Roger's shot of Frances on page 60. As you can see, it is not loss of shadow detail which is the problem. It is the exact opposite: excessive contrast, so that the flowers are burned out to a featureless white. Shadow detail is remarkably good. The picture was taken with a Pentax Z-1 and the 28-80mm zoom: exposure was probably 1/2000 at f/16, or even 1/4000 at f/11. We took some pictures at 1/8000, and when we examined the negatives, it did not seem that there was any evidence of reciprocity failure. (FES)

Today, the very best multi-coated lenses can easily reduce the light loss at each air/glass interface to about 0.5 per cent, or 99.5 per cent transmission. This means that complex zooms are feasible, with maybe fifteen or twenty glasses in ten or a dozen groups. With a dozen groups, and two dozen air/glass interfaces, 99 per cent transmission at each interface implies an overall transmission of about 80 per cent, and 99.5 per cent transmission raises this to almost 90 per cent. With the old 95 per cent transmission at each interface, you would be looking at a laughable 30 per cent or so: everything would look as if it was photographed in a fog. Indeed, some older zooms with less efficient coatings were not too good: even 98 per cent transmission at each glass/air interface implies just over 60 per cent transmission for a twelve-group lens, or just over 70 per cent for an eight-group.

Simpler designs, though, are inherently much more contrasty than zooms. A six-glass, four-group lens has eight glass/air interfaces, and with 99.5 per cent transmission, this equates to better than 96 per cent transmission of image-forming light. Lenses for Leica rangefinder cameras are famed for their contrast, and this is why: they are for the most part straightforward six- to eight-glass designs, with relatively few air/glass interfaces, and they have the best multi-layer coating around. It seems that the first-ever lens to be multi-coated was the 50mm f/1.4 Leitz Summilux in 1959.

The difference that the Leica's high-contrast, high-transmission lenses can make to your photography is impressive. In black and white, most printers reckon that the difference is equivalent to one whole paper grade, while in colour, a British reviewer attacked one of Roger's books for its 'over-contrasty, over-polarised' images. If he had bothered to read the text, he would have seen that the inconvenience of using polarisers on Leicas was

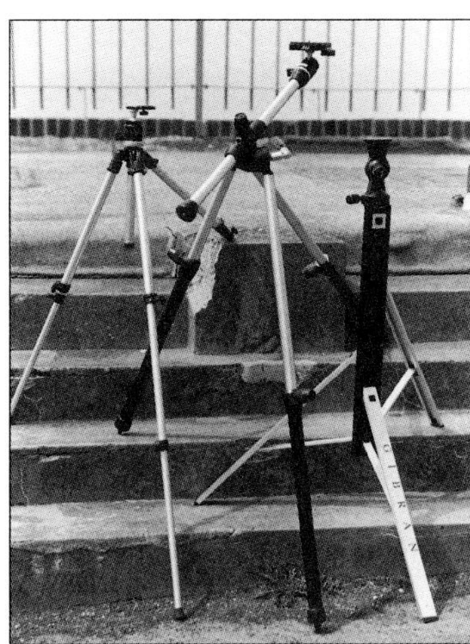

Tripods
No matter what film you use, you can greatly improve the quality which you will get from it if you use a tripod. Three of our most useful travelling tripods are shown here. All three have variable leg splay, so that they can be set up on uneven surfaces. On the left is a Manfrotto Bogen with a Kennett ball and socket head. This is the lightest reasonably solid tripod we own, and the one which collapses to the smallest size. In the middle is a Benbo, which is our most versatile tripod – it can be set up in the most extraordinary positions – but which is rather bulky and knobbly: the legs are two-section instead of three-section, and the control knobs are quite large. The sealed-leg design does however mean that it can be used in bogs and similar inhospitable surroundings. The head is again a Kennett ball and socket, though we would more often use the Benbo with a ProBall head, which is seen on the Gibran on the right. The Gibran is not only very beautiful – It is the only piece of photographic equipment in the New York Museum of Modern Art – but it is also very sleek and quick to use. The ProBall is an incomparably versatile head, though rather large and bulky: we use another ProBall on our monster Linhof tripod, which normally never leaves the studio.

specifically cited as a reason why they had not been used...

COLOUR SATURATION

This is closely allied to contrast, but it is not quite the same thing – and since the late 1980s, it has become increasingly important.

Traditionally, most photographers preferred fairly low colour saturation. When colour televisions became popular, it was something of a joke that you could always tell a photographer's set, because the colours were turned down until they looked reasonably natural, instead of the rather garish displays which appeared in shop windows and in the homes of the less discerning. In those days, Kodachrome 25 was treated warily, because of its very high colour saturation.

Today, the TV generation seems to have taken over. Colour saturations are much higher than they used to be, and as we were writing this, we read a review (presumably by a very young and inexperienced photographer) saying that while Kodachrome 25 was super-sharp, it lacked the punchy colours of modern films such as Fuji's Velvia.

As we have said elsewhere, there are times when high-saturation colour films are great. They allow you to make dramatic, colourful compositions, even on dull days and under flat lighting. But in our view, they are a device to be used sparingly: they should not be the everyday norm which they have become. This may be a matter of personal taste, and it may be a matter of differences between the generations, but if you find that your colour pictures lack subtlety, you might just want to take a step back and use a less saturated film.

COLOUR BALANCE

Colour balance is a rather less controversial matter. It is a matter of common experience that the human eye is enormously adaptable, and can read all kinds of light as 'white', from daylight (in all its hues) through to candlelight, which is very much yellower. It is also a matter of common experience that pictures taken with daylight-type film under tungsten lighting are much yellower than pictures taken by daylight or with electronic flash.

This is simply because a film cannot adapt in the way that our eyes can. If you want to read yellow light as white, you must either use a blue filter, or use a film which is designed to be exposed by tungsten light. If you expose a tungsten-light film to daylight, the result will be very blue.

Films are nominally balanced to given colour temperatures, which are a surprisingly complex area of study, but which equate pretty closely to straightforward heat. If you heat a black body to 1750°K, you will get a yellowish light rather like that of a candle. Heat it to 2600-2800°K, and you get something very like a domestic light-bulb. Heat it to 3200°K, and you get 'Type B' photographic lamps (100 hour lamps). Heat it to 3400°K, and you are looking at a Type A photoflood. As an interesting aside, this is only about 200° below the melting point of the tungsten filament.

Standard daylight equates to 5400-5800°K, depending on whose standard you are using, though the actual colour temperature of daylight ranges from about 2000°K at dawn if the sun is unobscured, to about 6500°K for the usual mixture of noonday sun, clouds and blue sky. Sky-light from a pure blue sky can be as high as 18,000°K. This is why shadows on snow look so blue, especially on a sunny day.

Correcting Colour Print Films – and Fluorescent Lighting

With colour print films, it should in theory be possible at the printing stage to filter out most or all of the yellow cast that you get from exposing daylight films to tungsten light. In practice, most labs do not, and some even put infuriating stickers on telling you that the picture is yellow because it was exposed by tungsten light. You can get tungsten-balanced colour print films, which are also designed for longer exposures (typically 10 seconds to 1/10 or even 1/100 second) when compared with daylight-type films (typically 1 second to 1/1000 second).

It is however inherently impossible to filter or balance any film, whether colour slide or colour print, for exposure by fluorescent lighting, because the spectrum is not continuous: there are bright lines at certain wavelengths, and the phosphors inside the tube only do a rough job of approximating to daylight. You will generally get better results with faster films, and you may also find that FL/D (fluorescent light/daylight film) and FL/W (fluorescent light/tungsten film) filters work. An alternative to an FL/D is a CC30M.

Colour Fidelity

Regardless of colour balance – and colour films may be balanced for as much as 6000°K – it is important to remember that the colours on a modern film are not true colours; they are merely a representation of the colours falling on the film. There have been a couple of systems of colour photography based on true colour, but they are very complex, completely obsolete, and not very convincing. In fact, they look less convincing than the colours on a modern film.

Because today's colours are not true colours, they can of course be increased or decreased in saturation, as already described, and they can also be made 'warmer' or 'cooler'. Traditionally, European films were the most neutral in colour; American films were inclined to be blue; and Japanese films were warm or golden. Psychologically, the Japanese got it right: in the words of Terence Donovan, a very great photographer, 'Have you ever heard a client complain because the pictures were too [expletive deleted] warm?' Today, almost everyone makes films which are warmer than they used to be.

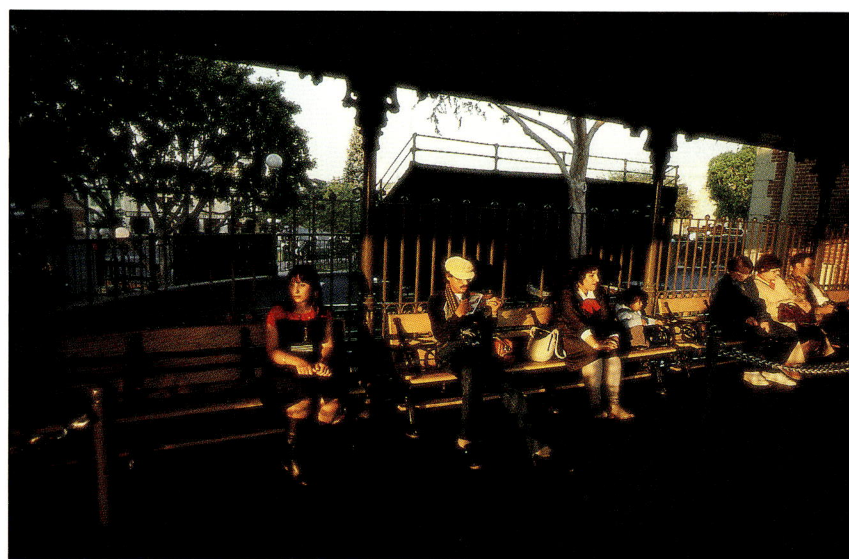

Disneyland Station

When the sun sinks low on a clear day, the colour temperature of direct sunlight falls lower than the colour temperature for which tungsten films are balanced: lower, indeed, than the colour temperature of domestic tungsten lamps. In other words, it would have been perfectly feasible to shoot this on tungsten-balance film, and it would still have looked slightly warm. Although it is possible to 'correct' this lighting balance, by using filters, few photographers would even consider it: the warmth of evening sun is almost invariably an enormous bonus, with its connotations of relaxation and peaceful comfort. This was shot on Kodachrome 64, which is of course daylight balanced. The camera was almost certainly a Leica M2, probably fitted with a 35mm f/1.4 Summilux. (RWH)

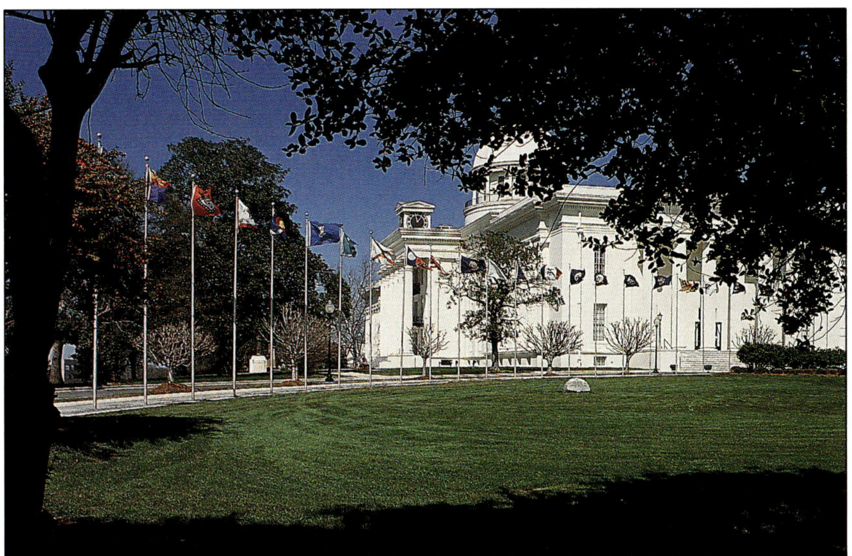

Alabama State Capitol
There is not a film made, black and white or colour, which can accurately represent this sort of tonal range. The grass and the sky are pretty much mid-tones (in fact, you can use a clear blue sky like this to take your meter reading), but the stonework of the capitol itself is glaring white and the undersides of the leaves in the foreground are very dark indeed. Because the white stonework occupies so much of the image, and would look awful if it were over-exposed any further, the trick was to give it the maximum exposure which would be acceptable without losing all detail (which corresponded to a straight incident-light reading). The grass and sky would then look natural, while the leaves in the foreground would go jet black; a convention with which most photographers are happy. It would have been possible to use fill-in flash to lighten the leaves and turn them green, but that would have made for a worse picture rather than a better one. (RWH)

As with speed, colour fidelity can vary from batch to batch, and it also varies according to how film has been stored. Again, professionals used to batch-test film, but today professional films are held to very tight colour balances during manufacture, and then aged to a specific colour balance before being chilled, which effectively halts any further colour change. Normally, young or 'green' films are literally greenish or yellowish in their colour balance, while old films go magenta.

'Professional' Slide Films – A Warning

There is absolutely no point in buying 'professional' slide films unless you treat them as they are intended to be treated, namely, stored in a refrigerator until a few hours before use; allowed to come gently to room temperature overnight; exposed in a single session, or at most in a day or two; and then either processed immediately, or chilled again until they can be processed. If you are travelling under arduous conditions in hot weather, you may actually get worse results from 'professional' slide films than from 'amateur' ones!

There are however two other things you need to know about 'professional' films. Both are concerned with projection because, of course, 'amateur' films will normally be projected, while 'professional' films are normally scanned for photomechanical reproduction.

First, some 'professional' films (particularly from Fuji) have a higher base density than 'amateur' films, which would in theory make them slightly dimmer when projected. In practice, no-one ever notices the difference, which is very slight.

Second, Kodak's newest generation of 'professional' films (introduced at the time of writing) were warmer in colour than the 'amateur' films, which were slightly more blue. This was to compensate for the warm, red light of the projector lamp. The difference is slight, and given the accommodation of the eye to different colours, it is almost certainly unnecessary; but there may be some shots where the colour balance looks odd if you mix old and new, or 'professional' and 'amateur' films.

THE D/LOG E CURVE

If you really want to understand films, you need to know about D/log E curves. Every film has its own 'characteristic curve', which plots density against exposure. Strictly, it plots density (on the vertical axis) against the logarithm of the exposure, which is why it is generally called a D/log E curve. Yet another name for it is an H&D curve, after Hurter and

Driffield, who did the original research in this area in the 1890s.

Although learning to read all the information from a D/log E curve is a major undertaking, you can learn quite a lot from just a quick glance. What follows may seem intimidating at first, and you can always skip it if you wish, but you may find it worth your while to come back to it at your leisure.

You can see that at the beginning, the curve starts out just above the base line. This is the minimum density or D_{min}, which is the base density of the film base and the unexposed emulsion taken together. For a perfect film, of course, D_{min} would be zero; but as there are no perfectly clear film supports, and as even unexposed and processed film has some opacity or turbidity, the D_{min} is always greater than zero.

Then, the curve rises slowly for a while. This is called the 'toe' portion of the curve, where density rises quite slowly even with significant increases in exposure. This is a measure of the threshold sensitivity of the film.

The 'toe' then yields to the so-called 'straight-line portion', where the relationship between exposure and density is fairly constant. A perfect film would have only a straight-line portion, but once again, there are no perfect films. Also, the straight line is not always dead straight: it may have a slight curve to it, like a very flattened S-shape. The straight-line portion of the D/log E curve is the part where you want (if you can) to get all the important tones in the subject.

The steepness of the straight-line portion is a measure of the contrast of the film. You cannot tell much in isolation, but if you compare two or more curves, you can see the difference. A contrasty film has a steep straight-line portion, because quite small increases in exposure result in quite great increases in density. A less contrasty or 'softer' film has a less steep straight-line portion, because a given increase in exposure results in a smaller increase in density.

Towards the top of the straight-line portion, the curve flattens out again into the 'shoulder'. At this point, once again, quite large increases in exposure are bringing only minor increases in density. The highest point of the curve is the maximum density or D_{max}.

Finally, the curve may actually start to fall again, implying that a further increase in exposure is actually resulting in a *decrease* in density. This is very rare with modern films, but it can happen, and when it does it is called 'true solarisation'. The reason why it is called 'solarisation' is clear enough – it used to be seen most clearly when the sun was in shot – but it is called 'true' solarisation in order to distinguish it from what most photographers call simply solarisation, which is more properly called the Sabattier effect. The Sabattier effect is achieved by briefly exposing a part-developed print, and then continuing development.

You can change the shape of the D/log E curve by changing the development conditions. Longer development, or a stronger or more energetic developer, will give you a steeper curve (higher contrast) and a higher maximum density, and shorter development or a weaker or less energetic developer will give you a shallower curve (lower contrast) and a lower maximum density. This is why developers and development times have

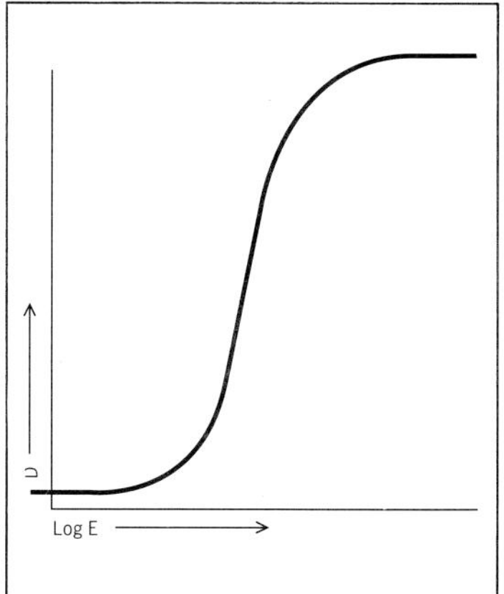

D/log E curve

The D/log E curve plots density (D) against the logarithm of the exposure (log E). Its shape differs for each film and each developer, and not all manufacturers use the same units when they draw D/log E curves; for that matter, they do not necessarily give units at all. The main variables are the steepness of the curve, and the maximum density. A steep straight-line portion means a contrasty emulsion, while a gentler slope means a less contrasty emulsion: the 'gamma' (G) of the developer/emulsion combination is a measure of contrast. Increasing development means increased density for a given exposure, and therefore increased contrast. Black and white films for normal use are almost never developed 'to completion', ie to the extent where the film reaches the maximum density of which it is capable. A colour density curve in a reversal film is the mirror image of a D/log E curve, because the areas which receive the least exposure are darkest and those which receive the most exposure are lightest; the D_{max} of most colour slide emulsions is in excess of 3.0, though for high-speed films (over ISO 500) it can fall below 3.0. A colour slide must of course have the lowest possible D_{min} and the highest possible D_{max}, which is why colour films are inherently contrasty.

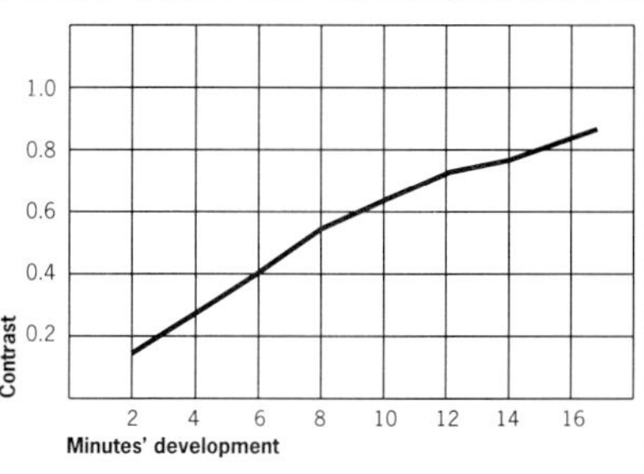

Contrast/Time Curve

An under-developed film lacks both density and contrast, while an over-developed one has plenty of both. Like D/log E curves, contrast/time curves are empirical. They vary according to the film/developer combination chosen, and also according to the agitation used: intermittent agitation (typically for 10 seconds every minute) gives a flatter contrast/time curve. Black and white films were traditionally developed to a contrast ('gamma' or G) of about 0.55, for enlargement with condenser enlargers, but today they are often developed to a G of around 0.70, because diffuser enlargers are widely used. This corresponds to an increase in contrast of about one paper grade. The amount of extra development from G = 0.55 to G = 0.70 is normally about 50 per cent. Both G = 0.55 and G = 0.70 are marked on this curve.

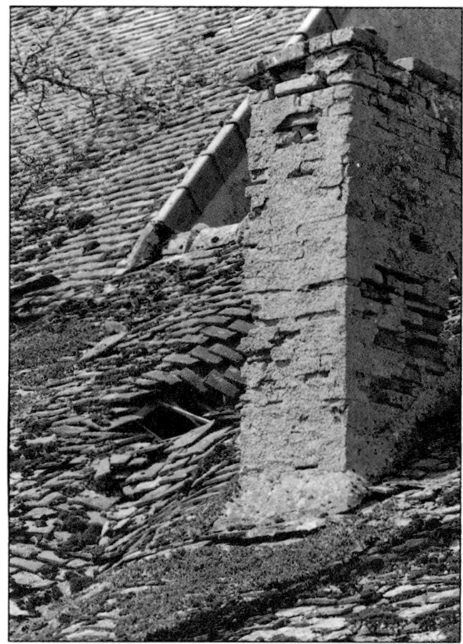

Collapsing roof

This is the sort of picture which simply works better in black and white than in colour: a study of shapes and textures. In colour, the mosses and lichens below the chimney would almost certainly have been too intrusive, as would the branch on the upper right of the picture. In any picture which depends on texture, though, you will normally do better to use a larger format than 35mm, which can lead to problems. For this picture, Roger used a tripod and set the lens to a very modest aperture (f/11 or f/16), both for sharpness and for depth of field; but it is still not quite as sharp as he would have liked. It is unlikely that it was the fault of the lens, which was the Sigma 70-210mm f/2.8 zoom, one of the sharpest zooms we have ever encountered. The film was however Ilford XP-2: this dates from before our adoption of Delta 100, which would have improved matters. Ideally, we would have preferred to use the Linhof and the 6x7cm format, but that would have run us into problems with focal lengths: this was probably shot at about 180mm, which is the equivalent of about 380mm on 6x7cm. A 360mm Tele-Xenar would have been perfectly feasible, but there were two difficulties: we don't own one (though at the time of writing we were seriously considering buying one), and we didn't have the Linhof with us... (RWH)

to be carefully matched to different films, to give the best possible D/log E curve. Thin, slow emulsions develop faster than thicker, faster ones.

The D/log E Curve and Colour

Because a colour film consists of three emulsions stacked on top of each other, as described earlier, it has three D/log E curves. For obvious reasons, these three must stay in step. If they do not, then a variation in exposure will result in colour casts, as one curve (corresponding to one colour) registers a greater variation in density than the other two.

When the curves of colour films get out of synchronisation like this, the result is often referred to as 'crossed curves'. Problems resulting from crossed curves cannot be filtered out, because the colour varies with the density. Suppose, for example, that there is too much magenta in the darker areas, but the lighter areas are all right. You can filter out the unwanted magenta quite easily, either by adding magenta if you are printing from colour negatives, or by removing magenta (or adding green) if you are dealing with colour slides. The only problem is that when you do so, you will also change the colour balance of the lighter area, which was previously satisfactory: it will now go green.

The most usual cause of crossed curves is poor development or some other processing fault, which is one of the many reasons why it is worth going to a good lab with first-class chemical monitoring. Another possibility, though, is grossly outdated or very poorly stored film (it usually goes magenta, though you can often filter out the worst of it), and yet a third possibility is using a film outside its designed exposure parameters. For example, some films are designed for long exposures in the 1/2 second to 10 second range, typically by tungsten light. You can get around the problem of the colour of the light with filters, but you may have problems if you try to expose the film by electronic flash, because the exposure will be a tiny fraction of the design exposure of the film.

'MAGIC'

Last of all, we come to something completely unquantifiable, a sort of Holy Ghost of photographic quality. It is not constant, and it does not belong to any one manufacturer. It is even independent of everything else which is traditionally regarded as 'quality'. For example, some (but not all) shots on the 3M/Scotch ISO 1000 daylight-balanced film will display it. Objectively, this is a rotten film: grainy beyond belief, with a very poor D_{max}, extremely subdued colours, and an actual speed which is about two-thirds its rated ISO. Its only merit, objectively, is that it is cheap; it is also available from a number of discount dealers as an 'own-label' film, at even lower prices. But subjectively, it can be one of the most magical films available. There are others, but it is always a personal matter to each photographer. Also, as we have said before, films are constantly changing, and what is bad today may be replaced with something that is good tomorrow. The information in this chapter should help you to make objective judgements, but subjectively, you are on your own.

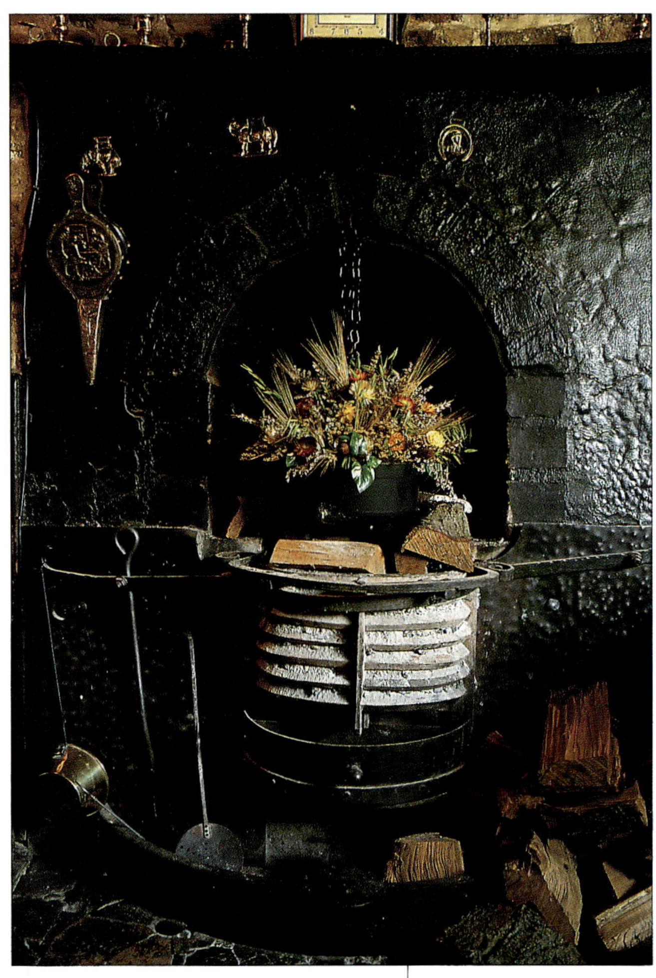

Fireplace

The Bell Inn, at St Nicholas at Wade in Kent, is such a superbly English pub that it is almost a parody of itself: beamed roofs, flagged floors, dark wood, a log fire... The food is excellent, too. In the summer, this colourful arrangement of dried flowers sits in the fireplace, crying out for a sharp, saturated, contrasty film to make the colours and textures spring out against the darkness. Even so, Roger opted to use a conventional ISO 50 film (Fuji RFP) rather than a higher-contrast film, because there was plenty of contrast there already. With the film we used, we were able to get a superb maximum black and very highly saturated colours, together with detail in the black-painted fireplace surround, which we might have lost with a more contrasty film. A subject like this is very demanding indeed, especially if you are using print film, because the darkness can 'fool' the meter (we used an incident-light meter) at the taking stage, and it can 'fool' the automatic printer again at the printing stage, leading to weak, greenish blacks and quite possibly to colour casts, which would be extremely visible in the neutral-grey wood ash. In such a case, a high-contrast film might give a better result – but it would only be better than a badly made print from a low-contrast film. A well-made print from a lower-contrast film would be the best option of all. (RWH)

3 PROCESSING

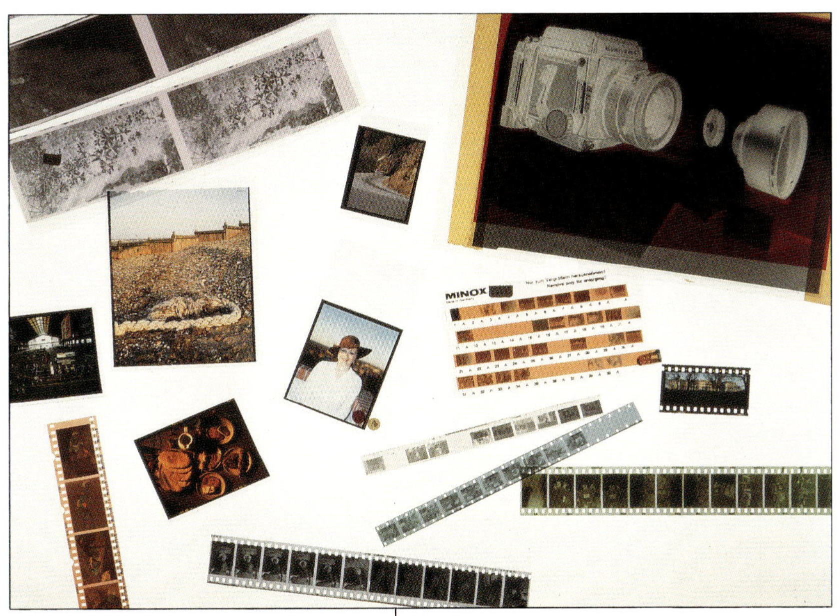

Film formats and types

Maybe this belongs in the next chapter, 'Film Sizes and Packings', but it also gives a very good idea of the different requirements for care in processing. The big image in the upper right-hand corner is an 8x10in negative, masked with 'Ruby Lith' film to remove an unwanted background. Below that is a sleeved 36 exposure Minox film with its 8x11mm images; a 24 x 56mm panoramic shot, made with a 35mm Horizont camera; two kinds of 16mm sub-miniature negatives (Minolta 16 and Mamiya 16); and two lots of half-frame 35mm negatives, one on early Ilford XP-1 with the characteristic greenish cast which it took on if left too long in the camera, and the other on Kodak Tri-X. To the left, from the top, there are 6-on-120 negatives on Ilford FP4, with a pinkish tinge; transparencies in 16-on-120, 10-on-120 and 4x5in formats; and a strip of 35mm full-frame colour negatives. The colours in the black and white films are interesting, too: they are inherent in the film/developer combinations used, but they mean that the different films need to be printed very differently, both for exposure and contrast.

Processing is an essential component of using film, and the availability (or otherwise) of professional lab services may also be an important consideration when choosing film. Where and how you have your films processed will depend on what sort of film you use (colour print, colour slide or black and white); on what you want to do with the pictures after they have been processed; and on how much money you want to spend.

CHOOSING A LAB

Before you use any new lab, you should give them at least one specially shot test roll to process. Ideally, you should give them two rolls, a few days apart. Examine the film for dust, fingerprints, scratches and other unwanted surprises, and decide for yourself whether you want to entrust more important films to them. Having said this, there are times when a quick mini-lab turnaround is more important than ultimate quality, either for holiday snaps or because you want to test a new camera.

To find a professional lab, the Yellow Pages are a good start – except that labs who advertise themselves as 'professional' may turn out not to be so. A better solution is personal recommendation. If you know any professional photographers in your area, just ask them what lab they use. We have even telephoned people 'cold', explaining that we are out-of-town professionals who need a professional lab, and asking them if they can recommend anyone.

Mail Order

We much prefer to deal face-to-face with our labs, even if it means a long drive. It reduces the chance of the film getting lost; it greatly speeds turnaround; and it means that if things do go wrong, you can find out why. Even so, we have used mail-order labs, especially for Kodachrome processing (we would have to go into London otherwise), and we have also tried some of the big discount colour print labs, which deliver very good quality at unbelievably low prices. They did not get big by being bad!

COLOUR PRINT PROCESSING

Although you can process colour negative film yourself, it is generally a better idea to have it processed professionally. It generally costs no more, and takes no longer, and any half-way decent lab will be able to keep a closer watch on time, temperature and chemical composition than you can do at home.

Labs catering for the professional

photographer will always sleeve the negatives, either in a long roll (more common in the United States) or in strips (the general practice in Europe). Amateur labs may or may not sleeve the film: many of them simply put all the film together in a pocket. It is a very good idea to sleeve them yourself if the lab does not do so, as it makes them very much easier to handle, especially when it comes to ordering reprints or to printing from the negatives yourself.

The care with which amateur labs handle film varies enormously; there was one lab in Santa Maria in California (near where we used to live) where we have seen negatives dragging on the floor, and where the staff had apparently never been told to handle film by the edges. The dirt and fingerprints defied belief. Needless to say, we used the other lab, which worked to professional standards.

A major distinction in any lab is between roller processing and spiral processing. With roller processing, the film is fed through in a continuous strip; with spiral processing, the film is wound onto a spiral wire frame, on which it is transported through the processing line. There is far less risk of scratching with spiral processing, and it is always worth asking any new lab which kind of film handling they use. If they use roller or continuous processing, and you decide to use them anyway, examine your test roll carefully for scratches. For 'happy snaps' and 5x7in/13x18cm prints, we have no hesitation in using good roller-processing labs (all mini-labs are the roller-processing type) but if we want professional quality prints, we habitually go to our regular professional lab.

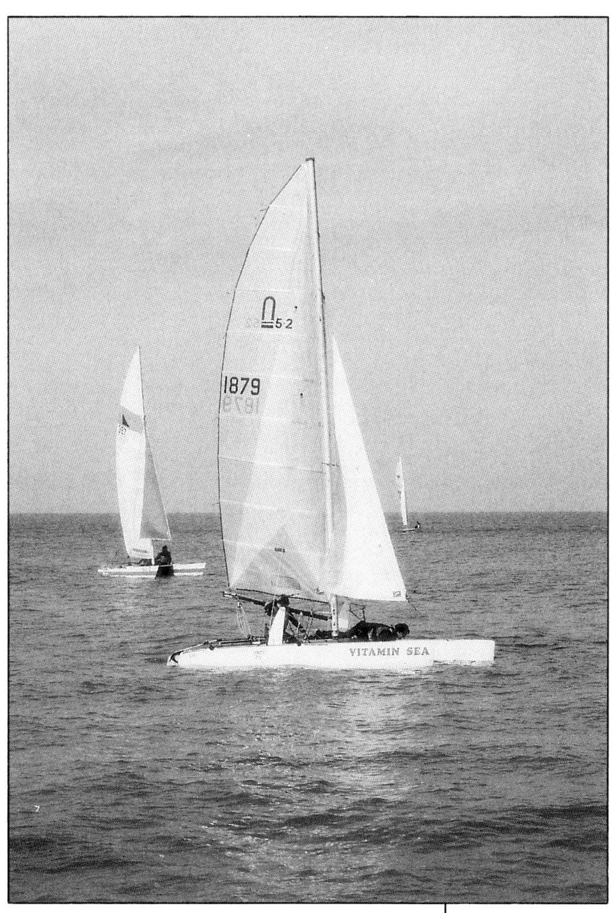

'Push' Processing

There is no point in 'pull' processing colour print films which have been over-exposed, because they can stand a very high degree of over-exposure. Nor is it possible to 'push' most colour print films. There are however a few high-speed colour films which are specially designed for 'push' processing at one or two stops faster than the base ISO speed. Not many labs offer this service, and it is always better to buy the fastest film you can get rather than to try push-processing a slower film. Some ISO 800 films can however be rated at EI 1600 and EI 3200.

Sailing dinghies

The quickest and easiest way to process film – albeit at a price – is to use Polaroid films. This was shot on Polaroid PolaPan, an ISO 125 direct-reversal black and white material. Like most other Polaroid materials, the real attraction for most photographers does not lie in the instant processing, but in the curiously vintage tonality of the image. If you over-expose fractionally, as Frances did here, the tonality is rather like that of a late-Victorian albumen print. This was a hand-held exposure, using a Nikon F and a Vivitar Series One 90mm f/2.5 macro lens. Exposure was 1/125 at f/11. (FES)

Bukowski Died For Your Sins

For some reason, the last time we were in New Orleans neither of us took very many of the traditional tourist subjects. The weather was very good, and we were staying in a delightful hotel, but someone had been writing all kinds of strange graffiti. This was one example – which presumably refers to the poet – and another simply said, Thirsty, miserable and always wanting more. *Was the person who wrote this mentally ill? Or perfectly sane, and writing it for shock value? Or was he pointing out, by a subtle irony, that Jesus would probably be about as welcome in twentieth-century America as Bukowski? Is there some significance in the use of the backwards 'E'? Whatever it was, Frances decided to photograph it 'straight', with the subtle tone and texture of the brick and the dense, black-marker graffiti. Only if you do your own printing can you make this sort of decision: otherwise, you get what you are given. (FES)*

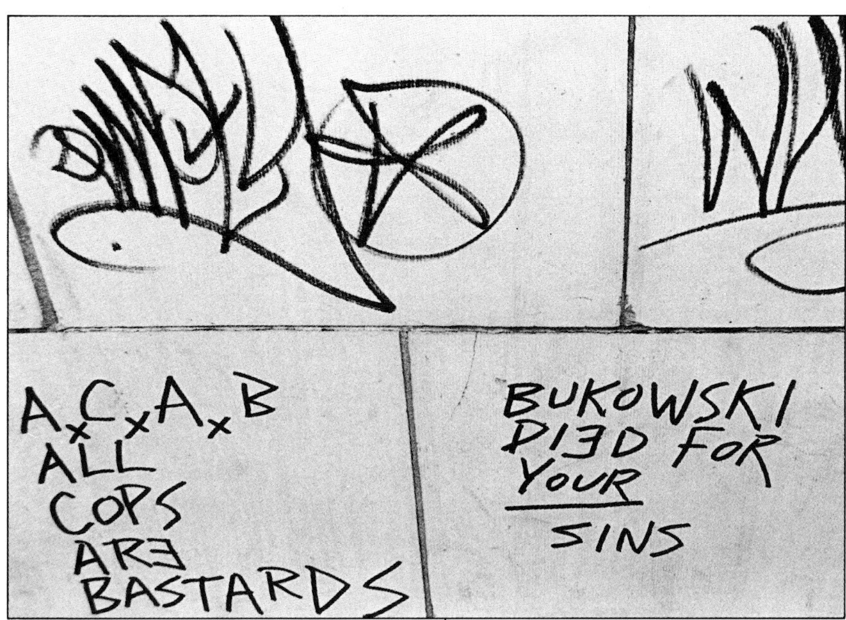

Print Packages

Most low-cost labs offer an astonishingly good, incredibly cheap service, and if all you want is snaps, you should have no hesitation in using them. The improvement in quality which you get from a professional lab will often be negligible if all you want is a standard package, but the price will typically be several times as high – at least two or three times, quite likely five or six times, and possibly as much as ten times. Also, rather than ordering reprints from a low-cost lab, you would do well to order duplicate sets of prints at the time of processing. Typically, to have duplicate prints made from a whole 36-exposure roll will cost no more than having six or eight reprints of the same size, and it involves much less film handling. If you know in advance that you are going to want five or ten shots of a particular subject to give to someone, it is usually cheapest and quickest to shoot several identical frames on the original film.

One problem with most amateur-oriented labs is that they crop quite a lot around the edges of the negatives. They do this in order to avoid having to worry about centring negatives too precisely in the film gate, and to take care of different sizes of negatives: the nominal 24x36mm of a 35mm frame can range from about 23x35mm to 25x38mm, and their masks are smaller than the smallest size they are likely to encounter. Usually, this doesn't matter, but there are some labs where you lose so much of the image that you begin to notice. The solutions are either to change your lab, or to allow a bit more room around the edges of your pictures. Very few camera viewfinders show the full area of what will appear on the film, in any case.

Reprints and Enlargements

When it comes to ordering reprints and enlargements, most professional labs

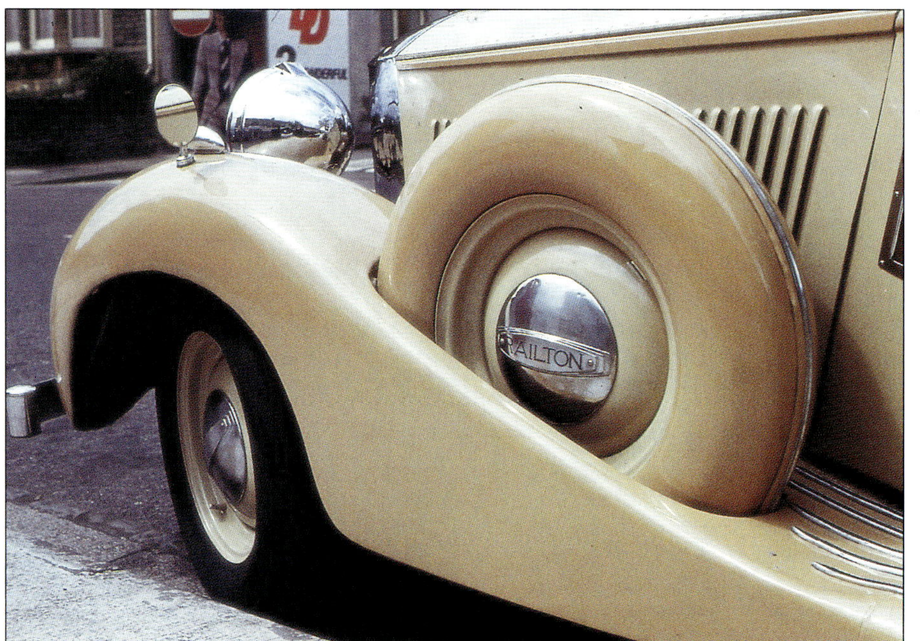

ORWO slide, mid-1970s

If you buy process-paid films when you are travelling, make sure that the pre-paid processing is (a) possible and (b) honoured when you get home. This old ORWO film dates from many years before the reunification of Germany, and was made in what used to be the DDR. It was readily available in most of Europe, but the editor of any American photographic magazine will confirm that there used to be a steady stream of plaintive letters from readers who had bought their film on vacation and then found that it could not be processed when they got home. It is also possible to buy process-paid films in good faith in one country, and then to be charged for processing when you return home, even though the manufacturer processes it! The official reason for this is to prevent 'grey' or 'parallel' importing, though the supporters of 'grey' imports maintain that the whole 'official importer' system is merely a thinly-disguised rip-off on the part of the manufacturers, who charge a fair rate in some markets and an exorbitant rate in others. We usually buy non-process-paid films, in the interests of speed (a two-hour turnaround instead of several days in the mail) but also because we can then have them processed in whatever country happens to suit us best. Modern ORWO films are much better than this stuff, which was grainy, contrasty and off-colour when it was new, and which has not kept well. (RWH)

offer two or three grades of service. The cheapest is the machine print, which is what its name implies: an all-in, machine-made print. The quality will obviously depend on the quality of the original negative. The next level up is the hand print, where a technician puts the negative in a normal enlarger and takes some personal care over it. In some labs, he or she will also crop, burn, dodge and otherwise modify the print in accordance with your instructions: the easiest way to give these instructions is to mark up a reference print to show what you want. In other labs, you do not get this degree of service with a standard hand print: you have to order a custom print, or deluxe print – the term varies from place to place. Typically, a hand print costs 50 to 100 per cent more than a machine print, and a custom print adds another 50 to 100 per cent to the price of a hand print.

Incidentally, if you ever order a 'poster print' from any lab, check first what they call a 'poster'. It may be as small as 11x14in (about 28x35cm), or it may be as large as 20x30in (50x75cm).

'Super-amateur' Labs

In the backs of many photographic magazines, there are small ads for custom printers. On the basis of very limited research, it seems that these are often keen amateurs who make very good prints as a means of supplementing their income. They are a good deal cheaper than professional labs, and they can represent superb value. The downside is that quality is very variable. Find a good one, and you should be very happy; but be warned that bad ones lose negatives and make rotten prints, leaving you with no real recourse. A test roll or print is even more important than usual in these cases.

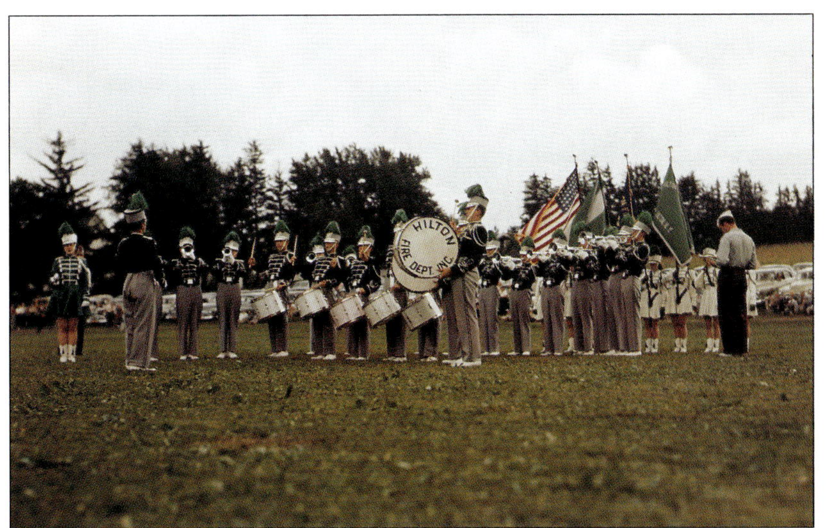

Drum and bugle corps

Frances's father, Artie Schultz, shot this in the very early 1950s. The interesting thing about it is that it is a quarter-plate (3¼ x 4¼ inch, 8.25 x 10.8cm) Kodachrome. Sheet-film Kodachromes were only made for a very short time, maybe six or seven years at most, and this must have been towards the end of their life. The reason they were discontinued was that it was extremely difficult to ensure even processing across the full area of the film. This is why rollfilm Kodachrome was so long in coming: for two or three decades, Kodak's scientists argued that 35mm was the widest format which could reliably and conveniently be processed. The longevity of Kodachrome is however very clear in this shot, which must have been about forty years old when we used it in this book: we also had other old films of Artie's, including 35mm Ektachromes, which had faded appallingly to a sort of uniform magenta. For that matter, Roger has Ektachromes from the 1960s and early 1970s which do not look too good. (W. A. Schultz)

Making Your Own Prints

If you want to print the films yourself – which, once you have mastered colour printing, will give you the best possible results for the least cost – you may still find it worth your while to have proof prints made by the lab that processes the film. This saves you a great deal of time and effort in making test prints: you can see from the machine prints where you need to dodge, burn, crop and so forth. If you have a good amateur lab whom you can trust, by all means use their package services. Alternatively, use your local professional lab.

Cross Processing

You can process slides as negatives, and negatives as slides. Not all labs will be willing to do it, so you may have to do it yourself, and not all films react the same way; but you may find it interesting to try. It is a technique which is quite popular in rock music photography, where everyone imagines it is something new each time it is rediscovered.

COLOUR SLIDE PROCESSING

Much the same is true of colour slide processing as of colour negative: a professional lab will do a better, quicker job than you can do yourself, for much the same money.

The first question you need to ask is what their turnaround time is. Any lab which takes much more than two hours to process any normal reversal film (except Kodachrome) cannot really call itself 'professional'. At worst, they may have one or two runs a day – one lab we used in California had a ten o'clock run and a three o'clock run – but if they cannot under any circumstances offer a same-day service, they are not a professional lab.

The other thing that is worth checking is whether or not they habitually mount slides. In Britain, 'chromes are normally returned unmounted, and mounting is either unavailable or costs quite a lot extra. In the United States, they are normally mounted, but the mounts are often flimsy heat-sealed plastic things or (worse still) cardboard. We habitually specify unmounted slides.

Kodachromes

Kodachrome processing is hellishly complicated. Unlike most colour films, where the dye precursors are incorporated in the emulsion, the dyes are added during processing. The technical advantage of this – it is called 'non-substantive' technology, as against the normal 'substantive' technology – is that until the film is processed, it is effectively a black and white film. This means that it is very stable, and that the colours are far less affected by heat and poor storage than they are in other

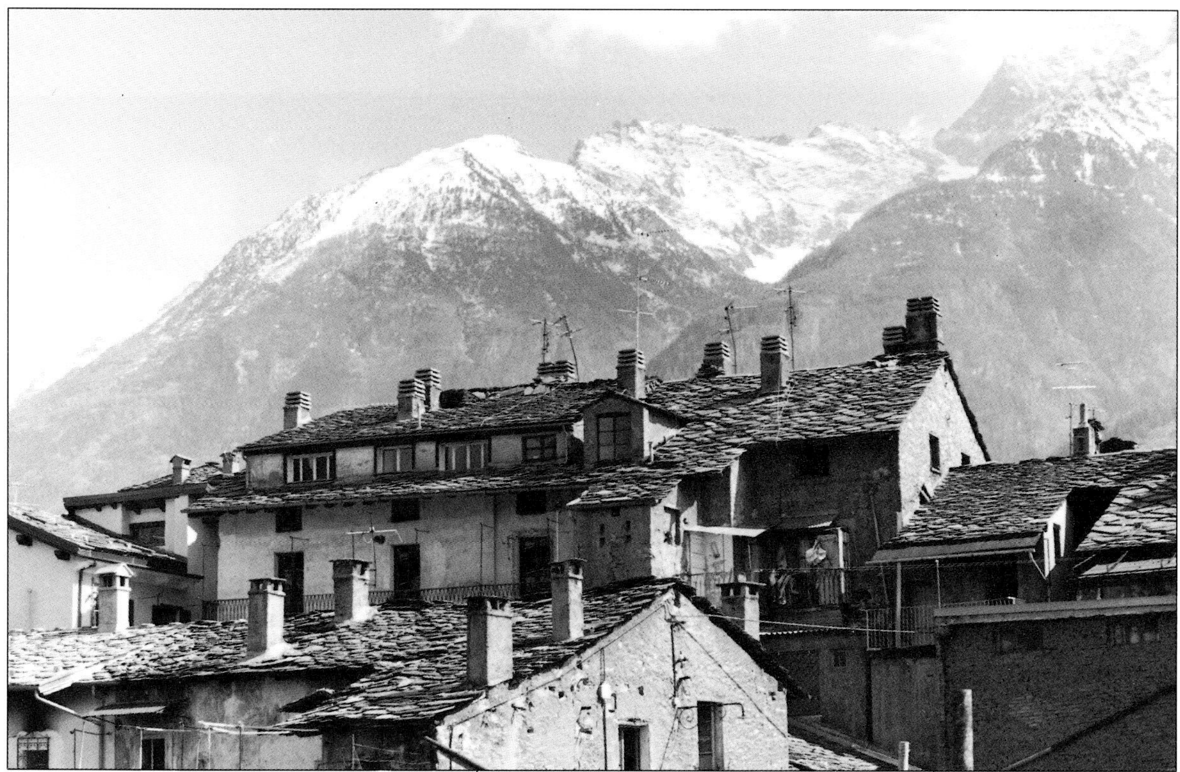

colour films. This is why we habitually use Kodachromes for travel photography.

The only inherent disadvantage to Kodachromes is the long turnaround time: you will be lucky to get same-day processing, even if you take the film in yourself, though you may get next-day processing. There is however a non-inherent disadvantage, which is that some Kodachrome labs are incredibly arrogant. There is (or was in the past) a rare problem with Kodachromes which can lead to processing stripes on the image. These are very faint, and can only be seen in pale areas of pure tone; unfortunately, such as a blue sky. The first time this happened to Roger, at the old Hollywood lab (now gone), they told him that it was his fault and that he must have rewound the film backwards! The second time, at the London lab, he was fortunately shooting a book for a Kodak subsidiary, so he was able to exert a little leverage. This time, they were more honest: they admitted that they did not know what caused it. This has only affected three films out of the thousands we have shot, but Roger has never forgiven Kodak's original attitude. When he has told this story to other photographers who use a lot of Kodachrome, they have been able to recount similar stories of their own.

At the time of writing, Kodak in Britain had moved Kodachrome processing back to London from continental Europe, and it was as good as it had ever been. For travel photography, we have reverted to

Streaky sky

For some reason, there is a streak in the sky of this picture of Aosta. The negative was shot on Ilford XP-2, processed commercially, and the streak looks like a drying mark – but it is invisible on the film. It also spreads across two frames, substantially identically. We were unable to figure it out. If you get this sort of problem, and the lab has no ready explanation (they didn't), then send the film back to the manufacturers, and ask for an explanation. Tell them that you are not necessarily interested in assigning blame, or in getting a replacement film: what you want to know is what caused the problem, and whether there is anything you can do to avoid it in future. (FES)

Kodachromes. But for general photography, especially where a rapid turnaround is important, we use substantive films.

'Pushing' and 'Pulling' Films

There are times when you inadvertently expose a slide film at the wrong EI; or when you need more speed than your film normally delivers; or when you simply get the exposure wrong. Most good labs will 'push' or 'pull' films to compensate for these problems. As a general rule, you can adjust the effective film speed during processing by half a stop or even two-thirds of a stop with impunity, and the best films will stand a one-stop 'push' or 'pull' without loss of quality. Going outside these limits is however risky. 'Pull' too far and you get flat, desaturated images; 'push' too far and you get big grain, excessive contrast, poor colour rendition and a weak, thin maximum black. Different labs may have different rules on how far they are prepared to 'push' or 'pull', and they may or may not charge extra for speed adjustment. In general, big-city labs in places like New York or London do not charge, and others do.

Two useful professional tricks are 'clip testing' and 'process one, hold one'. Clip testing is what its name suggests: the first few frames of the film (which are specially shot for the purpose) are clipped and processed, and the rest of the film is 'pushed' or 'pulled' to give the best possible image. This is obviously of use only when the whole film is exposed under substantially identical lighting conditions. 'Process one, hold one' is when you shoot two identical pictures on two pieces of cut film, and have the lab process one and hold the other. The second sheet can then be 'pushed' or 'pulled' to the desired EI. This is very useful when you are trying to match density precisely.

When requesting a speed change, always give the EI that you want, especially when 'pulling'. An ISO 100 film 'pulled half' is not EI 50: that would be 'pull one', but some people do not think like that.

Few labs offer 'push' or 'pull' processing for Kodachrome, though a one and one-third of a stop push to rescue Kodachrome 25 exposed as Kodachrome 64 has long been available. This translates into EI 160 for Kodachrome 64 and EI 500 for Kodachrome 200 – if you can get them to do it.

BLACK AND WHITE PROCESSING

The rules change completely when it comes to black and white processing. As a general rule, it is far better to process your own films, because you can use the very best combination of developer, film, and processing time. Unlike colour films, where there are two major standardised processes and one minor (one for colour print and one for colour slide, plus one for Kodachrome), there are scores or perhaps hundreds of black and white developers, all offering different advantages: finer grain, higher speed, greater capacity, greater longevity, high acutance, and so forth. Also, the time and temperature requirements, and the way in which the chemicals must be compounded, are nothing like as demanding as for colour.

In a commercial lab, there will usually be one or two developers which

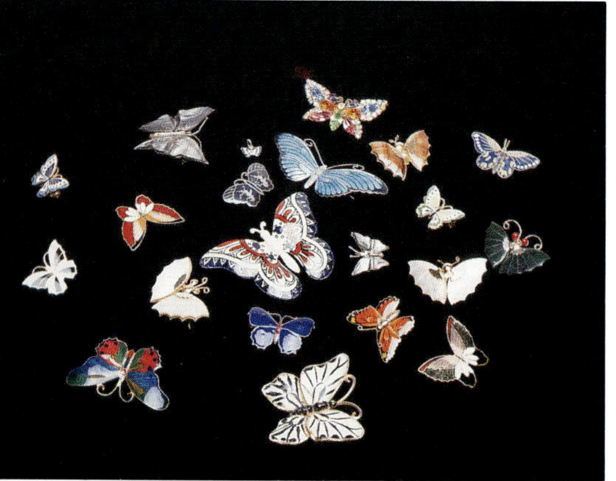

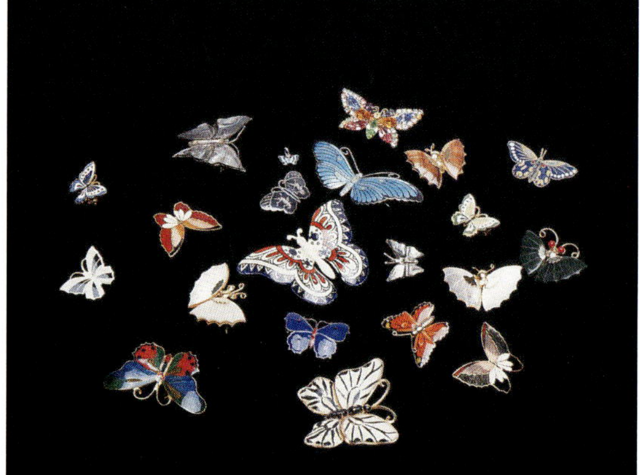

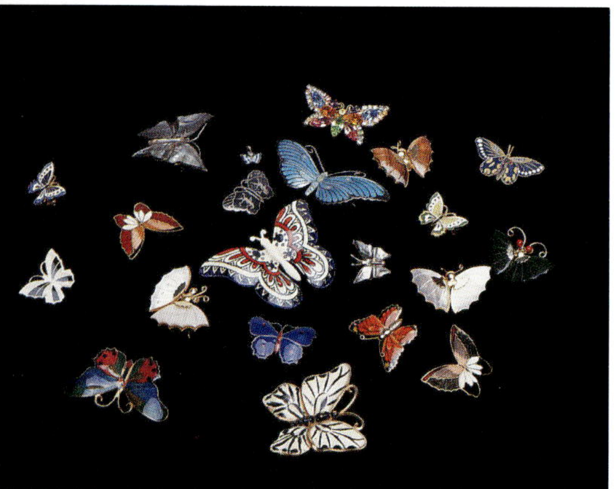

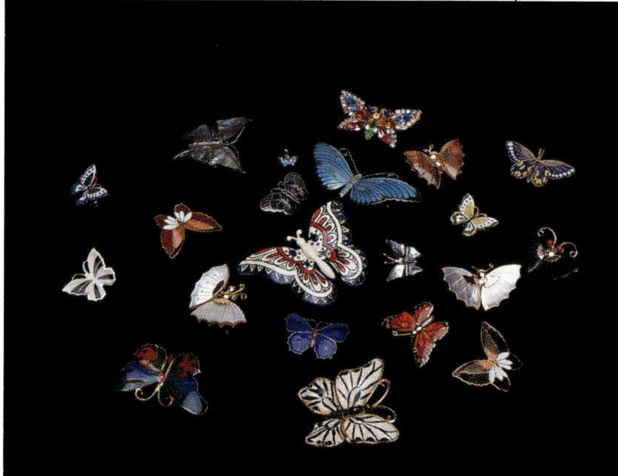

Butterflies

Modern films are so incredibly tolerant of over- and under-exposure that most people fail to pay enough attention to first-class processing. These butterflies from Frances's collection differ by two-thirds of a stop from one exposure to the next. Initial exposure determination (for Fuji RDP 100 rollfilm, exposed in a Linhof Super Technika IV with a 100mm f/3.5 Xenar) was by Gossen LunaPro F, confirmed with a test using Polaroid Pro 100; it was f/16. The first frame is one stop lighter than this (f/11); the second is a third of a stop lighter (f/14); the third is a third of a stop darker (f/18); and the last is a full stop darker, at f/22. As you can see, all four would be usable, and the best exposure for reproduction is probably the image that is a third of a stop dark. The flare on the enamel wings is deliberate: it would have been possible to remove it with a polarising filter, but this would have meant more saturated colours and a less challenging decision on exposure. To see why the one-over and one-under exposures are unacceptable, look at the top right-hand butterfly in the lightest exposure ('Tibet' is barely readable) and at the wings of the butterfly below it in the darkest exposure. You need to be aware of what colour films can do before you can order 'pushing' or 'pulling' on clip tests or on 'hold one, process one' pictures. Most labs allow speed control in third of a stop or even quarter of a stop stages.

may or may not be suited to the film you are using, and in which the film may or may not be processed for the correct length of time. If you have to have black and white films processed commercially, you have three choices. One is to find out what the lab is set up for, and use that. The second is to use something like Ilford FP4 or HP5, which is enormously tolerant of out-of-specification processing. The third is to use Ilford XP-2, which is processed in standard colour negative film chemistry; this is the path we take when we want to shoot more than four black and white films on a particular subject. Four films is the most that Roger can conveniently process at a time, using two twin-spiral tanks. He does the film processing, and Frances does the printing.

'Pushing' and 'Pulling' – and Contrast Control

Increasing development time for almost any black and white film will result in a higher effective film speed (EI), but it is invariably obtained at the expense of increased contrast, which makes the negative somewhat harder to print. Also, you will eventually start to lose shadow detail.

With the right films, such as Ilford HP5 Plus, and the right developer, you can get an acceptable image (even with some shadow detail) at 'push' speeds as much as three stops greater than the ISO speed: in the case of HP5 Plus, EI 3200 instead of ISO 400. In practice, even the best films tend to run out of steam at about EI 1600, though quality at this speed can be amazingly good. It is a better idea, though, to buy the

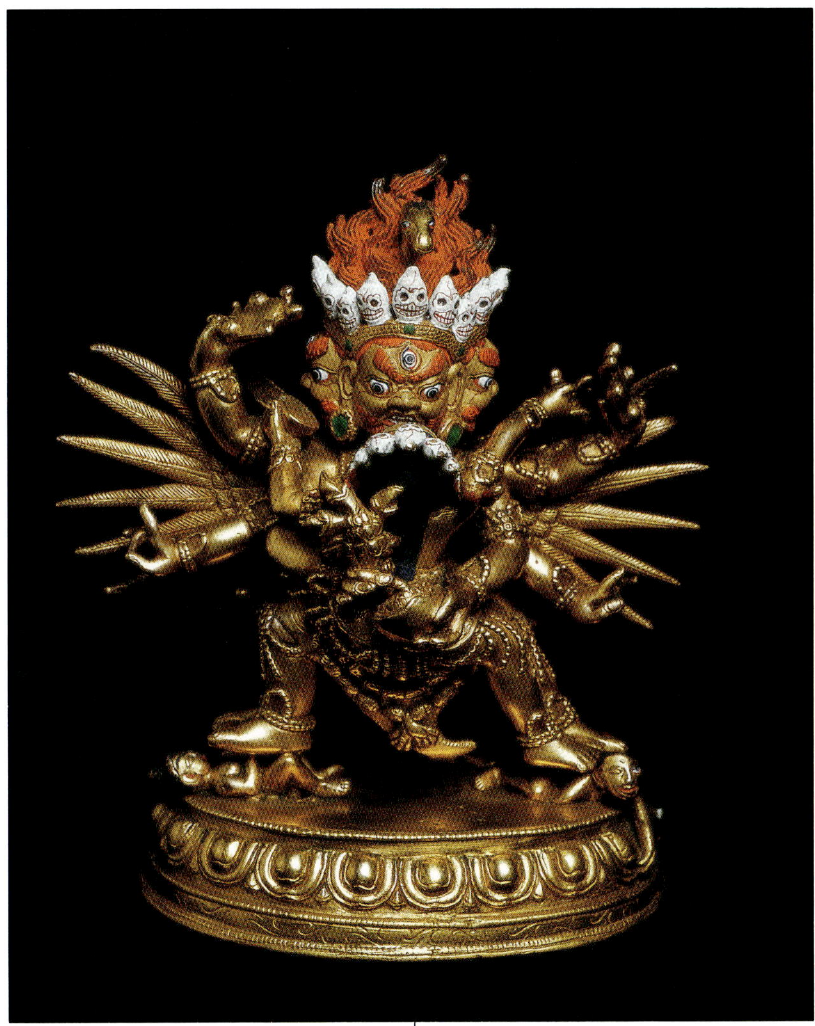

Hayagriva Rupa

If you want the best possible detail, especially in colour, you need to go to rollfilm or even 4x5in. This Tibetan rupa of high-gold bronze was borrowed from an antique shop in the King's Road, Chelsea, and shot in a friend's studio using a 'baby' Linhof and the 105mm f/4.5 Apo Lanthar, one of the sharpest lenses ever made. The format was 6x7cm, which although it has only about one-third of the area of a 4x5in transparency can still be enlarged with confidence to 20x30in or 40x50cm provided, of course, it is shot with the best available lenses! In this case, where no camera movements were required and the extra depth of field of the smaller format is welcome, there is little technical reason to use 4x5in or larger unless you know that the picture is going to be blown up to a very large poster indeed. There are however two non-technical reasons for using 4x5in. One is that art directors and designers like it better, and the other is that the bigger format on heavier-base film is harder for hamfisted separation houses to damage when they are scanning it for reproduction. (RWH)

fastest film you can get and to push it as little as possible.

The real use of varying development time is for contrast control. Increasing exposure and cutting development will 'compress' contrast and allow you to capture a very long tonal range on film, while decreasing exposure and increasing development will expand a limited tonal range (on a dull day, for instance) and give the prints extra 'sparkle'. Most manufacturers give development recommendations for this technique, but a good rule of thumb is 'fifteen-fifty'. To compress contrast, give one stop extra exposure (ie rate an ISO 100 film at EI 50) and cut development time by 15 per cent. To increase contrast, give one stop less exposure (ie rate an ISO 100 film at EI 200) and increase development time by 50 per cent.

Processing for Minimum and Maximum Grain

For minimum grain, there are many proprietary developers which can deliver excellent results. Many of these entail a speed loss of between a third of a stop or a stop (eg an ISO 100 film becomes EI 80 or even EI 50), and they give the very finest results when they are diluted to the limits permitted by the manufacturers.

For maximum grain, which you may sometimes want to use for effect, get an 'old-technology' ISO 400 film – Tri-X is good, or (if you can get one) an ISO 400 Chinese or Eastern European film – and develop it in paper developer. You will need to experiment, but an EI of 1000 for an ISO 400 film is a good starting point, and try three or four minutes at 20°C/68°F as an initial development time.

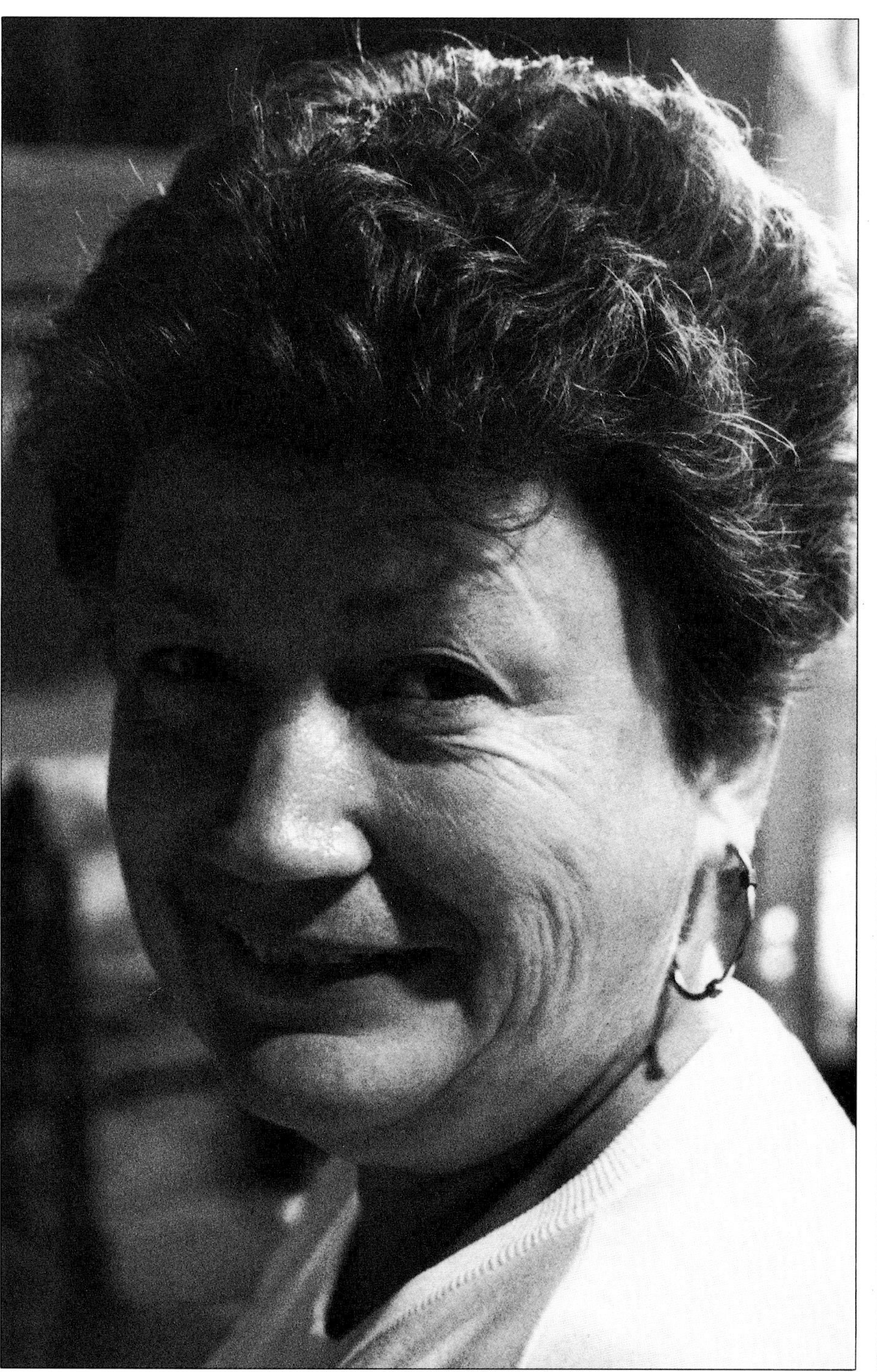

Frances

This is not a very good picture of Frances, and it is hardly a portrait which warrants inclusion on its own merits; but it has some technical interest in that it was shot on Ilford HP5 Plus rated at EI 3200, a three-stop 'push'. As you can see, lack of shadow detail is not the problem: it is lack of highlight detail, caused by excessive contrast. The grain is surprisingly modest in the original 6x enlargement, and in reproduction it may not be much in evidence at all. Although it is possible to get EI 3200 and shadow detail out of HP5 Plus, results are very much better at EI 1600 – or, of course, you could use one of the films rated at EI 1600, such as Fuji or Kodak. The advantage of these very high speeds is that you can make available-light exposures in poor light even with slow modern zooms: this was shot with a Pentax Z-1 and a 28-80mm f/3.5 to f/4.5 'standard zoom'. Of course, you would get the same shutter speed with a 50mm f/1.4 lens and ISO 400 film as with an f/4 zoom and EI 3200. In our experience, no film delivers really good quality at EI 3200. (RWH)

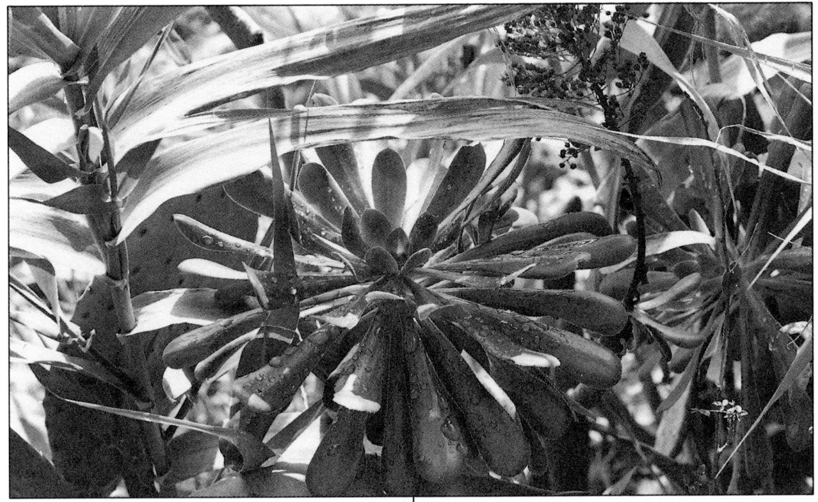

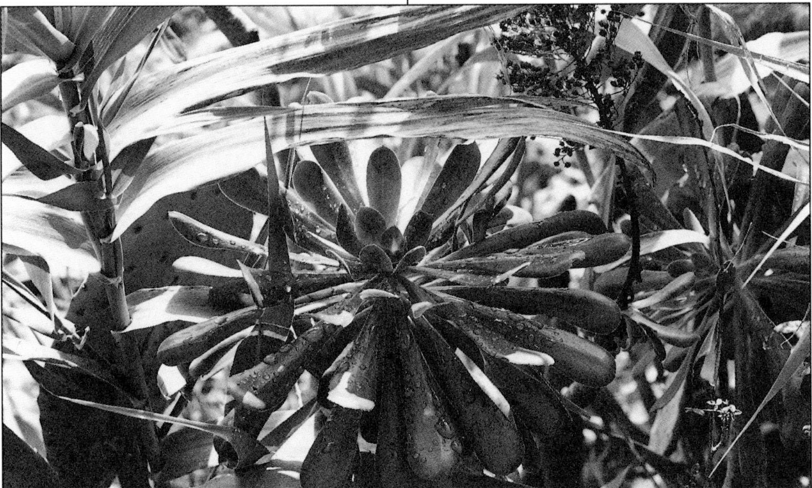

Succulent xerophytes, Gran Canaria

To see what a D/log E curve means in practice, look at these two prints from the same XP-2 negative. The prints are only one paper grade apart, 1½ for the low-contrast version and 2½ for the high contrast version, with a minimal difference in exposure (12 seconds and 10 seconds respectively). The main difference is in the mid-tones and dark mid-tones, which are very important in exhibition prints, though less so for reproduction, where they tend to block up. The tones which are assigned to Zone IV (dark mid-tones) in the softer print are pretty much in Zone III (darkest tone with texture) in the harder print: even with slightly less exposure, the steeper D/log E curve means that they have gone very dark. The two prints differ in mood: the softer print has a sort of richness which is missing from the harder one. For exhibition, using Multigrade FB (fibre-base), Frances would try to get a little more detail in the highlights, while accepting that there are parts which are going to remain substantially burned out, and she would try to get plenty of rich subtle detail in Zones III and II. (FES)

Black and White Printing

Custom black and white printing costs a fortune, and non-custom prints are hardly worth bothering with: they typically come out either in shades of cigarette ash, or in soot-and-whitewash. The only way to get good black and white prints affordably is to do them yourself. Once you have made the investment in the darkroom, the cost of making prints is not great – you can make half a dozen 8x10in prints for the price of a single cinema ticket, or a couple of pints of beer – so it is not an expensive hobby, and if you want to sell your work, it is the only path to take.

Nor is it necessarily expensive to set up a darkroom; in 1992, for example, we bought an enlarger, developing trays, safelight, and just about everything else we needed to set up a darkroom except for the paper and chemicals (and a thermometer), for $25 (about £18). Admittedly, our 'real' darkroom would cost more like £1000 ($1500) to duplicate, with a Meopta enlarger and both Meograde variable-contrast head and Meocolor colour head, Nova processing tanks, electronic timers and so forth, but once you have such a set up, it will last you forever. This is why you can often buy second-hand darkroom equipment cheaply: it does not wear out, and if someone gets tired of it, they are often happy to take whatever they can get. This is how we bought our $25 darkroom; it is a cheap way of seeing if you want to get into processing your own black and white. You can always upgrade later, and if you decide that it is not for you, you lose the price of a decent meal in a restaurant.

It is worth adding that a well-processed black and white print on

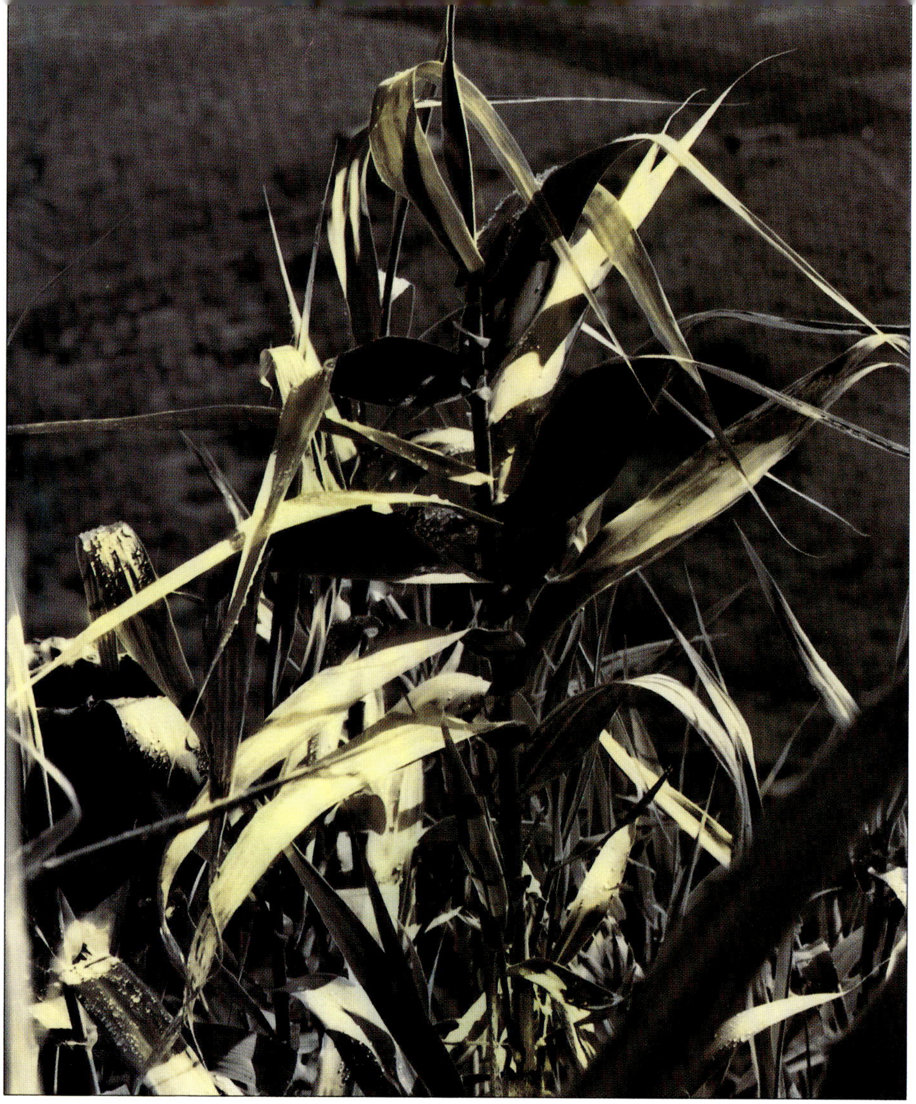

Corn, Gran Canaria

If you do your own processing, you can also get into such areas as hand-colouring and toning. Frances shot this corn in Gran Canaria, then selectively toned it using Edwal toners. The yellow toner was painted on neat, then the whole of the picture was briefly toned in blue toner to increase the contrast. The result is quite different from the original picture, which was principally a study in textures and chiaroscuro: this version captures the brashness, almost the violence, with which things grow in the Canaries. It emphasises the spikiness of the corn, and the way in which foliage suddenly catches your eye. The original shot was taken with a 90mm f/2.5 Vivitar Series One lens on a Nikon F; the film-stock was Ilford XP-2. (FES)

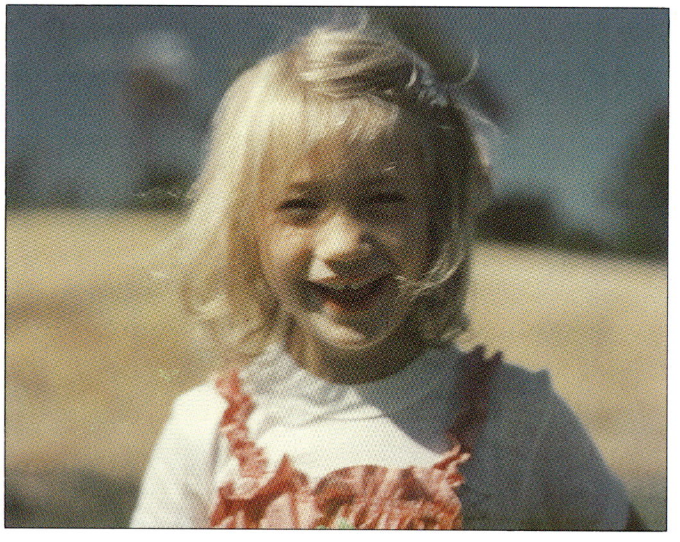

Lucille Schultz

This Anscochrome shot is a little older than the Kodachrome on page 55, dating probably from 1945 to 1948, and you can see how in those days the non-substantive Kodachrome was a vastly superior film to the substantive materials such as Anscochrome: sharper, more saturated, and (although it may not show in reproduction) a lot less grainy. We are not quite sure why the quality of this picture is so bad: the lens is actually quite sharp, as you can see from the hair on Frances's sister's forehead, but colour saturation is very low and (we suspect) halation was pretty bad. Nor have matters been helped by a modest dose of over-exposure and almost five decades of indifferent storage. (W. A. Schultz) fibre-based paper should last for a very long time without significant deterioration. If you take the trouble to fix and wash the prints carefully, they can last for many centuries. This 'archival' permanence is very important to some people; others just shrug and say, 'Nothing lasts forever.'

Reversal Processing

You can reversal-process black and white films yourself, to get black and white slides, or you can buy Agfa Dia-Direct, a black and white reversal film with the price of processing included (this film is not available in the United States). We find that the effort of doing our own black and white reversal processing is not worth the candle, but Dia-Direct gives wonderful quality and gradation, especially for technical shots.

CONTRAST CONTROL IN PRINTING

In black and white, you can use more or less contrasty enlarging paper to expand or compress the tonal range of the final picture. This is in addition to controlling the contrast of the film itself. You can also buy high- and low-contrast colour printing media from some manufacturers.

The ultimate in contrast control in printing is achieved by sandwiching the negative (or transparency) with a contact mask. Although this can be done in black and white, it is normally used for making colour prints, because (as already noted) the tonal range which can be recorded on a colour film is very much greater than the range across which colours are acceptable. The principle is simple enough: the mask is dark where the original is light, and light where the original is dark. The mask is normally made unsharp: it is a thin, slightly out-of-focus black and white image which is sandwiched with the original for printing. You can even buy reusable masks which use heat-reversible photochromic glass: the mask is made by contact printing to ultra-violet light, then returned to clarity by heating. Such masks are however very expensive.

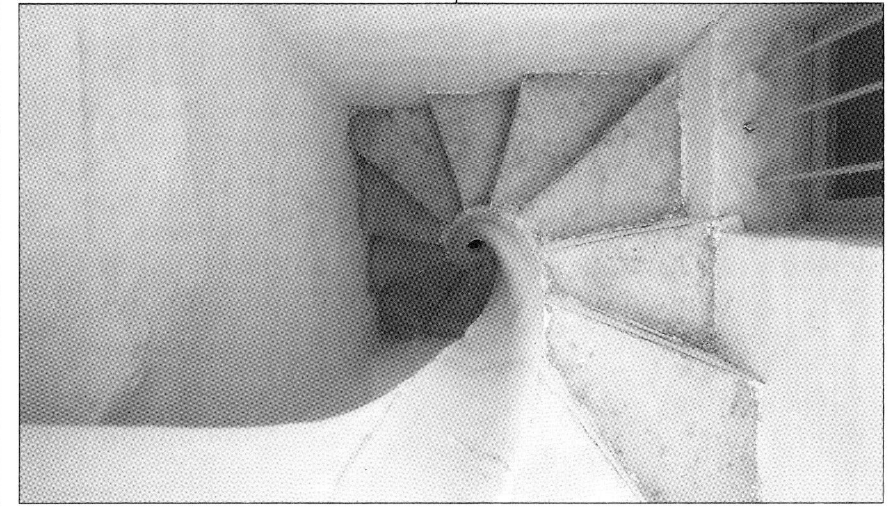

Stairs, Malta

These stairs in Malta date from when the house was modernised – in the fourteenth century! Roger shot them using a 21mm f/2.8 Elmarit-M on a Leica M2, but today he would almost certainly use either the 17mm f/3.5 Tamron SP or the 14mm f/3.5 Sigma, neither of which we owned in those days. The film-stock was Agfa's unique Dia-Direct, which is possibly the sharpest general-use film on the market but which is deadly slow (ISO 12, best used at EI 20 to 25) and which, as its name suggests, is a direct-reversal film. At the time of writing, we had used very little Dia-Direct for a long time: it is not available in the United States, where we were living for five years, and shortly after we returned to England, the lab which processed it in the UK suffered a fire, so all film had to be sent to Germany for processing. We were however looking forward greatly to the resumption of UK processing. (RWH)

4 FILM SIZES AND PACKINGS

The smallest standard film size was established by the tiny Minox and has since been adopted by a number of sub-miniature cameras. Each frame is 8x11mm, on a piece of film 9.5mm wide and about 500mm (say 18in) long for the 36-exposure roll.

The largest standard size is 11x14in sheet film; about 280x355mm. The area of the 'eleven-fourteen' image is over one thousand times greater than the area of the Minox image. Still larger cameras, up to 20x24in (50x60cm) have been made in limited production runs, but they have never achieved widespread acceptance. There are studio cameras which use even larger sizes of film, but they are for copying only and have no real relevance to general photography.

There have been countless sizes of films, plates and even disks in between 8x11mm and 11x14in, and often, different image sizes appear on the same film. It would be impossible to survey all these sizes and to advise every reader what film to use in every single camera. In fact, it makes sense to concentrate on 35mm, current rollfilm sizes, and current cut-film sizes, and merely to nod at the other sizes in passing.

35MM FILM

The overall supremacy and versatility of the 35mm SLR is indisputable, even if there are other cameras which do specific jobs better. To a large extent, this is due to a happy synergy of the 24x36mm format (overwhelmingly the most common) and the resolving power of the lenses and the films used with it.

In a companion volume, *The Lens Book*, we have gone into resolution and lens selection in depth; all that needs to be said here is that for most purposes – exhibition prints, publication, happy snaps, scientific recording, or anything else – 35mm film and 35mm cameras deliver an optimum combination of sharpness, convenience and economy. There are times when you need more sharpness or more control, it is true, but for most people 35mm is all they need.

The original Leica prototype seems to have taken 40 or maybe 50 pictures, loaded into the camera in the darkroom, but by the time they put the camera into production and made a film cassette to allow daylight loading, they could only get 36 exposures into it. This became the standard 35mm load.

The 18 exposure 'half load' was soon introduced for those who found 36 exposures too many: in those days, remember, 8 exposure rollfilms were the norm. Then, the 18 exposure load was lengthened to 20 exposures, and after that, someone introduced the 12 exposure 'week-end' film. A little while after that, the 20 exposure load was lengthened to 24 exposures. Somewhere in the middle of all this, Ilford introduced a 72 exposure load on

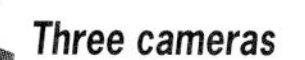

Three cameras

The old Nikon F is of course a 35mm camera, the sort of thing that most people are familiar with – though they probably use something a bit more modern! The 4x5in camera is a Linhof Technikardan, an enormously versatile machine which is however terrifyingly expensive: it costs more than even the most expensive Nikon, Contax or Leica SLR bodies. The little black blob in the foreground is a Chadt, one of the tiniest cameras ever made, which uses Minox film in the 8x11mm format. These represent the extremes of film size which we normally use, and we have to admit that the Chadt is really just a snapshot camera, through which we put maybe one or two films per year. Results are amazingly good at postcard size, and the camera comes with a wrist-strap and a small LCD watch, so it is no trouble to carry anywhere. We used to shoot both 8x10in and 11x14in, but for the sort of work we do, there was really no excuse for owning such large cameras – and film handling and processing were a real nuisance. Today, the largest cameras we own are 4x5in (Linhof Technikardan and Toho FC-45A).

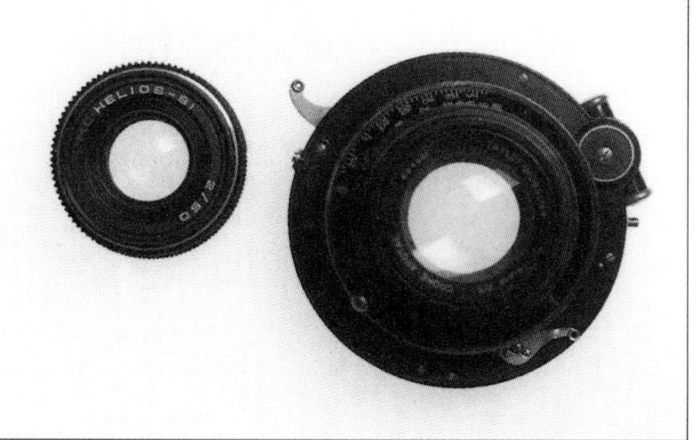

Two standard lenses

A 'standard' lens is defined as one with a focal length roughly equal to the diagonal of the negative. For the 24x36mm format, this is 43.5mm, and anything from 35mm to 50mm (this is a 50mm f/2) is regarded as 'standard'. For 11x14in, the diagonal is about 400mm, and 'standard' lenses range from 14in or 360mm (as seen here) to 450mm. The drawbacks of the monster formats are all too clear: lens speeds are necessarily slow, or the lenses would be unmanageably huge (this is an f/9), and working apertures have to be small, or depth of field would be negligible. Depth of field depends on aperture and on the size of the image on the film, and as a frame-filling shot of a face would be about one-tenth life size on 35mm and approximately 1:1 on 11x14in, apertures of f/45 and below are commonplace. We used to own an 11x14in camera (for which this was our standard lens) with an 8x10in reducing back; and although the contact prints were wonderful, the expense and effort of running the camera were just not worth it to us. As far as we can see, the main use for 11x14in cameras is for landscape photography and fine art; even for advertising, they are overkill, and for editorial work, no-one is ever going to appreciate the quality you can wring out of them.

special thin-base film, still in the standard-sized cassette; but it never caught on, and was discontinued a few years after it came out. With the 18x24mm 'half frame' format (also called 'single frame', because it is the size of a traditional movie frame), the various loadings were of course 24, 36, 40, 48, 72 and 144. Those of a mathematical bent can work out the equivalents for 24x24mm (Robot, Mecaflex), 24x32 (early Nikon and some others), 24x34 (Nikon again) and 24x56 (the panoramic Horizont format).

The 250 exposure long load was a Leica innovation in the 1930s, and has since become something of a standard for copying cameras and some other specialist applications. The original Leica 250 was known as the 'Reporter', but most 250 exposure backs for modern cameras are used in scientific or copying work.

Bulk Loading

You can save a good deal of money by loading film from bulk rolls, which are usually 30m long (just short of 100ft). Typically, a 36 exposure roll loaded from bulk costs one-half or even one-third as much as a full-price 36 exposure roll in the manufacturers' packing. For 36 exposures, you need about 165cm (say 65in) of film, so you can load eighteen rolls from 30m; the remaining 30cm (12in) is likely to be used up in cutting and trimming the film, and in adding 'a bit for luck'.

If you only need a few exposures, you can load those too, but the wastage will be significant: a single exposure calls for 30cm (12in) of film, after you have allowed for the film leader and the little bit on the end which attaches to the spool. Very roughly, six exposures calls for 50cm (say 20in); a dozen exposures calls for 72cm (29in); 18 exposures is 96cm (38in); and 24 exposures is 118cm (47in).

Another reason for loading from bulk is in order to take advantage of emulsions which are only available that way: some copying and high-contrast films are not sold in cassettes, because they are normally used in long-roll 250 exposure backs. These, incidentally, use approximately 10m (32-33ft) of film.

Whether you use velvet-lip cassettes or labyrinthine cassettes (illustrated on page 72), it is important not to 'cinch' the film or wind it too tight; this applies when you are rewinding, too. 'Cinching' can cause pressure marks in its own right, and will cause scratches if there are any tiny pieces of grit or dust present.

Other 35mm Loadings

There are a few 35mm cameras which do not take standard cassettes, though they are rare today. The Agfa Rapid cassette has no centre spool: the film is

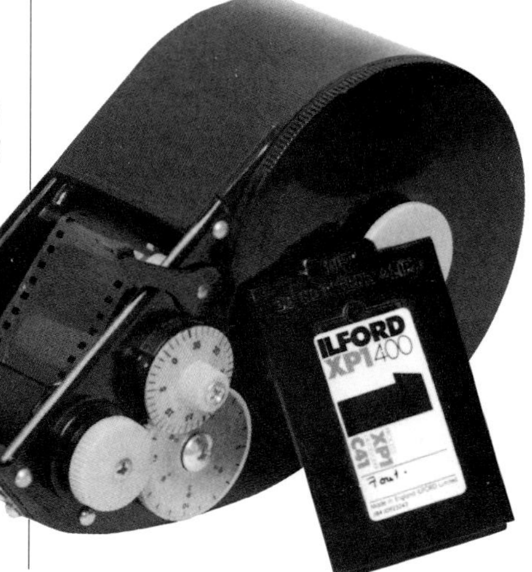

Bulk-film loader

You can see pretty much how the bulk-film loader works from this shot. The bulk (30m or 100ft) roll goes in the large chamber at one end, and the 35mm cassette goes in the small chamber at the other. The lid of the chamber containing the 35mm cassette can only be opened and removed when the bulk chamber is sealed: there is an interlock to ensure this. Likewise, the light-tight trap between the bulk chamber and the cassette can only be opened when the lid is in place, or at least when the lid retaining lever is pushed down. The small knob opposite the crank opens and closes manufacturers' cassettes – the one in here is for old Nikons – and the two dials record the number of exposures loaded into the cassette (upper dial) and the amount of film used altogether (lower dial).

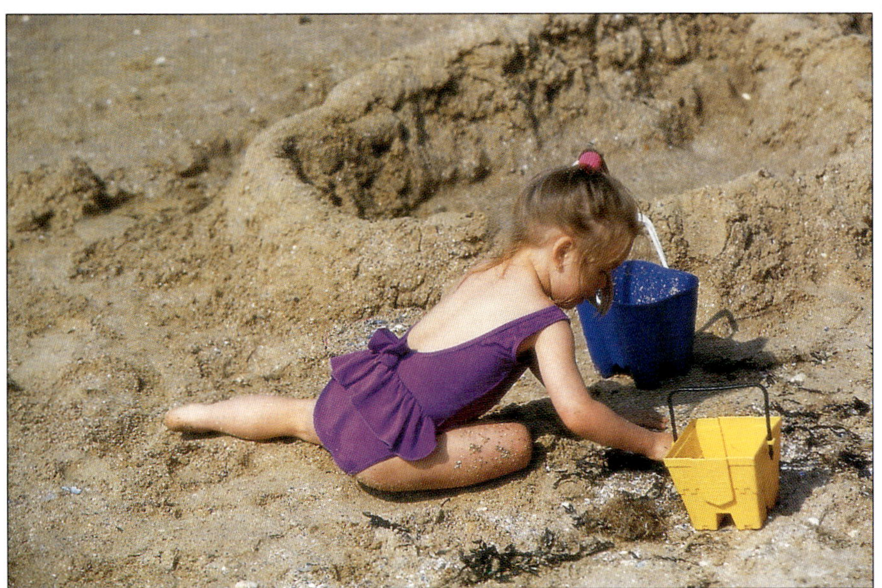

Sandcastle builder

Unless you go to the beach primarily to take photographs (as Roger does), you might do better to use a very short load such as 12 exposures. That way, the entire film can be exposed in a single day, and processed while the events are still fresh in your memory – next day at a one-hour lab, if you wish. Although we normally shoot colour slide film and black and white, we also use colour negative film for 'happy snaps', and we find that like the veriest amateurs, we can take several months to finish a film. After all, when it comes to snapshots, you do not normally want to shoot more than two or three pictures of each subject, if that; you are shooting for the memories, rather than for high aesthetic purposes or for commercial reasons. If you wonder how we as professionals can leave a film in the camera for months, the answer is simple. We have an old Nikkorex which cost us about $30 (under £20) at a camera show. It accepts Nikon lenses, and we use it as a snapshot camera so that we do not have to unload the films from our 'real' Nikons. (RWH)

just forced in, and curls of its own accord, though this is unsatisfactory for anything much longer than about 12 exposures. Some models of Robot use a special cassette, with velvet lips which are forced apart when the camera is opened. The Tessina, which is too small to use a standard cassette, uses miniature velvet-lip cassettes and takes pictures 14x21mm. There have also been 35mm films with paper leaders and trailers, like 220 film (see below), but these have not been available for decades. And, of course, a few cameras permit cassette-to-cassette loading: old Contaxes, the Russian Kiev copy of the Contax, Robots and a few others.

ROLLFILM

Overwhelmingly the standard rollfilm size today is 120. The film is 62mm wide and about 83cm (33in) long; it is backed with a piece of paper of the same width, but about 152cm (5ft) long. The long leader and trailer protect the film before it is loaded and after it is exposed (though it is a good idea to avoid direct sunlight) and the backing paper also has numbers for cameras using the old 'red window' system of film counting: numbers are provided for 8-on, 12-on and 16-on. The number of exposures and the nominal and actual dimensions of the most popular formats are as follows:

No of Exposures	Nominal Size Metric	Imperial	Actual Dimensions (Millimetres)
4-on	6x17cm	2¼x6¾in	55-7x155-70
6-on	6x12cm	2¼x4½in	55-7x110-20
8-on	6x9cm	2¼x3¼in	55-7x78-88
10-on	6x7cm	2¼x2¾in	55-7x66-72
12-on	6x6cm	2¼x2¼in	55-7x56-8
15/16-on	6x4.5cm	2¼x1¾in	55-7x42-5

Bouncy castle

Where you are shooting rapid action, and can reasonably expect that some pictures will be utter failures, then 36 exposure 35mm films are almost certainly the best bet. Ilford used to make a 72 exposure black and white loading, using a special thin film base, but demand was so low that they dropped it. The only other reasonably common loading that is longer than 36 exposures, unless you go to special 250-exposure backs for 35mm cameras, is the standard 70mm cassette. This holds just over 4m of film, or just under 15ft, and delivers rather over 50 exposures in the 6x7cm format. Roger shot half a roll or a roll of pictures of particularly spirited youngsters on a 'bouncy castle', and about a third of the pictures were usable. Even then, focus was not always perfect: choosing a high shutter speed in order to freeze the action necessarily implied fairly wide apertures. With ISO 100 film, exposures were around $^{1}/_{500}$ second at f/2.8 and f/4, using a 70-210mm f/2.8 Sigma Apo zoom at or close to its maximum focal length. It would be interesting to try to reshoot this, assuming one could find as lively a set of models again, on ISO 1000 film. This would allow $^{1}/_{1000}$ at f/8 or so – a useful improvement both in action-stopping and depth of field. (RWH)

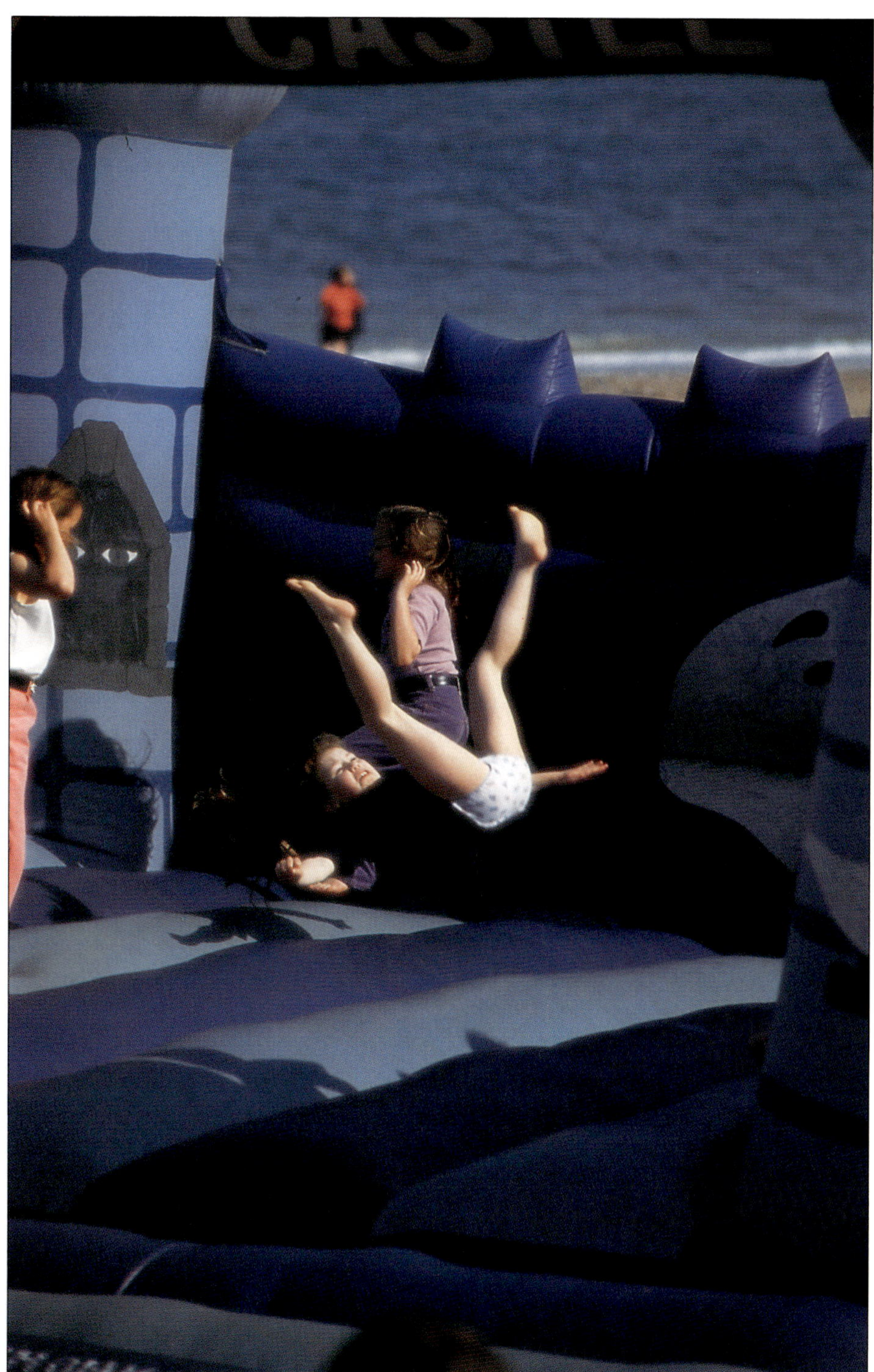

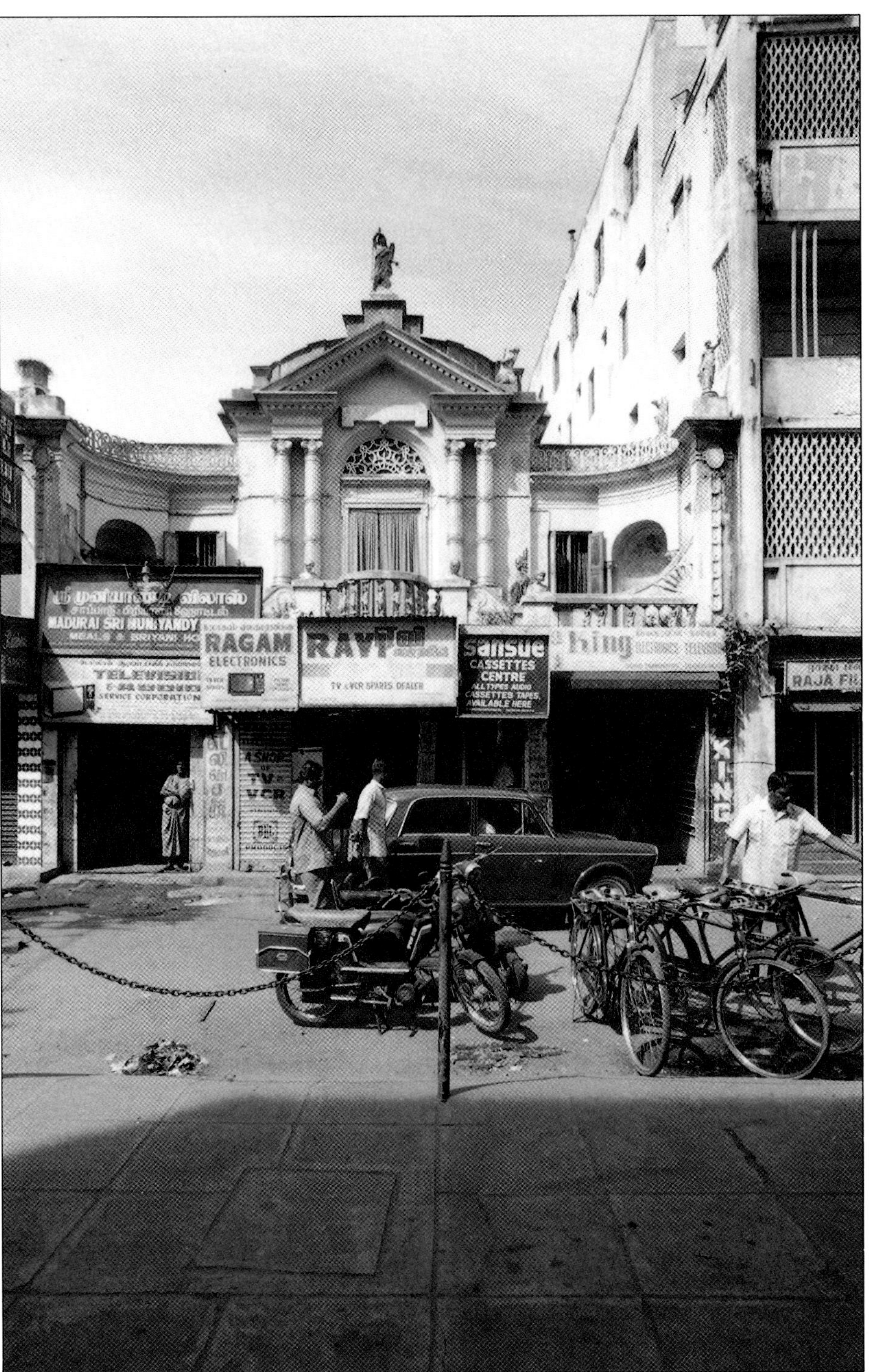

Street scene, Pondicherry

'Pondi' is a wonderful mixture of native South Indian influence, French influences (it was a French colony before Independence) and the pervasive British influence which is to be found all over India. Wherever you are travelling, though, 35mm is the ideal compromise for quality and portability. We have travelled with rollfilm cameras, and while the cameras themselves are not necessarily all that much bulkier than 35mm (especially the Mamiya 645 which Frances used extensively), carrying all those rolls of film is a real nuisance, especially on a long trip. Even with 15-on-120, you have to change films more than twice as often as with 36 exposure 35mm films, and of course you have to carry many more of them: to get the same 720 exposures you would get from 20 rolls of 35mm, you have to carry 48 rolls of 120 for the 645 – or 72 rolls for a 6x7cm camera. The only alternative which we would like to explore is 70mm, where 50-plus exposures per roll mean that 15 rolls of film give you almost 800 exposures, but the problem is that so few emulsions are available in 70mm. Also, the price of 70mm film is alarming. Frances shot this on XP-2, using a Nikon F with a 35mm f/2.8 PC-Nikkor; exposure was probably $^{1}/_{250}$ at f/11. (FES)

Foreshore, Gran Canaria

Until very recently, we would have said that there was little point in attempting 'fine art' photography with 35mm film: it was just so much easier to use rollfilm, where lens and film quality are far less critical. With the advent of Ilford Delta 100 – this was from the very first roll we ever shot – we are no longer sure that we would give the same advice. If you use a top-quality lens, Delta 100 can capture texture and detail which formerly were the preserve of rollfilm cameras. The enormous advantages of using 35mm, however, are that you have a far greater choice of lenses; that the cameras are very much faster-handling (though you should still mount them on a tripod for the very best quality); and that you have a much better choice of fast shutter speeds, which are ideal for 'freezing' movement like these waves. This was probably shot at 1/500 at f/8, using (probably) a 200mm f/3 Vivitar Series One. This is the equivalent of a 400mm on 6x7cm, or a 680mm lens on 4x5in – monsters, even if you could afford them. (RWH)

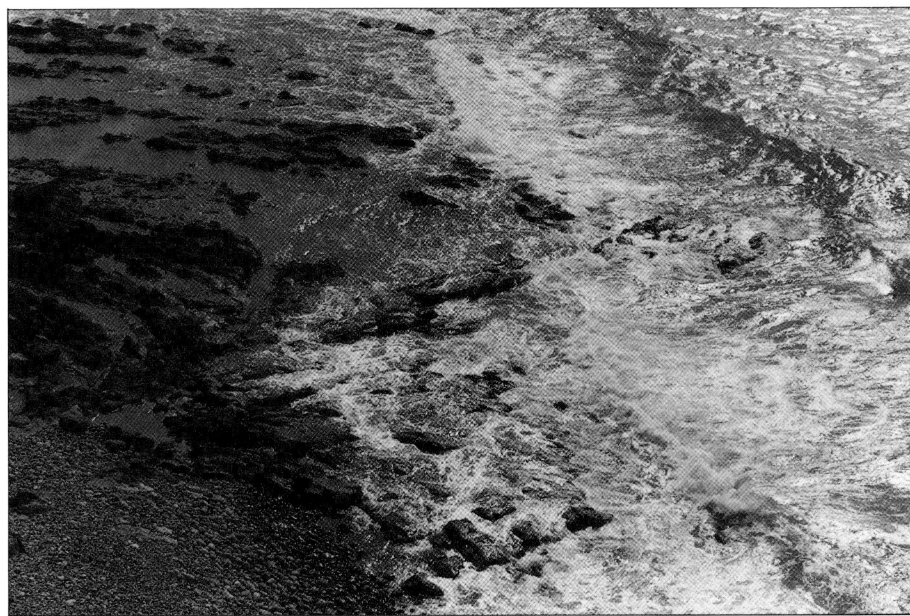

All modern cameras, except a very few old-fashioned models made mostly in communist or formerly communist countries, or in the Third World, use some form of automatic counting instead of the old 'red window'. There is an arrow near the beginning of the film, and this is lined up with an arrow or other mark in the camera; after that, film is automatically advanced the right distance, just as on a 35mm camera. This is how the '645' format is sometimes 16-on, but more usually 15-on; dropping one exposure allows significantly larger rebates between images, and slightly bigger negatives. There have also been 9-on (instead of 10-on) and 11-on (instead of 12-on) cameras for the same reasons.

The 220 format consists of a double-length strip of film (165cm/66in) with no backing paper but still with an opaque paper leader and trailer. Some cameras, and some interchangeable camera backs, can be adjusted to take both 220 and 120 film (the difference lies in the positioning of the pressure plate, as well as in the counter and wind-on) but others are designed for 120 only: either you need a separate back for 220, or you simply cannot use 220.

Although 220 means that you have to reload half as often, its limited popularity means that it is no cheaper to use than 120. Indeed, two rolls of 120 may well be cheaper to buy and to process than one roll of 220. Also, relatively few emulsions are available in 220.

Another 120-derived format is 620, which is the same film and paper as 120 wound onto a smaller-diameter spool. All 120 cameras can accept 620, but 620 cameras (and backs) will not accept 120 because the spool is too big. Also, automatic numbering systems designed for 120 will normally not work when used with 620, and vice versa. Some 620 cameras can be modified to accept

120, but most cannot – or if they could, it would not be worth the expense. Very few emulsions are still available in 620, and the main reason for mentioning 620 is to warn you to look out for what appear to be 120 cameras (or 120 rollfilm adapters for large-format cameras) but are not.

Finally, there is a half-length 120, though it is rarely encountered outside Japan. An 8-on camera gives 4-on; 10-on becomes 5-on; 12-on becomes 6-on; and 15-on or 16-on becomes 8-on. Emulsion availability is confined mostly to colour print films.

70mm Film

Once seen as the wave of the future, 70mm film has never enjoyed widespread popularity. Obviously, it is twice as wide as 35mm film, and it comes in big velvet-lipped cassettes which clearly owe a debt to 35mm. Formats are the same as 120/220, with 6x7cm the most popular. The standard loading is about 4.5m or 15ft: the precise number of exposures depends on the actual image size, but Linhof's 56x72mm '6x7cm' gives 53 exposures. Mostly, 70mm is used in special backs for a wide variety of cameras, though there have been a few 70mm-only cameras like the 'giant Leica' Combat Graphic.

Perhaps because of the large number of exposures per roll, 70mm film has found most favour in museums and scientific establishments, though it also has its merits as a film for stock (picture library) photography. As with 220, comparatively few emulsions are available in this size.

Choosing a Format

All rollfilm formats have their devotees, but the most popular are 12-on and 10-on, so it makes sense to deal with them first.

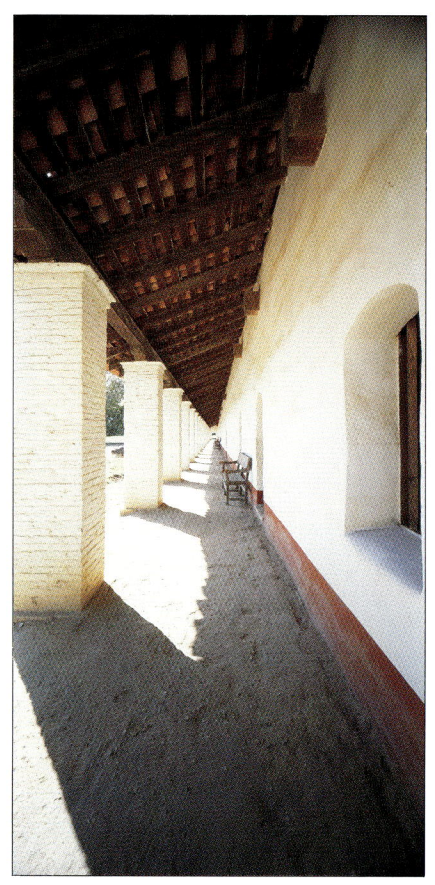

Mision de la Purisima Concepcion, California

This was one of our earliest experiments with Velvia, just after it came out, and it was also one of the first times we used the 6x12cm (6-on-120) back for our 4x5in cameras. The film was simply too contrasty to capture both the details in the wooden roof and the texture of the sunlit path under the colonnade, which you can see is quite burned out in the middle of the picture. Detail has however been retained in the lower left-hand corner, which was effectively exposed about a stop less than the centre of the image because of the extreme wide-angle lens used: a 47mm f/5.6 Super Angulon, more or less the equivalent of a 16mm lens on 35mm. For applications where even illumination is essential, you can buy a centre-graduated filter; but normally, the slight vignetting is an advantage. (RWH/FES)

12-on-120 The 'two and a quarter square' format was born of necessity. In the days before pentaprisms, it was very awkward indeed to turn a reflex camera on its side. With a square format, of course, there is no need to do this.

Since then, the position of the 6x6cm format has been consolidated chiefly by two cameras and their imitators: the Rolleiflex twin-lens reflex and the Hasselblad single-lens reflex. The legendary quality of both cameras ensured widespread professional acceptance, even among those who

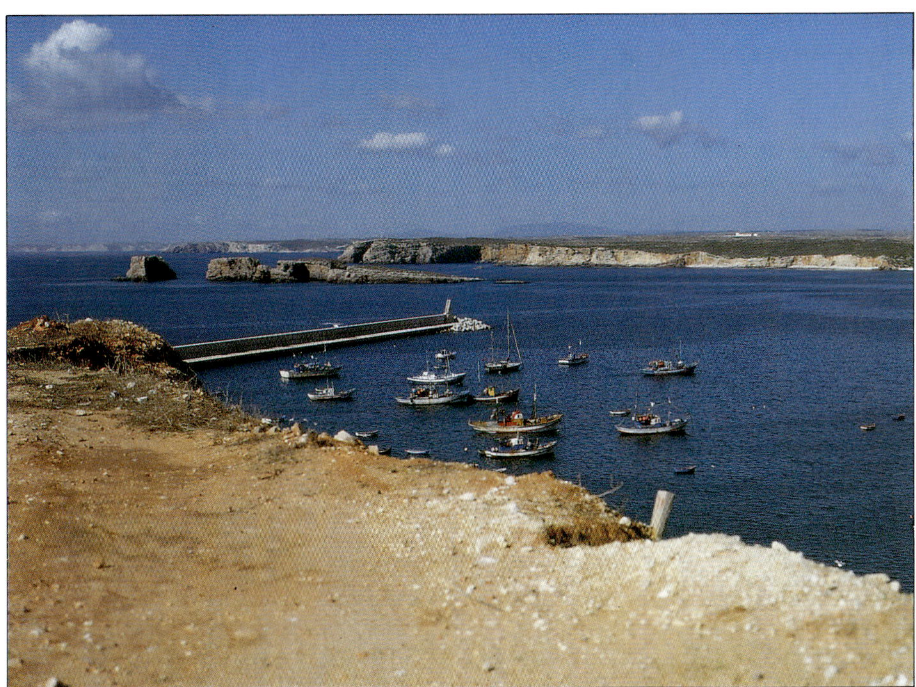

Fishing vessels, Algarve

For all that 120 film is a nuisance to carry and to reload, it can give you a useful selling edge if you want to get your work into picture libraries. This was shot with a Mamiya 645, using either the 80mm f/1.9 standard lens or a 150mm f/3.5 short telephoto, roughly the equivalent of 100mm on 35mm. What is important is not so much the increase in image quality with the larger format, which will only be detectable at about 5x7in /13x18cm or above; the real selling advantage comes from the fact that the bigger image is easier for the art director, designer, or picture buyer to see. This means that if the choice comes down to 35mm or rollfilm images of roughly equal artistic quality, the rollfilm image will normally sell better. Also, it has to be admitted that even the 645 image is almost three times the area of 35mm, while a 6x7cm image is more than four and a half times the area. In other words, if a 35mm shot looks good at 5x7in or 13x18cm, the 645 shot can go up to a full-size magazine page and the 6x7cm shot will look good at 11x14in or even 30x40cm. (FES)

were less than happy with the square format.

The argument that you can crop the same shot either 'portrait' or 'landscape' cuts no ice with the detractors of 12-on-120, who point out that a well-composed rectangle will discourage insensitive or incompetent cropping. One of the authors stopped using Hasselblads after he saw what art editors could do with square transparencies.

10-on-120 The 10-on-120 format was tentatively introduced by Graflex before World War II (as a 56x62mm/2¼x2½in format), but after the war the 6x7cm format was popularised by Omega (9-on, about 1950) and Linhof (10-on, 1959). Since then, it has become very popular indeed for two reasons.

One is that it enlarges conveniently, with minimum wastage, onto standard paper sizes and magazine page sizes: the old square 12-on format has to be cropped to fit a rectangle, so the effective area of Linhof's 56x72mm can be 65 per cent greater than that of a square image cropped to fit the same layout.

The other is that it allows bracketing of three exposures: one 'on the button' and one either side, for a total of nine. The 8-on-120 format is clearly less convenient in this respect. The 'spare' exposure allows for one error per film! For these reasons, 10-on-120 is often referred to as 'ideal format'.

15-on/16-on The 645 format is also called 'ideal format' by its proponents, who say that it represents the *usable* area of a 6x6cm image while allowing an extra three exposures on each roll: enough for five bracketed exposures, assuming no errors on a 15-on or allowing one error on a 16-on.

With modern film, 645 can deliver excellent quality – but of course, 6x7cm is even better.

Other Standard Formats The 8-on-120 6x9cm is the biggest convenient 120 format, with about the same shape as 35mm. It is much liked by architectural photographers (the extra height comes in handy) and by anyone whose pictures may be run 'double truck' across a magazine spread. There are few 8-on-120 cameras still being made, though there were many good ones in the past, most of which remain usable today. Now, this is principally a format for rollfilm backs on 4x5in cameras. The only real drawback is that you cannot bracket three shots on an 8-on back.

Both the 6x12cm (6-on-120) and 6x17cm (4-on-120) 'panoramic' formats have their devotees, but they get through film quickly and are not as useful as you might expect. There is also a 6x24cm format (2¼x9in, 3-on-120) available from one small Japanese company, Art Panoramic.

Obsolescent Rollfilms

In the past, there were many other rollfilm formats; some were vast, postcard sized or even bigger, while the old 828 'Bantam' size used imperforate 35mm film. All sorts of names were used to describe these films, including 116, 117 and 118, but never be guided by these numbers alone: sometimes, an unfamiliar number may turn out to be some long-forgotten manufacturer's designation for 120.

The only real survivor (which is dying fast) of the obsolete sizes is 127, a miniature version of 120 just 46mm wide. Cameras for 8-on, 12-on and 16-on were made, including such gems as the 'Baby Rollei' 4x4, but hardly any films are still available – mostly just colour print. This is in some ways a shame, because the '4x4cm' (actually about 38mm square) 'Superslide' made for impressive slide shows and could be projected in conventional 2in/5cm slide mounts in a 35mm projector.

CUT FILM

Once upon a time, and for no very clear reason, the standard size for a photographic plate was 6½x8½ inches (165x216mm). This size was therefore logically known as 'whole plate', and 'half plate' and 'quarter plate' were derived from it. Although quarter-plate really was one-quarter of a whole plate (3¼x4¼in/82x108mm), half-plate wasn't a half plate: instead, it was 4¾x6½in (121x165mm). Today, only half-plate and whole-plate sizes survive (as cut films), but with a steadily decreasing range of emulsions; in the United States, 'plate' film sizes are all but unobtainable.

On the Continent, metric sizes were adopted: the main ones were 9x12cm (sometimes known as 'continental quarter-plate'), 13x18cm and 18x24cm. Although these sizes also survive, they too are falling before the onslaught of American inch sizes, and even in Paris *'le five-four'* is becoming commonplace.

The common American (and to a lesser extent British) sizes are 4x5in (called 5x4in in England); 5x7in (rare outside the United States); and 8x10in (called 10x8in in England). Larger sizes are very rare, though 10x12in survives for new cameras made in India (the film is available elsewhere) and 11x14in is sometimes found in America, though few emulsions are

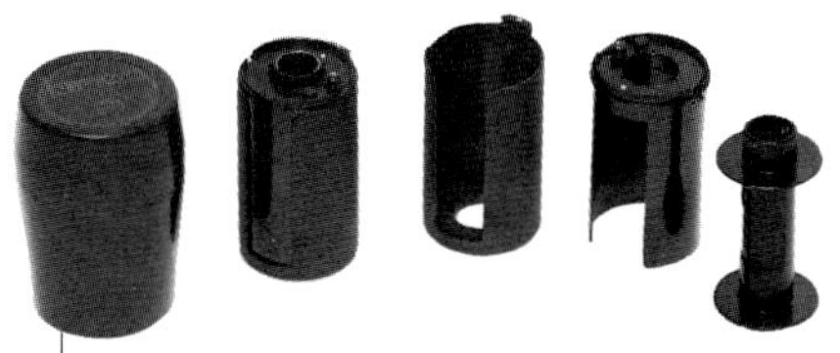

Nikon film cassettes

The cassette for the Nikon F derives from the pre-war Contax cassette (for rangefinder cameras), and is a simple and very nicely made piece of equipment. The film is of course wound onto the centre spool (extreme right), *which fits into the inner shell* (centre right). *This in turn fits into the outer shell* (centre); *a complete cassette is shown on centre left, along with its screw-top plastic container* (far left). *The two slots in the inner and outer shells are automatically opened by a key in the base of the camera when the back is locked, and they are automatically closed when the back is opened.*

Film cassettes

A rogues' gallery. From left to right, back row: conventional velvet-lip 35mm cassette; Shirley Wellard 'universal' cassette (works with any camera having a pull-up rewind crank); Leitz 'brass mushroom' cassette for screw-mount Leicas; Leitz 'chrome mushroom' cassette for M-series and screw-mount Leicas (you can just see the difference in the 'mushrooms', part of the locking apparatus, on the tops of the cassettes); Agfa Rapid coreless cassette. At the front, left to right: Russian copy of Contax cassette, to fit Kiev and Contax rangefinder cameras; Robot cassette, with sprung velvet lips; and Nikon cassette, clearly related to the Contax/Kiev cassette on the left.

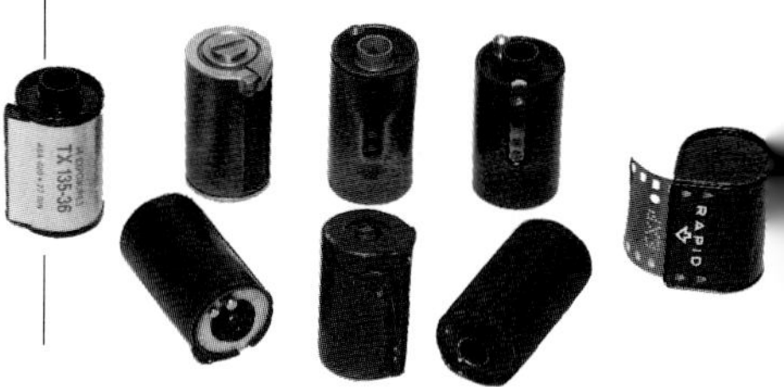

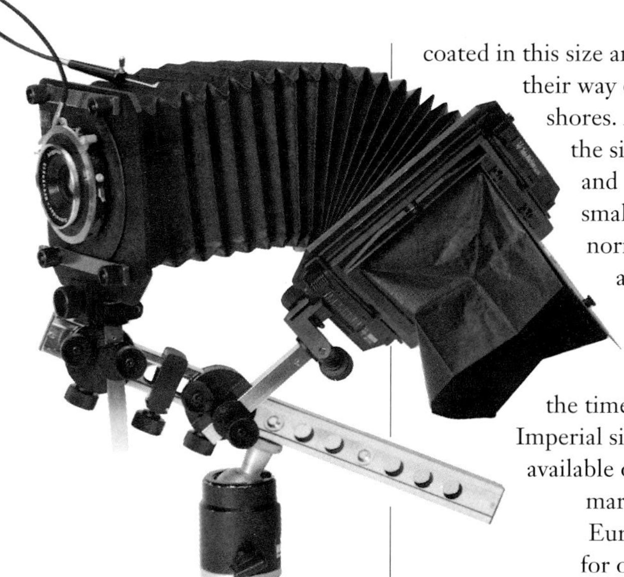

Toho FC-45A 4x5in camera

The principal advantage of a large format camera is often the 'movements' rather than the film size. This Toho monorail has all the movements: front and rear cross, rise, fall, swings and tilts. The swings and tilts are mainly used to hold a receding plane in focus (using the 'Scheimpflug Rule'), while the rise and fall are used principally to change the apparent viewpoint. The rising front (or falling back), for example, allows you to photograph a tall building without tilting the camera and getting the familiar 'falling over backwards' effect. Learning to use camera movements can take a while, though you can learn it in a couple of days from a good book – or, if you prefer, you could try a course of evening classes. Quite often, we use rollfilm backs (6x9cm and 6x12cm) on 4x5in cameras, so that we have the benefit of the movements and the convenience and (relative) economy of rollfilm. There are also 'baby' or rollfilm versions of a number of 4x5in cameras, including Linhof, Arca Swiss, Cambo and more. We own two 4x5in cameras, Linhof and Toho, and a 'baby' Linhof Technika with limited movements.

coated in this size and even fewer find their way outside America's shores. At the other end of the size scale, 2¼x3¼in and 6.5x9cm are the smallest cut-film sizes normally encountered, and film availability is declining fast: it is simply easier to use rollfilm. At the time of writing, the Imperial size was only readily available on the American market, while Europeans (including, for once, the British) used the metric size.

Just to make life still more interesting, the *external* dimensions of double cut-film holders (DCFHs) are not necessarily a guide to the film size they accept. The external dimensions of both 6.5x9cm and 2¼x3¼ in DCFHs are identical; so are those for 9x12cm and 4x5in; and so are those for half-plate, 13x18cm and 5x7in – so make sure that you have the right holder for the film. On the other hand, don't worry about a 9x12cm camera not accepting 4x5in film-holders, or about using 9x12cm film-holders in a 4x5: unless it is an old, pre-standardisation camera, there will be no problem.

Choosing a Cut-film Format

For the vast majority of purposes, 4x5in or 9x12cm is the best choice. Running costs are significantly less than for larger cameras, a vast range of emulsions is available, enlargers are not much of a problem, and you can buy standardised, affordable Polaroid backs with modest running costs (see Chapter 10).

Larger formats mean that enlargers are hard to find; running costs are high; Polaroids are a problem (8x10in Polaroids are available, but expensive); and the cameras are bulky. 'Ten-eight' is the biggest practical size, and even then comparatively few professionals (mostly in advertising) use them. If you love big contact prints, then by all means buy an 'eleven-fourteen', but its usefulness is limited. A few advertising photographers use 11x14in, and the transparencies are spectacular, but mostly it is an amateur's format, ideal for landscapes.

Quarter-plate is a delightful format, but film availability has declined to almost nothing, and the smaller cut-film sizes have mostly been replaced by rollfilms: again, only a limited range of emulsions is available.

Film Packs

Just occasionally, you may encounter film packs. These are ingenious devices which interleave several sheets of film into a rapid-change box that rather resembles a modern Polaroid film pack; but today, they are no longer made and it is not practical to try to reload them yourself. The film thickness was less than modern cut films, and the dimensions may even have differed slightly.

Plates and Plateholders

At the time of writing, plates were still catalogued by Kodak in the United States, at a staggering price, and they might also be available in some other countries; but it is many years now since their use was widespread. It is always worth checking, though, to make sure that film-holders really are film-holders, and not plate-holders:

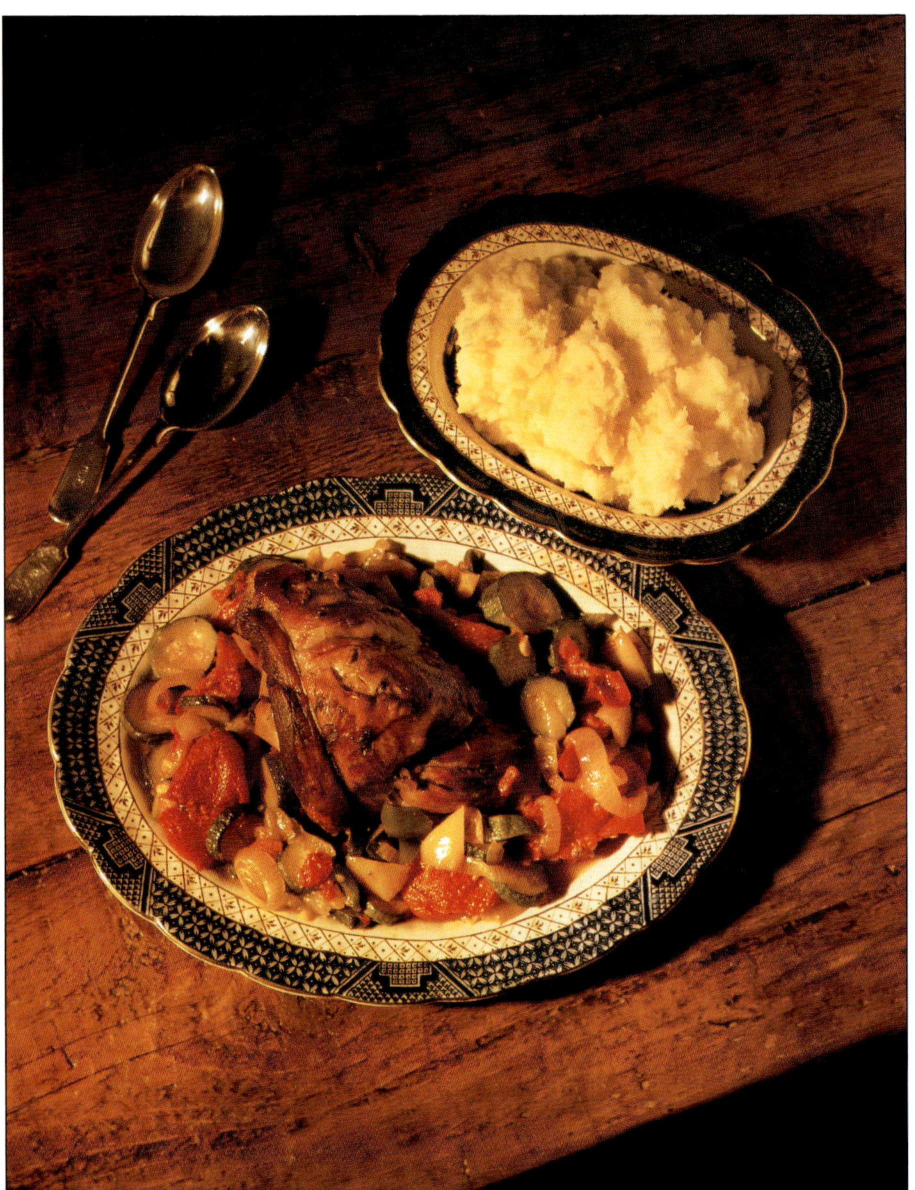

Lamb provençale

Food photographers almost all use 4x5in film, in order to capture the textures which make a good food shot so mouth-watering. In fact, it would be perfectly possible to shoot most of it on rollfilm – we habitually do – but there is certainly an extra 'edge' to 4x5in film. This is ISO 100 material: anything slower would have been excessively contrasty, and anything faster would have been unnecessary, because we were using a powerful studio electronic flash (Paul Buff 1800) which allowed us to work at f/32. In the studio, it is normal to use comparatively slow films, and just to pour on more light if you need it. While this was shot with quite an expensive camera, a Linhof Technikardan, it could equally well have been shot on the sort of second-hand technical camera that you can sometimes pick up very cheaply, and the lens was certainly not expensive: an elderly Kodak Commercial Ektar f/7.7. There was a heavy orange filter over the light source, which was 'snooted' and directed through a honeycomb grid to make it highly directional. (RWH/FES)

without an adapter (hard to find today), a piece of cut film will simply rattle about in a plate holder. A few manufacturers made dual 'film-plate' holders with spring-loaded pressure plates to accept either: we still use old Linhof film-plate holders.

'CARTRIDGE' AND 'DISK' FILMS

Although there have been many proprietary film sizes, the sheer marketing muscle of Kodak has allowed them to attempt to introduce a number of new sizes, most of which have met

Girl and crab

This extremely attractive young lady and her sister had caught four crabs on the beach near our house. She was explaining how, when you hold a crab like this, it acts almost as if it were paralysed. She had another crab in the other hand, so she could not tap this one with her finger to demonstrate – so she tapped it against her lips, as if she were kissing it. Roger had doubly the wrong film in the camera: a 24 exposure roll of print film, which we were testing for this book. The technical quality of the film (Konica 200, rated at EI 160 for extra saturation and finer grain) was superb, but Roger shot three frames of this pose alone, each with a slightly different expression, so it would have been much more convenient to have had a 36 exposure film in the camera. Also, because it is such an intriguing shot, it would have been better to have it on slide film. This is why we almost never use colour print film: if we want happy snaps, we can make them from slides, but making slides from colour negatives is altogether harder work and does not deliver the quality of a camera original slide. (RWH)

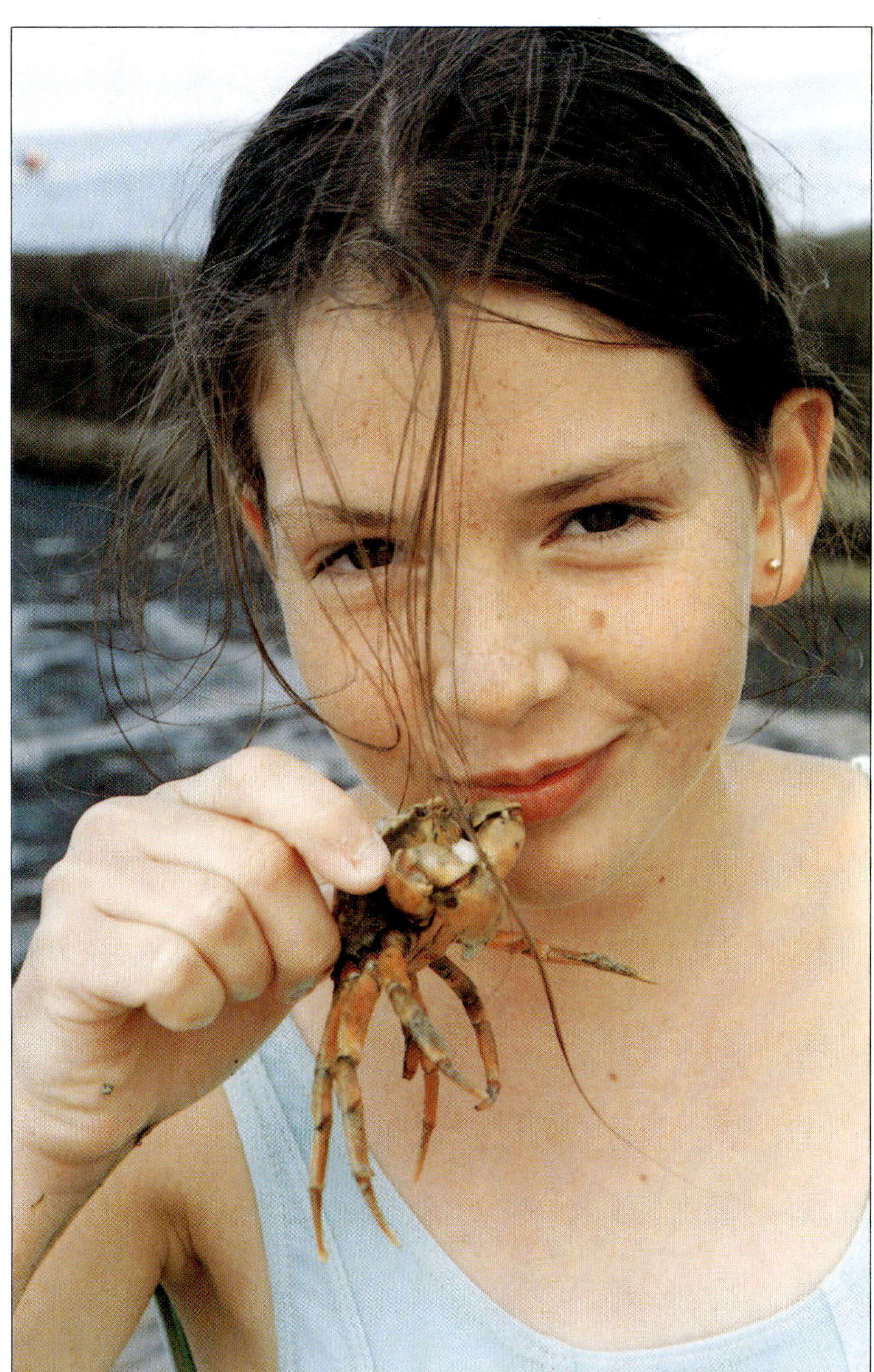

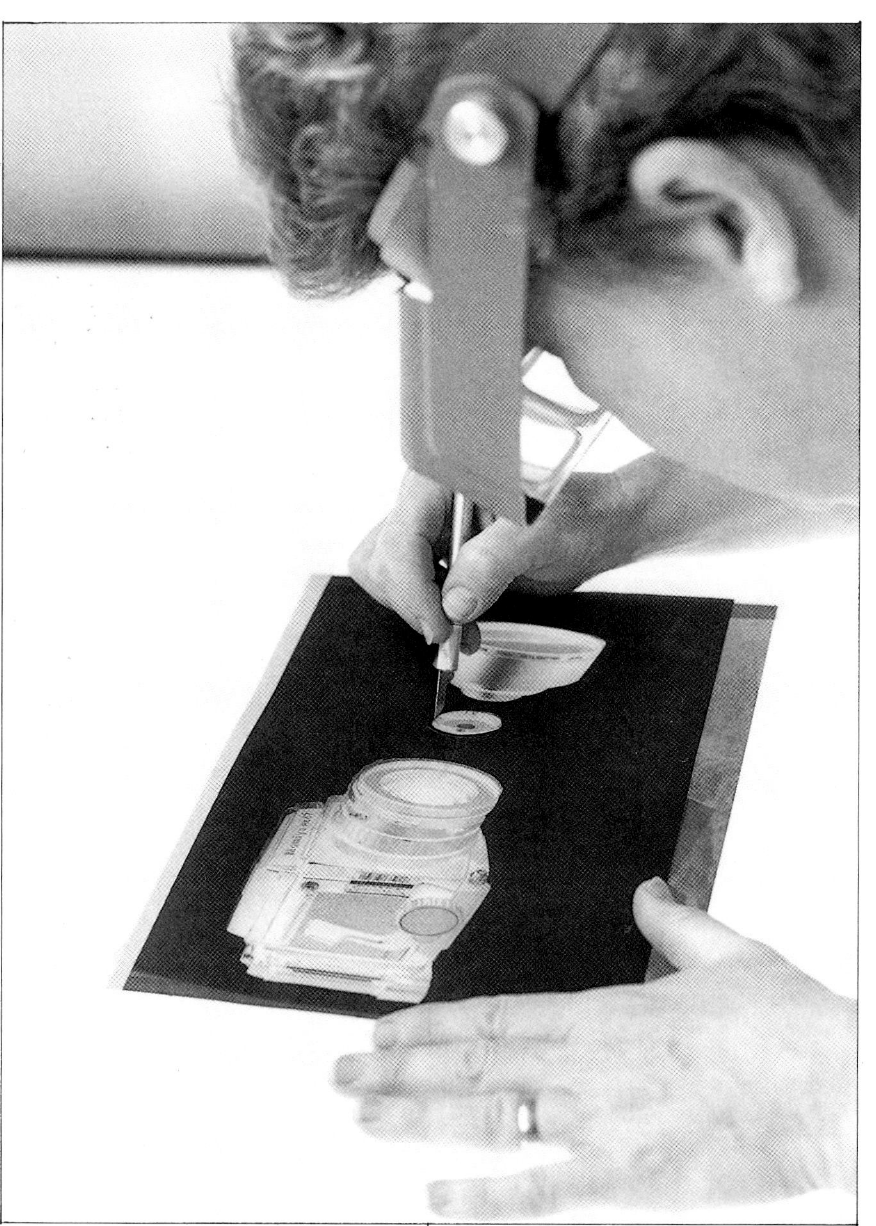

Cutting a mask on an 8x10in negative
It is just about possible to re-touch a 4x5in negative, and some people carry out limited retouching on rollfilm negatives; but if you want to do serious retouching, you need 8x10in or even 11x14in negatives. What we wanted here was a 'cut-out' of the Mamiya RB67, with the front element of the soft-focus lens removed and a 'tea-strainer' diaphragm apparently floating between the two. The easiest way to achieve this was with 'Ruby Lith', a low-tack red film. It acts as a safelight when you print the negative, so anything that has been coated with it will simply not record on the paper, while the places which remain un-masked print normally. In colour, retouching normally consists of opaque masking (obviously, you cannot use red film) and of dye retouching. If you want to see how cackhanded 'cut-outs' can be, look closely at advertising and fashion photographs: often, you will see how outlines have been very carelessly cut around, even in the most expensively-produced magazines. You might also care to look at models' eyes, where the whites are often 'cleaned up' by bleaching and the colour of the pupils is commonly enhanced to an unnatural degree. There is no doubt that electronic retouching is the wave of the future, but it is amazing how much a skilled retoucher can achieve with a big image and a few paintbrushes.

with only limited success. The 126 'Instamatic' format was Kodak's first easy-load cartridge film; its main drawback was very poor film flatness and film location, as several manufacturers found out to their cost when they tried to introduce 'proper' 126 cameras with all-metal construction and good lenses. The cartridge just wasn't up to it.

The 110 cartridge was a smaller and rather more precise version of the 126,

Film slitter

The 'Headliner' film slitter was originally intended, as its name suggests, to slice up photo-typeset headlines for paste-ups: some photo-typesetting machines used 35mm paper for this purpose. It uses two razor blades which can be set at varying distances apart, and it really can be used for slitting any 35mm film down to 16mm or 9.5mm. This means that you can load such improbable delights as Kodak T-Max P3200 or Ilford Delta in your Minox or Rollei 16, and if you have a tame lab (or if you do not mind getting into processing yourself) you can use such colour films as Fuji Velvia, Kodak Ektar 25, or Agfa 1000 RS. A word of warning, though: reaching carelessly into a drawer with one of these in it can result in a deep, painful cut.

and once again some quite good cameras were introduced to use the cartridge: Rollei, Pentax and Minolta are names that spring to mind. The big disadvantage of the 110 format was its small film size, though some newspaper photographers apparently used them. Then again, look at the reproduction quality in a newspaper...

Finally, the 'Disk' was Kodak's most recent attempt on the snapshot market at the time of writing: the tiny individual frames were arranged around the periphery of the eponymous disk. Apart from the tiny film size, the other disadvantage of disk cameras was that their shape made them hard to hold steady. Incidentally, putting several pictures around the edge of a circular disk was not a new idea: it had been tried on a number of sub-miniatures in the past.

SUB-MINIATURE

'Sub-miniature' is an odd term, when you think about it; how can something be 'less than miniature'? Even so, it is a widely-accepted term. Some people apply it to single-frame (18x24mm) 35mm, but in normal usage it means anything that is smaller still. The only remotely common 35mm sub-miniature is the Tessina with its 14x21mm images, and most of the others have used either 16mm or 9.5mm film.

The 16mm film may be double-perforated, single-perforated or imperforate, and the maximum film size varies accordingly from about 10x14mm (the smallest commonly encountered) to 14x17mm (the largest). Most 16mm cassettes fit only a single model of camera, though occasionally there may be two or three cameras in a 'family' which accept the same size, and even more rarely, one manufacturer may decide to use the same cartridge size as another. Most 16mm sub-miniatures are now long out of production, and new cassettes may be unobtainable: old ones have to be reloaded, if you can find them.

The news with 9.5mm is better, because most cameras use the Minox cassette and format (8x11mm). Processing is extremely fiddly, but a surprising range of films is available, especially if you go to a specialist dealer who may respool all kinds of emulsions. If you are really determined, you can buy (or build) a film splitter, and cut your own 9.5mm or 16mm films down from the middle of 35mm, but it is hard work.

5 METERING AND EXPOSURE

There is no such thing as 'correct' exposure: the best you can hope for (and indeed, the only thing you want) is a *pleasing* exposure.

If you think about it, this is inevitable. What would 'correct' mean, after all? A photograph is not the original scene; it is merely a representation of the original scene. It is two-dimensional instead of three-dimensional. In the case of a black and white picture, it is reduced to a series of grey tones; in the case of a colour picture, it is a collection of dyes which more or less recreate the colours of the original.

Even the most 'scientific' of systems, Ansel Adams's celebrated Zone System for black and white, allows the photographer to alter exposure (and development, and filtration) in order to get the tones where he wants them. By means of Previsualisation (Zone System believers always capitalise the word), you can create exactly the picture you have in your mind – if you are skilful enough!

In colour, exposure affects both tone and colour, and the results are less predictable. A colour film can record at least as great a total range as a black and white film, but in the final picture the colour will only be pleasing across a much smaller range of tones. Anything outside the range of colour reproduction may be represented accurately enough as a tone, but the colours will be hopelessly washed-out and desaturated at one end of the scale, and equally hopelessly murky and dark at the other. Within the range of pleasing colour reproduction, even modest variations in exposure – certainly one stop, and quite possibly as little as half a stop – can produce very

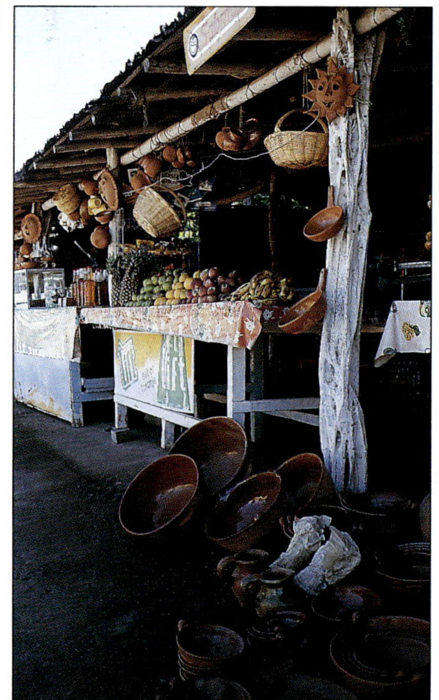

Red Square

It was a wet, nasty, horrible day with the rain turning to snow and back to rain again, so there was no way you could avoid this sort of hazy effect. Frances decided to make a feature of it, over-exposing slightly to make everything look even mistier, and using a longer-than-standard lens (the 90mm f/2.5 Vivitar Series One macro) to accentuate the atmospheric nastiness even more. The camera was on a tripod, partly to avoid any problems with camera shake, and partly so that she could take her time and compose the picture exactly. The shape of St Basilius is unforgettable, even though it is almost lost in the haze, and the factory on the other side of the Moscow river is much less visible than usual, which is a blessing. Because the people are nearer, they are well differentiated against the cathedral. (FES)

Roadside stall, Mexico

We are not sure to this day whether this picture of a typical Mexican roadside stall would look better with the sun shining full on it. There is certainly a slight problem in that everything is a little blue, which is a result of the stall being lit by sky-light rather than sunlight, but if the sun had been full on the stand the contrast would have been far too great and Frances would have lost the wonderful jumble of textures and colours which are the main attraction of the shot. In theory, she could have used an 81 series warming filter (probably an 81C), but in practice there is a limit to how long you can spend on a single picture. We must have done something right, because it made the back cover of a cook book. All too often, we both look at pictures and can see how we could have improved them; but at the time, you do not always think of these things. As it was, Frances simply took a reading with her trusty Weston Master meter and shot the picture, using the 90mm f/2.5 Vivitar Series One macro lens and Fuji RDP ISO 100 film. (FES)

Fireplace, Auberge St Hubert

Frances normally shoots much more black and white than colour, but she wanted to shoot this fireplace in a particular way. She used a 17mm lens (a Tamron SP) on a Nikon F, and Fuji 100 film. We took two incident-light readings with a Lunasix: one in full sun, where the light was streaming through the window, and the other a few inches away, out of the sun. The difference was impressive, about three stops. With a reflected-light meter, the difference would have been still greater (probably five or six stops, depending on where it was pointed), and the real reading would have been even harder to determine. Faced with this sort of lighting situation, the easiest way to handle it is to bracket widely: everything from one stop under the minimum reading to one stop over the maximum reading. This sounds extravagant, but it is still only five frames, and it was likely that several pictures would be usable: the only difference would be one of 'mood', which is always unpredictable. The aperture was set to give an adequate depth of field, so the bracketing was achieved by varying the shutter speed: the camera was obviously tripod mounted, partly as insurance against camera shake and partly because it is next to impossible to shoot five identically framed brackets unless the camera is bolted down. This was one of the lightest shots, which conveyed the sunniness of the place well; the darker shots were more brooding and dramatic, but less happy. When you have spent a lot of money to get somewhere, especially if it is somewhere you have never been before and may never visit again, it is foolish to economise on film. (FES)

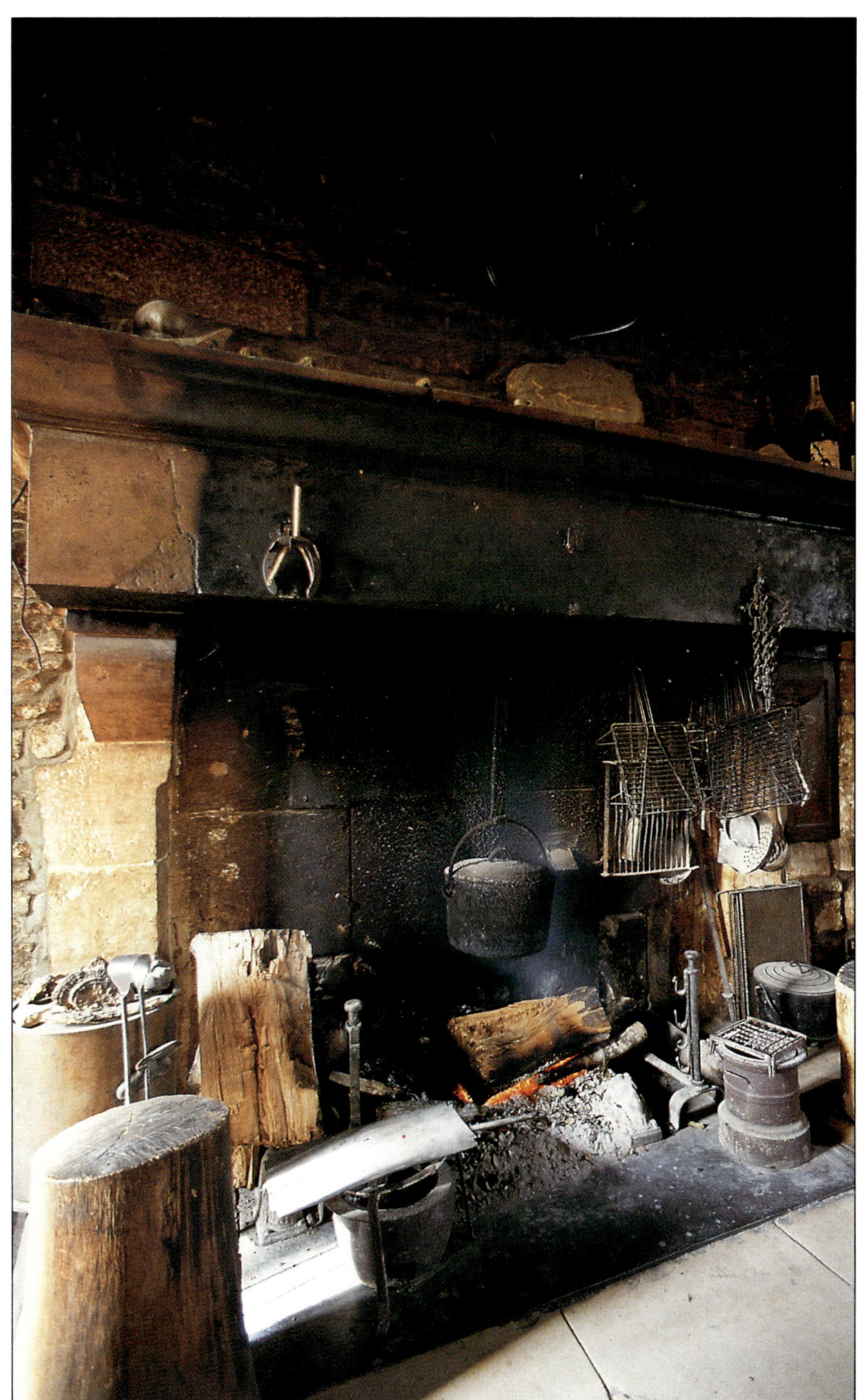

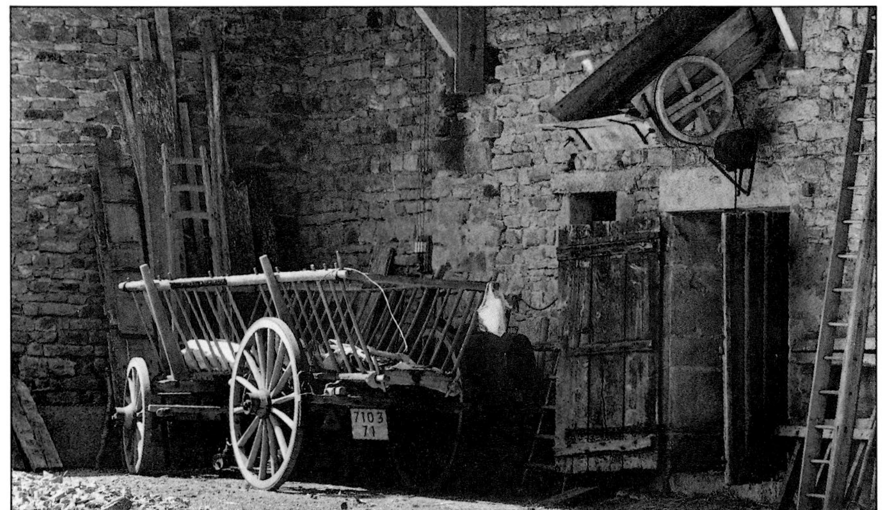

Farm wagon

One of the problems with being almost totally dependent on incident-light metering is that you have to be able to take readings either at your subject position, or in a place where the lighting is equivalent. On this occasion, we could not do this: not only was the farmyard entrance muddy, but there was a large dog which probably would not have been anything like so playful if we had opened (or climbed over) the gate. We compromised. An incident-light reading was perfectly feasible for the sunlit portion of the wagon – this was pretty much a joint shot, though Frances deserves most of the credit – and we knew that we would have to sacrifice some detail on the brightly lit wheel. We therefore guessed that we would need to give another two or maybe three stops, compared with the incident-light reading in the sun. Then, Frances took a reflected-light reading using the through-lens meter on her Nikkormat, which told her that she needed to give four stops more. This persuaded us that three stops was the ideal compromise, and so it turned out to be. The lens was a 70-210mm f/2.8 Sigma APO; the film was Ilford XP-2 (we would probably use Delta 100 if we reshot it now); and the exposure, as best we can remember, was 1/60 at between f/8 and f/11. The camera was on a Manfrotto/Bogen tripod. (FES)

significant variations in colour rendering. These in turn can greatly affect the mood of the picture: light and airy, bright and sunny, dark and gloomy, murky and mysterious.

Much of what follows is pretty hard going, and requires a degree of effort to understand, but there is light at the end of the tunnel. If you do not want to know *why* an incident light meter is so useful, just skip ahead to the heading 'Incident-light Meters' on page 90. There, you will learn how to use them - which is dead easy. If you want to understand exposure, though, read the rest of the chapter too.

TONAL RANGE

The tonal range of a typical outdoor subject can easily exceed 10,000:1. That is to say, the brightest highlight can easily be 10,000 times brighter than the darkest shadow. Even greater ratios, as much as 100,000:1, are perfectly possible, and 1,000,000:1 is feasible. Unfortunately, the maximum tonal range of a black and white print is only about 128:1 (seven stops), and while a colour picture can record about the same range of tones, it will only give pleasing colour across a range of 32:1 at most (five stops), and quite possibly over a range of as little as 8:1 (three stops). If the subject brightness range is outside the limits that you can reproduce in a picture, you will just have to sacrifice some of the highlights or some of the shadows – or both. It is worth while to look at these tonal ranges in terms of stops:

Tonal Range	Tonal Range (Stops)	Tonal Range	Tonal Range (Stops)
1:1	0		
2:1	1	2,048:1	11
4:1	2	4,096:1	12
8:1	3	8,192:1	13
16:1	4	16,384:1	14
32:1	5	32,768:1	15
64:1	6	65,536:1	16
128:1	7	131,072:1	17
256:1	8	262,144:1	18
512:1	9	5,24288:1	19
1,024:1	10	1,048,576:1	20

Cooking pot, Auberge St Hubert

This looks like the original pot that called the kettle black! Metering very dark, black-on-black subjects like this is very difficult indeed with a reflected light meter: there is so little light from the black surfaces that it can be hard to get a reading at all, and when you do, you need to give two stops less exposure than the meter indicates. What you are doing, in Zone System terms, is 'assigning' the pot to Zone 3 so that you will get some texture in it. A much easier system is to use a film with a very wide tonal recording ability (Ilford XP-2), take an incident-light reading (with the film rated at EI 200, in this case), then give an extra stop of exposure to compensate for the fact that most of the detail is in a very dark area. The print was made on Ilford Multigrade paper, with the contrast grade set at three. (FES: Nikon F: probably 90mm f/2.5 Vivitar Series One macro, tripod mounted)

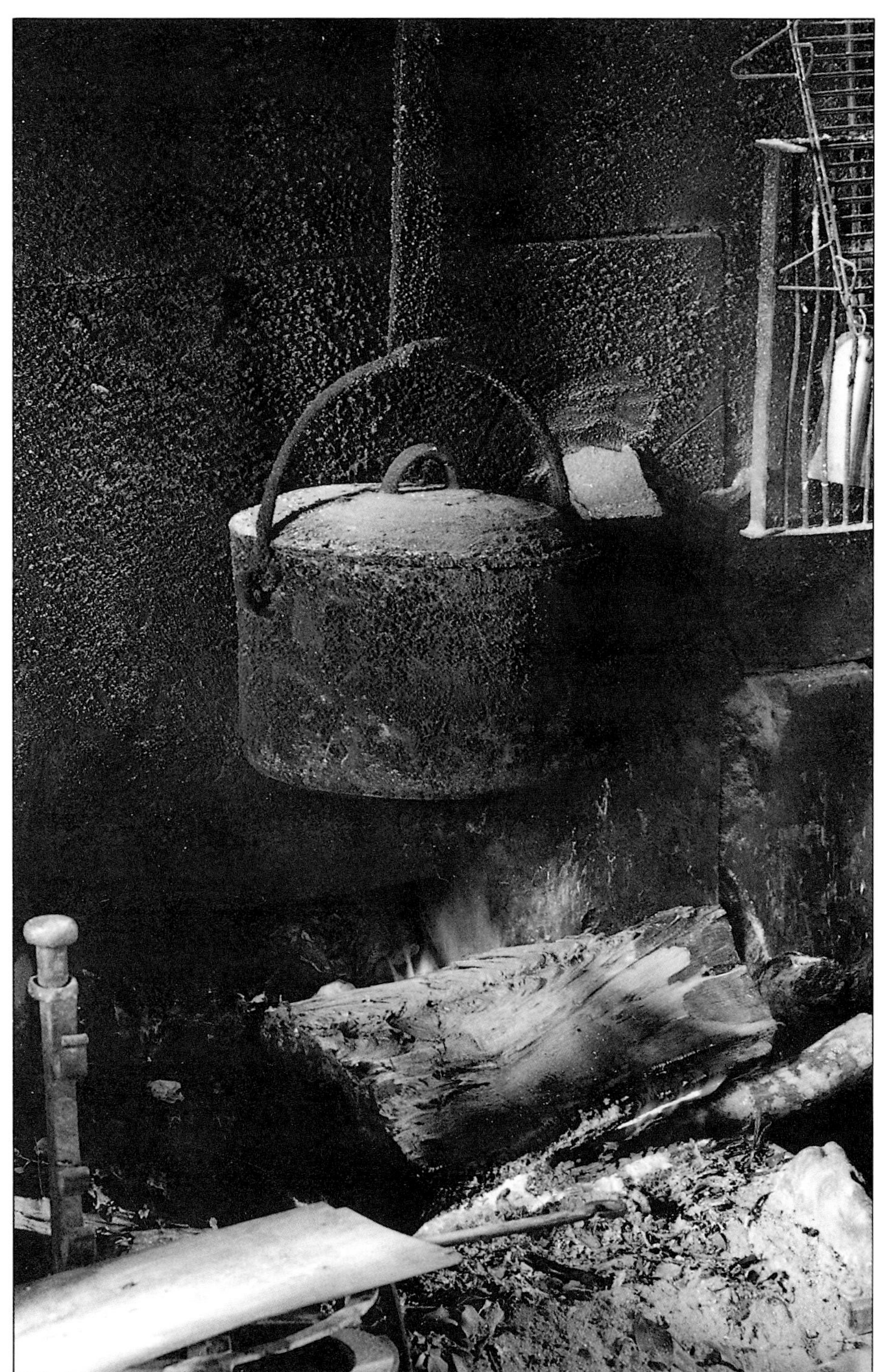

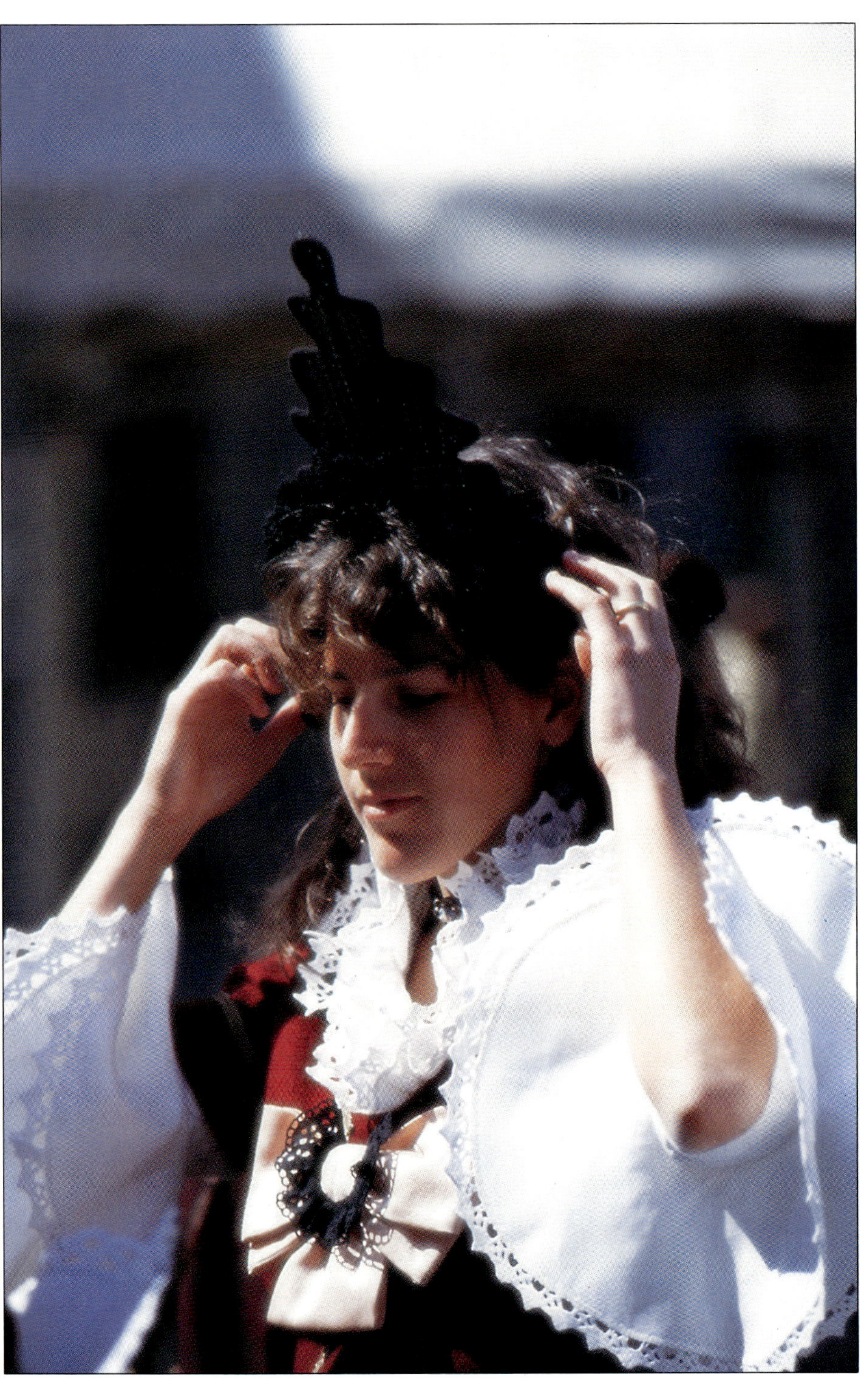

Groupe Folklorique du Val d'Aoste

Contre-jour (against-the-light) metering is always a problem, because you need enough detail to register on the unlit side of the subject without burning out the part that is in full sun. This girl in traditional dress provides a particularly demanding example, because she is wearing a mixture of pure black and pure white, and of course the main interest lies in the flesh tones. As it is, the exposure could hardly be better. Her forearms are right on the edge of burning out, it is true, but there is a good deal of detail in the white of the sleeves and collar and the black of the head-dress and the lace on the pink bow on her breast. And, of course, her face is adequately exposed on both its sunlit and its shadowed side. Exposure was based on periodical sun and shade readings with a Luna-Pro F, with adjustments for individual exposures made on the basis of experience. This is a stop and a half wider than the full-sun reading: there was no time to bracket. Film was Fuji RDP ISO 100, and the lens was the remarkably sharp and contrasty Sigma 70-210mm f/2.8 Apo mounted on a Nikon F. (RWH)

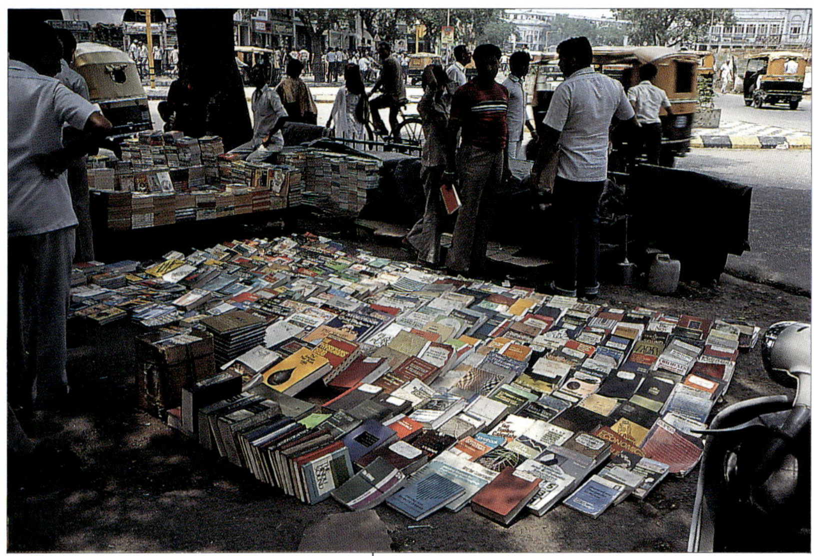

Bookseller, Connaught Place
Connaught Place in New Delhi has an extraordinary range of shops and pavement vendors. You have to admire a nation which regards learning highly enough that they sell sociological treatises next to Enid Blyton next to the works of Dickens, all from a roadside stall, even if half the editions are pirated. The easiest way to deal with lighting conditions like this is to take the occasional incident-light reading, just to check that you are in the right ballpark, and pre-set the camera accordingly. Then, if need be, you can modify the aperture or shutter speed in a fraction of a second, according to experience and to previous meter measurements; or alternatively, you can use a modern matrix-style metering system such as that fitted to the latest cameras. The exposure here, on Kodachrome 64, was obviously for the books themselves. Not only do we habitually pre-set the exposure on our cameras: with the aid of the depth of field scale, we also pre-set the focus, so that we can shoot in a fraction of a second if we see something interesting enough. Autofocus is fast, but a pre-focused camera is even faster. (RWH)

Obviously, you have to decide which seven-stop (or five-stop, or three-stop) 'slice' you want to select from that massive tonal range – and, which is less obvious, you have to decide how you want to reproduce that 'slice' on film.

An example makes the latter statement clear. Imagine that you are photographing a couple of friends on a sunny day, with a few white puffy clouds in the sky. If they were standing in the sun, the exposure might be 1/125 second at f/11. If they were standing somewhere cool and shady, it might be 1/125 second at f/5.6. This is a difference of two whole stops. Now imagine that one is standing in the shade, and the other is standing in a shaft of sunlight. You can photograph both of them on one frame. What is the correct exposure? Is it the 1/125 second at f/11 for the one in the sun? Or the 1/125 second at f/5.6 for the one in the shade? Or do you split the difference, and make it 1/125 second at f/8? If you do that, the one in the sun will (you hope) be only a little too bright, while the one in the shade will (you hope) be only a little too dark.

In Zone System parlance, this is known as 'assigning' tones. You choose a tone in real life, and you 'assign' it to a tone in the final picture. Give it some extra exposure, and you 'assign' it to a brighter tone in the picture. Give it less exposure, and you 'assign' it to a darker tone. At this point, we really need to look at the Zone System.

EXPOSURE IN BLACK AND WHITE: THE ZONE SYSTEM

Unless you have at least a nodding acquaintance with the Zone System, it is very hard either to understand or to put into words the technique of exposure in black and white; and although the Zone System is not directly applicable to colour, there is a fair amount that can be carried across. Even a photographer who never uses black and white at all should be aware of the basics of the Zone System.

This does not mean that he or she should necessarily become fanatical about it, which is one of the problems of the Zone System. Fanaticism seems to be the fate of all too many of those who do make the effort to understand it: there seems to be a fatal appeal in it to obsessives. In its essence, it is not hard to understand; and in so far as you choose to apply it at all, you really do not have to learn very much.

The Zone System divides the tonal range into nine, ten or eleven Zones, but the easiest to understand (and to apply) is the original nine-Zone system. This consists of a mid-tone, Zone V, and four tones on either side of it, disposed symmetrically. In the final print, Zones I to IV are dark tones, and

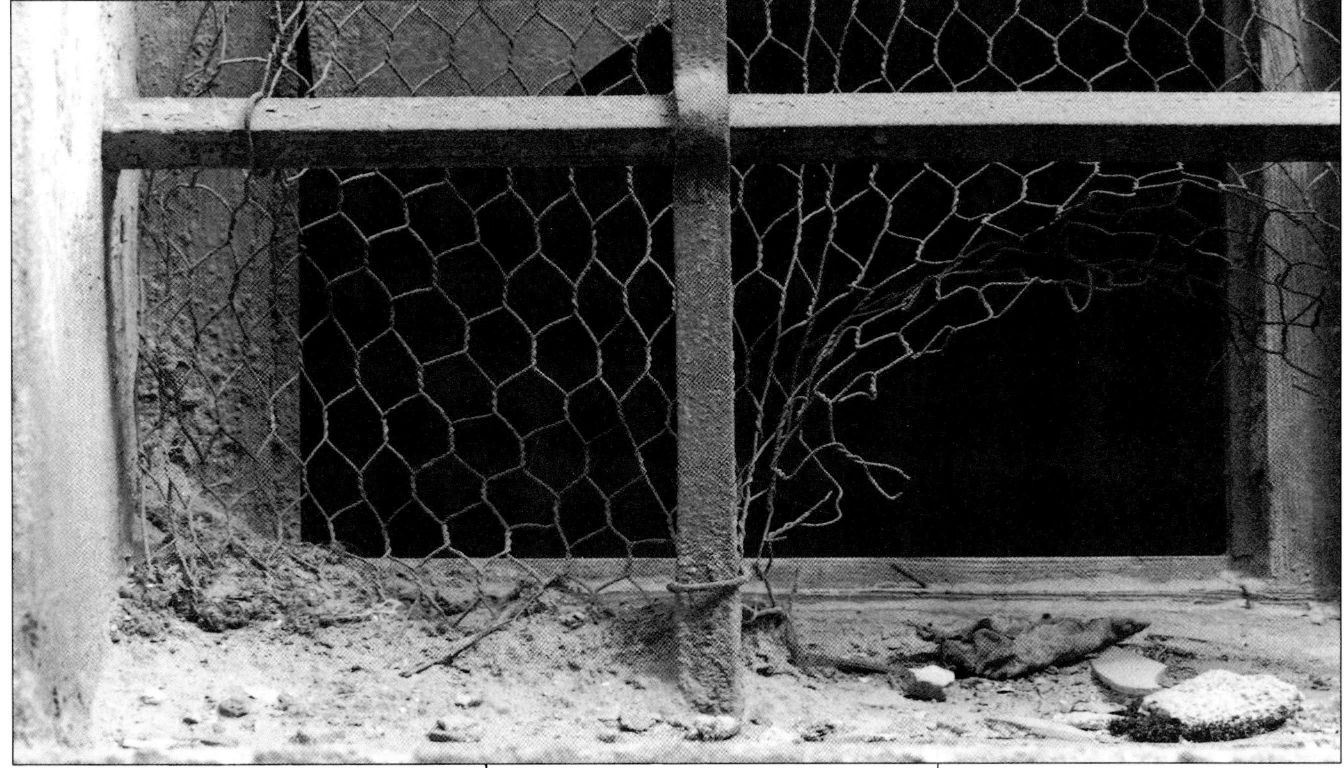

Zones VI to IX are light tones, as in the table below.

The most obvious and immediate problem with the Zone System is that you can (and indeed must) get tones within tones, which leads to such gems as 'Zone VI1/2' (the Romans never mastered fractions, so you have to switch to Arabic numerals). Also, with modern films, you can retain detail in Zones II and VIII – though unless you use a soft grade of printing paper, you

Zone I	The darkest black of which the paper is capable. Anything darker than Zone II.
Zone II	The darkest tone distinguishable from Zone I. One stop darker than Zone III.
Zone III	The darkest tone in which texture is discernible. One stop darker than Zone IV, and one stop lighter than Zone II.
Zone IV	Dark mid-tones. One stop darker than Zone V, but one stop lighter than Zone III.
Zone V	The mid-tone, by definition. A 'Grey Card' is an artificial mid-tone, which reflects 18 per cent of the light falling on it.
Zone VI	Light mid-tones. One stop lighter than Zone V, but one stop darker than Zone VII.
Zone VII	The lightest tone in which texture is discernible. One stop lighter than Zone VI, but one stop darker than Zone VIII.
Zone VIII	The lightest tone which can be differentiated from a pure, paper-base white. One stop lighter than Zone VII.
Zone IX	Pure, paper-base white. Anything lighter than Zone VIII.

Window, Aosta

As usual, exposure determination here was much easier with an incident-light meter than it would have been with a reflected-light meter. Using XP-2 (this was before we started using Delta 100 seriously), Frances took an incident-light reading and then gave an exposure which was one full stop less than the indicated reading, because she wanted detail in the pale-coloured wall. Normally, the lighter parts of the wall would be in Zone VII in the print, but the extra exposure moved them well into Zone VI. This sort of reduction in exposure normally means that you lose some shadow detail, and we were rather surprised when Frances printed this and found that there was still some detail inside the window – in Zone II, to be precise – though it probably will not 'read' in reproduction. This shows that it is actually possible to use a 10-Zone or even 11-Zone system, provided you work with the best available materials, careful exposure determination and original prints. For reproduction, where the extra Zones are invariably lost in the printing process, we stick with the old 9 Zone system. (FES)

Cane, wall and window

The different 'Zones', and the way they interact, can be seen particularly clearly in this photograph. The brass head of the cane reflects the sun and is a pure paper-base white, Zone IX. The lightest portions of the wall, just to the right of the window, are detectably darker than Zone IX, but with no detail: they are Zone VIII. Much of the rest of the upper part of the wall is Zone VII, the lightest tone in which texture can be seen, while the lower section of the wall is mostly Zone VI, a light mid-tone, with some parts (for example, the dark part immediately to the right of the window) in Zone V, the mid-tone. Zone V is also where the cane itself falls. The shadow on the lower left is Zone IV (dark mid-tone) and Zone III, the darkest tone in which texture is still visible; the shadow of the cane is also Zone III. The shadowed portion of the window itself is for the most part Zone II, just lighter than maximum black but without any real texture, while the upper right corner of the window is close to Zone I, maximum black, as are one or two of the cracks in the wall. There are however no true blacks (Zone I) in the whole picture, because there were not in the original scene. Not all of this tonal detail will necessarily 'hold' in reproduction. (RWH/FES)

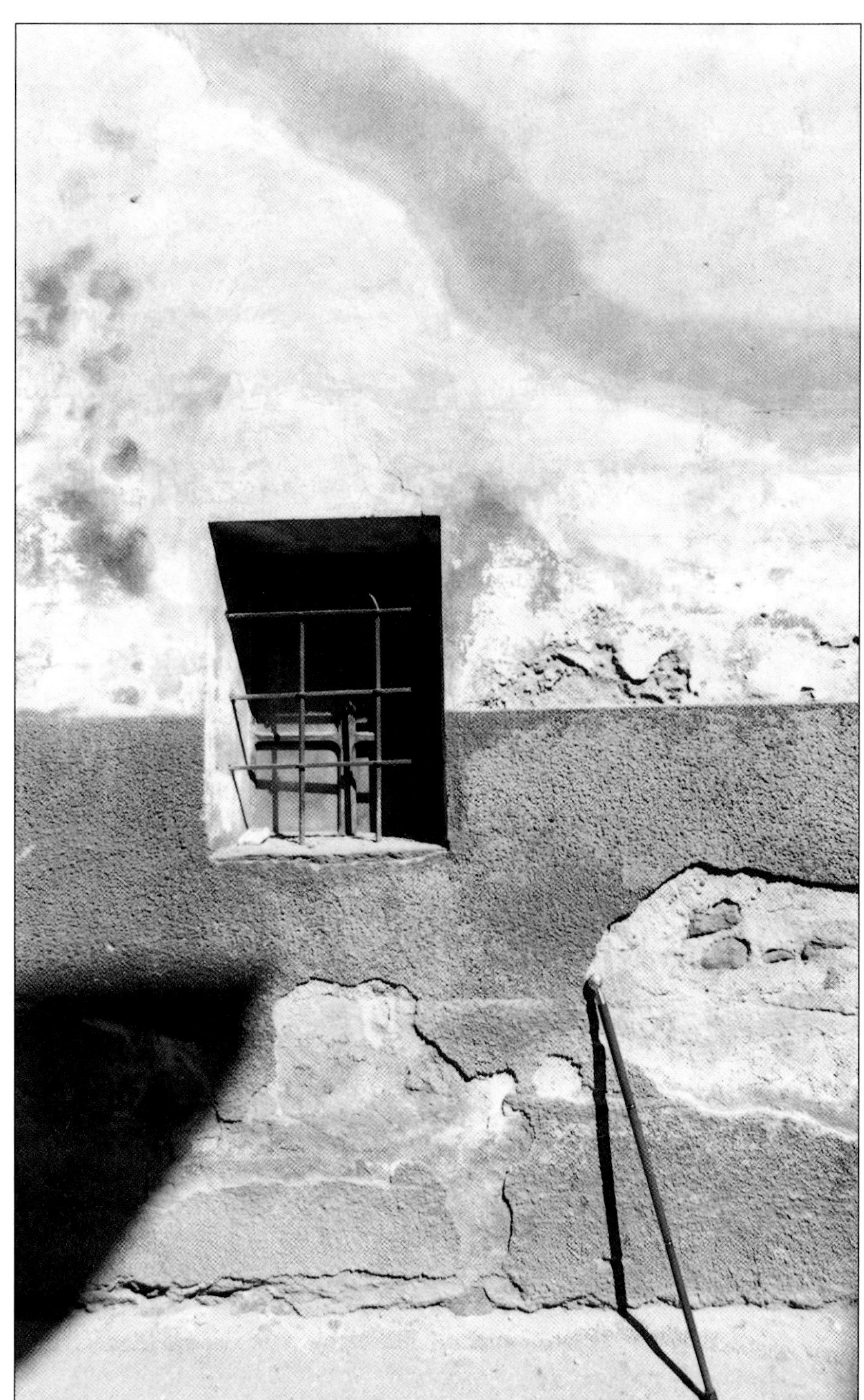

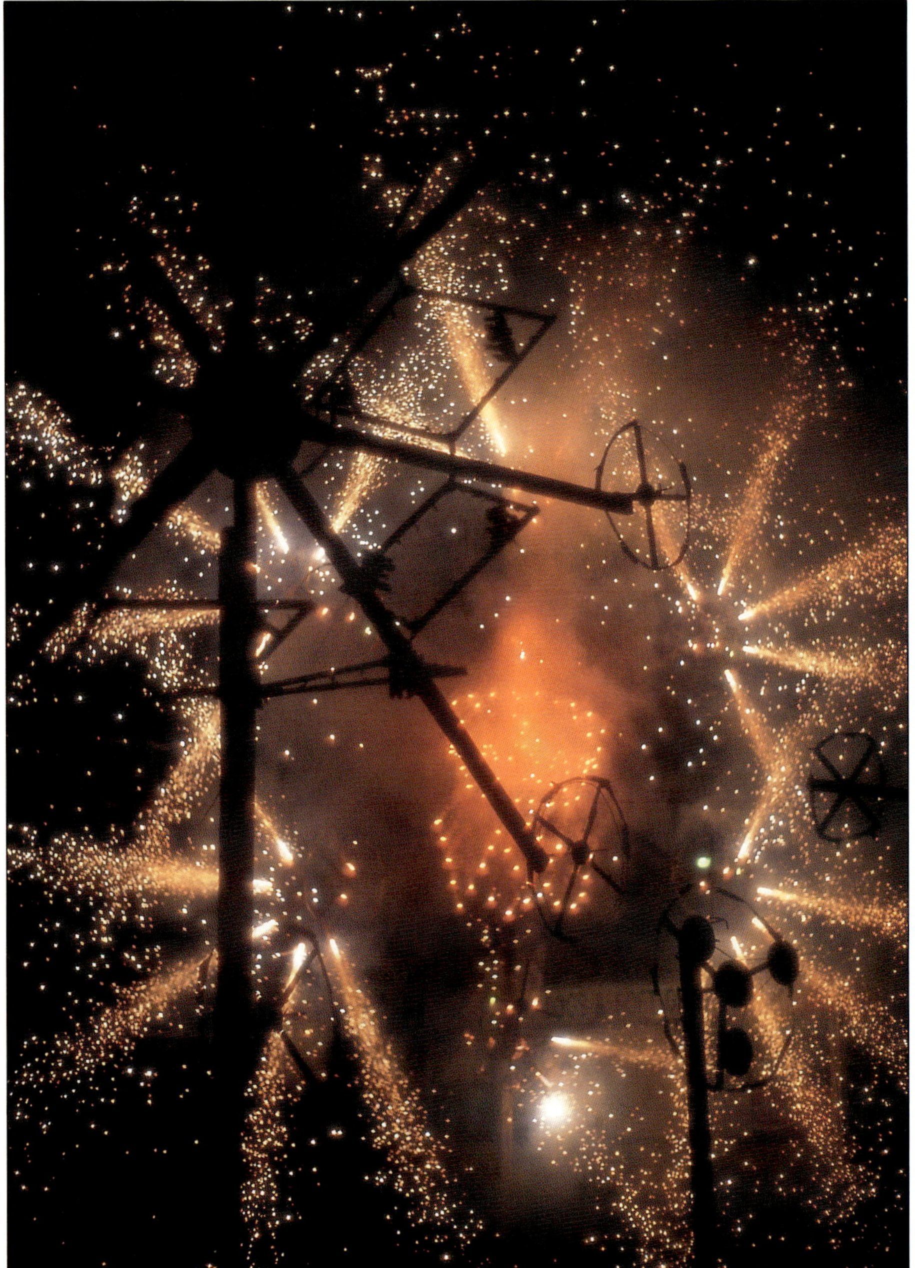

Fireworks, Rabat

Fireworks and other self-luminous subjects are very hard to meter, and the best way to determine exposure is by experience. Slow films – ISO 50 or ISO 100 – are necessary to give the best possible colour saturation, and indeed 'high saturation' films are a good idea. The light given out by fireworks varies widely, however. With ISO 100 film you will need to shoot at 1/30 to 1/60 at f/1.4 if you want to capture a child's face lit by a sparkler, but if you are capturing bright air-burst rockets against a dark or evening sky, you can use an exposure of several seconds at f/5.6 to f/8 or even f/11. The exposure in this case, again with ISO 100 film, was about 1/125 at f/2, using a 50mm f/1.2 Nikkor to facilitate focusing. The camera was hand-held: the Maltese are wonderfully relaxed about safety regulations and crowd control, taking the view that anyone with a functioning brain-cell should be able to figure out what is safe and what is not, and that it is the parents' job (not the organisers') to keep children under control. This is the Festa San Giuzepp, 19 March, in Rabat outside the walls of Mdina, which is the ancient capital of Malta. (RWH)

can still only retain nine Zones on the print. If you do use soft paper, of course, the reflectance of the print no longer bears a 1:1 relationship with the brightness of the original picture elements.

Even so, those different Zones – the lightest area in which textures are visible, the dark mid-tones, and so forth – are an extremely useful tool for analysing what is where in a print, and why a given print is successful (or otherwise). They are also useful when you want to point out the limitations of photomechanical reproduction, in which Zones I and II are almost invariably run together; Zone III is often muddy and indistinct, except in

Dawn, Kovalam

In India, fishermen in the south still use some very primitive boats. This one is no more than a few logs lashed together – something between a boat and a raft. They set out at dawn, which is a time when metering is very critical, especially if you do not want to lose the very subtle tones in the sky and water. The light is rapidly changing, and colours change almost as fast. We normally prefer to rely on frequent incident-light readings, combined with bracketing as necessary: one frame at the indicated exposure, one at a stop over, and one at a stop under. Often, two of the exposures will be perfectly usable, but even then, one of them will usually be detectably better than the other. Exposure is not a precise science, especially in colour, where quite small changes in density can also mean quite large changes in colour saturation. Bracketing is not a way of wasting film: it is a way of saving pictures. (FES)

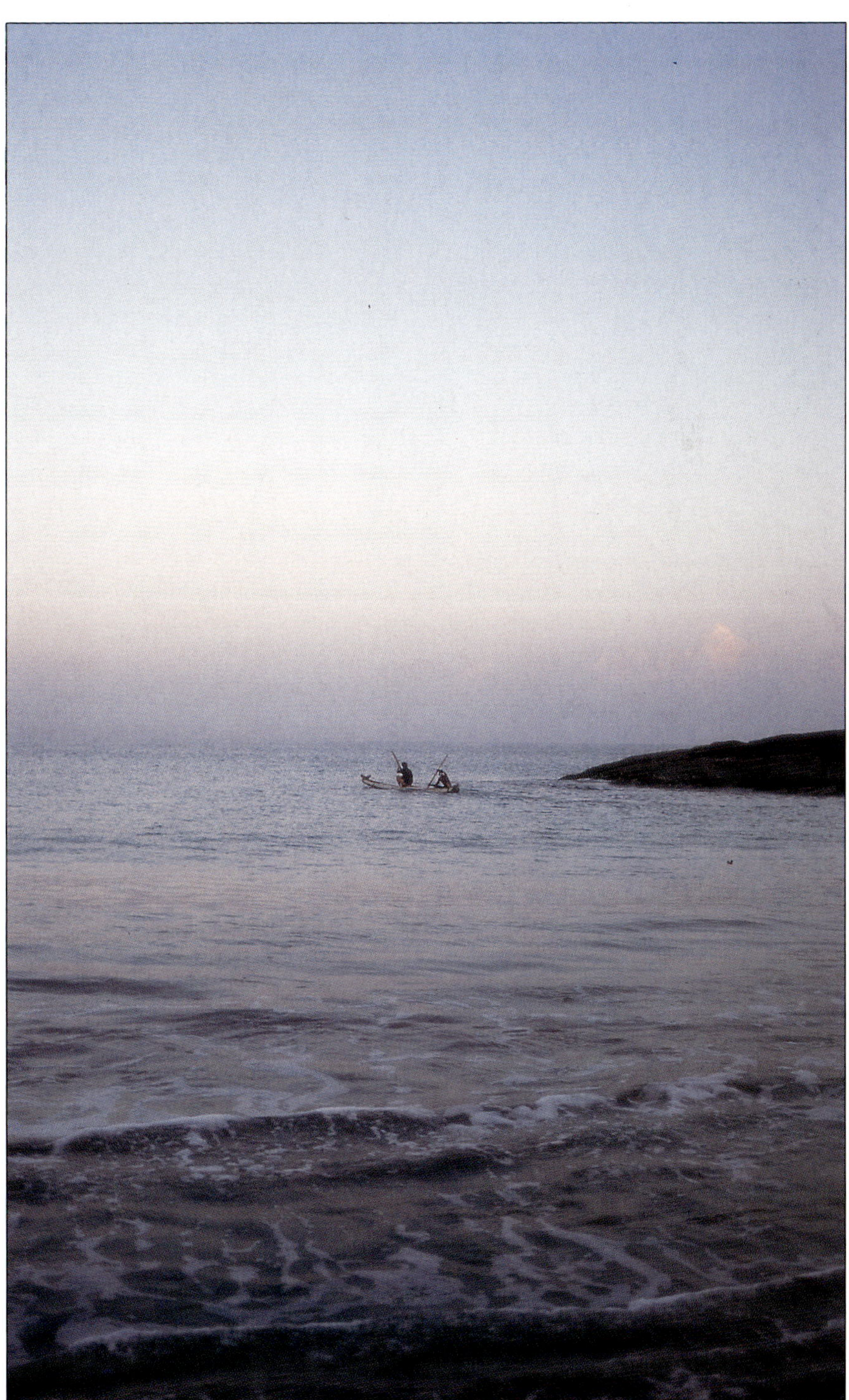

high-quality reproduction; and even Zone IV is at risk if the reproduction quality is bad enough. To be on the safe side, a print for reproduction should have the vast majority of its information in Zone V, Zone VI and Zone VII – at the top end Zones VIII and IX may run together. In an exhibition print, on the other hand, the glory of the picture often lies in the subtle tones in Zone III and even Zone II, and in Zones VII and upwards.

Now, imagine that you are photographing a whitewashed California mission, a subject dear to Ansel Adams's heart, may he rest in peace. It is a matter of common experience that the whitewashed walls will be blindingly white, and that in a normal photograph, they would have no detail in them: they would be in Zone VIII, or possibly even Zone IX. But you want detail in those walls – so you simply 'assign' them to Zone VII, the lightest tone with texture. This means under-exposing by a stop. The only question is exactly how you do this.

EXPOSURE METERING

Exposure meters are based on the rather surprising principle that an 'average' subject reflects 18 per cent of the light falling on it – a figure which is remarkably constant. There are, however, a couple of flies in the ointment. One is that there are plenty of non-average subjects about, such as our California mission. The other is that most exposure meters are not, in fact, calibrated for 18 per cent reflectance: they are calibrated for 10 per cent reflectance, Zone IV, a dark mid-tone.

Pause to consider for a moment the implications of this latter statement. Take it to its extreme. Instead of measuring a mid-tone or a dark mid-tone, imagine instead that you measure something really dark: a soot-blackened pot, for example. The meter will recommend an exposure which will give a print with an 18 per cent reflectance. You do not want an 18 per cent grey, though: you want something more like 5 per cent reflectance. The meter is therefore recommending an over-exposure of about two stops, and you have to cut the exposure by two stops. For most people, this is 'counter-intuitive' – you expect to increase the exposure for a dark subject, not to decrease it.

The same would apply if you took your reading off the whitewashed wall of the California mission. The meter would again give you a reading which would give an 18 per cent grey tone in the print – but you want something more like 60 per cent reflectance, so you need to increase the exposure by two stops. Again, most people would expect to cut the exposure for such a bright subject, rather than increasing it. If you took this natural-seeming course, though, the result would be even worse under-exposure.

A meter calibrated to 10 per cent reflectance will therefore always 'err' on the side of over-exposure; which is fine for colour print film and for black and white, but not so good for colour slide. Variations in meters, calibrations, personal preferences and even in metering technique, all explain why it is by no means unusual for a photographer to establish personal exposure indices (EIs), which may not necessarily match ISO speeds, and why some photographers habitually begin

Hand-held meters

For many years, we relied almost exclusively on the extremely accurate and very reliable Weston Master series of selenium-cell meters, switching to a LunaSix (LunaPro) for very low light levels. Today, given the cost of repairs to Weston Masters, we rely mostly on an older LunaSix (not shown) and on this LunaPro F, which doubles as a flash meter. The other disadvantage of the Weston Master is the bulky, detachable 'Invercone' incident-light attachment: the best ever made, but distinctly unhandy. We both find moving-needle meters easier to understand and to read than LCD-display meters, which are often made over-complicated: their designers' philosophy seems to be, 'We can do it, therefore we must do it'. The spot meter is a Russian model which we bought very cheaply in Moscow in 1991; it cost us under $5 (say £3), brand new. Now that we are getting used to it, we are considering buying a better model, but the price is a major deterrent. Spot metering is tricky at first, but after a while, the mental gymnastics become second nature – and when they do, it is the most accurate form of metering in the world.

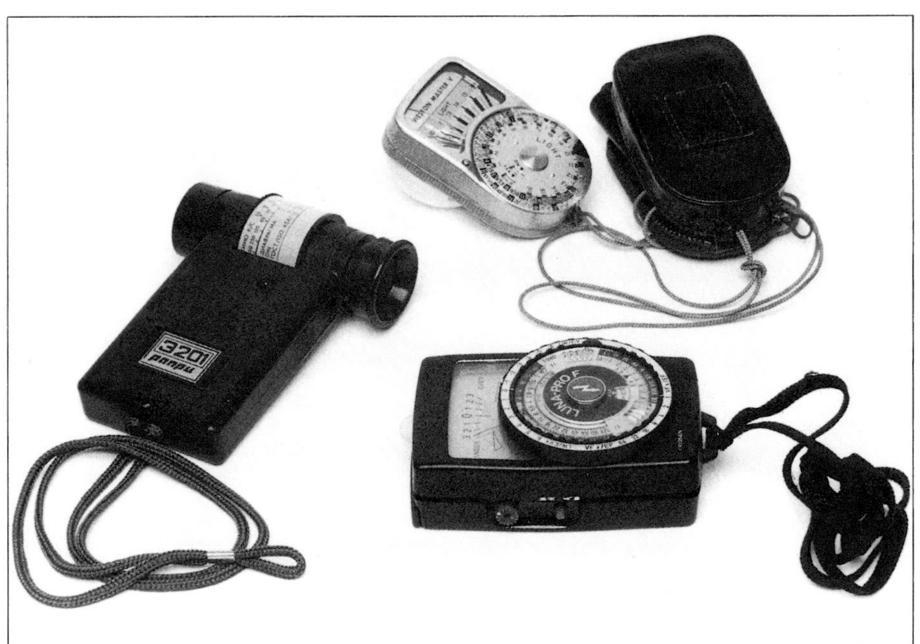

by setting film speeds to (say) one-half of the manufacturers' recommendations.

Modern in-camera meters get around the two objections of calibration and non-standard subjects extremely well, but even the very best of them are not perfect. What is worse, you never really know quite how much correction the ingenious gentlemen in Japan or Germany have introduced; so you do not know how much correction you have to make for yourself. It is, therefore, arguably better to have a meter with known limitations, even if they are apparently quite severe, rather than to have one where you are never quite sure what those limitations are. In fact, you can get two such types of meter. Both will give very similar results in normal use, but one is immensely easier to use than the other. The difficult one is the spot meter; the easy one is the incident-light meter.

Spot Meters

A spot meter, as its name suggests, reads a very limited area. If you understand the Zone System, you can read *any* given subject tone and assign it to the Zone you want in the final picture. For example, if you take a reading off someone's face, you might decide that you wanted to assign that face to Zone VI½. This would mean that whatever reading you took from the face, you would need to give 1½ stops more exposure, because VI½ is 1½ stops more than Zone V, the mid-tone. Or with the Californian mission wall, you could assign it to Zone VII (give two stops more than the meter indicates) or Zone VIII (give three stops more). Going the other way, and taking your reading off the pot, you could assign it to Zone III (the exposure is two stops less than the meter indicates) or Zone II (give three stops less than the meter indicates).

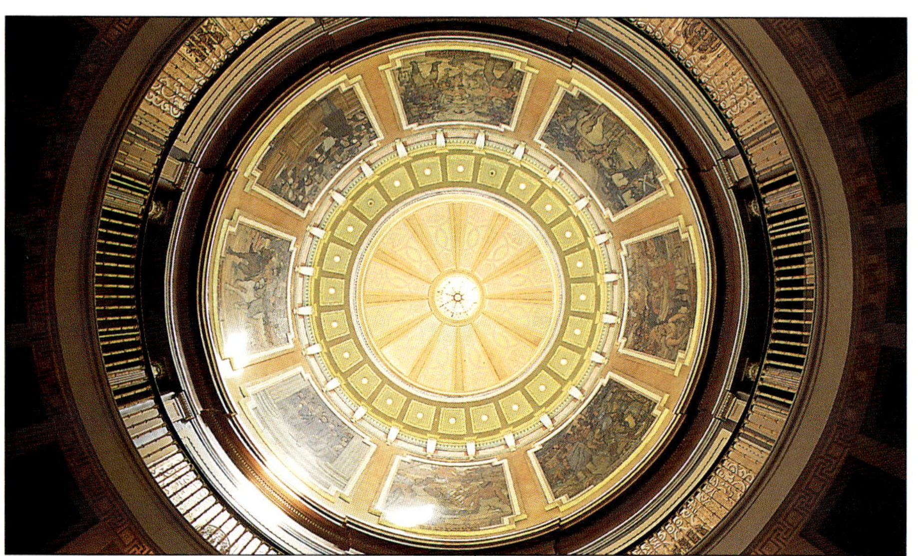

Dome, Alabama State Capitol
As so often when we bracket our exposures, we were amazed at how many different exposures of this dome were acceptable. We were shooting straight upwards, with the camera only about a foot above the floor, and there was no way we could take a reliable reading with the equipment at hand: a spot meter would have been the only sensible solution. Roger took a general reflected-light reading, and bracketed two full stops either way, a total of five exposures – and at least three of them, and possibly four (all except the very lightest) were usable. Whenever we contemplate buying an expensive spot meter, we reflect that the cost of bracketing is small, and spread out thinly, while the cost of a spot meter is high and comes all at once. We can afford the one much more easily than the other, and frequently we get an interesting and useful range of exposures which we would not get if we tried being more accurate and scientific about exposure determination. (RWH/FES)

This is an extremely accurate method of exposure determination, and it also allows you to measure the overall tonal range of your subject; but it is slow, and requires quite a degree of mental gymnastics.

Incident-light Meters

The incident-light meter skips around all the problems associated with varying reflectance, by the simple expedient of measuring the light falling on the subject. If you cannot get to the subject itself, you measure the light somewhere else, provided it is identical to the light falling on the subject. Out of doors this is normally very easy, and it is rarely that difficult indoors either. It also removes the problems of 18 per cent reflectance, effectively by incorporating a filter in the incident light measuring dome, which reflects 72 per cent of the light falling on it and allows only 18 per cent to fall on the meter cell.

The only problems which remain are first, when you cannot take a reading even of equivalent lighting (in

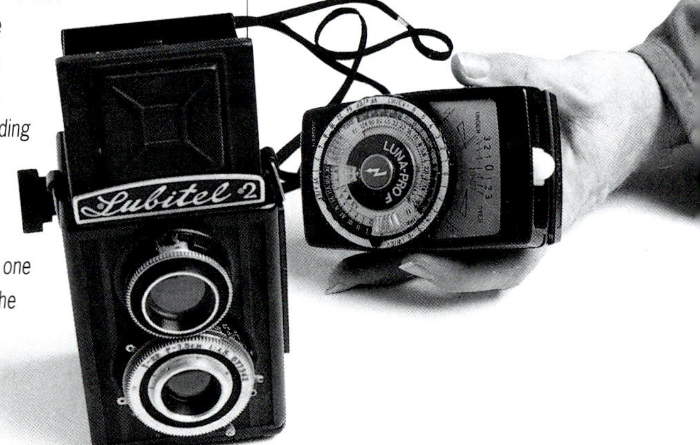

Taking an incident-light reading
This is the classic example of a difficult subject to meter: a black object on a white background. Using an incident-light meter gets around the whole problem, though. You point the meter towards the camera, from the subject position. Then, if you know that you are going to want a bit more detail in the dark areas of the picture (such as the black leatherette on this Lyubitel TLR), you simply give an extra stop of exposure: this was shot at f/11 instead of at the f/16 that the meter recommended. With flash meters, incident-light readings are the norm, and indeed most purpose-built flash meters without an ambient-light facility are built only to take incident light readings. The little white bobble or dome on the LunaPro F has to be slid into place to get an incident-light reading; a reflected-light reading from the camera position recommended two stops under-exposure, even before allowing for the extra one stop which was needed for the leatherette.

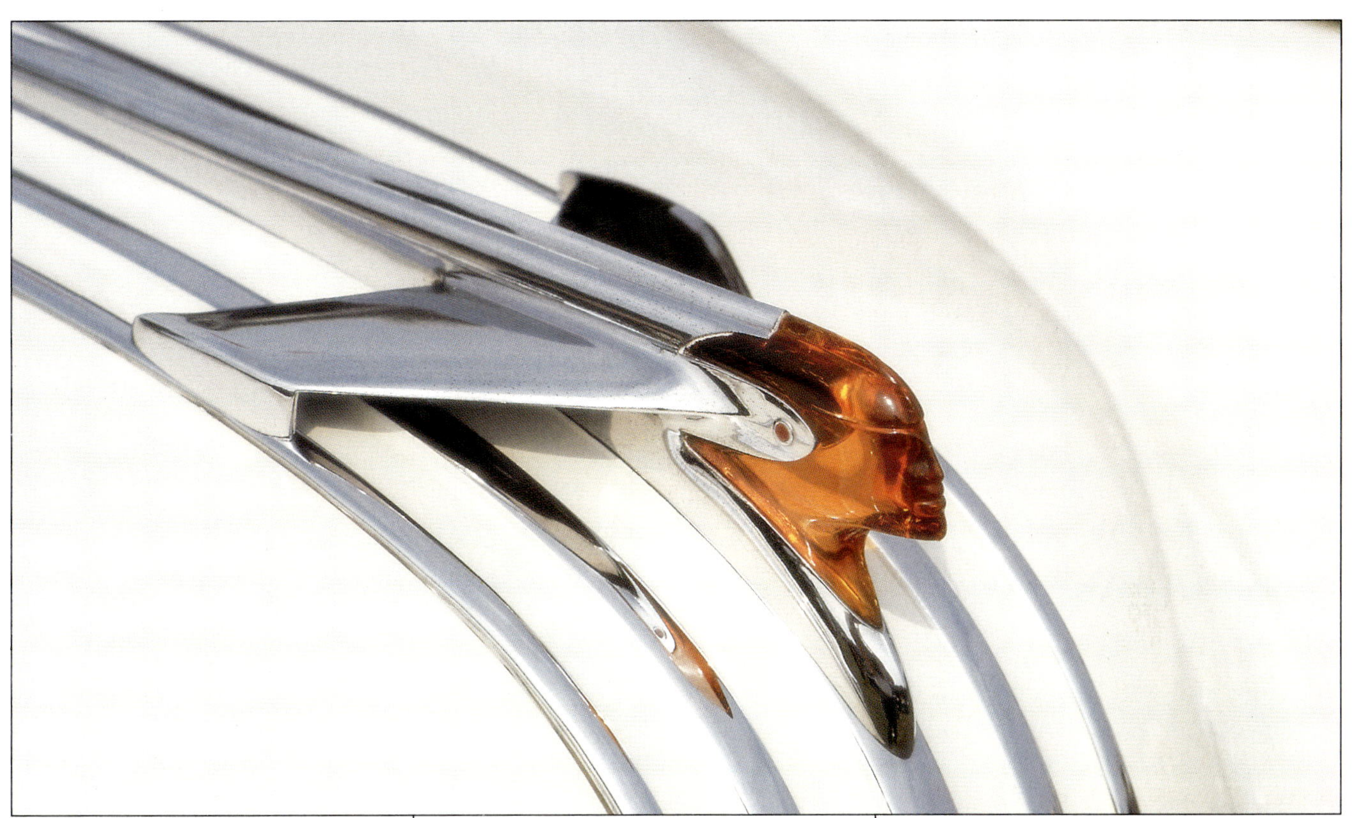

Pontiac hood ornament
This is a classic argument for incident-light metering. The white paint and chrome ornamentation on this old Pontiac would completely mislead any reflected-light meter, even the cleverest multi-segment system, but an incident-light reading was simplicity itself. Roger used an old Weston Master selenium-cell meter with an Invercone incident-light attachment, and then gave one stop less exposure in order to darken the whole image a little. This is a true 'high-key' subject, with a limited range of important tones: probably only two or at most three stops. It is true that there are dark tones reflected in the chromium and in the head on the hood ornament, but the picture loses nothing and indeed arguably gains somewhat from the fact that they are recorded darker than they 'really' were. The film was Kodachrome 64 and the camera and lens were a Leica M-series with a 90mm f/2 Summicron. The hand-held exposure was probably 1/250 at f/5.6 or thereabouts. (RWH)

which case you have to take a reflected-light reading, preferably with a spot or semi-spot meter), and second, when you want to 'reassign' values. Going back to our Californian mission, you would just cut the exposure by a stop, in order to darken the white wall. As for the soot-blackened pot, you would just increase the exposure by a stop, in order to lighten the dark pot. This is easy to remember, and easy to do. This is why almost all competent professional photographers have at least one incident-light meter, and know how to use it.

Most modern incident-light meters have a dome, which reads all the incident light for 180° or more, but a few are also available with flat diffuser plates. What follows is most useful with flat-diffuser meters, but it will do no harm if used with dome diffusers.

Take your first reading with the meter pointing straight towards the camera, from the subject position. Take your second reading with the meter pointing towards the strongest light source falling on the subject, again from the subject position. If there is a difference (and there may not be), then split it. That is all.

EXPOSURE IN COLOUR

With a colour slide film, you have to get the exposure dead right at the time of exposure, but with a colour print film, you can compensate to a large extent at the printing stage. The total range across which colour is acceptable in the print will however be much the same as for the transparency, about 16:1, unless you use negative masking when you make the print (page 63).

While an incident-light reading will always give an excellent basis for exposure, if you are shooting colour transparencies, you may wish to give

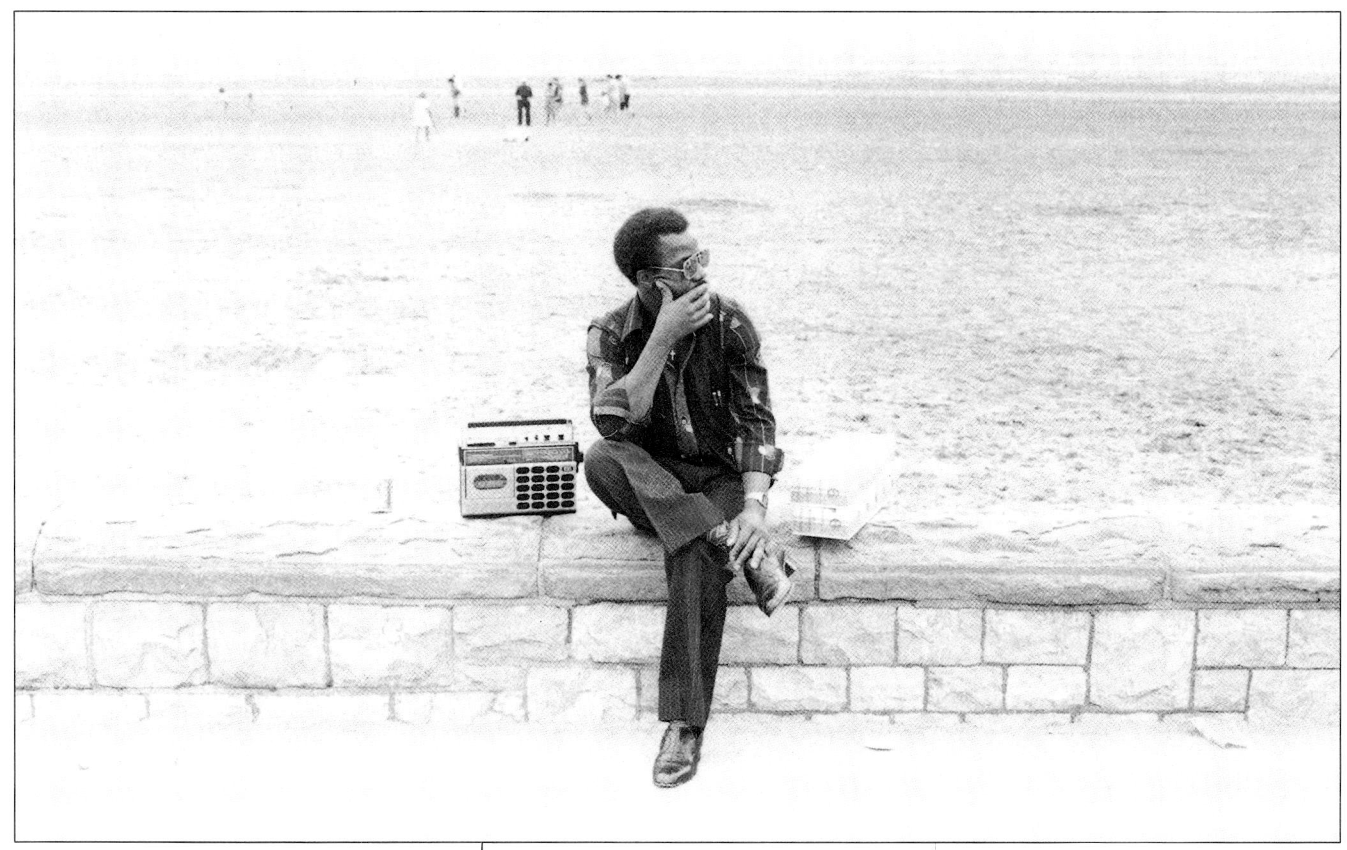

more exposure or less exposure than the meter indicates, or both. If you give more exposure, you will have a lighter transparency which might look cooler, or airier, or mistier, or more romantic. Over-exposed ballerinas are a clichéd example. If you give less exposure, you will have a darker transparency which might look richer, or moodier, or gloomier, or more forbidding. Because the effects of more or less exposure are far less predictable in colour than in black and white, it is also normal to bracket one's exposures.

Bracketing with Colour Slide

The three reasons for bracketing are to produce colour transparencies which closely match one another in density, colour and 'mood'; to make up for errors in exposure determination; and, as noted a moment ago, to vary that mood.

For matching density, half-stop rests are advisable. After careful metering, you make one exposure at the recommended exposure; one at half a stop more; and one at half a stop less. If the subject is a very difficult one, you might make two more, at one full stop more and one full stop less. You might even go further, both ways: some photographers will use half a roll of film in brackets, from three or four stops over to three or four stops under.

For covering errors in exposure determination, one-stop rests are normally adequate, because the greatest possible error across a three-stop range is half a stop. If any one of your three exposures is spot-on, you have no problems; and even if your exposure determination was one-and-a-half stops away from the optimum, either the over- or the under-bracket will be within half a stop of the optimum.

Weston-super-Mare

When Roger lived in Bristol in the 1970s, he used to go quite often to Weston-super-Mare to take pictures. As with many of Britain's seaside resorts, there is a fascinating contrast between its former elegance and the depths to which its once-handsome buildings have sunk, and it was (and still is) a great place for people-watching. Unfortunately, he was a lot less technically competent in those days, and the harsh contrast of beach lighting was something he did not always master. Frances found this negative, which was shot on the old HP5 in the days before HP5 Plus, in his files; she liked the sense of alienation which it conveys. There is actually a fair amount of detail in the background, but the picture was obviously exposed for the figure, and the contre-jour lighting has isolated him very well. The camera was probably one of Roger's old Leicas – he had five or six pre-World War II Leicas in those days – and the lens would almost certainly have been either a 50mm f/3.5 Elmar or a 90mm f/4 Elmar. The meter reading was most probably incident-light, using a Zeiss Ikophot T Export meter, one of the best-designed and most accurate ever made, but also unfortunately one of the least reliable. (RWH)

Again, you can extend the bracketing range if the subjects are really difficult: make five exposures, at two stops under, one stop under, at the reading, one stop over, and two stops over. This is a five-stop range, which is within the realms of guesswork, never mind exposure metering.

The kind of bracketing you need to do to vary the mood will depend on the film and on the effect you want. If you want lightness, try one stop over and two stops over. If you want darkness, try one stop under and two stops under. You will rarely need more.

Bracketing with Black and White and Colour Print

Unless you are really bad at exposure determination, or the subject is really hard to meter, there should be no need to bracket with either of these. If you are really worried (as we sometimes are!), then make an additional exposure at two full stops more than your best guess: under-exposure is usually much more of a risk in black and white than over-exposure.

Autobracketing

Some cameras have a built-in autobracketing facility, so they take three photographs in a row. Although one of our cameras has this feature – the Pentax Z-1 (PZ-1 in the United States) – it is not something we ever use, as we find that for most photographs it is better to take each picture at the optimum time, pressing the shutter-release ourselves at the 'decisive moment'. Autobracketing action shots, in particular, is a complete waste of time with even the fastest motordrive, though it arguably has its place in landscape photography.

Other Exposure Techniques

Clip testing and the technique of 'hold one, process one' were dealt with in the last chapter. A useful variation on 'hold one, process one' is to use two or more identical (or at least similar) cameras to make your two 'brackets' simultaneously, especially when you are photographing anything unrepeatable.

Polaroid test shots are the ultimate way of checking exposure, but they are covered at much greater length in Chapter 10.

FILL-IN FLASH AND REFLECTORS

A good way to reduce the contrast range of a picture is to use additional lighting (typically flash) to fill in the shadows; hence the expression 'fill-in flash'. This used to be quite difficult to work out, but most modern top-rank cameras (and some lesser ones, including a good number of compacts) offer automatic fill-in flash: our Pentax Z-1 is an example. Unlike the autobracket, this is a decisive feature: if we want fill-in flash, we do not even consider our old Nikons, but grab the Pentax automatically. Of course, most modern Nikons have this feature too.

An older, cheaper and easier solution is to use reflectors to kick extra light into the shadows. Anything will do: a white sheet, a towel, even a newspaper. Two especially useful tools are a sheet of board covered with aluminium foil which has been crumpled and then flattened (this gives a bright diffuse reflector with no 'hot spots') and collapsible reflectors such as the excellent Lastolite, which folds down to a disc little more than 30cm (12in) across but expands to a full 1m (3ft) circle.

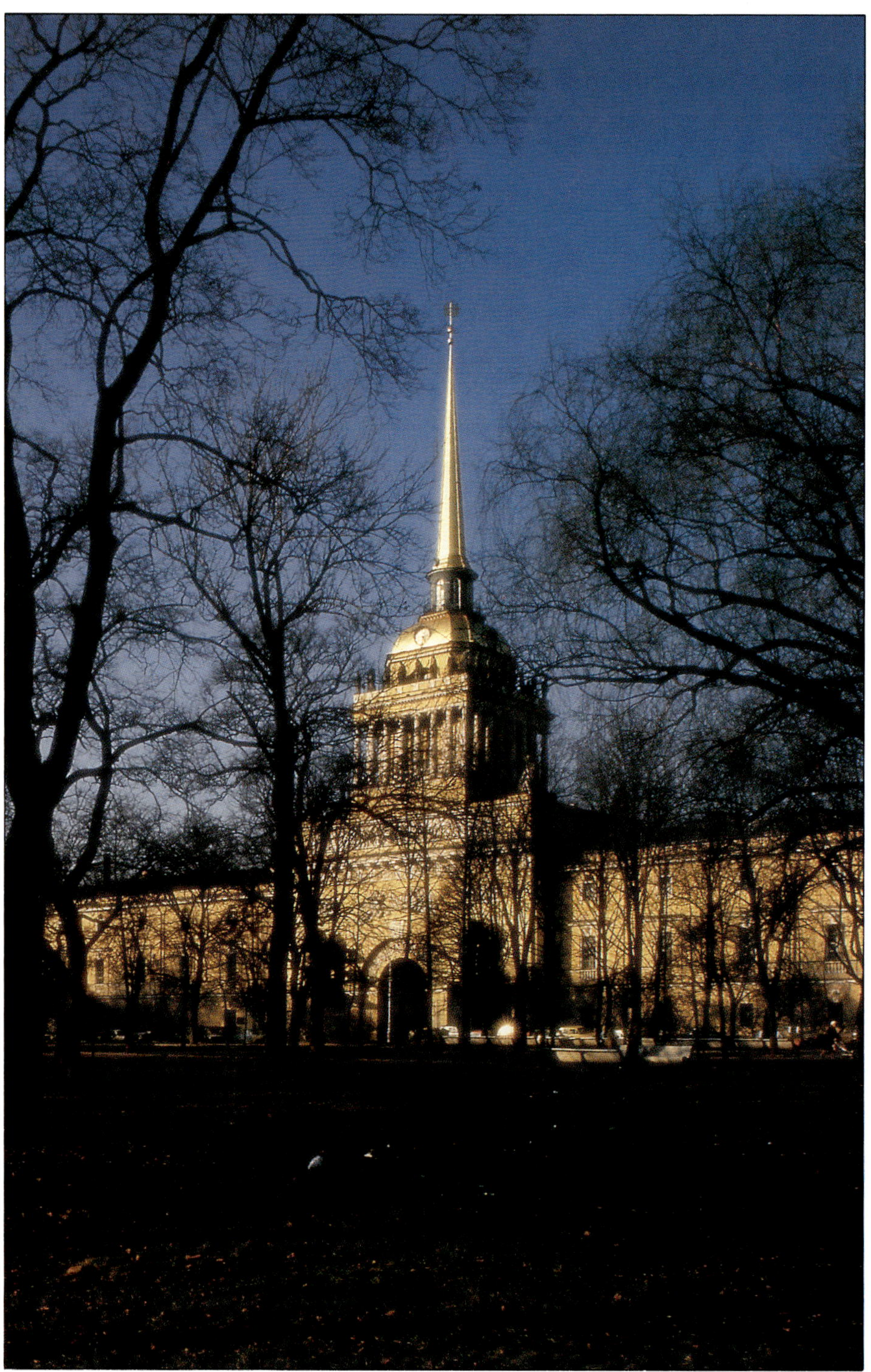

St Petersburg

St Petersburg is full of beautiful buildings, and quite frankly, we are not sure what this one was. The problem with it, as in so many cities anywhere in the world, is that cars are parked outside and spoil its beauty. Roger got around the problem in two ways. One was by shooting through a little park in front of the building, which allowed it to appear through the leafless autumn trees (this was late September), and the other was by under-exposing somewhat to emphasise the richness of the golden stonework and the gilded top. He took an incident-light reading in a sunlit clearing in the trees, then cut the exposure by a full stop. The flash of light from a car window was a pure bonus: he had noticed it as he was setting up the shot, and thought of changing the camera position slightly in order to lose it, but then he realised that it was all of a piece with the golden image he was trying to create. The lens was Frances's 35mm f/2.8 PC-Nikkor, on a Nikon F mounted on a Gibran tripod. Exposure was probably about 1/60 at f/11 to f/16, on Fuji RFP ISO 50. (RWH)

6 BLACK AND WHITE FILMS

Confederate cemetery

We were working on a book on the American civil war when Frances shot this. There are far fewer Confederate cemeteries than Union: so-called National cemeteries are mostly full of Union troops, with Confederates commemorated (if at all) by a single monument over the mass grave in which they were buried. Frances is a Yankee by birth: she was born in upstate New York, and she can remember when she was a very small girl seeing a veteran of the Civil War who at that time was over a hundred years old. Even so, she could not help being moved by the depth of Southern feeling, and the more she learned about the subject, the more she realised that the (Yankee) history she was taught in school was excessively simplistic and indeed often wrong. She hand-coloured this picture in several different ways, before deciding that colouring just the battle flag was the best in order to capture the way in which the South remembers what some still call the War of Northern Aggression. She used Veronica Cass photo-oils to do the colouring, applied with cotton buds. (FES)

Although most people start their photographic careers today with colour print films, it is not a bad idea to look at the theory behind black and white films first – mainly, because it is easier to understand. Black and white films share many characteristics with colour, such as speed and grain and sharpness and so forth, but the dimensions of colour saturation, colour balance and colour 'signature' are missing.

WHY USE BLACK AND WHITE?

There are two main reasons for using black and white instead of colour: love, and money.

Those photographers who use black and white for love are inclined to wax lyrical about the subtlety and abstraction of monochrome, and the almost limitless opportunities which it offers the creative photographer for imposing his own vision upon the medium. If you are already among their number, you will need no encouragement; but if you have never tried black and white, you really should – provided you do not mind running the risk of addiction.

The photographers who use black and white for financial reasons are a mixed bag. On the one hand, there is a steady demand for black and white because it is cheaper to reproduce than colour. Even though colour is becoming more and more pervasive, there are still plenty of magazines and indeed books which do not run to colour throughout. This book, for example, is printed in colour (four-colour separations) on one side, and

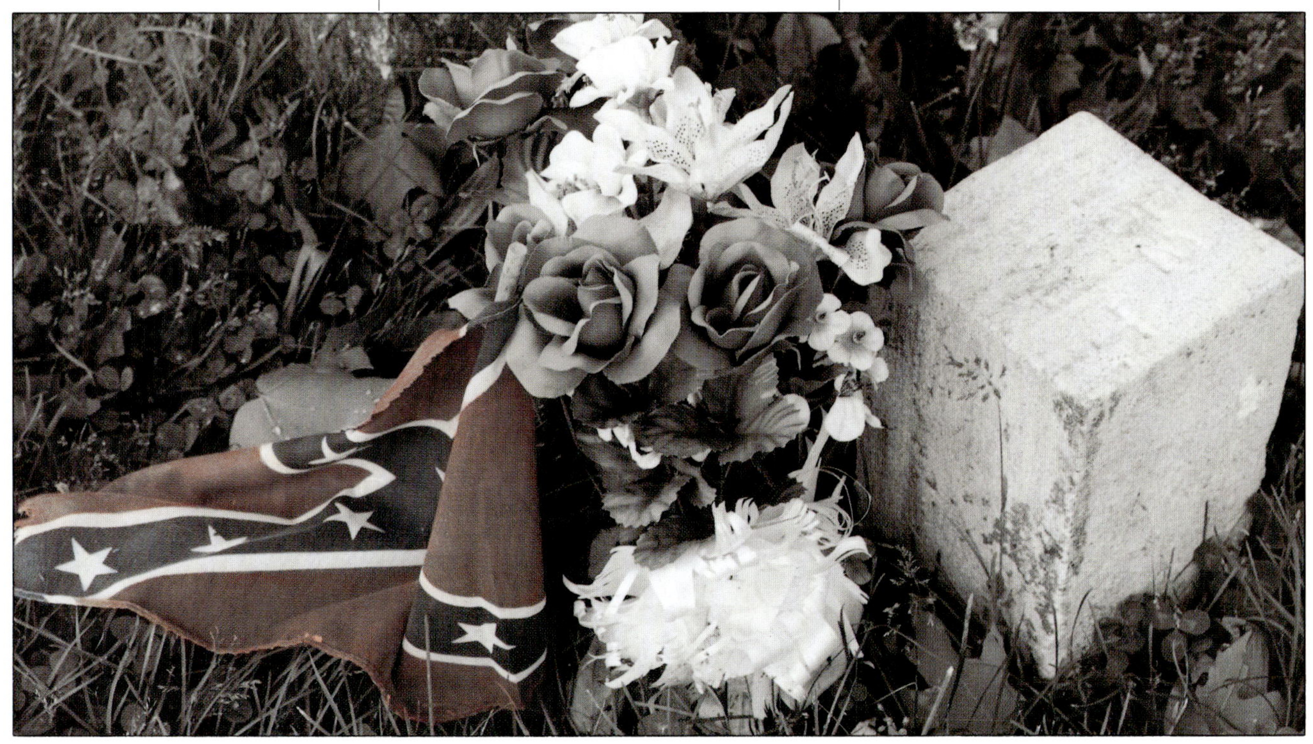

black only on the other. Because of the way that the big sheets are folded and cut to make the book – the 'imposition' – the pages are not simply alternated, but you will never find colour on both sides of the same piece of paper.

In addition to this somewhat utilitarian argument, there are also some applications where, regardless of expense, black and white has more impact than colour. To see this phenomenon at work, look at the more up-market magazines like *Vogue*. Both the advertisers and the editorial section could afford to use colour wherever they wanted, but they sometimes choose monochrome instead – and it works! Look at a down-market magazine, on the other hand, and they will use all the colour they can afford.

A third reason for using black and white is permanence. An archivally processed conventional print on fibre-base paper has a life which can be measured in centuries, unlike a colour print which will be lucky to last more than a few decades at best, under ideal conditions. Some artists feel that their work is so important that it must be made to last forever, but another reason for archival processing is the sheer interest value of very old pictures. The importance you attach to your pictures is up to you, but we compromise. Our RC-base prints should last for many decades, and we process our fibre-base prints to last as long as reasonably possible, without getting obsessive about it: they should last a century or two, at least. We are not arrogant enough to believe that the majority of our pictures are important enough to be kept longer. If they turn out to be so, a future generation can copy them before they disappear!

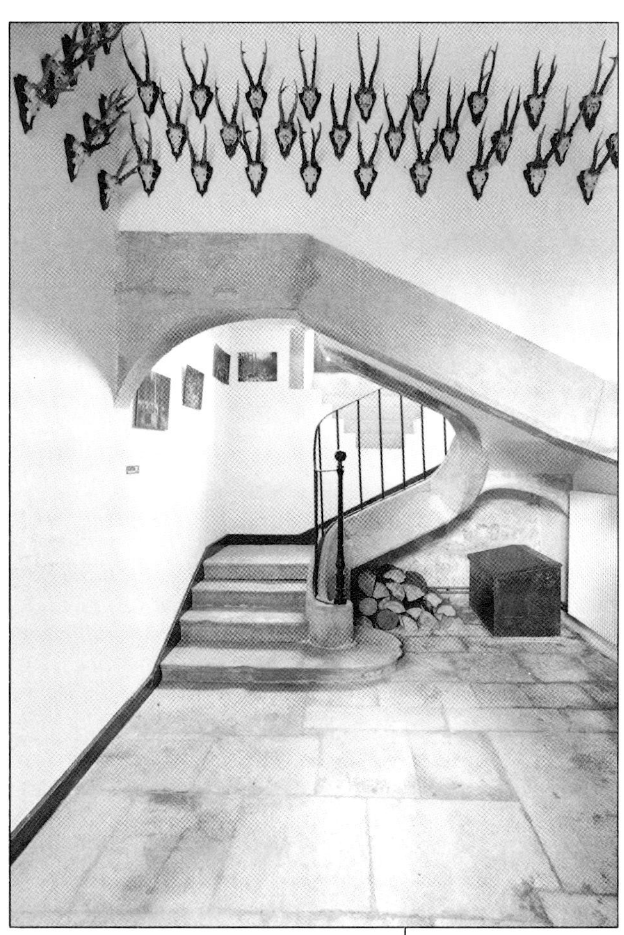

Interior, medieval abbey, France

A constant problem with taking pictures for magazines is that the reproduction is often 'muddy' and flat. The usual advice on how to get around this is to make contrasty or 'bright' or 'snappy' prints – the euphemisms vary. This is not the answer. All you will get is a muddy version of an excessively contrasty print. What you need to do, if you possibly can, is to make sure that all the important detail is in the light mid-tones, as it is in these two pictures. This is Zone VI, if you remember the Zone System from Chapter 5. Sometimes you can do this by selecting your subject carefully; sometimes you can do it by careful exposure, 'assigning' the important tones to Zone VI; and sometimes you can do it in printing. Sometimes you cannot do it at all!

The other thing you need to do, if there is any possibility of confusion, is to use the caption to make it clear what the picture is about. The close-up of the stairway is clear enough, but in the other shot the odd-looking things on the wall are the skulls and horns of the local small deer: the abbey-turned-chateau, which is about 700 years old, is a museum of hunting. In a book like this, they will reproduce clearly enough, and they are still hard to recognise without being told; but if the picture was run on newsprint, they might be reduced almost to silhouettes. The film was XP-2 (again, dating from before we started using Delta 100); the camera was a tripod-mounted Nikon F; and the lenses were a 17mm f/3.4 Tamron SP and a 35mm f/2.8 PC-Nikkor. Exposure details forgotten. (FES)

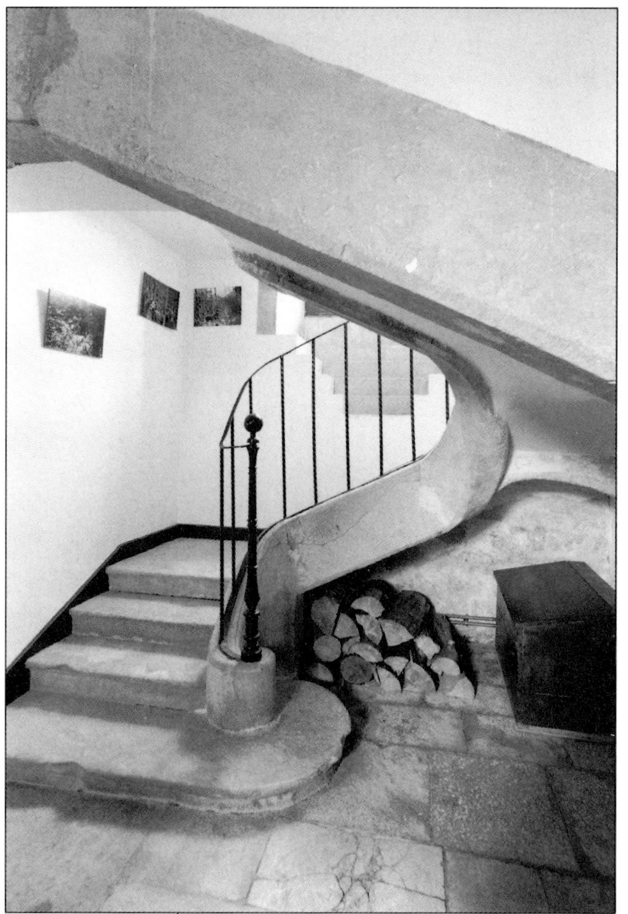

THE COSTS

When colour was first introduced, advertisers and editors paid more for it because of its rarity value, and because it was expensive for the photographers to produce. The old differentials between colour and black and white still survive today in many places, which is utterly ridiculous, because providing black and white prints actually costs the photographer *more* than providing transparencies. Either way, the film and processing are normally a small part of the cost of a shoot – the photographer's expertise is (or should be) what the client is paying for – but once the colour slides are processed, there is very little more that the photographer needs to do: just put them in mounts (or sleeves), and send them to the client. With black and white, though, the photographer has to maintain a darkroom, and to spend additional time producing prints; or alternatively, he or she has to pay someone else to do it.

For the amateur, colour slides are now the cheapest way to produce first-class work. Good-quality package prints from a decent lab are next (and the price is very close), while black and white printing (even in your own darkroom) is more expensive again. Even so, it is not really very expensive, once you have your darkroom set up. The only type of photography which is more expensive than black and white is producing your own colour prints, or having them made in a custom lab. So much for the economics, though: what about the films themselves?

ULTRA-SLOW FILMS (BELOW ISO 100)

These are not films for general, everyday use. The biggest problem is that they are mostly very contrasty, so they can only really be used on overcast days (when they are inconveniently slow, and have to be used in a camera that is mounted on a tripod), or in the studio where the lighting is under control. We use Ilford Pan F (ISO 50) for photographing cameras and similar things, for illustrations in magazines and books like this, but we do not normally use it outdoors.

Having said this, there are some photographers who do use ultra-slow for general photography, but they tend to be rather obsessive types who use obscure developers and take pride in wrestling with difficult films. A great favourite among these people is Kodak Technical Pan film, which is a super-fine-grain film designed for document copying and similar applications, which was hijacked by people who manage to extract more quality from 35mm than you would have thought possible. Another slow film which is very highly regarded is the deadly slow Orwo 25, which seems to have less ferocious contrast than most other slow films. Agfapan 25 is yet another. The limiting factor with most of these films is neither the grain nor the resolving power of the film: it is the resolving power of the lenses.

It is also worth making the point that you can get much better results with a medium-format camera and medium-speed or even fast film than you will get with any but the finest 35mm cameras and the best slow films available. This is what most professionals do if they need big black and white prints. Only a masochist would use slow films and a medium-format camera: you just do not need the extra quality that the films can deliver.

MEDIUM SPEED FILMS (AROUND ISO 100)

These are the films which are traditionally recommended as 'standard' films – but a lot depends on what you want to use them for. For a long time, 'standard' was synonymous with 'dull', and many photographers accepted a minimal loss of quality in return for the extra speed of ISO 400 film: only traditionalists and studio photographers used ISO 100 or ISO 125 films.

Then, two films came along which reawakened interest in this hitherto moribund section of the market. One was Kodak T-Max 100, which has already been mentioned as a 'love it or hate it' film, but which in the opinion of those who love it was a major improvement over anything which had gone before. The second was Ilford's Delta 100, which again has already been praised to the skies. Until Delta 100 came along, we simply did not bother to use medium-speed films at all. Today, we use Delta 100 whenever we want the best possible quality in monochrome.

During the life of this book, it is of course possible that something even better may come out; but when it does, the magazines will make much of it, because it is going to have to be very good indeed.

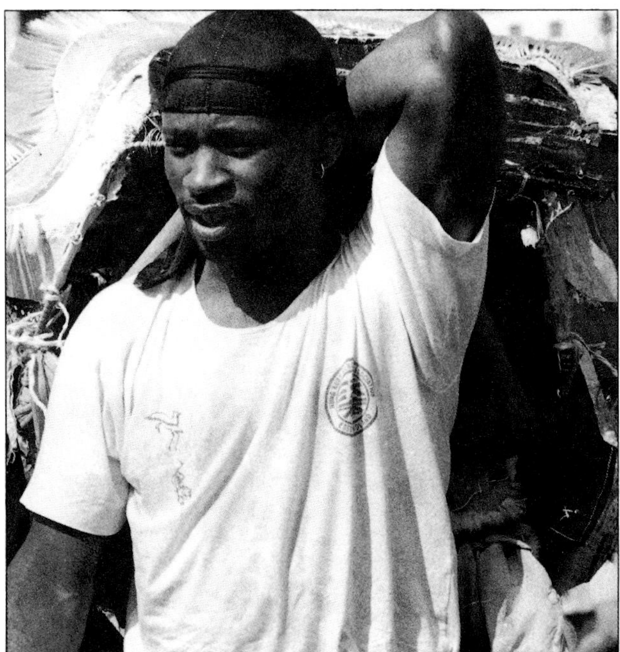

Martial artist/Lion Dancer
A versatile gentleman, this: not only a martial arts expert, but also a Lion Dancer – he is carrying the lion's head, after the dance was over at the Ramsgate Chinese Festival. He has a very photogenic face, and the way he was carrying the lion's head (a light framework with a highly stylised lion on it) is a classic 'carrying' pose. If you do not know all this background, though, this picture looks even more exotic than it is: the high sun might be over some heat-soaked Mediterranean port. The only thing which slightly spoils the picture, from the point of view of exoticism, is his Essex martial arts T-shirt: otherwise, he could be some stevedore from the 1930s, or a sailor in the South Seas... The great thing about black and white is that it cuts you loose from too literal an interpretation of the here and now. He was photographed on Delta 400 using a Nikon F and a 90mm f/2.5 Vivitar Series One macro; exposure was about 1/250 at f/8 or f/11. (FES)

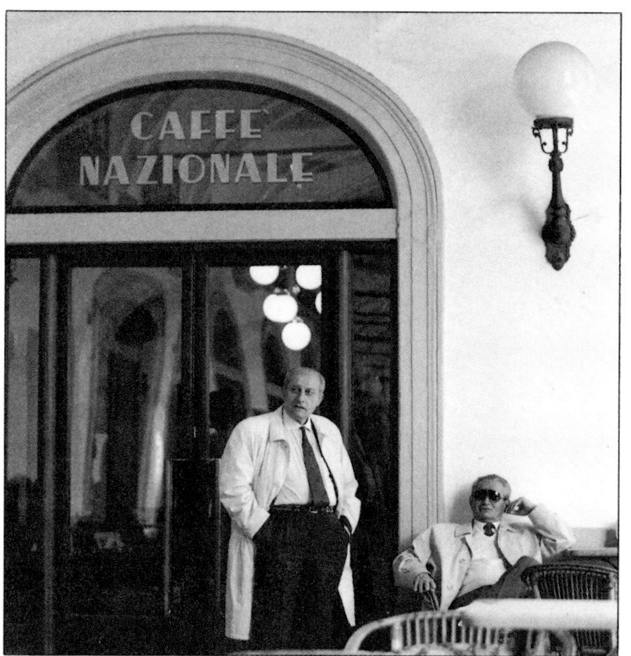

Café, Aosta

No doubt these two gentlemen are eminently respectable citizens; but countless movies have given us certain expectations about respectable-looking Italian gentlemen of a certain age. The wonderful 1930s architecture and lamp (Fascist Deco), the cane chairs, and of course the name of the café itself all set this clearly in Italy. In colour, it would be just another snapshot, or at best a Chamber of Commerce advertising shot to tell you what a nice place Aosta is; but in monochrome, everything has an archetypal quality. Roger shoots far less black and white than Frances, but there are times like this when he gets it right; and when you do get black and white right, you understand what its advocates are always saying, about its inherent superiority to colour. The camera was a Nikon F and a 70-210mm f/2.8 Sigma lens, probably at 210mm and probably wide open, or at f/4 at the smallest. The film was Ilford XP-2, rated at EI 250. This is a sectional blow-up from maybe two-thirds of the negative. (RWH)

FAST FILMS (ISO 400)

For many photographers, these are the standard films in black and white. Everyone has his or her own favourite, often based as much on geography as on logic: traditionally, Americans used Tri-X, and Britons (and many Europeans) used HP5. These are however 'old-technology' films, even though they have been through a constant process of refinement and improvement. The 'new-technology' films, such as Kodak's T-Max 400 and Ilford's Delta 400, offer finer grain and better gradation, but at the expense of slightly more critical exposure. They also require processing in the right chemistry to give the best results: old-technology films were less fussy. If you process your films yourself, do not shrink from the 'new technology' films, but unless you have a lab you can really trust, stick with the old standards. They can very nearly be processed in vegetable soup and still deliver an acceptable image.

An alternative to all of them, though, is Ilford's XP-2. As mentioned elsewhere, this is a 'chromogenic' film, processed in the same chemicals as any normal colour negative film, and it offers enormous exposure latitude and reliable processing. We find that it is the perfect film for reportage, though some people find the dye-cloud 'grain' a little disturbing, and judge the film to be less sharp than it is. Even those who do not like it in 35mm, however, tend to love it in rollfilm or (better still) in 4x5in.

All of these films are effectively grain-free up to about a 6x enlargement, which is all that most people ever need, and if they are blown up any bigger, some people find that the grain adds a sense of immediacy.

ULTRA-FAST FILMS (OVER ISO 400)

We find these to be useful more often than ultra-slow films, because we keep finding ourselves in situations where we are running out of light. On the other hand, because we own quite a lot of super-speed lenses, we do not have the same need of ultra-high-speed films as the users of zoom lenses. For example, a typical modern 'standard zoom' might have an aperture of f/3.5 to f/4.5. At f/4.5, you need film rated at slightly over EI 1600 just to equate to ISO 400 film used with an f/2 lens – and we have lenses as fast as f/1.4 and even f/1.2. Combine these with ultra-fast films, and you really can take pictures in next to no light!

Most ultra-fast films are actually ISO 400 or ISO 800 films designed for

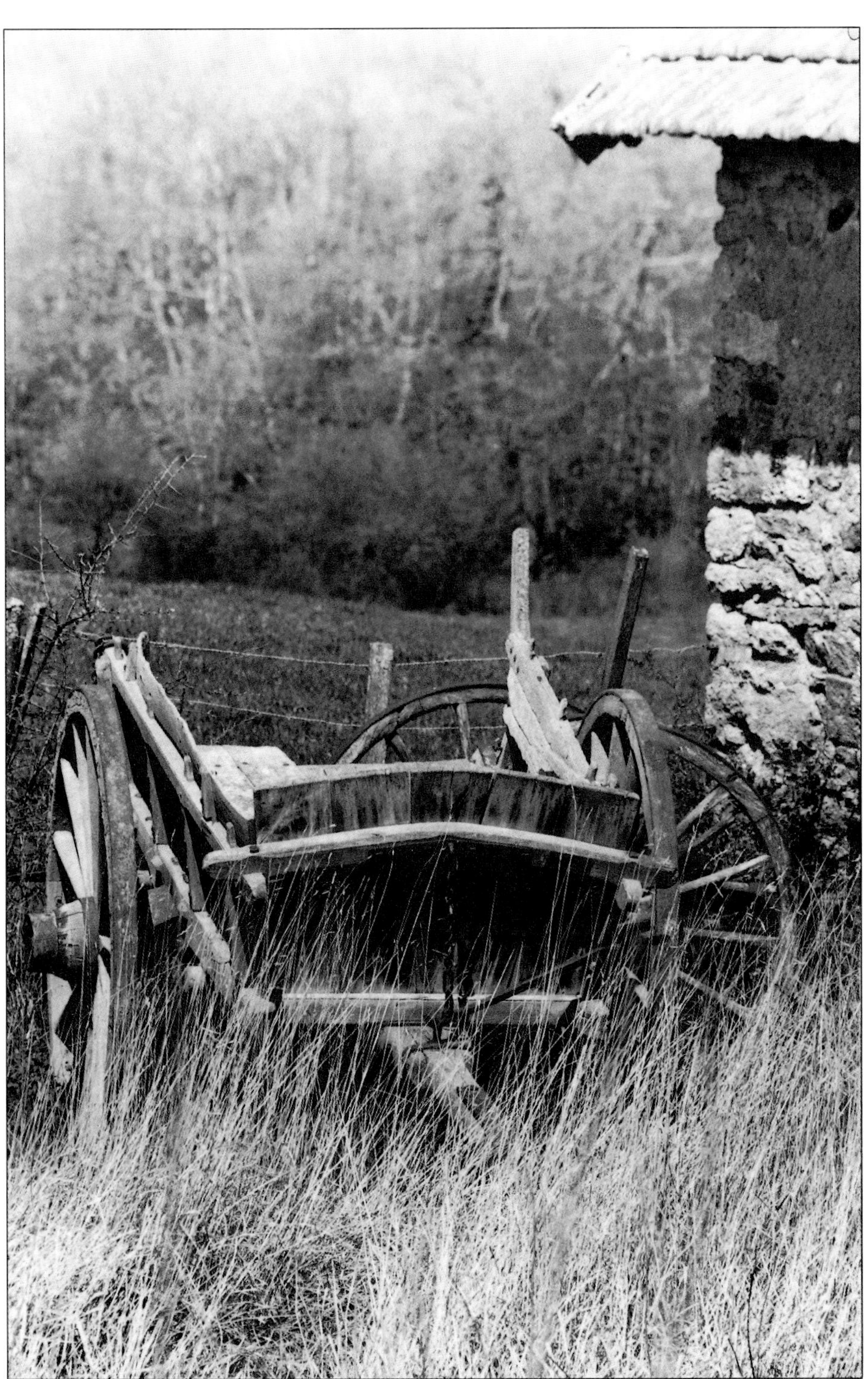

Wagon, rural France

You can worry too much about holding detail everywhere in a print. The temptation in a picture like this is to try to hold detail even in the brightest parts of the wagon; but if you do, the whole thing will be too dark and too dull. We made that mistake! When Frances reprinted it, she increased the contrast by one and a half paper grades and cut the exposure by a third, from 15 seconds to 10 seconds. The net result was that she still held texture – just! – in the upper surface of the wagon-rails, which are therefore in Zone VII, while the grass in the foreground is Zone VIII with highlights in Zone IX. In the original print, you can see variations in tone in the front surface of the wagon-board (Zone II), though this will probably have disappeared in reproduction, and the shadows under the wagon are as black as the paper can deliver: Zone 1. The contrast of the dry, pale grass against the shadows makes the print look contrasty at first glance, but if you look carefully, you see that there is a very full range of tones in it. Film was Ilford XP-2, exposed in a tripod-mounted Nikon F with a 70-210mm f/2.8 Sigma Apo zoom. Exposure was probably 1/250 at f/11 in slightly hazy sunlight. (FES)

Birchington Carnival

This is the sort of picture which would be almost impossible to shoot on colour slide film, unless you used fill-in flash to lighten the girl's face under the hat. Even then, you would need a pretty powerful flash-gun, because this was shot with a Sigma 300mm f/2.8 lens at a distance of maybe twenty feet, at an aperture of f/5.6 or so: and, of course, you would run into synch-speed problems, even with modern cameras which synchronise at 1/250 second. With the old Nikons we use, the maximum synch speed is 1/60, which would have meant working at f/11: this implies a guide number of 220 (feet) or 70 (metres), which is about the limit for hand-portable electronic flash used out of doors. In black and white, using Delta 400, there is a little detail missing on her right arm, but there is still texture in the veil and in most of the blouse. You could probably get an acceptable colour print if you were prepared to do a good deal of dodging and burning, but in any case, monochrome suits the vintage dress. (RWH)

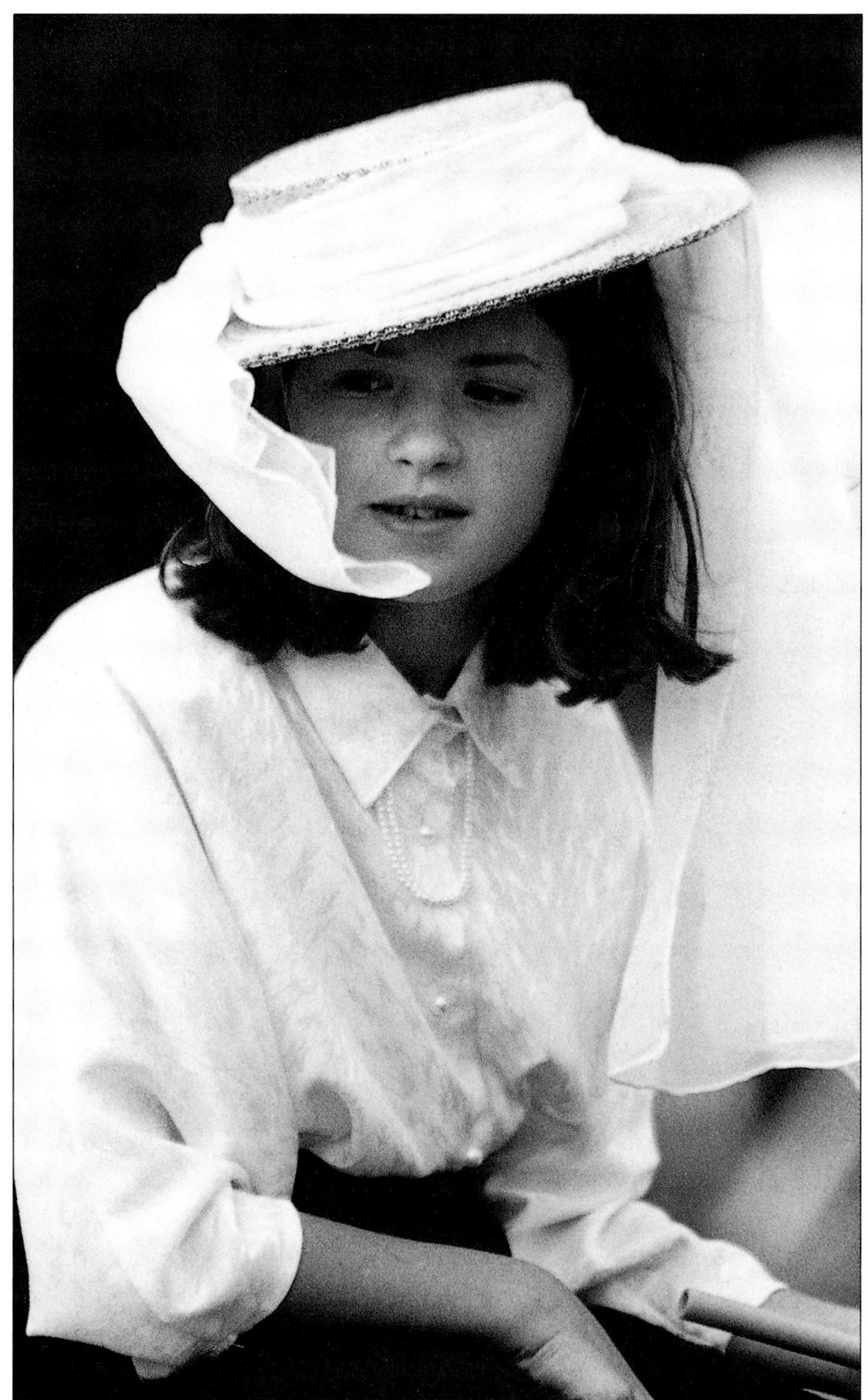

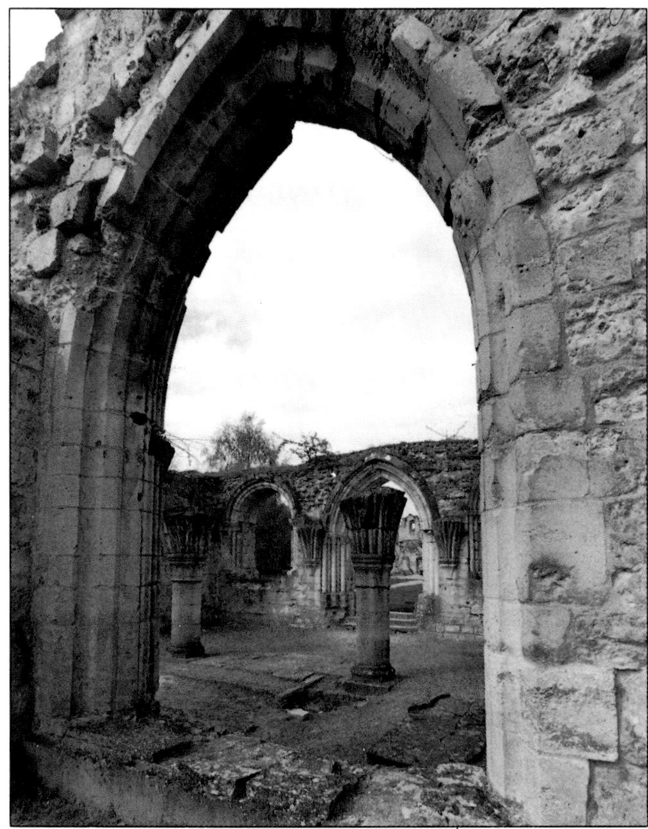

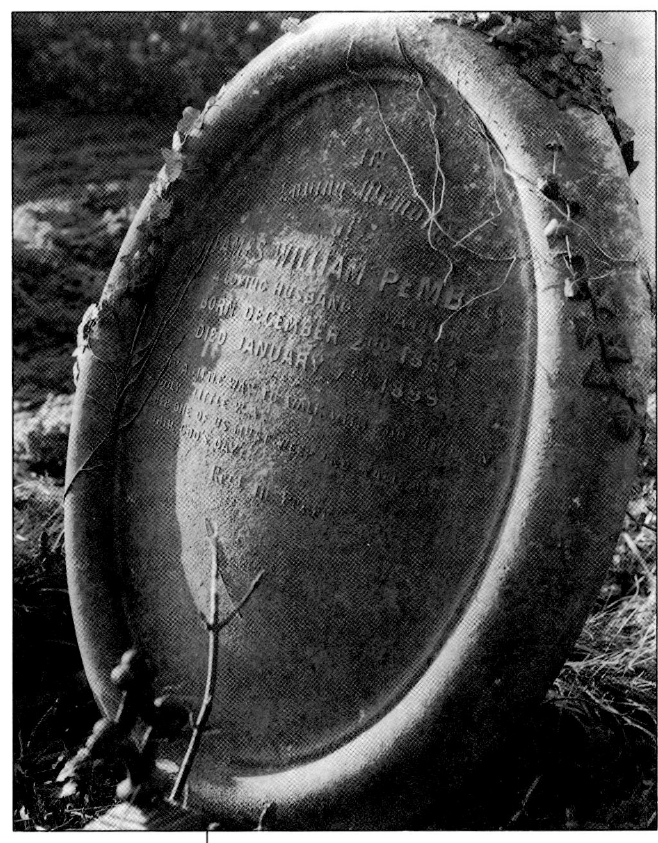

Ruined church, France

This ruined abbey church had a very 'gothick' feel which cried out for black and white – and besides, it was rather a dull day – but it was extremely difficult to get even the modest amount of texture which is held in the sky in this print. The way to get it is to use a split-contrast technique on Ilford Multigrade paper, with very low contrast for the sky (Grade $^{1}/_{2}$) and very high contrast for the walls (Grade 5). In order to get maximum depth of field when she was shooting the original picture, Frances stopped her 35mm f/2.8 PC-Nikkor well down, using the index marks for the next largest aperture as a guideline. In other words, given that she was shooting at f/16, she used the depth-of-field indices for f/11. The exposure, on Ilford XP-2, was about $^{1}/_{60}$ or maybe even $^{1}/_{30}$ at f/16: there was a lot of patchy cloud, and even on those rare occasions when the sun broke through, it was not very bright. A yellow, red or orange filter would not have helped much with the sky, because there was not enough blue for it to work: the clouds were merely grey on white. (FES)

Gravestone, Parish Church of All Saints, Birchington

We very rarely shoot rollfilm black and white, because modern 35mm films are so good that we really have no need to do so. Our work is only occasionally reproduced larger than A4 (210x297mm, about $8^{1}/_{4}$x$11^{3}/_{4}$in), and almost never larger than 10x14in (254x355mm), which is the page size of Shutterbug, *the magazine we both write for in the United States. If we habitually produced large exhibition pictures, we might however feel different: there is no doubt that a 16x20in or 40x50cm picture from a 6x7cm rollfilm negative is an altogether more luxurious sort of thing than you can get from even the finest 35mm cameras, lenses and film. Sometimes, though, we shoot medium-format black and white just for the fun of it. This was shot with the Linhof in the churchyard of our parish church, and it may be that even in reproduction and at this modest size you can see the improvement in quality. We had tried shooting the same subjects in 35mm, and we felt that the larger format was somehow called for: not just for quality, or even for the camera movements (we have a shift lens for the Nikons, after all), but more for the sense of tradition and occasion. Next time, we shall try shooting on ortho film (see Chapter 8) for an even more vintage approach. (RWH/FES)*

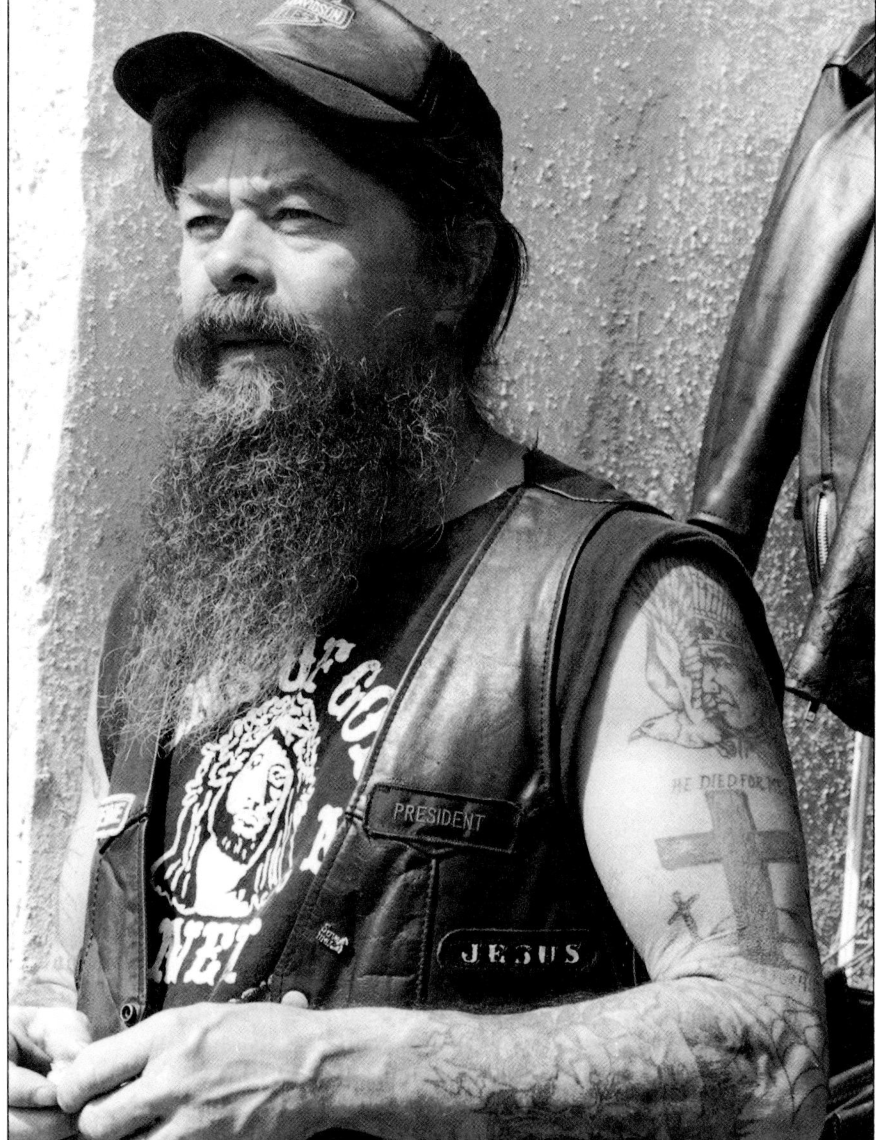

President, Sons of God Motorcycle Club
At Daytona during Cycle Week, you can find just about every variety of hairy biker that you can imagine. Most of them are posers who only ride a few hundred miles a year, but there are still thousands who really live the biker lifestyle. The President of the Sons of God Motorcycle Club wears an INRI T-shirt, and one of the tattoos on his arm reads 'He died for me – I live for him'. Frances's Nikon F was loaded with Ilford XP-2, our standard reportage film, and exposure in the bright Florida sun was 1/250 at f/11. The lens, as far as she can remember, was her 90mm f/2.5 Vivitar Series One macro. She asked if she could photograph him, and he was more than willing. Most real motorcyclists (like most real Christians) are not aggressive, 'bad-ass' types, even if they look it. (FES)

'push processing' to higher exposure indices, and some of them are significantly better than others. They all deliver their best quality at their lowest permitted speed rating, with surprisingly good quality when pushed one stop and barely acceptable quality when pushed all the way to their limit which is EI 1600 for some, and EI 3200 for others. The grain can be very large, though for many photographers this is actually one of the attractions of such films. At their maximum speed ratings, they can also be quite hard to print. The biggest single drawback of these films, which are great fun to play with, is that they are quite a lot more expensive than ISO 400 films, which are in turn rather more expensive than ISO 100 films. They can also be quite hard to find: many camera stores do not bother to stock them at all.

As we said at the beginning of the chapter, though, most people use colour print film today; so it is time to look at these.

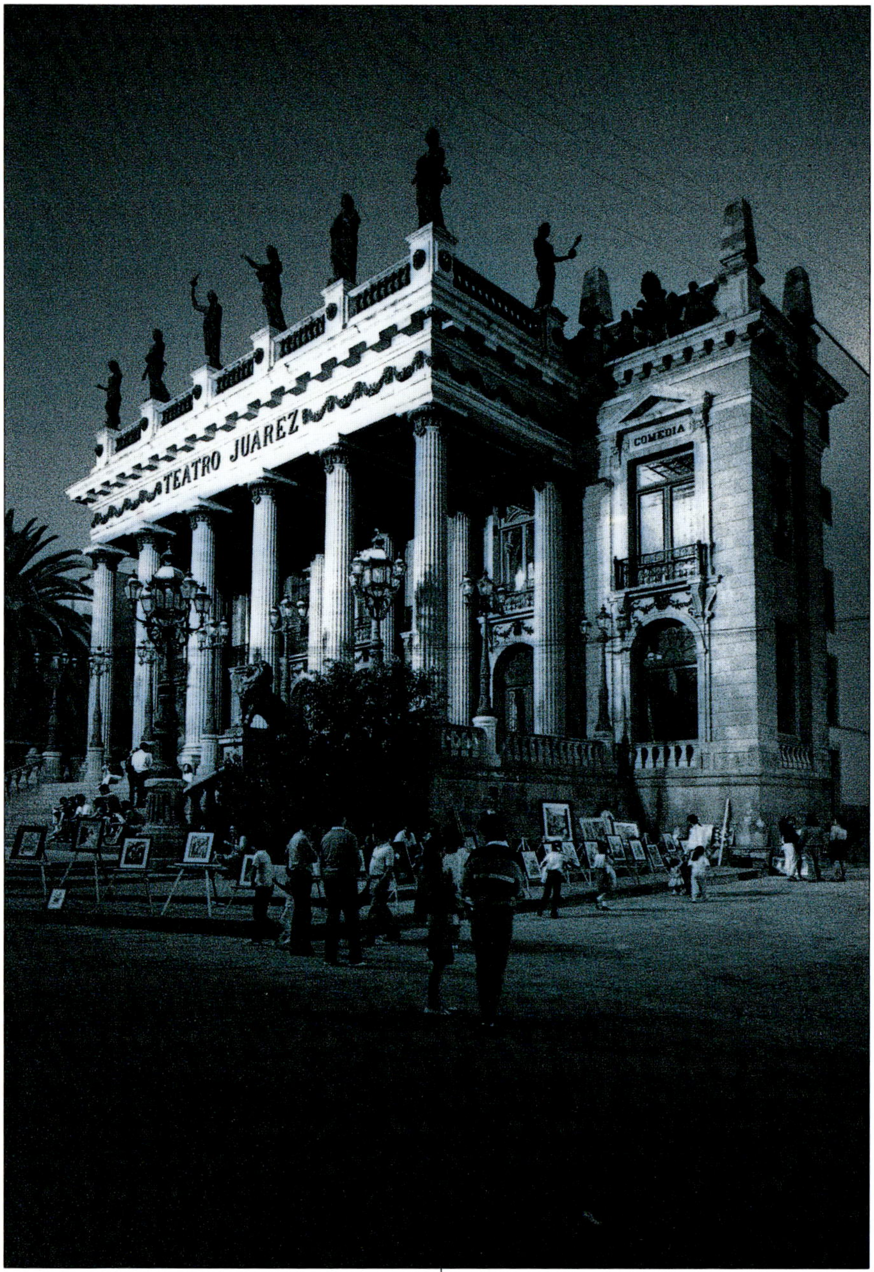

Teatro Juarez

Using black and white does not mean that you have to give up colour! Although sepia-toning is the most common way to add colour to black and white prints, there are many other forms of toning available. This was done with Edwal blue toner, a fast-acting single-bath toner which converts the black silver image in a print (or black and white slide or movie film, for that matter) to a blue dye image. You can stop the process at any point, from the slightest 'cooling' of a black and white image to a chalky blue tone. Frances shot this on Kodak T-Max P3200, rated at EI 1600, in early twilight – the exact exposure is forgotten – and we hoped that blue toning would capture the deep, velvety blue of the Mexican night sky. In fact, blue toning worked so well for this theatre that we have since tried blue-toning other architectural shots, and it generally seems to work very well for such subjects. (FES)

theBottomline camera bag

Pan F Plus is a film which we normally use only in the studio, for shots like this one. There is little or no point in using medium format: 35mm is quicker, cheaper, easier, and gives excellent gradation and resolution – provided you use the right lens, film and lighting. The lens must be sharp: this was shot with a Vivitar Series One 90-180mm f/4.5 Close-Focusing Flat-Field lens dating from the 1970s, which is not only one of the sharpest zooms ever made but which also focuses to one-half life size on the film. We find that ultra-slow films give us the kind of gradation we want, provided we are using our big 'soft box', also known as a 'northlight' or 'idiot light' (the last because it is so easy to use). This is simply a big diffuser, about 4x3ft (130cm x 100cm, say) through which we punch the light from a Paul Buff Ultra 1800 professional flash unit: this was shot at about f/16, so you can see that there is plenty of light to play with! We could of course use a rollfilm or even 4x5in camera with a faster film, such as XP-2, which would allow f/45; but the depth of field with the 35mm camera is better, even at the larger apertures. The bag comes from theBottomline (sic) and is Frances's favourite hard-shell case.

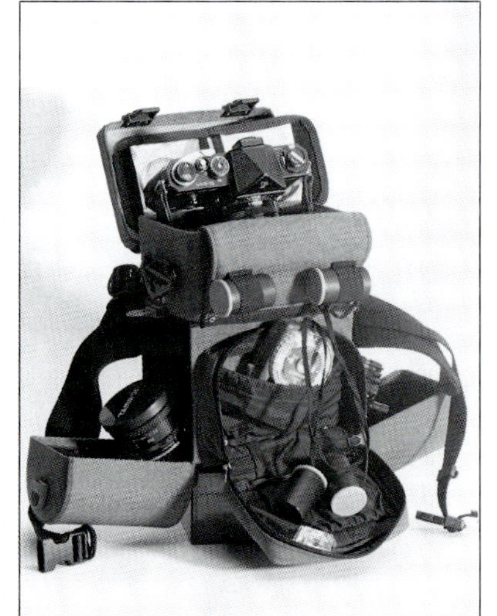

7 COLOUR PRINT FILMS

Colour print films are overwhelmingly the most popular films available today, and account for over 90 per cent of the market. As described in Chapter 1, they can even be used as 'universal' films, for colour prints, black and white prints and colour slides. With colour print films more than any other, though, the film that you choose must be influenced by the purpose to which you intend to put it.

The main uses for colour print films are for the family album; for exhibition prints; for commercial 'social' photography (weddings, bar-mitzvahs and portraits); and for publication. Because the choice of colour films depends so much on the use to which they are to be put, it makes more sense to analyse things this way than to look at them in terms of film speed.

Before we look at the different applications, though, it is worth mentioning that colour negative films are probably the least stable of all modern colour materials, though they are improving all the time. The negatives should last for many decades – quite possibly a lifetime – if they are stored in the dark in modest humidity, and small changes in colour balance can be filtered out in printing, though eventually you may run into problems with crossed curves (page 49) as light areas fade faster than dark ones, or vice versa. The prints themselves may however display detectable fading in only a few months, and will certainly fade in a very few years, especially if they are on display in an area where they are in direct sunlight. A darker corner will always prolong the life of

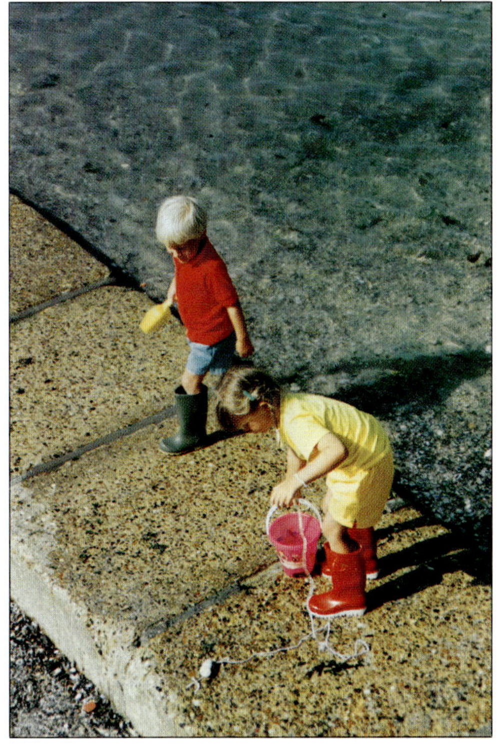

Children playing at the seaside

Increasingly often, we are knocked out by the quality that is obtainable from medium-speed print films. This was shot on ISO 200 Konica film, rated at EI 160 for extra saturation and finer grain, and in the original 5x7in machine print the quality is almost beyond belief. Grain is invisible – it is barely obtrusive even if you put a 6x magnifier on the print, the equivalent of a 30x enlargement – and the colours are superbly saturated, though in this particular case rather biased towards cyan: we suspect that the picture was reprinted to get the sea to look blue. The tonal range runs from the bright white of the soles on the little girl's boots (a tiny amount of cyan is visible under the magnifier) to a remarkably good black inside the top of the little boy's boots, with very acceptable flesh tones on the children's arms and faces. The degree of enlargement is limited more by the lens, a modestly priced zoom, than by the film. Exposure was fully automatic, using a Pentax Z-1, known as a PZ-1 in the United States. (RWH)

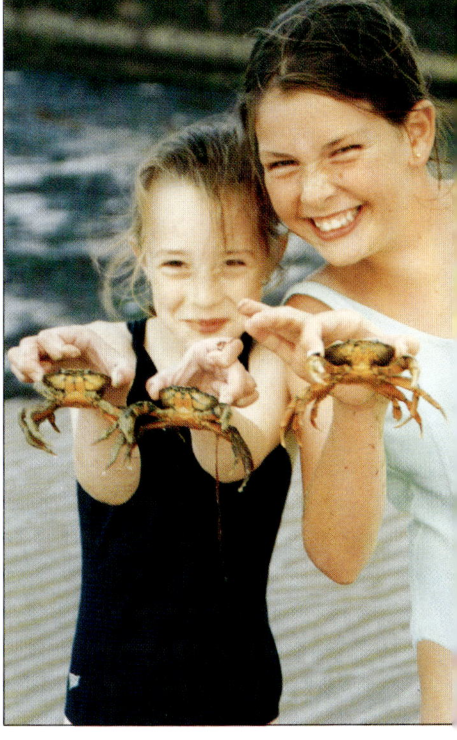

Crab-catchers

This was shot on Konica 200 rated at EI 160, one of our favourite colour print films, but it shows the potential advantage of using yet faster films. If it had been shot on Konica's ISO 400 material, the difference in grain and colour saturation would have been negligible with the 5x7in colour prints which we normally have made by our local happy-snap lab (Supasnaps in Margate), but there would have been a worthwhile increase in depth of field, holding both the crabs and the girls without the detectable loss of sharpness which maybe is apparent here: just look at the younger girl's hair and eyes. It may seem perverse to use high-speed films for this sort of picture in bright light, but the cost penalty is very small – the film price is about 10 per cent more than ISO 200, or 15 per cent more than ISO 100, and processing costs the same – and for most purposes, the faster film will actually deliver better quality, with greater depth of field and less camera shake. We generally rate ISO 400 colour print films at EI 320 or even EI 250, for the reasons stated in the text. (RWH)

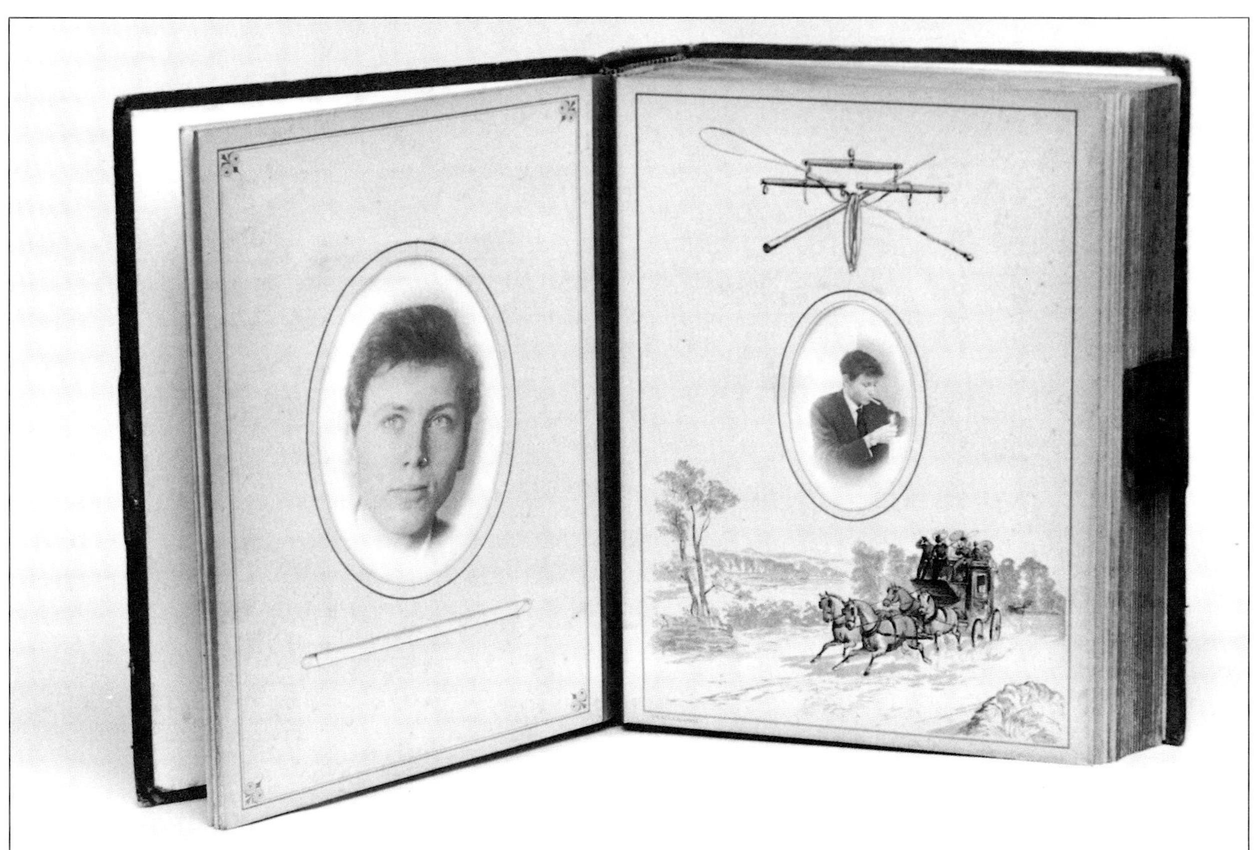

any print. If you keep your prints in an album, choose one with acid-free paper and an 'archival' method of securing prints, if you want to enjoy them in your old age. Alternatively, stick with black and white.

THE FAMILY ALBUM

Anyone who says that he or she never takes snapshots is either very dull, very unhappy, or a liar. We all take snapshots, amateurs and professionals alike, to remind us of weekends spent with friends, happy times with lovers, the way our children grow up, and so forth.

Most professionals we know adopt the same approach, and give the same advice: use the fastest film you can comfortably afford. While slower films deliver superb quality, so do faster ones, and they are much more versatile. We normally use ISO 400 film, rated at EI 200 to EI 320 as described elsewhere in the book. Even with the 5x7in or 13x18cm enlargements which we normally specify, the results are absolutely first class: with 4x6in or 10x15cm pictures, they would be unbeatable. We have used a little ISO 1000 film, rated at EI 500 with the occasional excursion to EI 1000, and again, we have been astonished by the quality: it is only the price that stops us using ISO 1000 all the time. Yes, you can see the beginnings of grain in a 5x7in or 13x18cm enlargement, but we do not find it obtrusive. On those rare occasions when we want bigger blow-ups, we simply accept the grain as a small price to pay for the sheer versatility of the film.

With fast films, you can take the most wonderful available-light shots, especially if you use a compact camera

Old photo album

An excellent way to display prints is in a traditional Victorian album – if you can find one in good order. This one, which is leather bound with a silver-plated brass hasp, probably dates from the 1880s. Roger has used it for many years to store his favourite pictures of friends; the pictures on these two pages are of Nicholas Andrew Gill Hayes, and were taken in the 1960s. If you do your own printing, you can even vignette the prints (as Roger did here, somewhat inexpertly). You can mix plain black and whites, sepia-toned prints, hand-coloured prints, and modern colour prints quite happily, for something which is uniquely yours and which your friends (and, as you and they grow older, their children) like to look at. A useful tip for preserving leather and preventing it from cracking is to use 'hide food', a preparation designed to keep leather furniture and clothing supple.

with a reasonably fast lens. One of our snapshot cameras (we have several) is an old Yashica Lynx 14, a rangefinder camera from the 1960s or early 1970s. It is not very compact – in fact, it weighs about a kilogram, just over two pounds – but it only cost us $20 or so (under £15) at a photo-show in California in the early 1990s, and it has an amazingly sharp f/1.4 lens. Exposure determination is via the built-in meter, or by guesswork (more often the latter), and we can take pictures with it in next to no light.

If this sounds like too much trouble, then by all means use a camera with built-in flash. If you do, there is no point in using anything faster than ISO 400, and quite honestly, there is no great advantage in re-rating it; just stuff it into the camera, let the DX coding do its work, and you will get very good results. This is true whether you use a modestly-priced autofocus compact or a full-featured super-SLR like our Pentax Z-1.

If you cannot afford faster films (and they can be quite a lot more expensive than slow ones), don't worry about that either. It is almost impossible to buy a bad film from a modern manufacturer. Any ISO 100 'standard' film will deliver superb quality at an unbeatable price.

We are assuming, of course, that you are using a 35mm camera of some kind. If you are using 126 or 110 or disk film, there are very few cameras which will deliver reasonably sharp results, but this is the fault of the cameras rather than the film. Going the other way, there is really not much point in using anything bigger than 35mm. Processing will be time-consuming and expensive, and the extra

Film reminder window

For the most part, we are just as happy with our elderly Nikons and Leicas as with modern cameras; possibly happier, because we are used to them, and therefore find them easier to use than modern wonders with hundred-page instruction books. One common feature of modern cameras which we really would like to have 'retro-fitted' to our dinosaurs is however the film reminder window, seen here on a Pentax Z-1. If you do not use a great deal of film, or if you have several camera bodies, it is extremely useful to have an incontrovertible reminder of what film you have in them. All other types of film reminder rely on your remembering to reset them, or on your replacing the film-box end in the pocket. This one is foolproof: if you have film in the camera, you can see what sort it is. There are only a few films which do not have the information in the right place for the window, including (surprisingly enough) Polaroid.

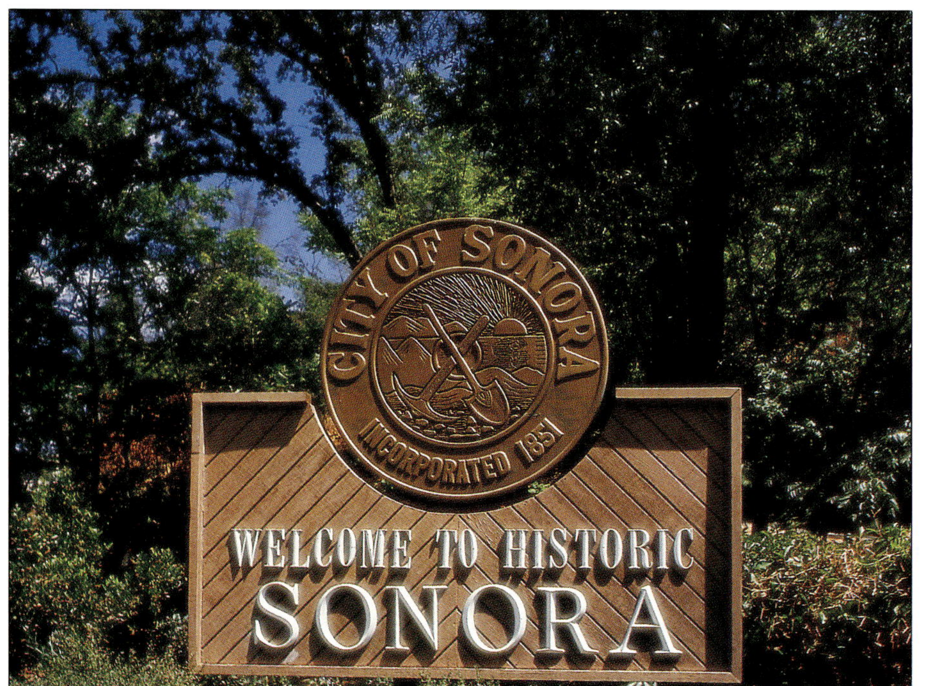

Welcome to Sonora

We are in an unusual position in that many of the pictures which most people would shoot for their albums, we shoot for publication. Either way, shots like this one are a useful continuity device to make sure that people can follow your itinerary, but you obviously want to make them as attractive as possible. In this case, the light came from almost directly overhead and gave wonderful sharpness and clarity to these two signs. Only a sharp, highly saturated film could do full justice to the subject – but as there is plenty of light, you can afford to over-expose quite drastically (at least one stop) in the interests of fine grain and saturated colours. Some labs might then print the picture too light, but you can point to the detail in the image and tell them to reprint it and get the exposure right. If you want high quality from colour prints, you must find a good lab who will do what you want. (RWH)

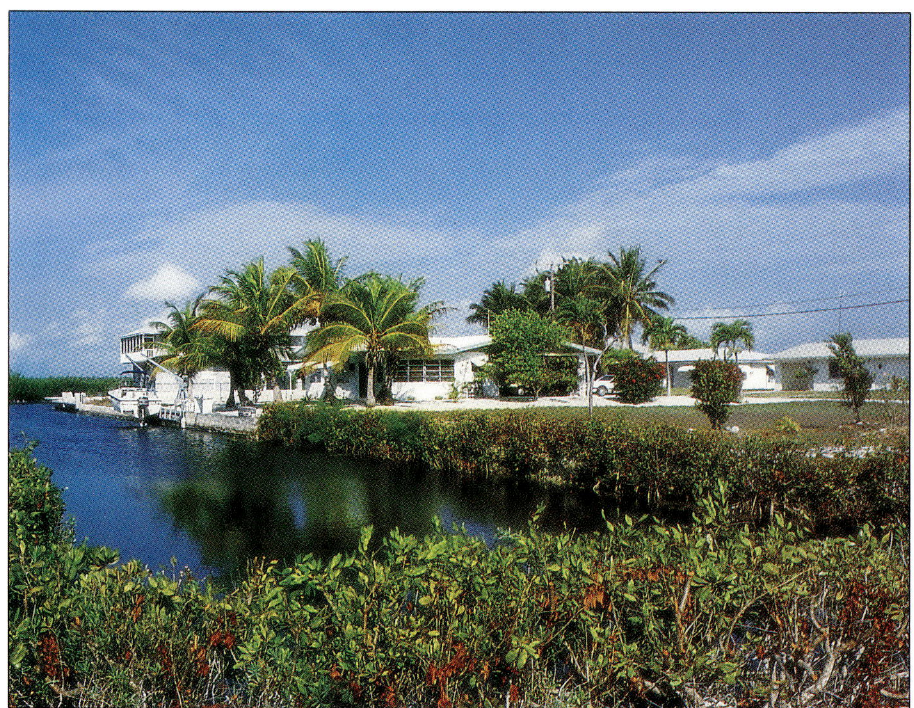

House, Florida Keys

Most automatic printers are set up to deal with precisely this kind of picture, and the results which they can deliver are likely to be first class. All the colours will probably be spot-on, with good saturation and precisely the kind of bright, sunny image which you wanted to capture in the first place. The only trouble is that the picture itself is not very interesting. It might be useful as part of an advertising brochure for the Florida Keys, and it makes an adequate souvenir of the affluence and indeed luxury which characterise the popular perception of the Sunshine State; but pictorially, it is somewhat lifeless and it is further marred by the power and phone lines on the right. America can be positively Third World when it comes to such matters: burying power cables costs too much money, so the companies would rather save a few bucks and ruin an idyllic view instead. (RWH)

San Andreas city limit

There are some pictures which you shoot purely for amusement, and it really does not matter what sort of film-stock you use: you just scatter them through your album like little humorous landmines, waiting for people to laugh when they come across them. The joke here is that this is the San Andreas that the San Andreas Fault is named after, the geological fault-line which (some say) will one day cause California to disappear into the Pacific Ocean. The idea of calling 9-1-1, the local equivalent of the British 999, in the case of an emergency on that scale is pure bathos. Often, when we are travelling, we keep one camera ready and loaded just to shoot this sort of amusing aside. Other city limits signs which we have shot are Dorky, Kansas and Dull, Tennessee; and the city of Pratt, Kansas, home of the Pratt Beavers sports team, afforded any number of entertaining exposures. (RWH)

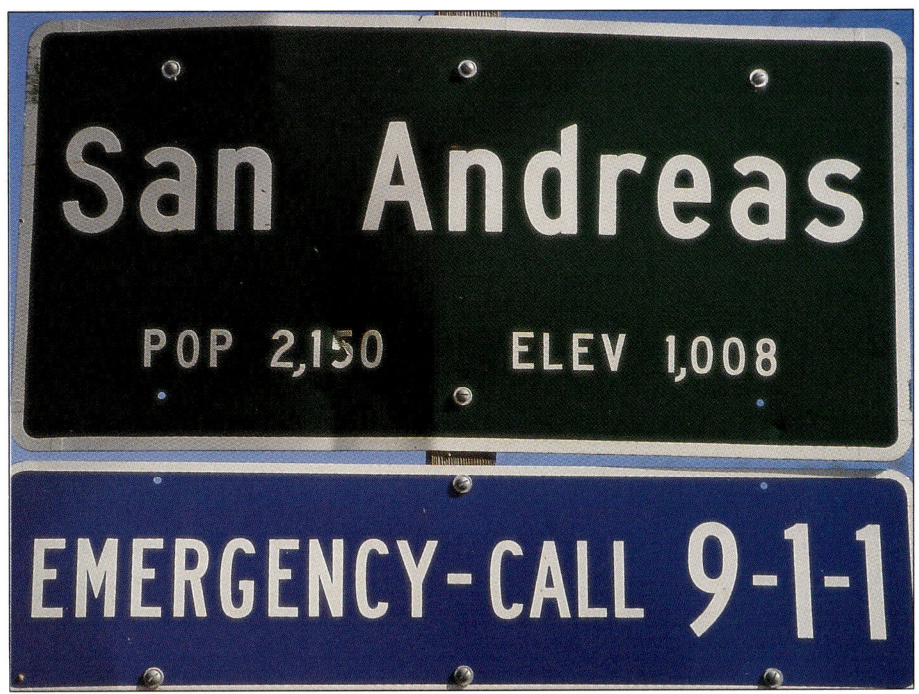

Abandoned car, Guadalupe, California

Different people have different views on what constitutes 'fine art' photography. We define it as something we would like to have on the wall. Roger, more than Frances, is something of a child of the 1960s, and this smacks of fashionable ecological concerns; but quite apart from the message, there is something compelling in the contrast between the man-made (but decaying) form of the abandoned automobile, and the burgeoning greenery around it. This was actually shot on Kodachrome 64, using a Leica M-series and a 90mm f/2 Summicron, but it would probably have made a better print if it had been shot on slow colour print film, preferably using a rollfilm camera, and then printed conventionally to maybe 16x20in or 40x60cm. (RWH)

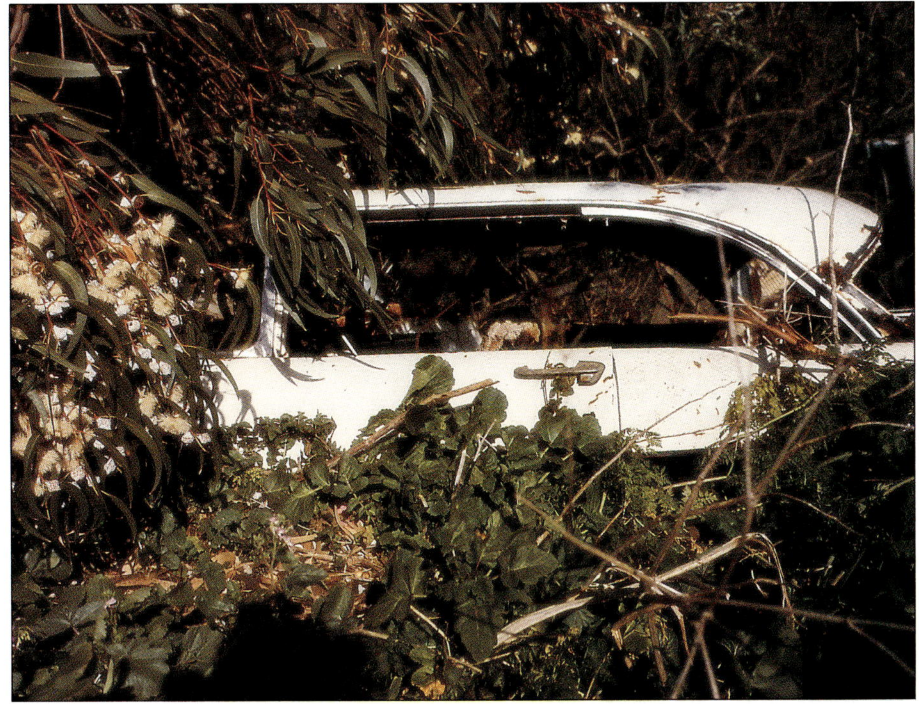

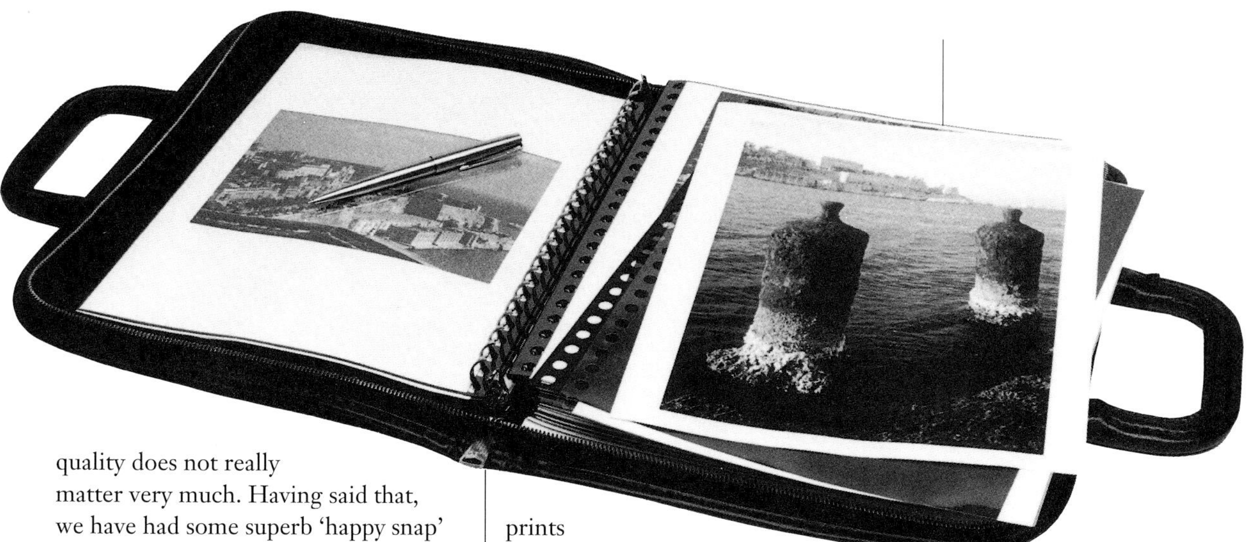

quality does not really matter very much. Having said that, we have had some superb 'happy snap' results from a Lyubitel TLR which cost us £5 ($7.50), and just to show it could be done, we also tried a 620 Kodak 'Box Brownie' which Roger's father bought in Gibraltar in 1948. It worked, but we cannot recommend it.

Video Disk

At the time of writing, video disks were a comparatively recent innovation, and it was unclear whether they would catch on. The advantages are obvious: easy storage, easy viewing on the TV, easy searching for specific pictures. The disadvantages are equally obvious: you need the video player, you cannot easily show other people the pictures without bringing them home, quality is modest, and there is always the risk that the whole system might become obsolete, leaving you with useless platters of metallised plastic.

Colour Photocopies

Modern colour photocopiers can deliver amazingly good quality, and indeed the same technology can be used to print pictures from video disks. You may care to try 'blowing up' colour prints on a colour photocopier: the results can be very impressive. We even use them sometimes for pictures to hang on the wall.

EXHIBITION PRINTS

If you want colour exhibition prints, you will of course do best to use either super-slow films such as Kodak's Ektar 25 or the various ISO 50 films on the market, or to do what the professionals do and switch to a larger format, in which case ISO 100 films will deliver all that you need – it will be far better than anything you can get from 35mm, because of the inherent limitations of 35mm lenses. Gradation will be better, too. In fact, with a 6x7cm camera you can go to ISO 400 and still get superb results at as much as 16x20in or 40x50cm.

SOCIAL PHOTOGRAPHY

Professional photographers who need to produce prints (wedding photographers, portrait photographers,

Portfolio

If you want to show off your work, you need a portfolio or 'book'. Opinions vary on the best way to present this, but we find that carrying modestly sized prints in a loose-leaf, ring-bound leather portfolio is ideal. The pictures should all be printed on the same size paper, in the interests of neatness and uniformity, though the actual image size may vary. We do not carry transparencies, because they are too hard to read, and we do not use very large pictures because we believe that if people are interested in your work, they are usually visually sophisticated enough to learn all they need from a relatively small picture. The pictures themselves are all oriented the same way, so that you do not have to turn the portfolio on its side, even if this means printing a picture very small indeed. When we lived in the United States, we mostly used colour photocopies (from Magoo's, in San Luis Obispo): scanned directly off 35mm transparencies, these looked very like the printed page. Now that we are out in the Kentish wilderness, Frances has begun to print from transparencies, using Paterson reversal materials.

etc) will almost invariably use medium format cameras. Because their subjects are normally people, they will also use special low-contrast colour films, mostly rated at ISO 160, which allow them to get good skin tones and still hold the detail in clothing from white brides' dresses to dark suits. These films are readily available from any good camera store. Processing will normally be 'professional packages' from a professional lab, though some photographers have in-house labs. Trying to break into this market on the cheap, with 35mm cameras and ISO 100 films and cheap, amateur lab-work, is a waste of time.

PUBLICATION

If the picture is interesting enough, it will not matter what it was shot on: it will be published. An example we have used elsewhere is a flying saucer landing in Times Square – do you really think that anyone would turn it down, just because it was a badly-exposed picture on out-of-date Polaroid?

A surprising number of newspapers use colour negative film for photojournalism, either scanning directly from the negative or having prints made. The main reason for their choice is the latitude of the film: not only are staff pressmen often working under difficult lighting conditions, but they are also notorious for being careless about exposure even when the conditions are right. In any case, most colour reproduction in newspapers is so awful that it would not matter what the original was shot on; there have been press photographers who used the old 110 format.

Most other colour pictures for publication had better be transparencies, though high-quality hand-prints just may be acceptable. They should be at least 5x7in or 13x18cm, and preferably 8x10in or 18x24cm. Larger prints are hard to handle and are much more susceptible to damage. They must be unmounted, or they cannot be scanned.

SLIDES AND NEGATIVES

Several companies advertise slides and prints from the same film. While there is nothing inherently implausible about this, what they are doing is selling respooled movie film which is not designed for use in still cameras. It is actually a negative film, which can then be printed both onto paper and onto positive film for slides. Not only is it reputed to scratch easily, but from the examples we have seen, we have never been very impressed with the results. These films are just about adequate for amateur use, but we would not care to use them professionally.

You can get slides from regular colour negative films by using appropriate duplicating films such as Kodak 5072. This approach requires a tungsten-light slide duplicating set up, and while it delivers surprisingly good quality, there is an inevitable loss of sharpness if you duplicate from 35mm to 35mm: 'duping down' from a larger format, such as 6x9cm to 35mm, is a much safer bet.

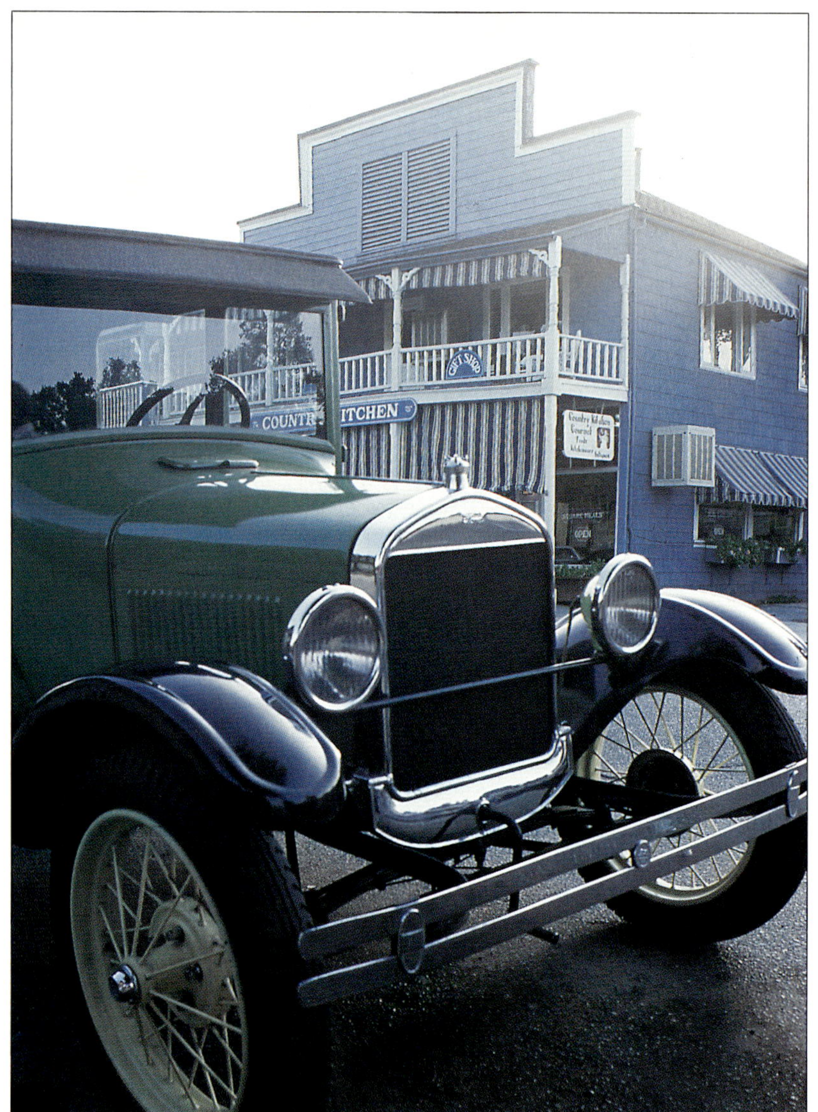

Old Ford car, Jamestown

This is the sort of atmospheric shot which can be very hard to capture on print film. We were staying in Jamestown, in California's Gold Country, and this old Ford car seemed to fit in very well with the timber western-style buildings. Frances decided to over-expose the picture slightly (it was on slide film) for two reasons. One was to get adequate exposure on the side of the car nearest the camera, and the other was to get a sort of faded, washed-out appearance which would suit the bygone subject matter. If she had been shooting on colour print film, though, this sort of over-exposure would have had precisely the opposite effect from what she wanted, as it would have increased colour saturation. She could have under-exposed, which would have meant that the picture was thinner and flatter, but it would probably have been printed too dark by any automatic printer. If you want to get this kind of effect, you must print your films yourself; or have expensive custom prints made; or (as Frances did) use slide film. (FES)

Town, Portugal

If you are interested in serious landscape photography, then (as for portraiture) you might do well to consider a medium-format camera: specifically, a technical camera like our 'baby' Linhof. The big 56x72mm image is more than four and a half times the size of a 35mm negative, and you can make exhibition prints of 16x20in or 40x50cm with confidence. What is more, you have the camera 'movements' – especially the rising front, which is invaluable for architectural photography – and if you buy second-hand, you are only looking at the same sort of money as a new shift lens for a 35mm camera! The range of available lenses is limited, it is true, and you will be lucky to find more than 65mm, 100mm or 105mm, and 180mm; but how much more do you need? We cannot recall whether we used a Technika IV or a Technika 70 for this picture – we owned both at the time – but we now use the Technika IV because although it is slightly less versatile, it is much more compact. Of course, a rollfilm camera costs slightly more to run than 35mm, but in landscape photography you are not normally shooting dozens of frames of every subject: a roll or two of film is often all you need for a very pleasant day out. (RWH)

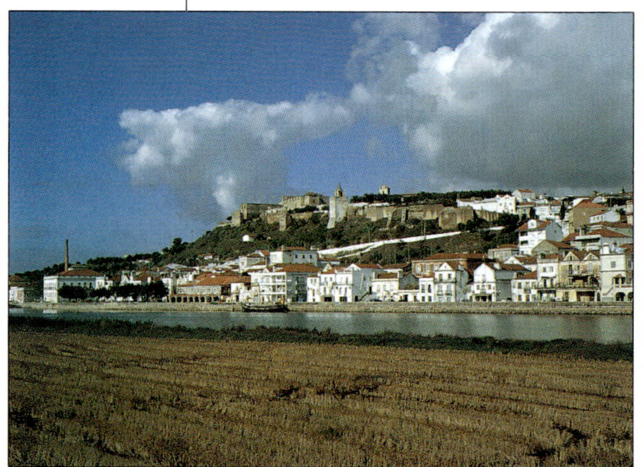

8 COLOUR SLIDE FILMS

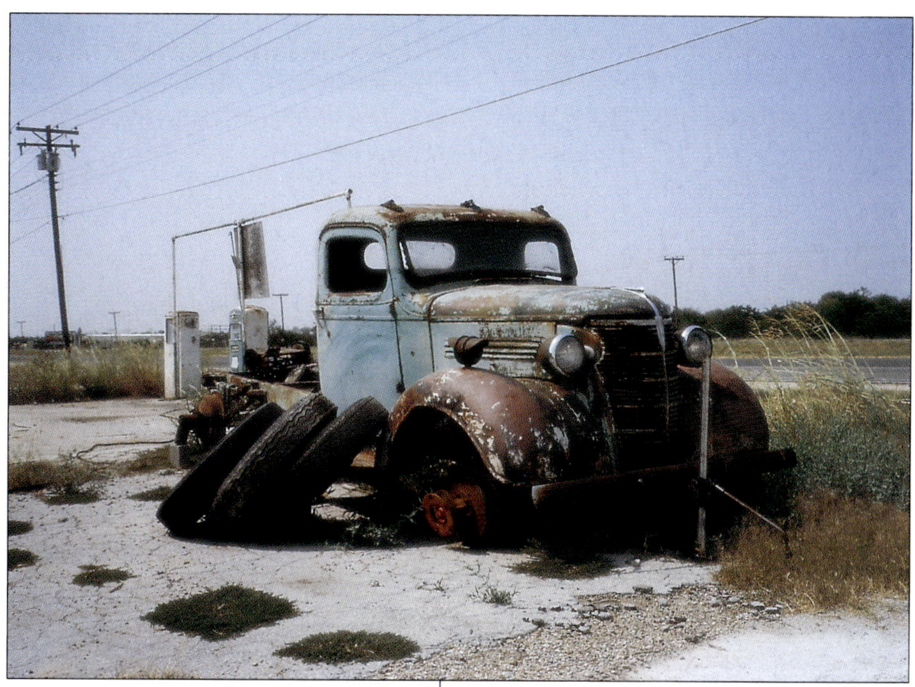

Truck at abandoned gas station

We have driven across the United States seven times in all. On the interstate highways, there is little to be seen – one strip of concrete looks much like the next – but on the older, smaller roads there are all kinds of subjects for the camera. It was presumably an Interstate which killed this old service station: with all its customers whizzing by on a new road, it just withered away and died. This was shot in the mid-1980s on the old Agfa 50RS film stock, a very neutral and moderate-saturation material which we liked a great deal. The pastel tones, rendered still paler by a slight degree of over-exposure (about half a stop), call to mind ancient postcards or old magazines, where the colours are faded and soft. The gas station probably only went out of business in the 1950s or maybe even the 1960s, but the overall mood owes much more to when it was founded: probably the 1940s. Pictures like these form a very strong argument for the 'palette' school of film choice described in Chapter 1. By the 1980s, Agfa had gone over to using Kodak Ektachrome-compatible chemistry, so their films were no longer so individualistic as they were in the 1960s, but they still retained (and retain to this day) a different 'colour signature' to both American and Japanese films. (RWH)

Colour slide films were originally designed for projection – a modern version of the old 'magic lantern' show – and indeed the first modern slide film was (like 35mm photography itself) essentially a spin-off from movie film: it was Kodachrome, which appeared in the early-to-mid 1930s.

For many years thereafter, colour photography was an expensive undertaking, whether you chose slides or prints, but slides soon established themselves as the preferred medium for reproduction. Because they were camera originals, they were inevitably sharper than prints, and this advantage is as true today as it was then.

As with colour print films, your choice of colour slide film will depend to a large extent on what you want to do with the final pictures. The main uses are for projection in slide shows and audio-visuals; for reproduction (overwhelmingly the most important professional use); and, to a very limited extent, as originals for making colour prints.

COLOUR SIGNATURES

'Colour signature' is not merely a question of colour balance, or even of the overall fidelity of colour. Rather, it is a question of how an individual film responds to individual colours. For example, Kodachrome was traditionally famous for its ability to differentiate subtle shades of red, and also for its inability to differentiate subtle shades of green. Ektachrome 64 is particularly good at blues. Konica 100 is wonderfully subtle, but (at least based on our experience when we last tried it) the saturation may be too low for some people's tastes, though we loved it. The old Orwochrome, in the days when

East Germany was still a separate country, reduced everything to a child's poster colours. Modern Orwochromes are incomparably better for most purposes, as well as being usable at the film's full rated speed, but there are times when you miss those garish hues. The fast Scotch/3M films are muted and grainy – the exact opposite of the old Orwo. And so on...

The thing about colour signatures, though, is that you can very rarely say that one is 'better' than another. It is very much a question of personal taste – and possibly even of national taste, because the Americans allegedly like bright, toy-box colours while the Germans traditionally prefer something a bit subtler.

It is also a matter of fitting the colour signature to the subject. There are some cases where you would have to be a masochist to try to use a particular film for a particular application, such as the old Ektachrome 64 for food photography. As recently as the 1980s, Ektachrome 64 was so blue that it was almost impossible to make food look appetising on it unless you used an 81EF warming filter, and even then you were pushing your luck. Modern Ektachrome 100 is an incomparably better film for this purpose!

OTHER TECHNICAL CONSIDERATIONS

Apart from colour signatures, the other technical considerations are pretty much what you would expect. For the most part, the slower films are more contrasty and finer-grained, though the traditional link between speed and colour saturation seems to be breaking down: some modern ISO 100 high-saturation films are at least as highly saturated as Kodachrome 64, and possibly more saturated than Kodachrome 25.

On the topic of the contrast and colour saturation of slow substantive films (ie all of them except Kodachrome), it is most intriguing to read Kodak's views as expressed in their catalogue. They describe almost all of their slow films (under ISO 100) as being 'for use under controlled lighting conditions', which is a virtual admission of what we have been saying all through this book: they are simply too contrasty and saturated for general photography outside the studio. Inside the studio, there is no doubt that they can deliver the most amazing quality; but using them as everyday films is like using a Formula One Ferrari for going to the shops. You can do it, sure, but there are other ways of doing it better.

PERMANENCE AND STORAGE

The permanence of colour slide films, like that of colour negative films, has improved rapidly since the 1950s and 1960s, and any reasonably sensibly stored slides should now exhibit minimal fading or colour shifts for several decades. Kodachromes will show the least deterioration, but like all films they should be stored in a dark,

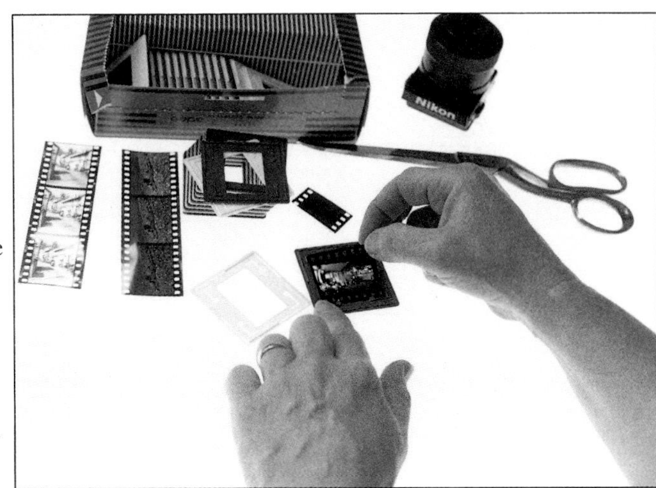

Slide mounting

There are numerous brands of slide mount on the market, to say nothing of the plastic or cardboard heat-seal mounting service offered by some labs. Some mounts are however downright flimsy, and if you want to submit slides for publication, you had better put them in mounts which can be opened without destroying them. The industry standard in glassless mounts is GePe, as shown here. Their mounts are available with and without metal masks; the masks give a very much crisper edge for projection, but we do not normally use them as our slides are intended primarily for publication. If you want to use glass slides, there are several choices, but the leading ones are GePe (again) and the alloy-clad Perrot mounts which we favour. Glass mounting is useful if you want to show the same programme again and again: the glass offers excellent protection and improves film flatness. Never send glass-mounted slides through the post (the glass sometimes breaks) and do not use curved-field projection lenses. Anti-Newton's-ring glasses will help prevent those infuriating 'crawling rainbows' which you sometimes see in glass mounted slides, and which are caused by the slide pressing against optically flat glass.

cool place with modest humidity. Prolonged exposure to light will cause any colour material to fade eventually, and Kodachromes will actually fade faster than many substantive films if they are exposed to light for long periods

Like most professional photographers and picture libraries, we store our slides in 'archival' multi-pocket sleeves. These are made by a number of manufacturers, and are chemically inert.

FILMS FOR FLAT COPYING

One last topic to cover before we go on to the various final uses for transparencies (projection, publication and printing) is the choice of colour slide films for copying original artwork, or for 'lifting' pictures from old books. You can use these as part of a slide show, or for publication (subject to copyright restrictions), or even as originals for making display prints.

We have found that slow films are ideal for this, and that in many cases the newer high-contrast films provide a useful boost in colour saturation. This is especially true when you are copying old chromolithographs, which can be a curious combination in which muted colours are used garishly. On lower saturation films, the colours can be altogether too flat.

A common problem, though, is that the white paper looks excessively blue. This is usually because of the whitening agents in the paper, which are akin to the 'blue whitener' so beloved of ancient washing-powder advertisements, though it is also true that a lot of printers' inks have a very high ultra-violet reflectivity. While we do not see this with the naked eye, some films do 'see' it, and record it as added blue. A UV or sky-light filter is normally a good idea for copying in colour.

Something we have also done in the past is to use slide film to copy monochrome originals. These can be scanned as black and white images, and the results are very satisfactory indeed. Remember, merely because you are using a colour film, you do not have to record colours on it! We found it much quicker and easier to make slides than to make copy-negatives and then prints. Not all publishers will accept them, so check first.

TRANSPARENCIES FOR PROJECTION

The most important thing in transparencies for projection is consistency. It does not necessarily matter very much what sort of film you use, as long you stick to the same sort throughout the slide show. If you suddenly switch from a fine-grain film to a coarse-grained one, or from a film with one 'colour signature' to another, it will stick out like a sore thumb.

Apart from this, the usual rules apply. If you have many pictures of people in your slide show,

Projectors

If you want to see your slides at their best, get a decent magazine projector. The old 'push-pull' type, where each slide is individually inserted in the carrier in turn from a box or stack, may be cheap, but they are very unsatisfactory. A magazine projector is much better. The professional standard today is usually the Kodak 'Carousel', with its circular magazines: the older 80-slide versions are generally the most useful, as they accept slides of any reasonable thickness and there is very little risk of jamming. Ours is a very old one, bought for $50 (about £30) at a camera show in California in about 1990. In England, Carousels are very expensive indeed, and you may prefer to buy one of the old straight-magazine types which (once again) you can often pick up for very modest prices if you watch the small ads, because many people have switched from slides to video. We paid £12 (under $20) for this one in 1992, complete with a screen – and all we wanted was the screen, which would normally cost twice as much as this if you bought it new!

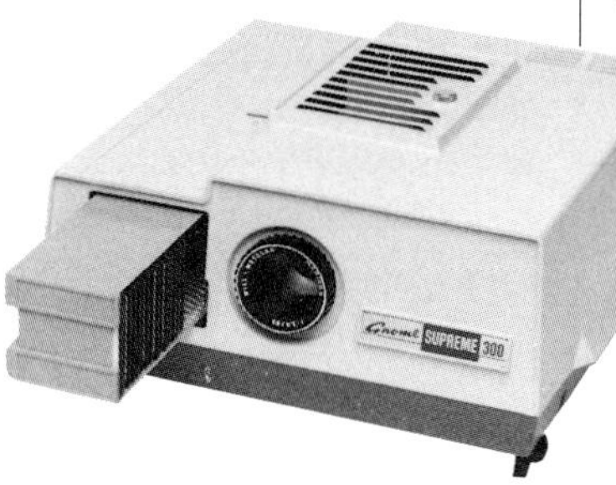

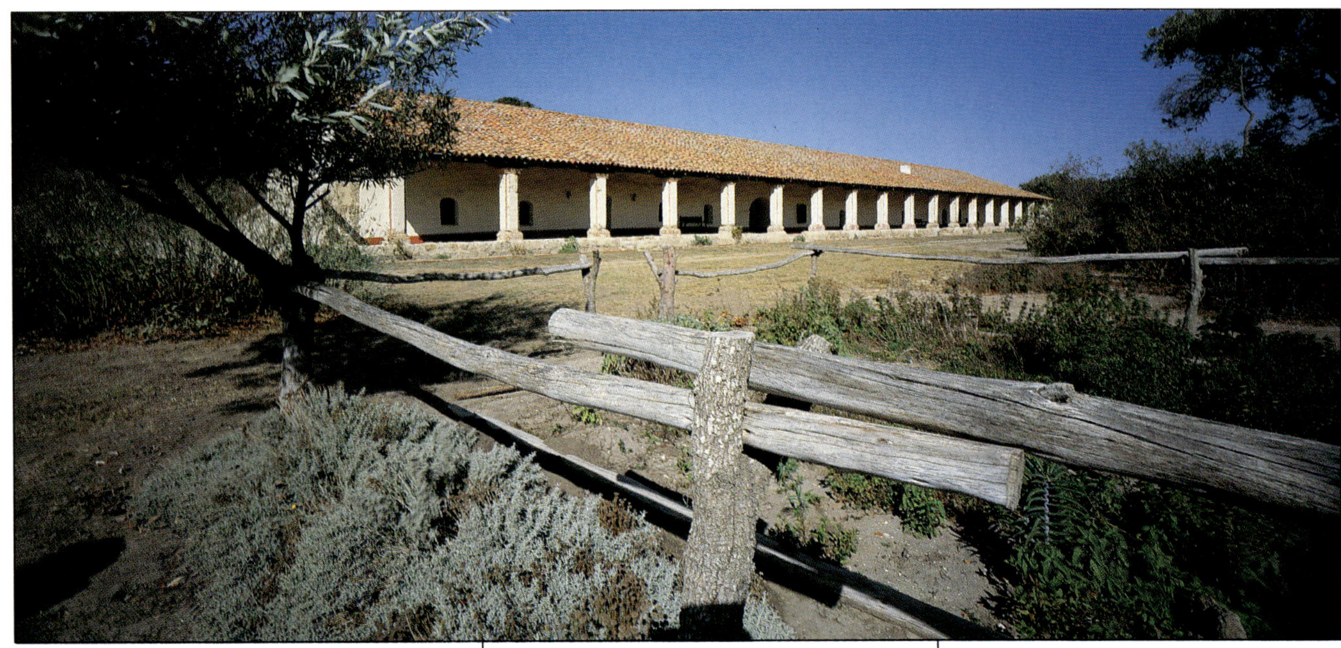

you would do better to stick with a film with more modest contrast; if you are photographing landscapes, you might do better with a high-contrast, high-saturation film. For general applications, any ISO 100 film, the 'universal slide film', will do very well, and so will Kodachrome 64. If you have a great deal of light to play with, then Kodachrome 25 is worth considering too.

If you must use different films, perhaps because some of the show was shot in good light and some in poor light, it is a good idea to try to stick with the same 'family' of films: all Kodachrome, say (25, 64 and 200) or all Agfachrome. Alternatively, you might even wish to duplicate all the slides onto one stock, using filtration to even out the variations in colour signatures.

Front Projection

A little-considered professional use of 35mm slides is for front-projecting backgrounds (and back-projection too, for that matter). Some photographers use figurative slides such as sunsets, the Manhattan skyline, and so forth, and others use abstract slides to liven up dull catalogue photographs.

Exposure for Projection

Transparencies for projection must be as carefully matched as you can get them, not just for colour balance but also for density – which means getting the exposure right! We have all seen slide shows where the picture on the screen jumped from glaring over-exposure to murky under-exposure and back again, with results which are almost physically painful when they happen and soon lead to headaches.

If you do have wildly differing densities, either as a result of poor exposure or because of the subjects you are photographing, try to put the slides

Mision de la Purisima, Concepcion

Learning to use the 6x12cm format is difficult enough, without compounding your problems by using a high-saturation, high-contrast film (Fuji Velvia) on a sunny day, and without using a super-wide lens (47mm f/5.6 Super Angulon, equivalent to about 16mm on 35mm) into the bargain. You can clearly see the effects of vignetting here: the corners of the image are quite significantly darker than the middle, though the effect is masked by the dark foliage. Given that this is from the very first roll of Velvia we ever exposed, and the very first time we used the 6x12cm back, it is not too bad; but we would have done a lot better to use ISO 100 film, which would not have exhibited anything like as much darkening at the corners, and we might also have done better to use a longer lens such as the 65mm f/8 Super Angulon or even the 100mm Symmar, both of which would also cover the format. (FES/RWH)

His Holiness the Dalai Lama

The technical quality of this shot is frankly awful, but that does not really matter very much. In fact, the weak yellow light and lack of exposure contributes to the mysterious and magical quality of the image. It was shot in Dharamsala in North India, where His Holiness has been in exile since 1959; Tibet is of course occupied by Chinese forces. The occasion was Losar, the Tibetan New Year, and these are the Losar celebrations at Thekchen Chöling temple, the 'Great-Teaching Dharma-Place'. There was next to no light – you can see a couple of feeble lamps to the right of His Holiness – and the only choice was to shoot wide open on the fastest film available, in this case using a 90mm f/2 Summicron and Scotch 1000 film, pushed one stop (which gave something like a true EI 1500); even then, the shutter speed was around 1/30 second, so there may be a hint of camera shake. If the opportunity to shoot the same subject arose again (which we hope someday will happen – or better still, we can go to Lhasa when the Chinese empire collapses), then the natural choice would be Agfa 1000 pushed to EI 2000, but the lens would still be the Summicron. To begin with, we cannot afford the 75mm f/1.4 for the Leicas, and in the second place, Roger finds that he can safely hand-hold his Leicas at one step longer on the shutter-speed dial than he can hold a reflex. This means that even if we did buy an 85mm f/1.4 for the Nikons, it would still have the same effective speed: he would have to use it at 1/60 where he would use the Summicron at 1/30. (RWH)

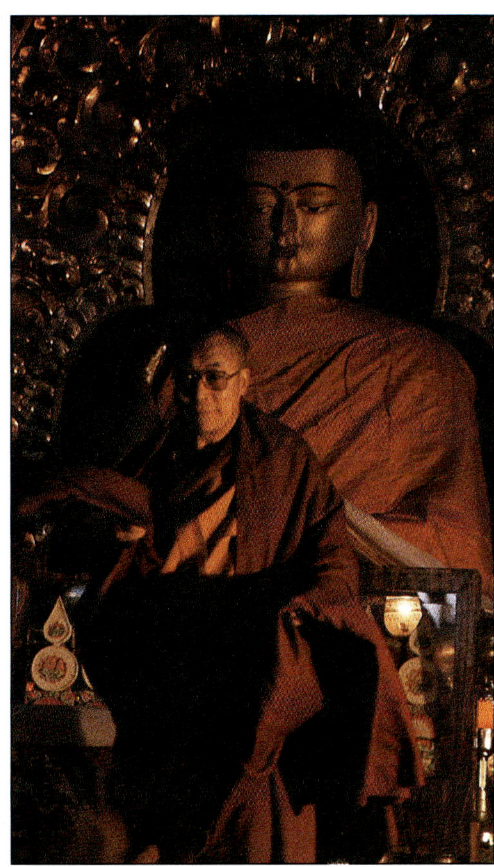

Wet rock face

By the time we took this picture, we had rather more experience of both Velvia and the 6x12cm format than we had when we took the pictures of the Mision. This is a disused railway cutting in Kilmacolm, just near Glasgow, and the weather was a mixture of showers and weak sunshine – exactly the sort of conditions where Velvia's ability to 'punch up' colours is at its best. The wet rock face and the foliage provide a riot of contrasting textures in close proximity to one another, and slightly generous exposure (we rated the film at EI 32) meant that we captured all kinds of subtle tones within the wet rock itself. The lens was a 135mm f/8 Schneider Repro-Claron, probably working at about f/16. This necessarily implied a long shutter speed of maybe 1/4 second, which explains the continuous streams of water which are visible against the cleft on the upper right. Obviously, our appreciation of the picture is coloured by our recollections of taking it, but it seems as if you can almost smell the wet earth and the rank vegetation, while the sunlight on the foliage cascading down from the upper part of the shot carries the promise of spring. This shot simply would not have been so successful on any other film stock than Velvia. (RWH/FES)

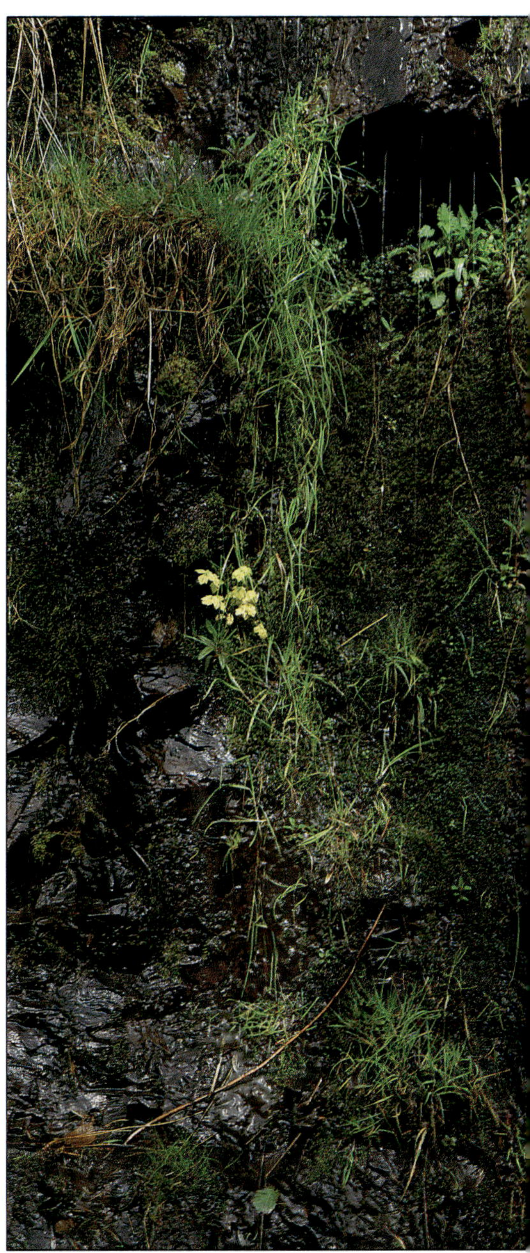

into a sequence where the transitions are reasonably gentle. A single slide of intermediate density, interposed between a very dark slide and a very bright slide, can make an immense difference; and if you can make the gradation subtler than that, so much the better.

Unless you have a very powerful projector, you will almost certainly find that the best slides for reproduction are not the same as the best slides for projection. Slides for projection should generally be a little lighter than slides for reproduction: anything from a third of a stop to two-thirds of a stop.

Projecting Larger Formats

The vast majority of slides for projection are of course 35mm, but there is something to be said for larger formats. A 6x6cm or (better still) 6x7cm transparency looks absolutely gorgeous on the screen, and of course the extra area means that not only is there more detail: you can also pour a lot more light through it.

Of course, all slides for projection should be in the same format – switching from 'landscape' (horizontal) to 'portrait' (vertical) and back again never looks very good – and square slides are a very good way around this. A superb format for projection is 'superslide', which is nominally 4cm square but which is actually closer to 38x38mm. The great thing about this format is that it fits into standard 2x2in (5x5cm) slide mounts, just like 35mm, and can be projected in the same projectors. With an area some 67 per cent greater than full-frame 35mm, it is a lot brighter on the screen. The traditional way to make 'superslides' was with 127 film, exposed in something like a 'Baby Rollei', but now that there are no 127 slide films left on the market, you have to cut down larger formats – masked 645 is very effective, as it is already the right size in one dimension. You may even find 'superslide' backs for some 6x6cm cameras.

PUBLICATION

The vast majority of colour pictures which you see in books and magazines are made from transparencies. The slide is taped to the glass drum of a 'scanner', which revolves very rapidly. A xenon light source, mounted on a lead screw inside the drum, scans the transparency from side to side: the vertical component of the scan is of course handled by the revolving drum. Photo-electric cells outside the drum, opposite the light source, register both the colour and the density of the transparency, and the output is by laser to four sheets of black and white film: one each for cyan, magenta and yellow, and one for black. The printing plates are made from these films or 'separations'. The term 'laser scanner' refers of course to the output: the actual scanning cannot be done by laser, because a continuous-spectrum white light is required for scanning.

You can get quite extraordinary quality from 35mm originals if they are scanned – certainly far better than all but the best colour prints – but for the ultimate quality you need a very highly skilled printer and first-quality paper and inks. The main determinant of image quality is the dot size: obviously, the smaller each dot is, the better the final picture can be made. Dot sizes are still often referred to as 'screens', dating

Captioned slide

If you want to submit slides for publication, or even if you just want to keep them filed neatly, a slide captioning program is a good investment. We use SlideScribe's LabelBase, which gives four lines of highly legible caption per label and which also allows all kinds of search programs to help you find your slides – you can search by up to four key-words. The only drawbacks to this kind of program are that you need to have a dot-matrix printer (and a computer!) and that there is no room for a thumb-spot. A thumb-spot is a dot placed in the lower left-hand corner of the front of the slide: when the slide is correctly positioned in the magazine or carrier for projection, it is in the top right-hand corner as seen from the back of the projector – in just the right position, in fact, for the thumb of a right-handed person.

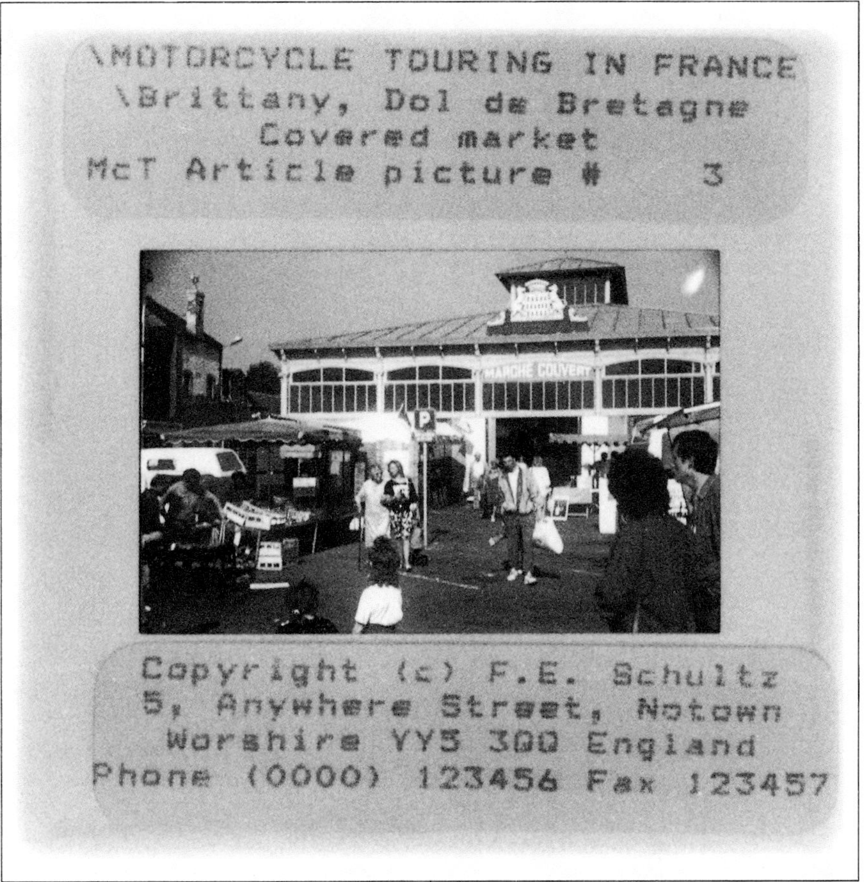

from the days when the separations were made with big process cameras, through screens which broke the image up into dots.

For obvious reasons, the old screens came with fixed dot sizes, also known as 'line' sizes because the screens were physically ruled with lines: a 133 line screen, for example, had 133 lines per inch. Today, dot sizes can be varied more or less continuously. Low-quality printing is typically in the 50-100 line range, though it can fall as low as 30 line, and normal good-quality printing (the sort found in this book) is typically in the range of 150 to 180 line, though it can fall as low as 130 or 120 line. The very highest quality printing can be well over 200 line and as high as 300 line, though the finer it gets, the harder it is to control: there is an ever-increasing risk of 'blocking' and 'bleeding', where the dots are too close together and the colours run together as a result. Very high quality printing requires special papers, which are far more expensive than the blade-coated papers used in books like this.

For anyone who wants to convert 'lines' to dots per centimetre or millimetre, the truth is this: like 5x4in film, this is one of those things which is

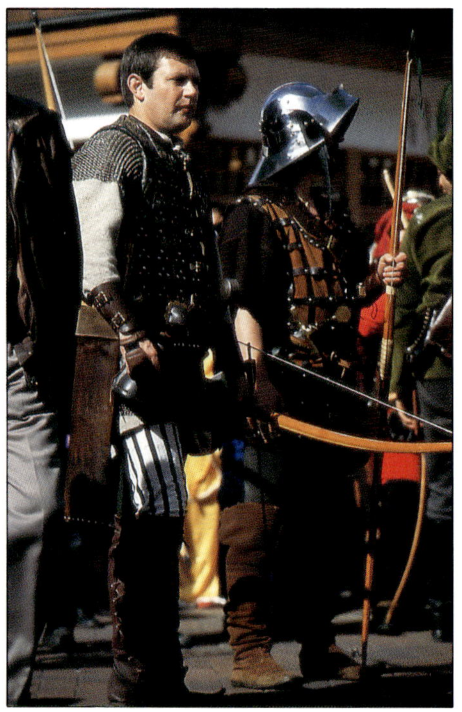

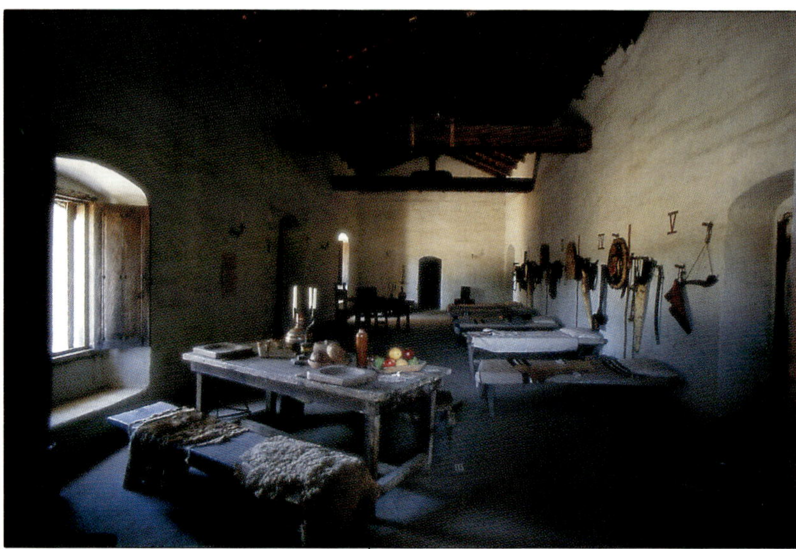

Re-enactors, Canterbury

When you are shooting subjects like these, you have to strike a balance between a natural desire to record the bright colours worn by the re-enactors, and the dangers of excessive contrast. So-called 'high-contrast' or 'high-saturation' films, used with high contrast lenses, can give you poster-like colours which look downright unnatural. They are all right with zoom lenses, where the contrast is inherently lower (this was shot on ISO 50 film with a zoom lens), but if you are using a compact camera with a high-quality lens of fixed focal length, you may well find that you will get very much better results with normal-contrast ISO 100 material. You will also save money into the bargain, as almost any good, modern ISO 100 print film should give first-class results with subjects like this if exposed in a compact camera – or, of course, in any camera with contrasty lenses, such as a Leica M-series. With really flary lenses, on the other hand, a high-contrast film would be the obvious choice: this would be the case (for example) with the 50mm f/2 Jupiter or the 85mm f/2 Jupiter for the old Russian Zorkii rangefinder cameras. (RWH)

Cuartel, *Mission de la Purisima Concepcion*

The cuartel (soldiers' quarters) of this restored mission near Lompoc in central California is made as far as possible to look as if the Spanish soldiers who once manned it might return at any moment. You can only photograph it through the windows, and the overhanging eaves, small windows and dark roof combine with white-painted walls to create a subdued, cool light with a surprisingly restricted tonal range. If Roger had used ISO 50 film, it would have emphasised the pools of light by the windows and the darkness of so much of the rest of the room, but using ISO 100 film captured the overall sense of coolness and darkness. The light coming through the windows is principally sky-light, which is why it is so blue: the sun is shining on the other side of the building. It would have been possible to correct this with an 81-series filter, but the blueness adds still further to the coolness. Earlier in the day, when the sun is on the window side of the room, the light is much harsher and the overall impression would be sunnier. In our own 100-year-old house, as in this 200-year-old mission, the rooms are arranged so that the early-morning sun streams through the windows and wakes you, while the evening sun lights the rooms where you would relax towards the end of the day, before going to bed in a room where the sun no longer shines. (RWH)

set up in inches, and always measured in inches. If you insist, 100 lines is about 40 lines per centimetre; you can work the others out from there.

Colour Fidelity in Photomechanical Reproduction

There isn't any. Photomechanical reproduction is as much an art as a science, and printers' inks are not pure colours. A master printer makes all his (or more rarely, her) adjustments by eye, and different printers' interpretations of what is best will vary widely. Also, the scanners themselves have to be set up to read different kinds of films, and if the film that is being scanned is not one that is on the list of master programs, it will probably be scanned as if it were the film that it looks most like.

On the other hand, in any given

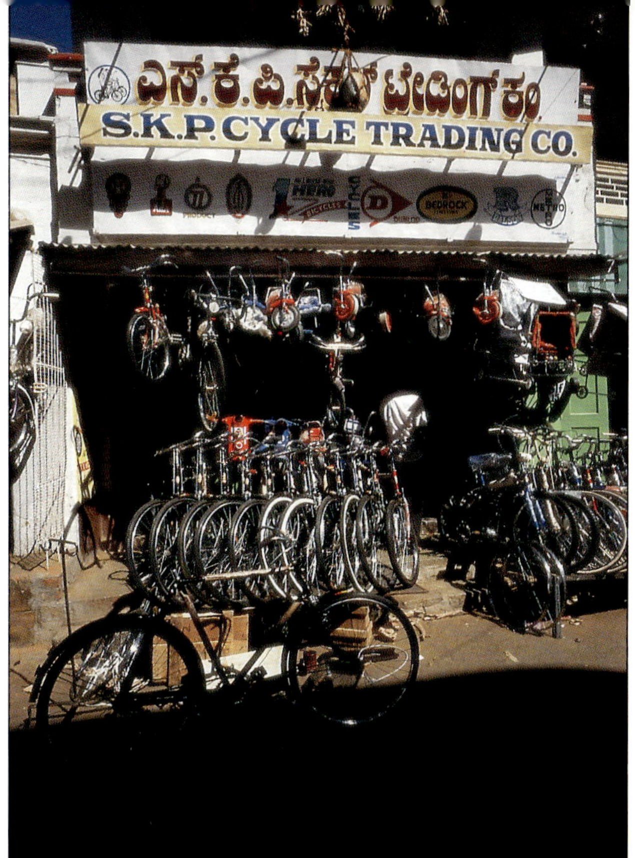

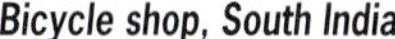

Bicycle shop, South India

Because the primary interest in this picture is in the bright colours and tropical light, the logical choice is ISO 50 Fuji RFP rather than ISO 100 RDP – though arguably, Kodachrome 64 could substitute equally well for either, and would have been less demanding when it came to storage. We were travelling by motorcycle, so we simply did not have room to carry as many camera bodies as we would have liked: normally, we carry two colour bodies and one black and white body, so that the colour bodies can be loaded with (say) ISO 50 and ISO 100, or ISO 100 and ISO 1000, while the black and white body is loaded either with Ilford XP-2 or Ilford Delta 100. The exposure in this case was based on a straight full-sun incident light reading, which guaranteed adequate exposure of the bright, white paintwork and bright, saturated colours for the bicycles, but necessarily implied inky-black shadows in the interior of the shop and very dark shadows in the foreground. High-saturation films (which are normally high-contrast as well) are generally much more useful in the studio or in temperate climes than they are in the tropics; where they are used at all in contrasty light, they must be used with discretion. (RWH)

Teatro Calderon, Zacatecas, Mexico

This picture was shot by Frances, but it is Roger's fault! Frances has a considerable interest in theatre – both her BA and MA are in theatre-related studies – and she wanted to photograph this nineteenth-century colonial-style theatre. She borrowed Roger's camera (he normally carries colour, and she carries black and white), but he inadvertently gave her a camera body loaded with tungsten-balance film. Exposing it by daylight, or at least by twilight, meant that the overall effect was very blue. Even so, the picture 'works' because the tungsten-lit entrance to the theatre looks very warm and welcoming, which is exactly the way that the theatre should be. The camera was a Leica M-series, mounted on a tripod; the lens was a 35mm f/1.4 Summicron; and the film was 3M/Scotch 640T, with a nominal ISO 640 speed, though we normally rate it a little slower. The exposure would have been bracketed, but we cannot remember what it was. This was the lightest bracket, because we both thought the camera was loaded with the rather faster ISO 1000 daylight material. (FES)

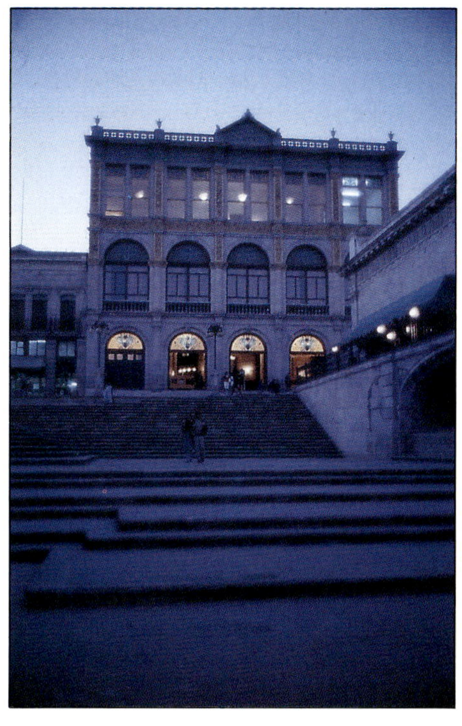

publication there is likely to be a high degree of consistency in the actual printing – at least on each sheet! You cannot, therefore, mix and match different film-stocks and expect the printing process to obscure the differences between them. In fact, the differences may even be accentuated in some cases. It is therefore advisable, though far from essential, to follow the same advice as for slide shows. Ideally, stick to the same film-stocks for a single publication, or at least, stick to the same 'family' (Kodachrome, Ektachrome, Fuji, etc). The only exception to this advice is when you want to achieve a particular effect in a particular picture – the 'palette' approach referred to in Chapter 1. You can see from this book how wide the variations can be between different stocks.

Reproduction from 35mm Originals

For photojournalism or reportage, and for many other applications where ultimate quality is not essential, 35mm has become the norm for colour reproduction. Indeed, some magazines insist on 35mm originals for editorial use, and will only accept larger formats if they really want the pictures very badly indeed.

Exactly which film you choose will depend on your subject, and the publication for which you are shooting. Historically, printers greatly preferred Kodachromes, but they are much more flexible today and will accept virtually any film.

The ancient advice holds good, that you should always use the film which will allow the best possible quality, and for most applications this will mean either Kodachrome or ISO 100 'universal' film. If there are no people in the pictures, or if you are shooting under controlled lighting conditions, or of you want high contrast and saturation for some reason, then by all means use an ISO 50 film; but as usual, it may be too saturated and too contrasty for some applications, even though it will also be sharper and finer grained.

Use faster films only when you need them, or when you want the particular effects that they give. To see what colour films can and cannot do, get hold of a recent copy of *National Geographic*. The standard of writing is generally abysmal, and the standard of photography varies widely, but the standard of reproduction is about as good as it gets in any magazine, and almost all the editorial material is shot on 35mm. The graininess of the different films is clearly visible.

Reproduction from Larger Formats

Although it is possible to get very good quality indeed from a 35mm original, it is possible to get even better quality from larger originals. For magazine advertising, larger formats such as 6x7cm and 4x5in are very much the norm, and most book publishers also prefer larger formats. So do most of the people who commission corporate reports and the like.

To some extent, this is a matter of conservatism and living in the past, especially when it comes to the difference between top-quality 6x7cm and ordinary 4x5in: at normal reproduction sizes (up to about 8x11in or A4), with ordinary reproduction, there really should be no discernible difference. On the other hand, the difference between rollfilm and 35mm will be readily discernible.

In the United States, there seems to be a much greater willingness to work from 35mm originals, even for studio photography, but in the rest of the world, rollfilm and cut-film formats are preferred. Indeed, using rollfilm or cut film in the United States will probably give you an edge there, too – and it is always worth remembering that in relative terms, the book publishing industry in the United States is far smaller than it is in Britain, which probably leads the world in the origination of photographically illustrated books.

Given that for studio use you are usually working with controlled lighting, you can cheerfully use any slow film. We find, though, that the extra speed of ISO 100 film is useful, because it allows us to stop down more than you could with ISO 50. This can be extremely useful in (for example)

Black and white conversion from slide

Quite often, publishers will want to use a colour slide as a black and white image in reproduction – a 'conversion'. The best conversions are very good indeed, but the worst of them are very bad, and you may find it a better idea to make copy-negatives from your slides, using the kind of copy set-up shown on page 127 or simply turning the head of your enlarger upside-down and putting a piece of opal acrylic sheet (Perspex or Lucite) across it as a diffuser: this was 'duped' using the colour head from our Meopta enlarger. You may wish to increase exposure by a stop, and cut development by 15 per cent, or you may find that the contrast of your 'dupe' is excessive. This picture appears by permission of Artie Schultz, Frances's father: it is from his quarter-plate Kodachrome which appears on page 55. This has been 'flopped' (or 'flipped' – reversed left for right) so that you can see the Kodachrome edge marking. (W. A. Schultz)

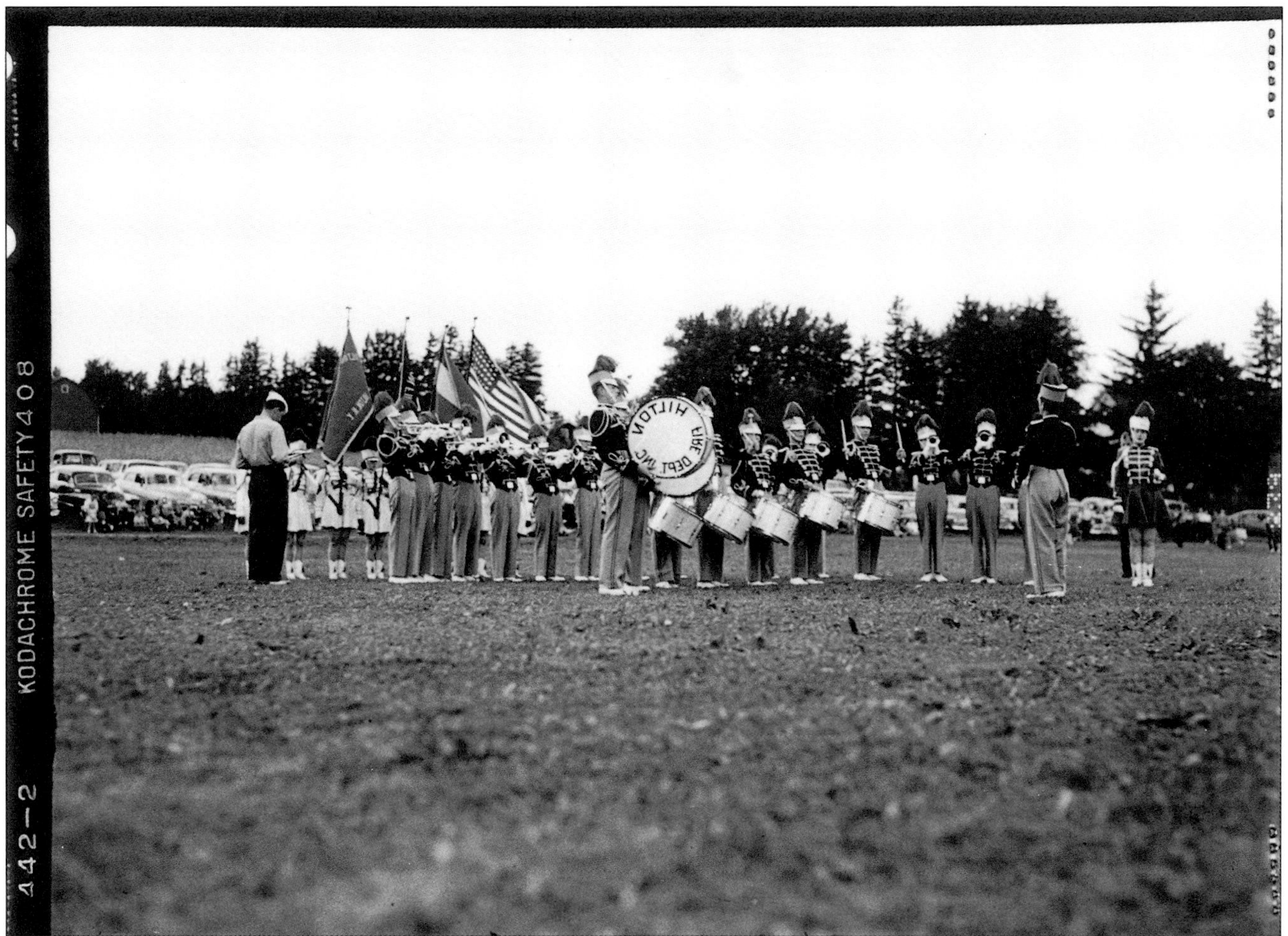

food photography, where the ability to use f/32 instead of f/22 translates into a welcome increase in depth of field. Because the lighting is controlled, you can effectively vary contrast and saturation by varying lighting ratios and exposure. There is, therefore, rarely any need for high-saturation films, though you can get them.

Only very rarely would a studio photographer consider using anything faster than ISO 100, and availability of fast 120 films and cut films is very limited in comparison with availability of fast 35mm films. We have however tried food photography with Agfa ISO 1000 on 6x7cm, and it gives an effect which may not be fashionable at the moment, but which could become so.

PRINTS FROM SLIDES

Several highly skilled photographers believe that the very best colour prints are made from slides, rather than from negatives. The Ilfochrome Classic process (formerly Cibachrome) is generally reckoned to lead the market,

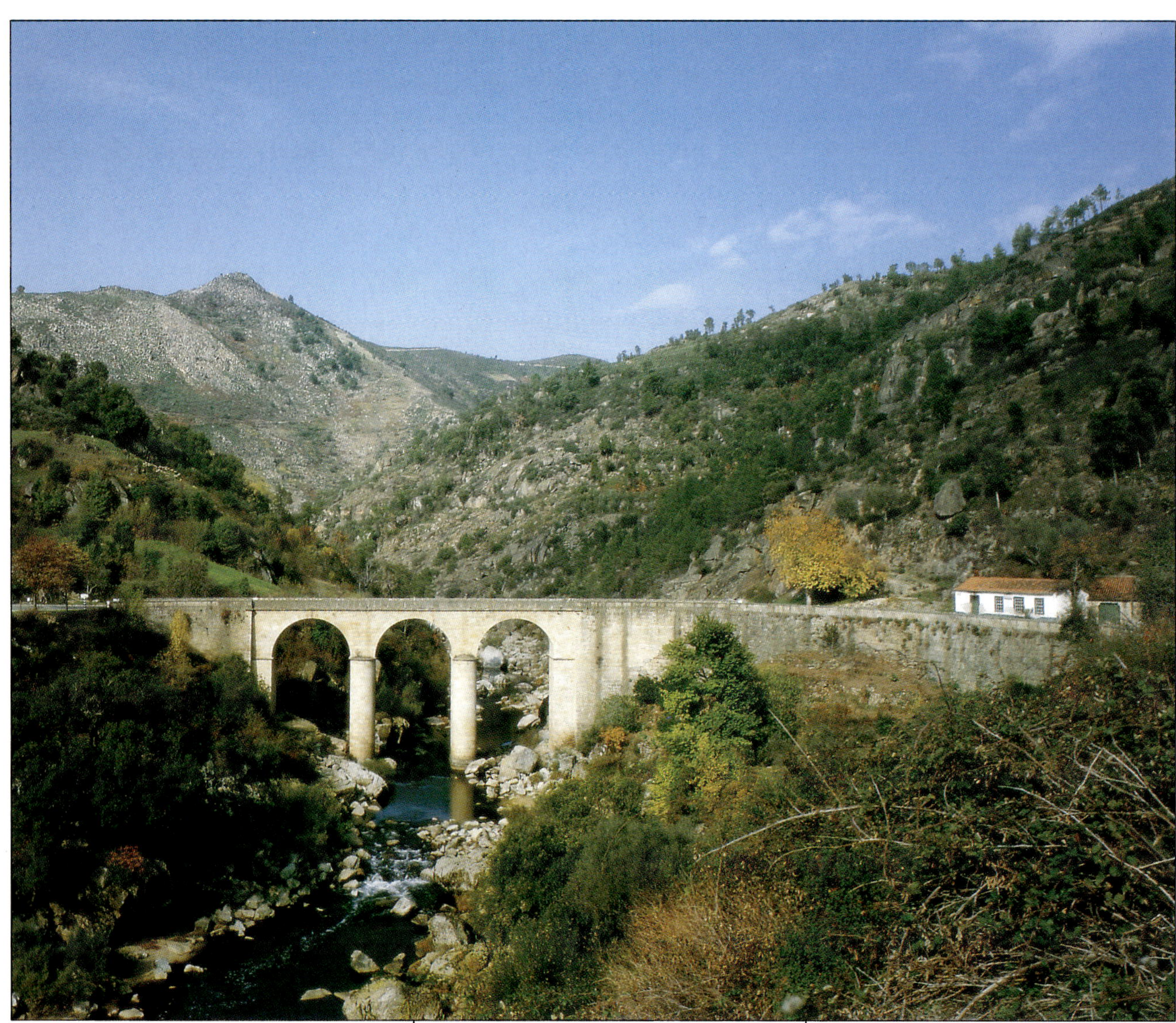

Near Chaves, Portugal

At one time, we used to travel quite a lot carrying our Linhof medium-format cameras. This was shot with a Linhof Super Technika IV, using Ektachrome 64 in a rollfilm back giving an image 56x72mm, Linhof's interpretation of the nominal 6x7cm size. Eventually, though, we realised that a great deal of the quality which we got from our rollfilm shots was not actually due to the larger format. Rather, it was the result of the extra time and effort which we put into taking the pictures: putting the camera on a tripod, levelling it carefully, taking numerous exposure readings, and so forth. If you mount your 35mm camera on a tripod, stop down to the optimum aperture (typically f/8 or f/11), and generally take the picture with the same degree of care and effort as you would use for larger formats, the results can be very good indeed. This is especially true if you are shooting for photomechanical reproduction, where a camera original can be scanned and output to film without any quality loss. If you are more interested in making colour prints, where there is an inevitable loss of sharpness at the enlarging stage, then you would probably do better to stick with the larger format. (RWH)

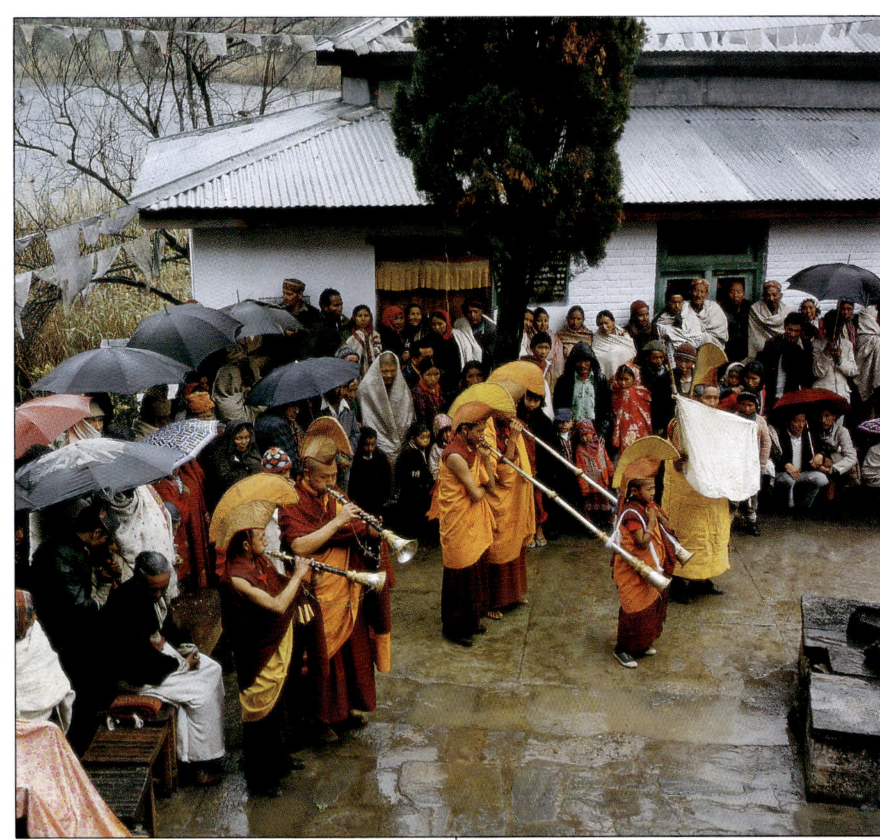

Cham Dances, Tso Pema

In the early 1980s we did quite a lot of work for the Tibetan Government in Exile. With Ngakpa Chögyam, Roger wrote Great Ocean, *an authorised biography of the Dalai Lama, and we also produced a propaganda book,* Hidden Tibet. *This is one of the few travel photographs that Roger ever took with his Hasselblad – a superb camera, but one which (for some reason) he was never terribly comfortable with. In those days, we used Ektachrome 64 out of habit, and when we look back at the pictures now, they seem very blue. This one is particularly blue, because of the weather. If we were reshooting now, there would be a strong argument for using either a Linhof or one of the big rollfilm Fuji rangefinders to make master negatives on colour print film using ISO 400 material, then duplicating these negatives onto 35mm slides. The reason for this somewhat roundabout path is to make sure not only that the master negatives would never leave our possession, but also that there would be almost no temptation for anyone to try to borrow them. It is all too easy to borrow a slide and not return it, and one might be tempted to loan it to avoid the bother of making a duplicate; but with a negative, where a print or a duplicate has to be made anyway, the temptation is very much less. Where multiple copies of a picture are required for library or propaganda use, this is a useful approach. (RWH)*

though it is very expensive, and other reversal processes are also very good. When a friend of ours, Lewis Lang, conducted exhaustive experiments to try to get the very best results from 35mm, he found that Kodachrome 25 printed on Ilfochrome Classic was detectably superior to conventional prints made from Ektar 25. He showed us the results, from originals shot using Zeiss lenses on a Contax, and with 16x20in (40x50cm) prints, he was undoubtedly right. The only question is, how many among us make exhibition colour prints this size from 35mm? Or use equipment this expensive?

Another advantage of Ilfochrome Classic is that it is an extraordinarily stable material, which should outlast any conventional colour print by a factor of ten or more. The dye-destruction chemistry is unique.

The problem in making prints from slides lies in contrast control, and you need either to use masking techniques (touched upon at the end of the last chapter) or low-contrast 'paper' – we use quotation marks because Ciba-chrome/Ilfochrome Classic is in fact coated on a white plastic base. It also helps to use a low-contrast original, which (apart from its sharpness) is why Lewis used Kodachrome 25 rather than any of the newer high-contrast materials. There is more about making prints from slides in the next chapter.

9 WORKROOM FILMS AND SPECIAL TECHNIQUES

There are many workroom and special-application films and techniques which can be exploited to solve technical problems, as well as for creative purposes. These films and techniques include making prints or display transparencies from slides, and slides from negatives; duplicating transparencies; copying black and white images; making small copy negatives from unmanageably large old negatives; making high-contrast black and white images; and seriously specialist activities such as photomicrography, cathode ray trace recordings, and so forth.

PRINTS AND DISPLAY TRANSPARENCIES FROM SLIDES

It may seem a trifle perverse to want to make prints from slides, but there are strong arguments for doing so. Prints from slides can be sharper and more permanent than prints from negatives. A display transparency is like a print, except that it is designed to be transilluminated: it may have a clear film base, so that it has to be displayed on a light box, or it may have an opal base. There are several ways of making display transparencies and prints from transparencies.

Internegatives

The traditional way to make a print or a display transparency from a slide was via an internegative. The slide was re-photographed onto negative film, and usually enlarged in the process, then printed onto conventional colour print film. We have no hesitation in saying that we cannot see why this process survives. The final print is a third-generation image, and quality is always inferior to a first-class reversal print, made directly from a transparency.

Ilfochrome Classic ('Cibachromes') and R-Types

As mentioned in the last chapter, the acknowledged leader among exhibition and display materials is Ilfochrome Classic, commonly referred to by its old name of Cibachrome, often abbreviated just to Ciba (pronounced 'Seeba' – the Ciba-Geigy company used to own Ilford). A Ciba made off a high-quality transparency is a joy to behold, and the only real objection to the process is the price. Another advantage of a Ciba, which is made by a dye-destruction process, is that it is one of the most permanent forms of colour print yet devised. This material is available both on an opaque ground and on an opal ground for use as a display transparency.

There are various other reversal processes, generically known as 'R-types', though this strictly refers to Kodak's materials. Although R-types are not quite as good as Cibas, they are still superb: we know of one amateur who never won a print contest until he switched to R-types, since when he has been a regular prizewinner. R-types are cheaper than Cibas, but still not cheap.

Dye-Transfer and Related Processes

Another possibility for making prints from slides is dye-transfer printing, which is based on colour separations

Duplicating set-up

Sometimes, if you are lucky, you can find old professional equipment like this Bowens Illumitran duplicator for very modest prices: maybe as little as a tenth of the new price. For the most part, amateurs do not know what they are and do not realise how useful they could be, while professionals may not frequent the places where you find them. The main purpose of the Illumitran is copying slides, but we also use it for making slides from negatives (using a special Kodak negative film); for making black and white negatives from slides (generally using Ilford FP4 rated at EI 50 and under-developed to reduce contrast); and even for making 35mm negatives directly from negatives which are inconveniently large to print. The choice of a Leica-plus-Visoflex may seem a little eccentric, but (as so often) it is the result of historical accident. To begin with, the Visoflex shows 100 per cent of the 24x36mm format: many SLRs 'trim' the edges. Second, the motor is extremely useful, as it means you do not have to touch the camera (and perhaps move it) in order to wind on. We do not normally use motor drives, but we just happened to have one for the Leica. Then, the Leica bellows (which we bought silly-cheap) is a very good unit, with its own focusing track so that the whole bellows and camera unit can be moved up and down.

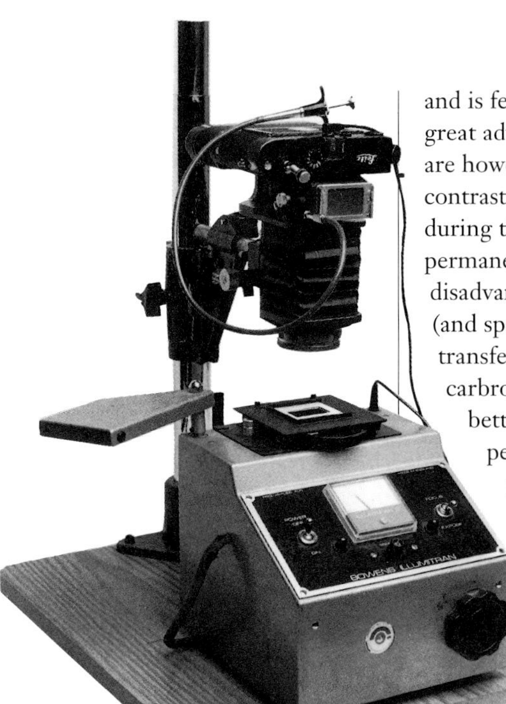

and is fearsomely complicated. The great advantages of dye transfer prints are however that the colours and the contrast can be manipulated extensively during the printing process, and that permanence is very good indeed. The disadvantages are cost, and the time (and space!) needed to make dye-transfer prints. The old tri-chrome carbro process arguably gives even better results and even greater permanence, but with a processing time of about two and a half hours, the process has fallen into disfavour.

There is an even weirder and more time-consuming French process, apparently based on the Fresson or Artigue processes: it involves abrading the image with a mixture of sawdust and water, but gives immense permanence and unparalleled quality. When we last checked, there was one lab in France capable of carrying out this process, and another in Canada, and both had waiting lists for processing; but details of the process were secret.

SLIDES FROM NEGATIVES

Slides made from negatives have two major advantages over camera originals. One is that you have the exposure latitude of the original negative, and the other is that you do not let your precious camera original out of your control.

The only convenient way to make slides from negatives, at least at the time of writing, was to use a Kodak Vericolor slide film. This was only available in bulk, at a rather stiff price, and you loaded it into your own 35mm cassettes. Then, using a tungsten-source slide copier (see below), you simply copied the negative onto this film and had it processed by the standard Kodak colour negative process.

SLIDE DUPLICATING

There are various types of slide duplicator on the market, ranging from cheap devices which clip onto the front of a camera lens (or replace the lens entirely) to very expensive stages which are used with a copying stand.

If you are serious about slide duplicating, you would do well to look out for a second-hand professional unit such as the Bowens Illumitran (which uses electronic flash) or one of the tungsten-source units which is effectively an enlarger head turned upside down. In fact, you can do just that: take a colour enlarger head, and turn it upside down so that the light source becomes a light platform. Before you do so, though, make sure that the bulb will still give a normal life in this position: some bulbs are designed to burn in a particular position, and their life will be gravely shortened if they are held in another one (cap up, cap down, etc). The manufacturer can normally tell you whether a specific lamp-housing is suitable for use as a slide copier. We use a Meopta colour head when we want to use a tungsten-balanced film for copying.

A continuous (tungsten) source has two advantages. First, you can get a much wider range of duplicating films than are available for electronic flash, and second, you can simply dial in filtration instead of using separate filters. The countervailing advantages of the Illumitran, on the other hand, are that it is cooler and that there is much less likelihood of camera shake during exposure, because the exposure is made by flash.

Duplicating Films

The difference between a duplicating film and a 'normal' film is one of contrast. If you use an ordinary camera film to make duplicates, you will (unless you take special precautions) end up with an image that is significantly more contrasty than the original.

There are several duplicating films which are balanced for tungsten illumination and exposures in the 1/10 second to 10 second range – or even in the 1/4 second to 16 second range. Although you can filter a flash source to the right colour, the short duration of the electronic flash may mean that you end up with crossed curves (page 49) and more or less lousy duplicates. You would be well advised, therefore, to use tungsten-balance films only with tungsten-source slide copiers.

At the time of writing, the only duplicating film balanced for electronic flash and short exposure times came from Kodak: its code name was SO-366, though of course a policy of updating means that it could be replaced at any time. This film can for some reason be extraordinarily difficult to find. In the United States in particular, even professional dealers will tell you all sorts of lies: that the film is not available, that Kodak only make tungsten-balance duplicating films, and that the tungsten-balance films are in fact suitable for exposure by electronic flash.

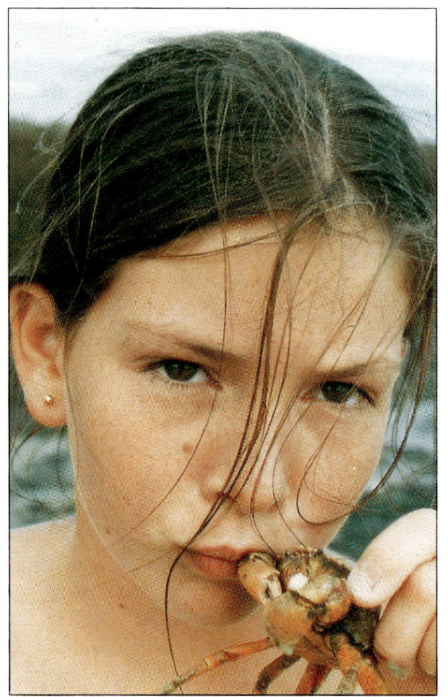

Duplicating with Ordinary Films

A couple of paragraphs back, we said that you could use ordinary films for duplicating, provided you took special precautions. The first precaution is to buy a film with normal contrast and colour saturation, ie not one of the current generation of high-contrast high-saturation films: duplicates made on Velvia would be a disaster. Films we have used with success include various Kodachromes, as well as tungsten-balance general-application films used with the appropriate filtration: tungsten-balance films seem to have lower contrast and colour saturation than daylight-balance films of the same or similar speed.

The second precaution is to reduce the contrast in some way, normally by allowing some white non-image-forming light to flatten the contrast of the image. You can get a contrast

Slide from negative

At the time of writing, the only film readily available for making slides from negatives was Kodak 5072, which was alarmingly expensive and which was only available in 100ft (30m) rolls. Processing was by the standard C-41 colour negative process, which tended to confuse labs mightily; they would process what they thought was a negative, and end up with a positive! It was not a convenient film to use, being balanced for tungsten light and requiring rather long exposures: on our makeshift duplicator, an enlarger colour head turned upside-down, exposures typically ran around 10 seconds at f/8. This is the sort of exposure that the film is balanced for, too: attempts to use it on the Illumitran, where the electronic flash illumination is a tiny fraction of a second, would run a severe risk of crossed curves (page 49). The colour balance in this duplicate is somewhat cyan, though this could easily be corrected by adding further cyan on the colour head; it is a negative process, of course, so if there is a colour bias, you get rid of it by adding the colour that is excessive. This is a blow-up of a section of the picture which also appears on page 75.

Frances's graduation picture

Victorian novels used to begin, 'It was in the summer of 18_ when I first saw Captain Mortenson..'. Well, this is the summer of 19_, which is certainly long enough for an Ektachrome to have taken on a distinctly magenta tinge. With copying film and the right copying set-up, you can however produce a considerably better and less evanescent copy: this copy should still be very acceptable in the year 2040, by which time the original slide will probably have gone a very nasty colour indeed. It was taken using the copying set-up shown on page 127, with Kodak SO-366 copying film. Compared with the usual copying filter pack for fresh Ektachrome, this was -

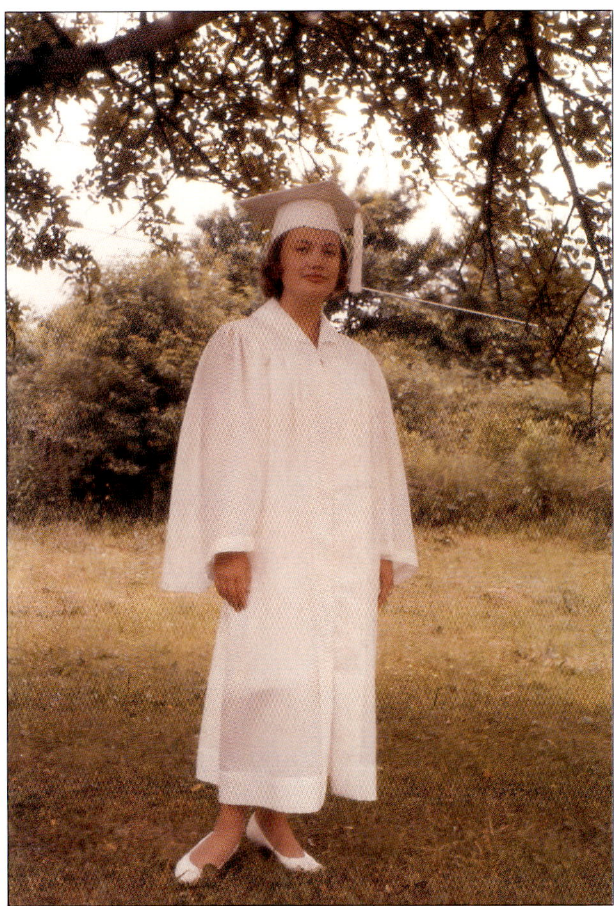

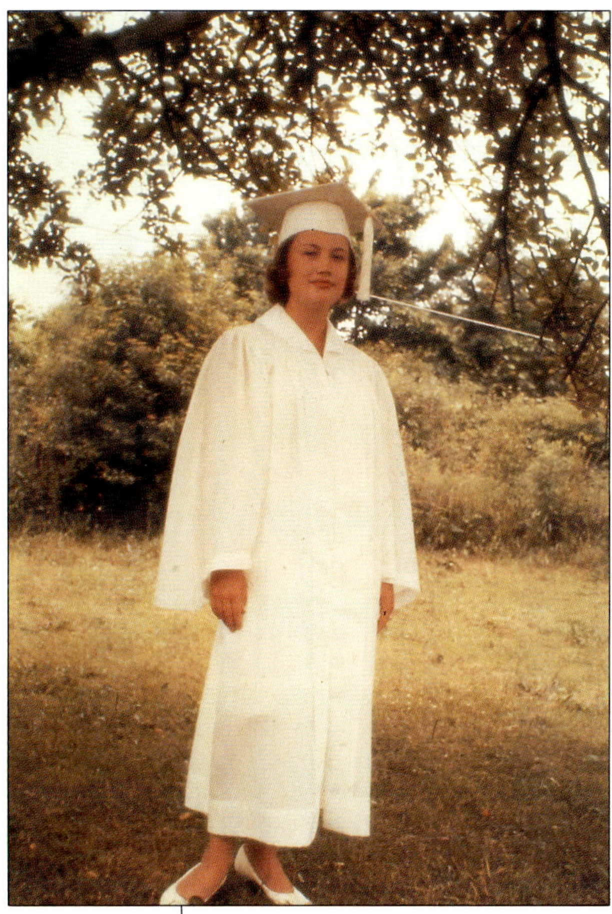

50M. It is now slightly yellow, with pinkish highlights in the robe, but further attempts to produce still better colour (by subtracting 20M as well) were doomed by the fact that the dyes used in the slide have faded differentially, so that the characteristic curves (D/log E curves, page 49) are now effectively crossed. This means that it is impossible to get satisfactory colours in both the highlights and the shadows, and we decided that this was a pretty good compromise. Given how difficult it can be to get a truly faithful copy transparency, it is very cheering to work with old, faded transparencies where you can normally produce a better result than the original.

control unit for the Illumitran which does this via a small secondary flash and a 45° sheet of glass between the original and the copying lens, but an easier and arguably better approach is not to mask the transparency as it lies on the copying stage. Instead of masking off the white light around the edges of the transparency, you simply leave it. This extra light bouncing around veils the contrast of the image: you may need to experiment, and to use some masking, to get precisely the contrast you need. This is how we used to get good-quality dupes using Kodachrome, and indeed they were among the best duplicates we have ever seen.

You could in theory pre-expose the film, always assuming that you have a camera which can handle double exposures. Once you have determined the correct exposure without pre-flashing (which you can only do by experiment), you take the transparency off the stage and give the film a white light pre-exposure of about 10 per cent of that exposure – three to three and a half stops down from the main exposure. You should also cut the main exposure by half a stop or so, as pre-flashing sensitises the film, quite apart from the extra exposure it gives. Pre-exposure would work with both tungsten and flash-balanced films, but we have never tried it: the information above is based on theory and analogy only.

BLACK AND WHITE COPYING

The problem with black and white copying – in other words, making negatives from flat copy – is often the exact opposite of colour copying: it is lack of contrast, rather than an excess, which causes the difficulties. In extreme cases, you can use lith or line films (below), but normally you will do better to use conventional film, cutting exposure slightly and boosting development slightly in order to get a contrasty image. About half a stop to a stop less exposure than indicated, and about 50 per cent more development, will be a good starting point for experiment.

Almost any film can be used for copying, but medium-speed films are generally best: the very slowest films can be hard to handle, with negligible exposure latitude and disproportionate contrast variations. An unusual and all but obsolete film which we sometimes use for copying is Ilford Ortho cut film: contrast can be controlled over a very wide range by choice of developer and developer time, and it can be quite convenient just to process a sheet or two at a time.

Ortho is also useful if you want to create a vintage *ambiance* in a portrait or even a landscape. The film is very low on red sensitivity, which means that the overall effect is similar (but not identical) to using a heavy red filter on a modern panchromatic film. This lack of red sensitivity also means that Ortho

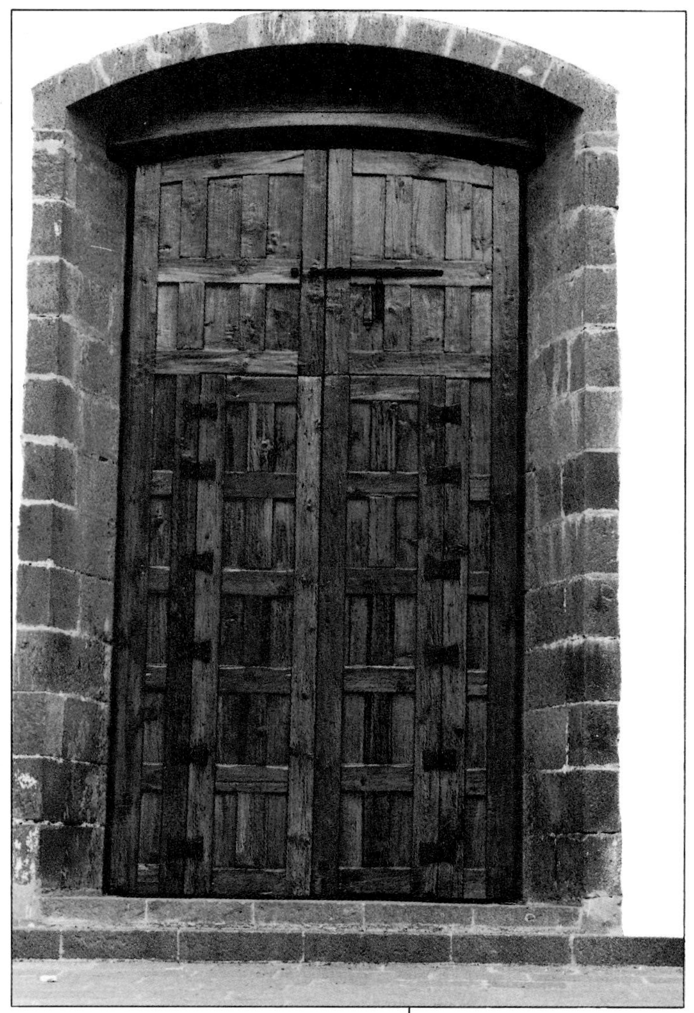

Door
The effect that you get when you shoot on an ortho film is not quite the same as the effect that you get when you use a blue filter on a conventional panchromatic film. The explanation lies in the spectral sensitivity curves, but it is enough to know that there is a difference. Using ortho film is like taking a step back in photographic history, to the days when sensitivity varied wildly according to whether you were exposing by daylight or by tungsten light, and also to the days when one film was asked to perform all sorts of tasks, with different developers and development times being used to control contrast. With a high-contrast developer, ortho film can give an almost lith-film effect, while with a gentle metol-only developer it can be surprisingly delicate and subtle. Because ortho film is so versatile, effective film speeds vary widely according to exposure, developer choice, and developer time: the same film might be rated by one photographer at EI 20 for one application, and by another photographer at EI 200 for another application. At the time of writing, Ilford Ortho was one of the few films available in 6.5x9cm, which meant that it could be used by the owners of 'baby' Linhofs and similar cameras. (FES)

is very much slower under tungsten light than it is under daylight or electronic flash: typically, about half as fast.

Copying Set ups

If you do much copying – or even if you do not – then it is much easier to have a proper copying set up with a copying stand; good, even illumination; and a good copying lens on the camera.

A purpose-built copying stand is expensive, but you can also make a perfectly good copying stand out of an old enlarger, and some enlargers can be adapted to do double duty as copying stands: for example, our Meopta Magnifax requires a small, modestly-priced adapter.

For illumination, a couple of photofloods in second-hand reflectors will be more than adequate: use fairly large reflectors to avoid 'hot spots', and set the lamps up at 45° on either side of the copy platform, about three feet (one metre) from the copy. You really do not need four lamps: neither of us has ever used a four-lamp copying set up in our entire lives.

Any SLR camera will do, but it is a good idea to use either a purpose-made 'macro' lens such as a Micro Nikkor, or a good quality enlarger lens on a bellows. A 50mm lens may be inconveniently short, but anything from 75mm to 105mm will allow a useful working distance and (more importantly) will produce extremely even illumination.

Do-it-yourself Soft Pornography

Every now and then, in the backs of photographic magazines, you will find advertisements for exposed, unprocessed film of nudes or 'glamour studies'. The implication, of course, is that somewhere there is a photographer cranking out images so steamy that they can only safely be sent through the post in unprocessed form. In fact, they are just copy negatives, usually (we are told) of 1950s bathing beauties. We say 'we are told' not out of prudishness, but because once you know the story, it hardly seems worth the effort of checking it out; it just sounds altogether too believable.

FINE-GRAIN POSITIVE

Fine-grain positive film, affectionately known as 'eff gee poz', is not a film which you would normally want to use for copying. Rather, it is a contrasty bromide-speed emulsion (about the equivalent of ISO 1/2 to ISO 2) coated onto transparent film-stock, in a variety of packings from 35mm to large cut-film sizes.

The main use we have found for it is in making ultra-large sectional blow-ups, via an interpositive. Enlarge a section of a 35mm negative onto the fg pos – we normally use it in the form of 70mm rollfilm or 2 1/4x3 1/4in/6.5x9cm cut film – and process normally in paper developer. Then contact print the fg pos onto lith or line film (see below) for really crisp, clear black and white grain. If you don't want to get involved with lith or line, then make the contact internegative on another piece of fg pos.

Most enlargers can blow a 35mm image up some 10 to 15 times, using a standard 50mm lens. If you now enlarge a 35mm-sized piece of your internegative to the same extent, you will have enlarged the image anything from 100 to 225 times. In fact, our

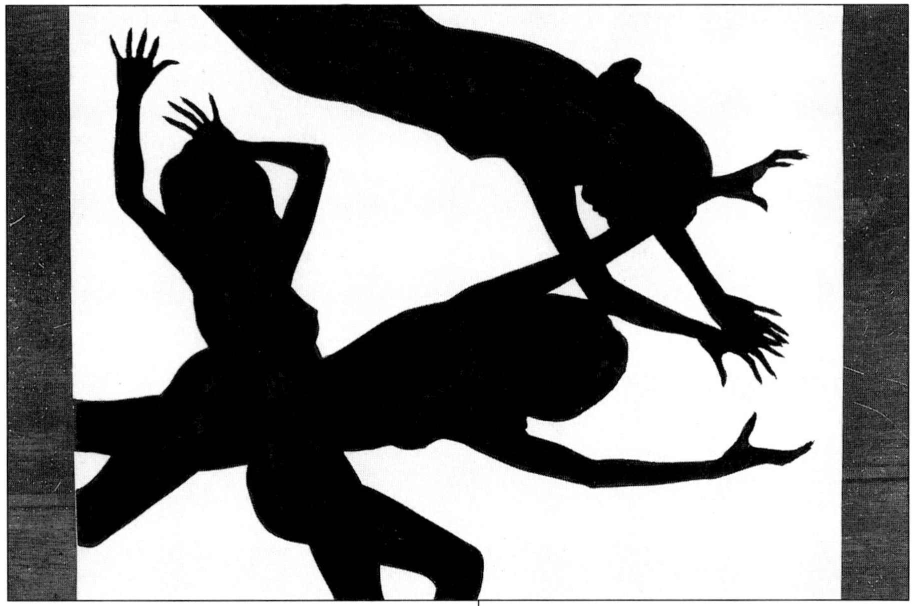

Lith

It is almost never a good idea to shoot lith film as a camera original of the subject itself: a much better idea is to use it to make copy negatives from prints. Furthermore, it is unusual for lith film to 'drop out' all greys in a single step: normally, you have to make the original neg, an interpositive, and then a further internegative, building contrast at each stage. A rather easier approach is to make a very high contrast print to begin with, either printing on Grade 5 paper or making a high-contrast Polaroid original, and then to copy that onto lith film. This picture by Colin Glanfield dates from the 1960s, when lith conversions were a fashionable technique; perhaps it is time that it was revived. (Colin Glanfield)

Magnifax can run to 18x with a 50mm lens, so the overall magnification is a staggering 324x.

ULTRA-HIGH-CONTRAST BLACK AND WHITE IMAGES

'Lith' and 'line' films are designed to give an ultra-high-contrast image. Ideally, you should end up with a very dark maximum black, or with clear film – and with nothing in between. These films have to be processed in special developers, and exposures are extremely critical: exposure latitude may be as little as a quarter of a stop. For this reason, they are normally used in the workroom, to make copies from existing black and white prints.

You can buy lith or line films in 35mm bulk rolls, but if you possibly can, you will do better to shoot larger formats: 4x5in is fine. This allows for limited retouching, which is very simple with lith film because you simply scrape off unwanted black spots, and fill in unwanted clear spots with lamp-black retouching medium.

To print lith films, go straight to the highest contrast grade of paper you can. If the results are still not contrasty enough, then contact print the lith film through two more generations: an interpositive, then another internegative. This will bump the contrast up to pure black and white. It is however much easier to do this if you are using sheet film rather than 35mm, where dust will almost certainly be a problem.

PAPER NEGATIVES

Strictly, paper negatives are nothing to do with film; but they are still worth a brief mention. You can load cut-film holders on large-format cameras with pieces of regular photographic printing paper cut to size; expose them like film (start with an EI of 1 or 2 – and note that ISO paper speeds are nothing to do with ISO film speeds); and then contact print them onto another sheet of paper. For best results, use single-weight or better still airmail paper, and consider oiling it after processing in order to get better translucency. The spectral sensitivity of the paper will vary widely: variable-contrast papers are probably more red-sensitive, and panchromatic papers like Panalure are of course sensitive to all colour. The grain of the paper negative will also intrude to a greater or lesser extent. This is a technique which can be used to create very interesting vintage-looking portraits, especially if you can get hold of a really large-format camera such as 8x10in, 10x12in or 11x14in.

SPECIAL-PURPOSE FILMS

There is a small residual category of films which does not fit in anywhere else in the book, and which you may either need to know about for their intended application, or may want to try for unusual effects.

Aerial Films

Aerial films are either high-contrast versions of ordinary films (available in both black and white and colour) or have extended infra-red sensitivity and reduced blue sensitivity, in order to help cut through haze. They are normally available in 70mm, 5in (127mm) rolls, and 9½in (241.3mm) rolls.

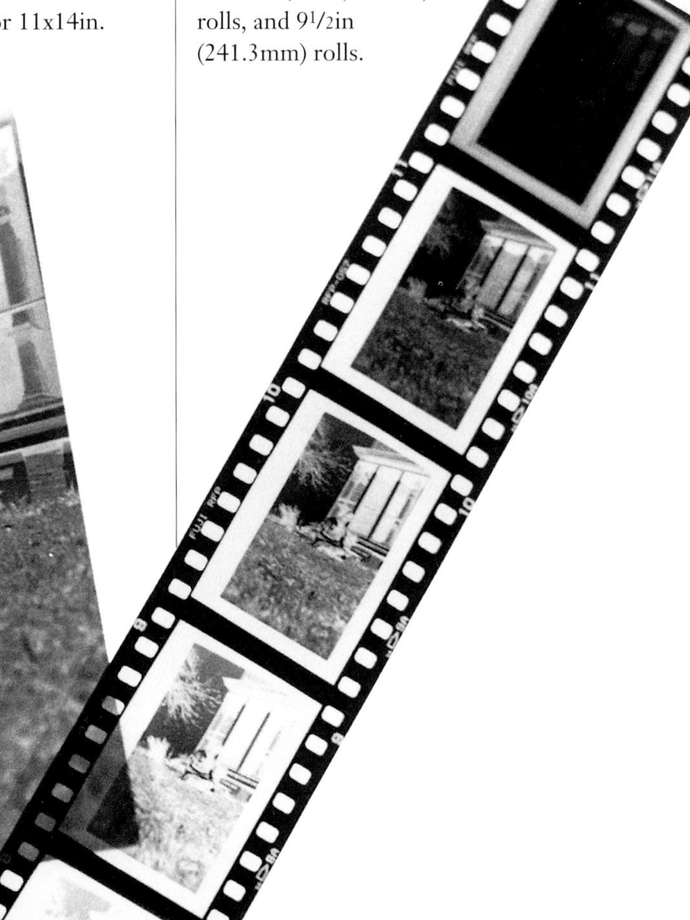

Copy negative

In the 1930s, Frances's father used a 116 camera – a long-obsolete format, nominally 2½x4¼in or about 6.5x11cm, but ideal for landscapes – and they accidentally came over to England with us when we left California, instead of going to Alabama with Frances's parents. Although we have an enlarger big enough to print them, it was not set up when we wanted to use it; in fact, it was in the attic, because we do not normally need to print anything bigger than 6x9cm. We therefore copied the negative onto slide film (Fuji 50 RFP) to create a 35mm negative which we could print easily. Normally, we would use Dia-Direct, but the British Dia-Direct lab was out of commission at the time. Reversal films create a direct positive, but if you are copying a negative, then of course you get a direct negative. Because the 35mm negative is about one-eighth of the area of the 116 image, the quality loss is negligible. We used the Illumitran (page 127), which can handle originals up to 4x5in (8x10in with an optional additional box), but you could equally well copy most big, old negatives using a light box or even a piece of opal acrylic such as Perspex or Lucite with a light underneath. The test exposures on this negative revealed that f/22 worked best on our Illumitran.

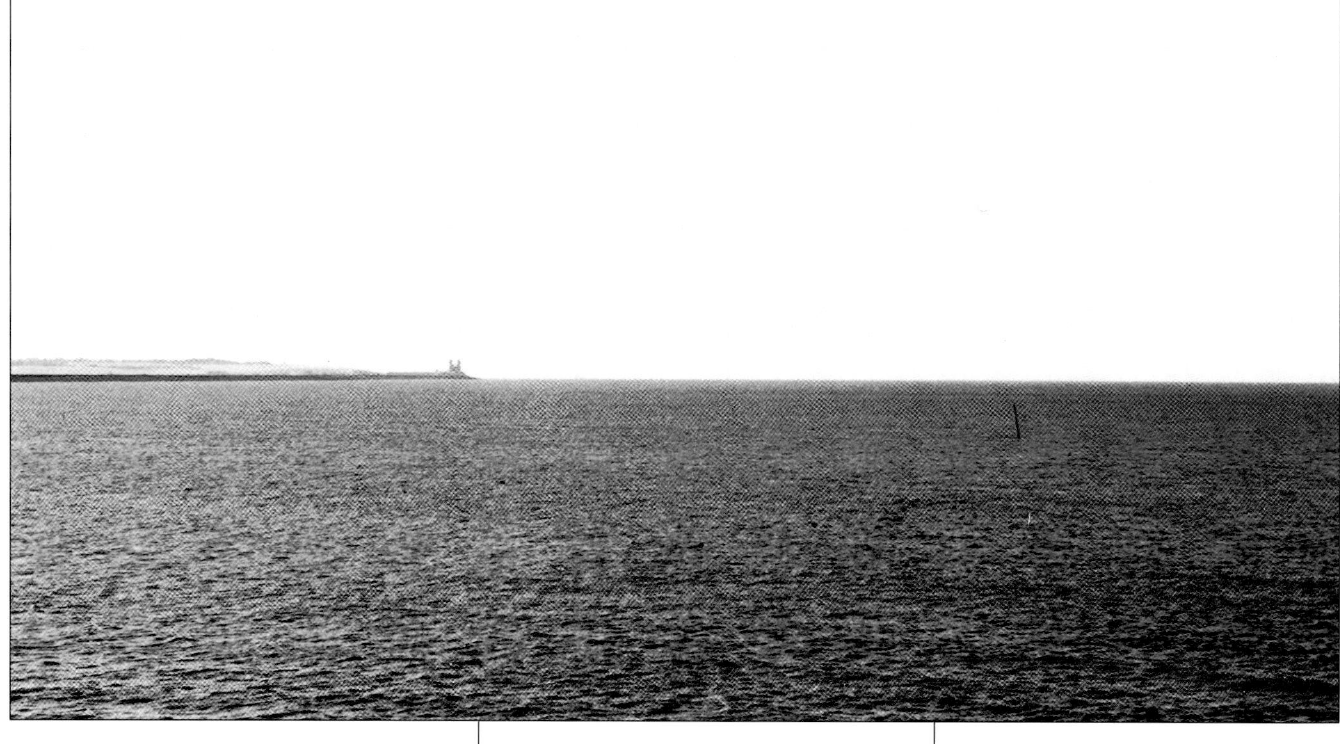

Cathode-ray Trace Recording

This is often done today on Polaroid films, the subject of the next chapter, but if it is done on conventional films they are normally of very high sensitivity and are processed to a very high contrast.

Electronic Output Film

These are designed for use with digital film writers and film recorders, when an image has been electronically manipulated and is then output to transparency film rather than as a set of separations. They are of extremely limited interest to anyone else: a 125ft (30.5m) roll of 9.5in (241.3mm) Ektachrome 7122 costs well over £1000, almost $2000, in 1993.

Holographic Films and Plates

As their name suggests, these are for making holograms. They are seriously expensive – the plates are sold individually – and we have never heard of anyone using them for anything except holograms.

Infra-red (IR) Films – Black and White

These are designed principally for industrial, legal, scientific and medical photography, but they are also widely used for their pictorial effects. When they are used for landscapes, most foliage comes out white, and there is an unearthly overall effect: one photographer used IR very successfully for a series of pictures of allegedly

Reculver Towers

The forensic uses of infra-red films are well known – we have all seen pictures of altered signatures, or of how the ink shows up on a burned cheque – but a less obvious application, which is particularly popular with the military, is cutting through haze. Infra-red 'light' is scattered far less by atmospheric moisture and dust than is visible light, even with a red filter. Because IR light is generally brought to a different focus from visible light, you normally focus by visible light and then reset the focused distance against an infra-red

focusing index. Filtration was a heavy 8x red, on both films: if you do not use a filter, there will be very little gain in haze-cutting ability. The darkest red filter we own is visually all but opaque: it is for use on a Leica rangefinder camera where, of course, you do not have to focus through the lens. In reproduction, the difference between these two shots may not be great, but the one that was shot on conventional film (FP4) had to be printed a grade and a half harder even to approximate to the infra-red shot, and it still has less detail and 'sparkle'. (RWH)

haunted castles. They are less successful for portraits, where corpse-like complexions are the rule. Every few years, someone (usually someone who is too young to know that it is nothing new) revives IR portraits for taking pictures of rock bands. Kodak's High Speed Infra-red is rated at about EI 50 to daylight, or EI 125 to tungsten light, when used with a Wratten 25 filter (deep red). Using IR films without some form of red or deep red filtration gives results which are disappointingly similar to any other film. Konica's IR 750 typically requires an exposure of 1/60 second at f/5.6 in bright sunlight, with a deep (8x) red filter.

At the time of writing, IR films were available in 35mm and 4x5in from Kodak, and in 35mm and 120 from Konica.

Infra-red Films – Colour

These are 'false colour' films: integral tripacks with the three layers sensitised to green, red and infra-red. Objects reflecting much IR, such as foliage, appear red/magenta. Like black and white IR, colour IR film is not primarily designed for pictorial applications, but some people still use it for landscapes and other purposes. We have never used it, because we really do not like the effects very much. There are examples of colour IR in Roger's book *35mm Panorama*, also from David & Charles.

At the time of writing, Kodak's IR

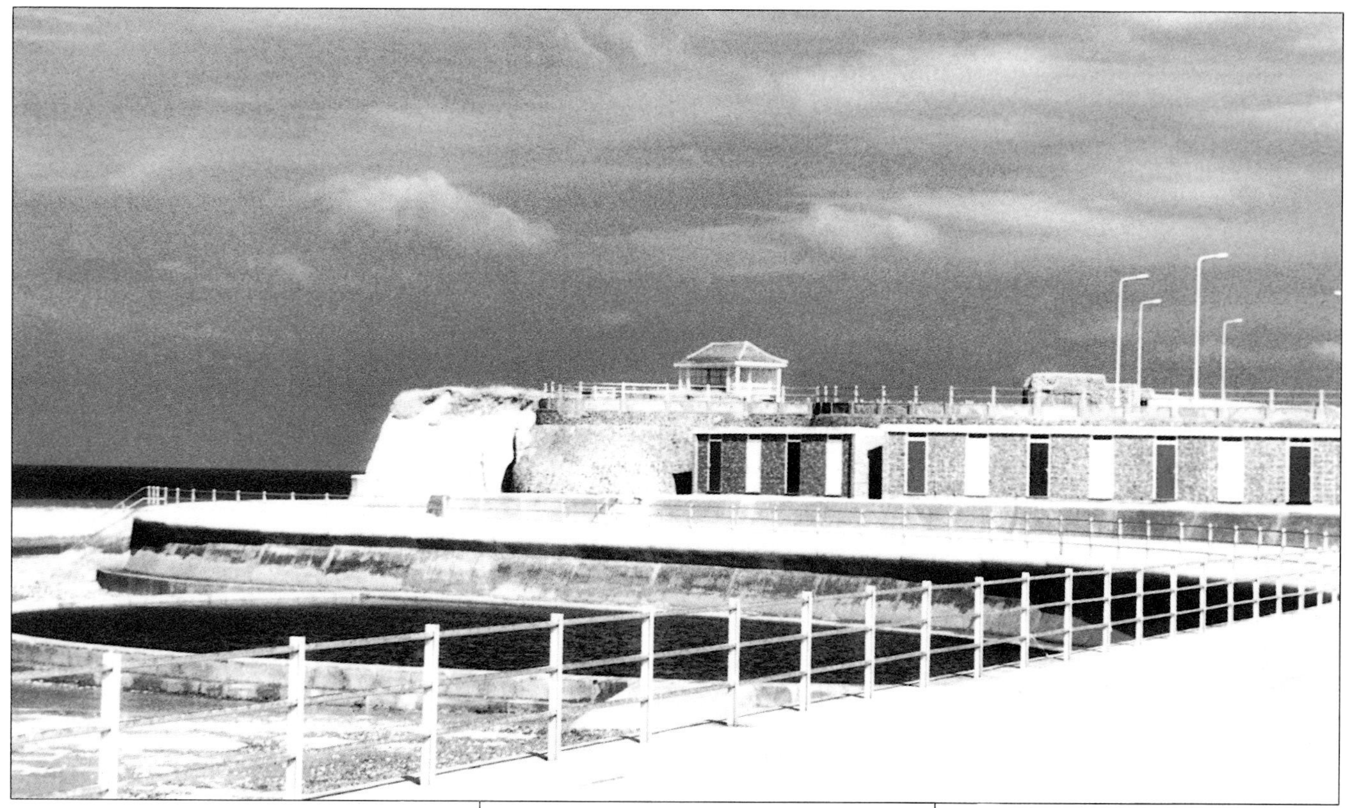

colour film (emulsion 2236, the only colour IR film readily available) still required the old E-4 process, which was hard to find and expensive when you could find it. The film was expensive, too – about three times the price of ordinary 36-exposure 35mm slide films. The main customers were the military, and teaching hospitals.

Nuclear Research and Monitoring Emulsions

These cannot even be used for normal photography, as they do not form an image in the normal sense. Monitoring emulsions are fogged by hard radiation, and help to monitor dosage; research emulsions typically record heavy particle tracks.

Photomicrography

There used to be a film called Kodak Photomicrographic Contrast Film, which was a super-high-contrast film for photomicrography. As far as we can discover, it was discontinued years ago. Today, people presumably use ordinary high-contrast, high-saturation slow films.

Short-wave Radiation Plates

All films are sensitive to ultra-violet radiation, though most lenses are not transparent to it. Normally, special quartz lenses are used for UV photography; and if you want to record very hard UV, Kodak will sell you their SWR Plate (Short-wave Radiation). The only standard size, at close to

Minnis Bay seafront

The harsh contrasts, unfamiliar tones, and dramatic skies characteristic of infra-red film are all obvious in this picture, which turns a typical English seafront into something strange and slightly frightening. The film was Konica's IR 750 film in 35mm size, exposed in a Nikon F fitted with a 90mm f/2.5 Vivitar Series One macro lens. Because the infra-red reflectivity of different surfaces is very unpredictable, and because IR films are normally used with filters, exposure determination is inevitably a mixture of experience and guesswork: Konica recommends El 32 without a filter, and (in bright sunlight) 1/60 at f/5.6 with an 8x red, like the one that was used to take this picture. (FES)

PolaChrome HC and Polapan HC

For photomicrography and some other technical applications, high-contrast colour films are used to emphasise colour differences. Exposure is normally very critical, and must be within a half or even one-third of a stop, but quite subtle variations in colour can be emphasised very effectively, as in the different colours of the gear-wheels in this Russian pocket-watch. The main purpose of PolaChrome HC is for making audio-visual slides from artwork or from electronic imaging systems, and we have yet to discover any applications for general photography. PolaPan HC is another matter. This is a high-contrast, high-speed (ISO 400) black and white film, designed primarily for copying line drawings and text, but it also has very strong graphic possibilities which are somewhere between lith films and ordinary black and white. It is also ideal for some kinds of technical illustration, as with this picture of the same watch, where both shape and texture are emphasised to a very high degree. There is much more about Polaroid films in the next chapter.

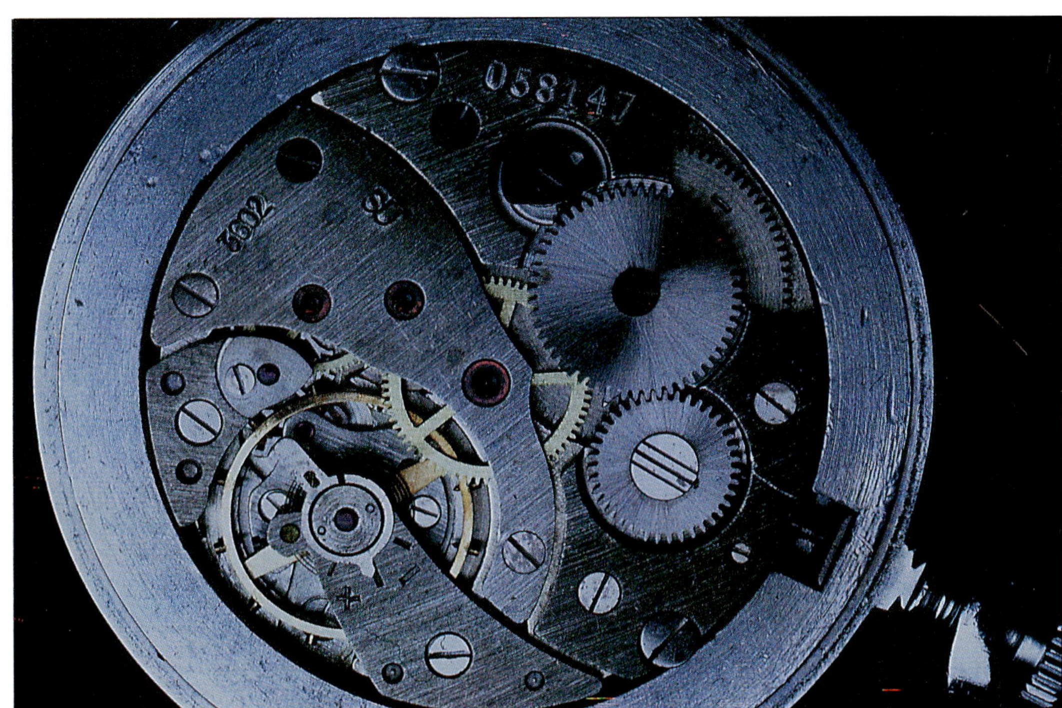

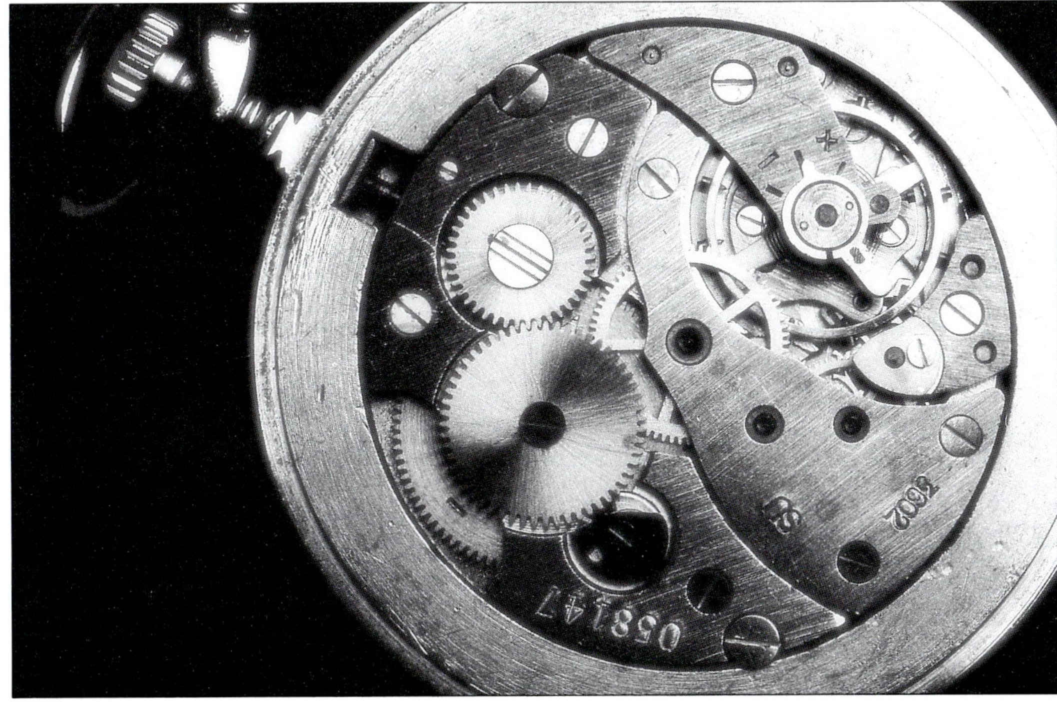

$1000, say £650, for 36 plates in 1993, was 2x10in (51x254mm); other sizes were available to special order, price on application, delivery in two to four months!

Spectroscopic Plates

These are about as special-purpose as you can get, in that they are generally manufactured to order, in custom sizes and with your preferred combination of speed, spectral sensitivity, resolving power and contrast.

Spectrum Analysis Film and Plates

If you are into spectroscopic analysis, these are for you. Otherwise, you are unlikely to have much use for them. Typical sizes include 2x10in (51x254mm) and 4x10in (102x254mm).

Surveillance

Gone are the days of super-fast surveillance films that were not generally available to the general public: films like Kodak's 2475 and near-mythical 2485 recording films. Today, if you are into serious surveillance, you do not place your faith in anything so *passé* as ultra-speed film and high-speed lenses. Instead, you use image intensifiers, high-gain video, and thermal imaging systems. Ordinary silver-based photography is relegated to the second rank: the sort of job which a friend of ours in MI6 dismissively referred to as 'the dirty mac brigade'.

Modern surveillance films are not even really fast; but then again, they never really were. They were designed to capture highlight detail, and let the shadows go hang. If this is your criterion for exposure determination, then any competent ISO 400 film can be rated at a minimum of EI 1600, and a good ISO 400 film will give you recognisable faces at EI 5,000 to 10,000. With T-Max 3200, you can get recognisable faces (if you can see them through the grain) at EI 25,000 and above.

In fact, unobtainable super-speed surveillance films which are made only for the intelligence services are one of the urban myths of modern photography. Anyone who works in intelligence will tell you that they use off-the-shelf films, batch-tested perhaps, but still the sort of thing that you can buy from the catalogues of Kodak or Ilford.

Underwater Film

One of Kodak's more bizarre ideas was a colour slide film balanced for underwater photography: Ektachrome 5019. It is balanced to remove the blue cast that is common at 3 to 6m (10 to 20ft), and to give higher contrast than usual. Then again, the speed is only ISO 50, so it would normally be used with flash – when the blue cast is not a problem anyway. It is a relatively new product at the time of writing, and it is unclear how successful it is going to be. All the divers we have spoken to, and all of the professional photographers as well, have wondered why on earth this stuff was made. Maybe it was for the CIA...

Teatro Juarez

In Mexico, as in many Spanish-influenced countries, the evening promenade is a well-established social custom. Frances wanted to photograph it, but without using flash: not only would it have been disruptive and rude, but it would not have conveyed the mood, and the lighting would in any case have fallen off very rapidly. She also wanted to keep reasonable depth of field, so although she used Roger's 35mm f/1.4 Summilux on a Leica M2, she stopped it down to about f/2.8. The film was Kodak's excellent P3200, rated at EI 1600 which we have found to be the maximum speed for normal-looking gradation. A different rendition of this picture, tinted blue, appears on page 104. (FES)

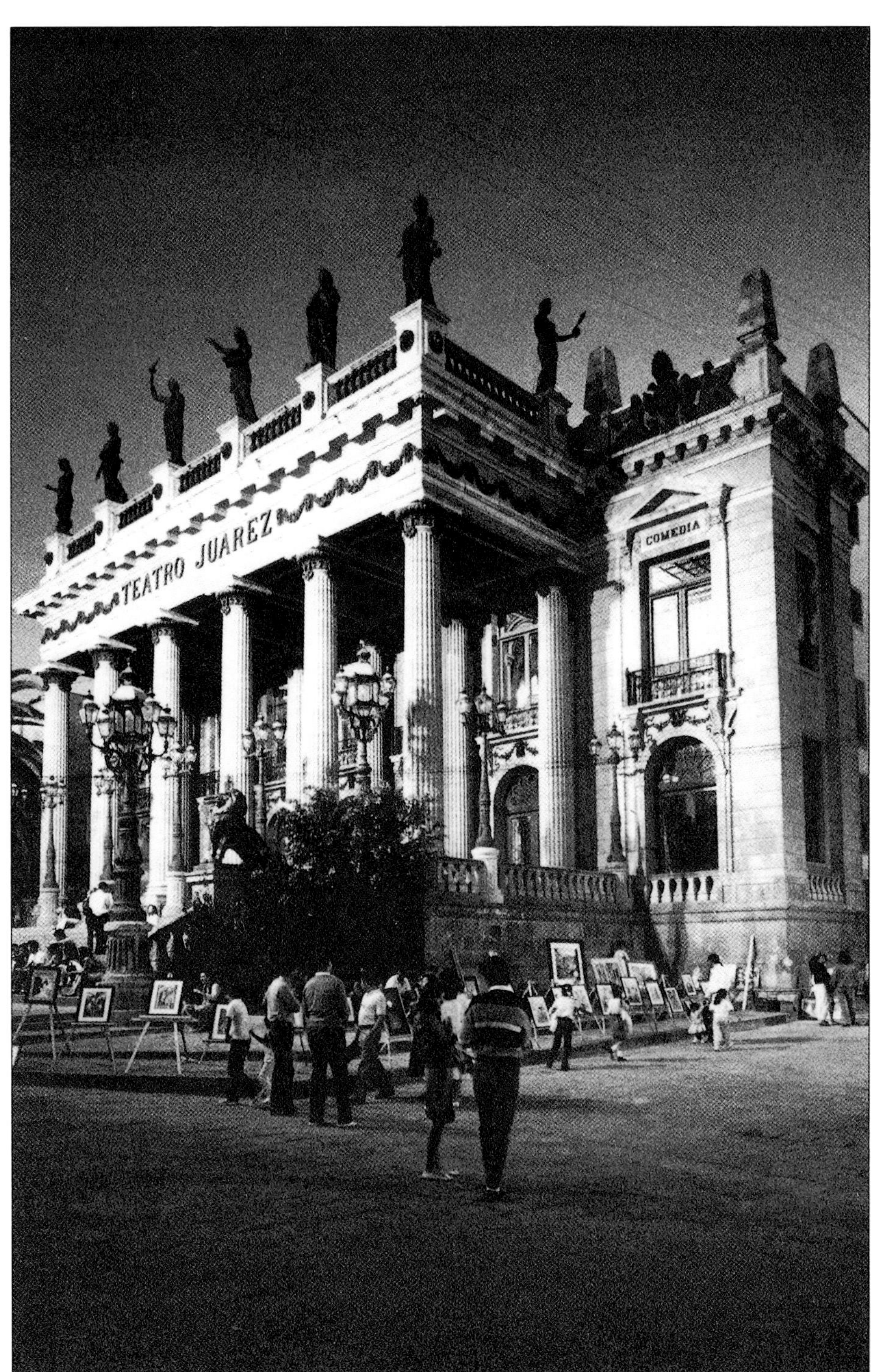

10 POLAROIDS AND OTHER INSTANT-PROCESS FILMS

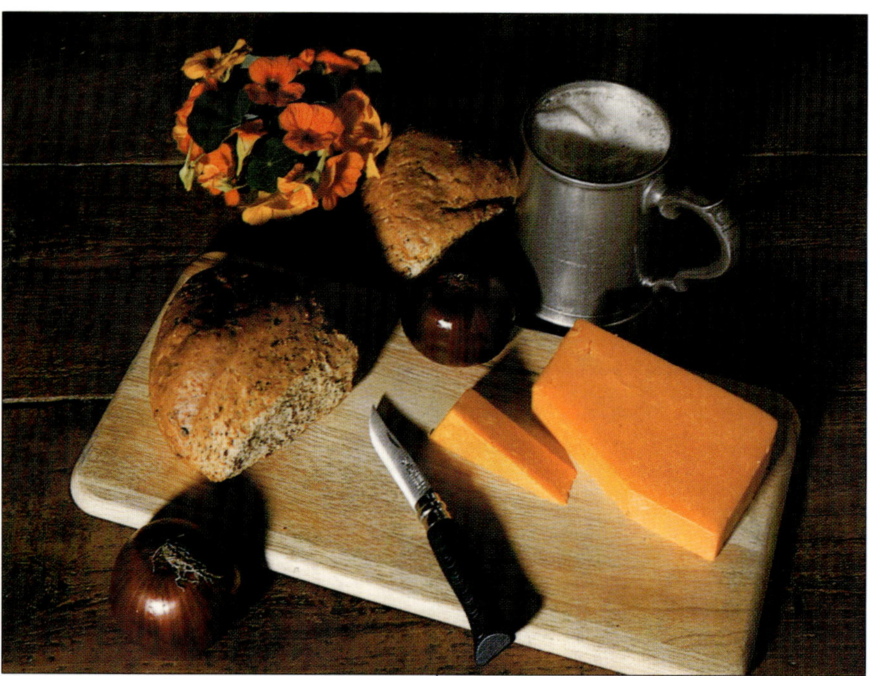

Still life, Polaroid Pro 100
The most common use for Polaroid materials among professional photographers is for proofing or testing before they commit the final image to conventional 'chrome. Even though we were setting up this shot only to demonstrate this aspect of Polaroid materials, and to compare the results from different emulsions, we still found that we made a number of changes to the composition and lighting on the strength of the first Polaroid. Polaroid Pro 100, the latest and best emulsion at the time of writing, was rated at a reliable ISO 100 at all exposure temperatures, and took 90 seconds to process at temperatures from 70-95°F, 21-35°C. At 60°F/16°C it rises to 120 seconds, and at 55°F/13°C to 180 seconds. Very small differences in exposure were readily visible: we found that as little as a quarter of a stop was detectable, and as the normal permissible variation in 'chromes is a third of a stop, matched Polaroids will always give well-matched 'chromes. Establishing the precise relationship between the optimum 'chrome exposure and the optimum Polaroid exposure is however a matter for experiment: some photographers find that they still do best by exposing their 'chromes at a third or even half a stop more or less than the optimum Polaroid. Once you have established the relationship, it remains constant; but you have to establish it by experiment. (RWH/FES)

Catullus, the Roman poet, wrote '*Nec sine te nec tecum possum vivere*': 'neither without you nor with you can I live'. Many photographers feel the same way about the products of the Polaroid Corporation. They complain about the price, and about problems which are as often of their own making as Polaroid's; but they would never go back to working without Polaroids if they could possibly help it.

Polaroid materials are expensive, it is true, but you are paying for sublime convenience and (if you use them for testing before you shoot on 'chrome) they give you the nearest thing you can get to total peace of mind. Their other significant drawback, apart from the price, is that they must be used while they are still in date: outdated Polaroid materials will almost invariably give poor results, often to the point of unusability. This problem is easily avoided by not keeping large stocks of Polaroid, but it is worth knowing.

One more problem with Polaroid is that the corporate culture, especially in the United States, seems to be secretive to the point of paranoia. Their technical literature is for the most part remarkably uninformative, and if anything goes wrong, the unspoken assumption is that it is your fault. On the bright side, they have a very generous guarantee policy: return anything which went wrong through no particular fault of yours, and they will replace it. The only way to learn how to use Polaroid products is by experiment (which can be expensive) or

Still life, Polaroid Type 59

Type 59 (Type 669 when in quarter-plate pack form) was the immediate antecedent of Pro 100. Even in reproduction, the greatly improved colours of the Pro 100 should be visible, and Pro 100 is considerably better at differentiating both highlights and shadows than Type 59/669, though still not as good as regular 'chromes; but if you are interested in image transfers or emulsion transfers, the older film works very much better. Another 'old-technology' aspect of Type 59/Type 669 is that the ISO 80 film speed holds good only across a relatively limited range of processing temperatures – around 75°F/24°C. At 90°F/32°C it is EI 100; at 65°F/18°C it is EI 50; and at 55°F/13°C it is EI 40. In other words, when you expose it (which you can do at any temperature), you have to know what the temperature will be when you process it; and also, processing times range from 90 seconds at 55°F/13°C to 60 seconds at 75°F/24°C. This has been known to prompt dark mutterings from European photographers about overheated American studios. Reciprocity is pretty bad, too: the recommended range is only 1/30 to 1/1000 second, with a third of a stop loss when exposed at 1/3000 second, or ever-increasing losses when exposed for longer than 1/30 second: one-third of a stop at 1/10 second, two-thirds of a stop at 1/4 second, one and a third of a stop at one second, and a staggering two and two-thirds of a stop at 10 seconds. Colour shifts start outside the 1/100 to 1/1000 range, and are trivial at 1/30 and 1/3000 (CC05C and CC05R respectively), but at 10 seconds the recommended filtration is a stiff CC50R + CC10Y. (RWH/FES)

by talking to Polaroid staff, who are normally extremely helpful and who will give you all kinds of hints and tips which really ought to be in the technical literature.

There are, and have been for some time, three distinct groups of Polaroid instant-process films. There are the 'traditional' peel-apart films; the integral or non-peel films; and the 35mm films. The peel-apart films are available in various sizes, and in a bewildering variety of emulsions, as well as in single-sheet form. There is also a Fuji version of the peel-apart film pack, and there was for a while a Kodak instant-picture camera. Unlike Fuji, however, Kodak neglected to pay Polaroid any royalties, and when they were convicted of contravening Polaroid patents, they were hit with very large damages and ceased production of their instant material.

More than any other manufacturer, Polaroid is constantly introducing new films and dropping old ones. It is therefore perfectly likely that by the time you read this, some of the films described will have been superseded by others. On the other hand, the general observations on the types and applications of the films will remain good.

PEEL-APART FILMS

These were originally introduced for taking snapshots, but in this field they have now been supplanted by the integral film types. They remain in production, however, because they are so extraordinarily versatile. Their main users fall into two groups: scientists and researchers who need quick pictorial records, and professional and advanced amateur photographers who use them for proofing or testing before taking

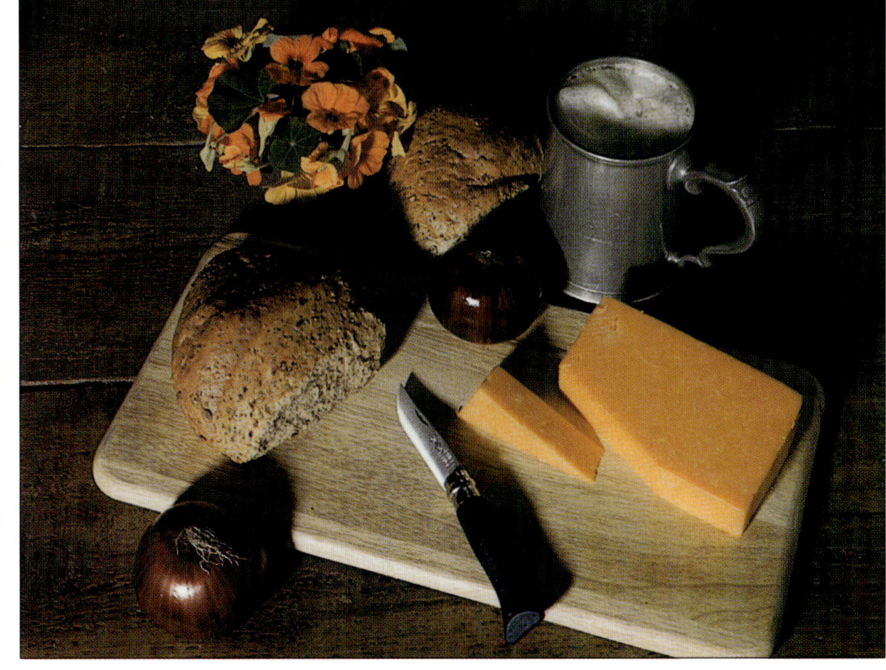

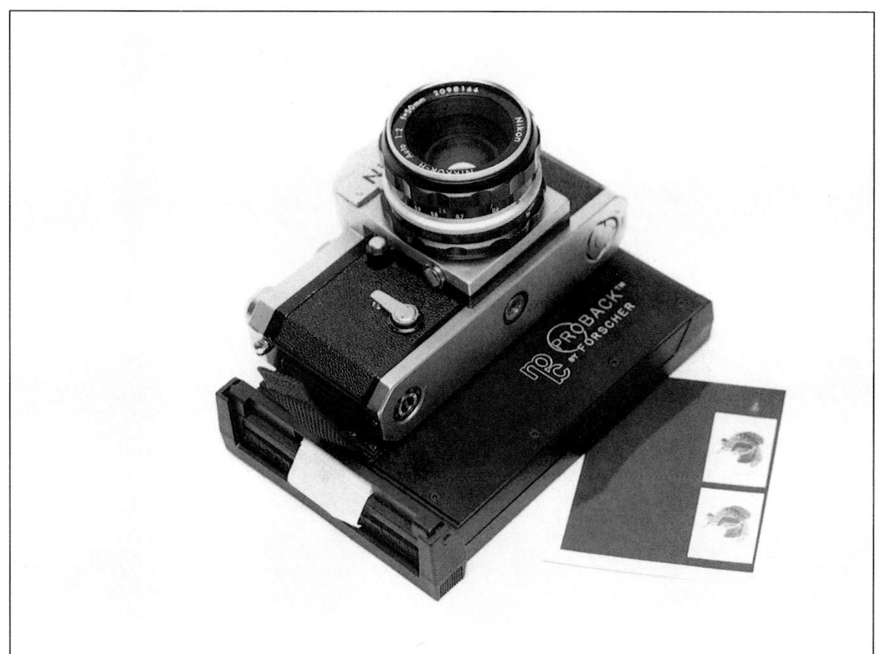

Polaroid back for 35mm

Newton Plastics Corporation of Newton, Massachusetts makes Polaroid backs for a number of 35mm cameras. The images are too small to allow you to judge sharpness effectively – you can make two exposures on one sheet, as shown, and there is still plenty of blank Polaroid – but they provide a first-class preview of composition, lighting and exposure. The backs use a fibre-optic image-transfer plate, which accounts for their very high cost, and some photographers are not convinced that they are worth the money. Our view is that if you can afford them, they are very worth while.

the 'real' picture. It is however possible to use some (though not all) Polaroid peel-apart films as original pictures for reproduction; and of course there are always photographers who use Polaroid materials for their unique qualities.

Overwhelmingly the widest choice of emulsions is available in quarter-plate and in 4x5in single sheet loadings. The films are available in both black and white and colour with speeds ranging from ISO 50 to ISO 20,000.

Development times range from 10 seconds to four minutes, and can further be varied widely according to temperature: some films are much more sensitive to temperature variations than others. The speed of the film can also vary according to the processing temperature, and if you depart significantly from the 75°F (24°C) at which Polaroid films are supposed to be used, you had better take account of the instructions packed with the film.

Most modern Polaroid peel-apart materials are 'coaterless', which is to say that they do not have to be coated after they are peeled apart. Some of the more specialised monochrome materials may however still require coating. Coaters are packed with those films that need them: they are like little squeegees impregnated with a sort of sealant. If you fail to coat a print which requires coating, it will fade quite quickly, but if it is coated it will last as long as most non-archival black and white prints. Coaterless films last very well without coating.

Scientific Uses

Little needs to be said about these. In general, if you need Polaroid films in your work, you will already know about them because they are so widespread. If

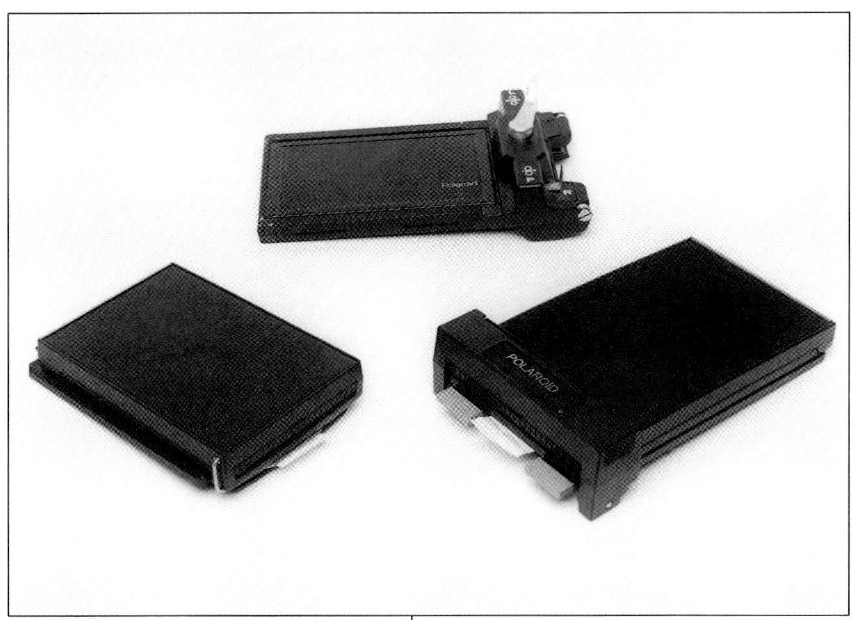

Polaroid backs
These three Polaroid backs all fit 4x5in cameras, though not necessarily equally conveniently. The single-sheet holder is the most versatile, but also the most expensive to run, the heaviest, and the most expensive. This is the one which also accepts regular 4x5in 'chromes from Fuji and (at the time of writing) Polaroid. The 4x5in pack holder is thin enough to slip under the ground-glass of most cameras, just like a rather thick cut film holder, or you can remove the ground-glass and fit it in the same way that you would a rollfilm holder. This is easily the best choice if you normally use just one type of Polaroid film for proofing and exposure checking, and it costs a bit less to run than the single-sheet holder. The quarter-plate holder is cheapest to run, but also the least convenient, because the back cannot be fitted under the ground-glass of most cameras – you have to remove the focusing screen – and because the image is both small and very offset. The single-sheet holder shown is the older metal version; it was replaced in 1993 by a lighter plastic version.

you do not know about them, Polaroid will be more than happy to tell you. There are all kinds of emulsions, including one for video image recording and another – the aforementioned ISO 20,000 material – for cathode ray trace recordings.

Proofing/Testing

Almost all professional cameras can be fitted with Polaroid backs. Rollfilm models, and even 35mm cameras, use the quarter-plate pack film. Backs are available either from the camera manufacturer, or from NPC of Newton, Massachusetts. Even when the camera manufacturer makes the backs, NPC backs are likely to be cheaper and just as good, and there are several cameras where your only option is an NPC back. Many professionals consider a Polaroid test facility so important that they will not buy a camera which cannot accept Polaroid backs; and this is also one of the reasons why rollfilm is so widely used. A 6x6cm or larger Polaroid test is big enough to see easily: a 24x36mm Polaroid test is rather more of a strain on the eyes, though still a lot better than no test.

The widest choice of holders is available for 4x5in and 9x12cm cameras: single-sheet holders (which fit any modern 4x5in camera with a Graflok back) and pack holders for both 4x5in and quarter-plate film, which can only be used with cameras having a removable ground glass or a very wide back opening.

When it comes to 8x10in cameras, the film-holder and the processor are separate; in all the other formats, they are combined, and the action of pulling the film out of the holder initiates the development process. With 8x10in, you take the film out of the holder and put it into the processor. Perhaps it is unnecessary to say that 8x10in Polaroids are expensive; but if you are shooting 8x10in commercially, you should be charging enough to cover the cost!

Whether you use colour or black and white for proofing is very much a matter of choice. We prefer colour, and so do most art directors, but many photographers are perfectly happy to use black and white, which is cheaper and develops faster. If you prefer colour, there are Polaroid films balanced both for electronic flash/daylight and for tungsten.

Origination from Polaroids

Most printers are irrationally prejudiced against Polaroids, but the medium-contrast black and white proofing materials can certainly be used as original 'bromides'. We have used Type 54 extensively, and we must have

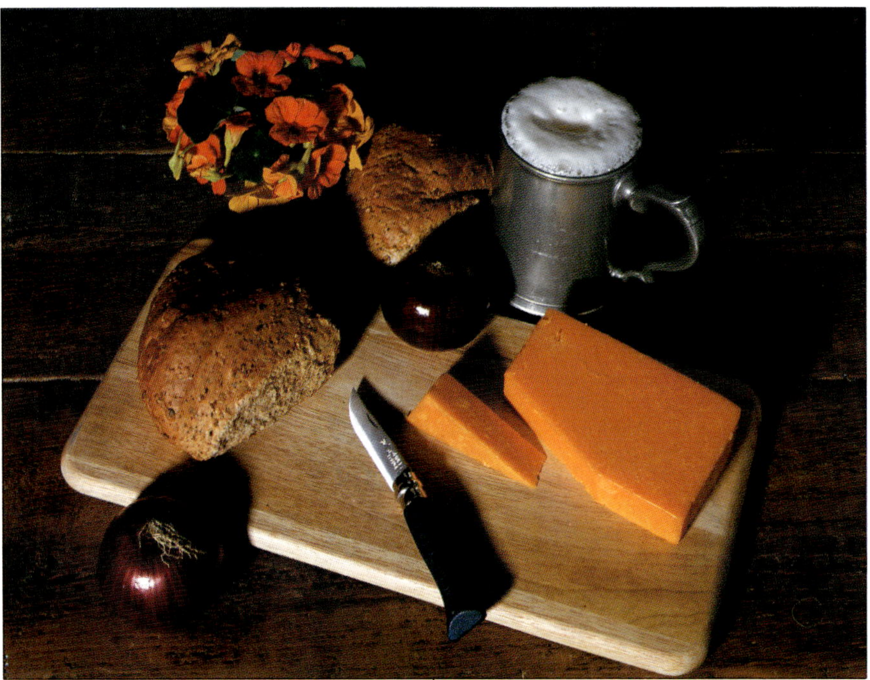

had scores of images printed from this material.

It is possible to originate from any other Polaroid material, too, but you may find it even more difficult to persuade the printers to do so. It is true that Polaroid colours are rarely as good as those from 'chromes, but they are usable.

Polaroid's Special Image Qualities

Fine art photographers use Polaroids for all sorts of reasons. Some like the immediacy of the medium: they just keep shooting until they see what they want. Others like the fact that each image is unique, and that shooting is relatively slow: not being able to 'machine-gun' the subject, as they could with a 35mm or even rollfilm camera, gives them a certain *frisson* which they feel is reflected in their work. Yet others use special-application scientific materials for general photography, such as the 'ordinary' (blue-sensitive-only) Type 51 or the ISO 20,000 Type 612. Yet others like to maltreat the material in different ways, in particular by image transfer and emulsion transfer.

Image transfer is covered briefly in the caption on page 18, and Polaroid have produced a booklet on the subject which they will send you on request. Emulsion transfer is (if anything) even more brutal than image transfer. You develop the film in the normal way, but you then float the emulsion off in hot water, wash it by transferring it from one hot bath to another, and finally transfer it to another substrate. Rips and wrinkles are almost inevitable in the emulsion transfer process, but its advocates see this as part of its charm.

Many fine artists prefer to use image transfer and emulsion transfer with

Still life, Fuji RDP

This was shot on ISO 4x5in Fuji RDP, for a number of reasons. One was to show how the final 'chrome looked after the various 'tests', because this is why most professionals shoot Polaroids. Another reason was however to point out that Fuji package this film (and also ISO 50 RFP) in single sheet holders which can be inserted in Polaroid 545 holders just like sheets of Polaroid film. You pay a handsome premium for the convenience of being able to use 'chromes in your Polaroid holder: it costs up to 50 per cent more per sheet than buying the film in boxes and loading it conventionally into cut-film holders, but on the other hand, you have no worries about light-tightness, and film in this form is much quicker and easier to use and (above all) much lighter than film in normal holders. Polaroid used to offer their own version of the same thing, but this was discontinued in about 1993 because demand was low and because Fuji's version was both more convenient and could be used in Kodak Readyload holders as well as Polaroid holders. (FES/RWH)

Toe shoes, Polaroid image transfer

To make an image transfer, you expose a colour Polaroid peel-apart film (it will not work with black and white film) in the normal way, but after 10 or 15 seconds, you peel it apart and squeegee the negative into contact with a sheet of heavy watercolour paper (or fabric, or a number of other media). A roller is the easiest way to press the film into intimate contact with the paper: some people also use the back of a spoon to burnish the darker areas of the image down onto the paper. Then, after anything up to two minutes, you very carefully peel the negative off, and if you are lucky, you will have a transferred image on the paper. We have found that the choice of paper is not as important as getting it soaked through, with hot water acidulated with a few

Rose photographed with PolaChrome
Even the standard-contrast Polachrome can be a tricky material for some subjects, as Frances discovered when she tried to photograph flowers with it. Somehow, it seems happier with manmade subjects, or with sunny views – another example of 'magic' or 'the x factor' or 'personality', those strange and unquantifiable aspects of films' behaviour which remind us that photography is both an art and a science, and that the art can raise its head at unexpected moments. Again and again, our experience with Polaroid materials is that you need to try them for yourself to see what they will do: unlike substituting (say) Fuji film for Konica, or Kodachrome for Agfachrome, the odds are that you will not just get something which is slightly different from anything you have seen before: you will get something which is completely different. (FES)

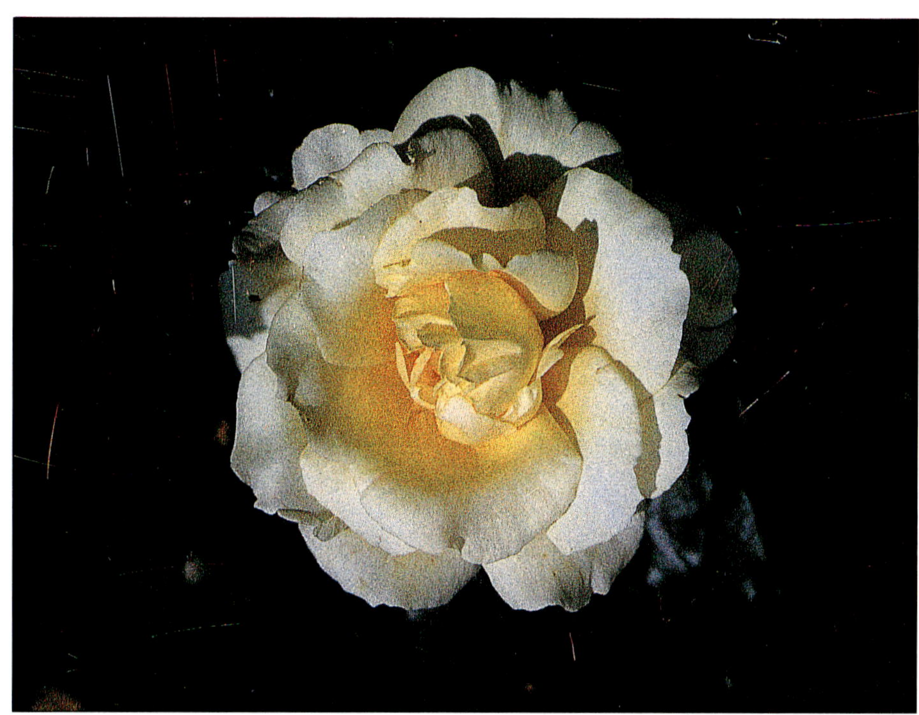

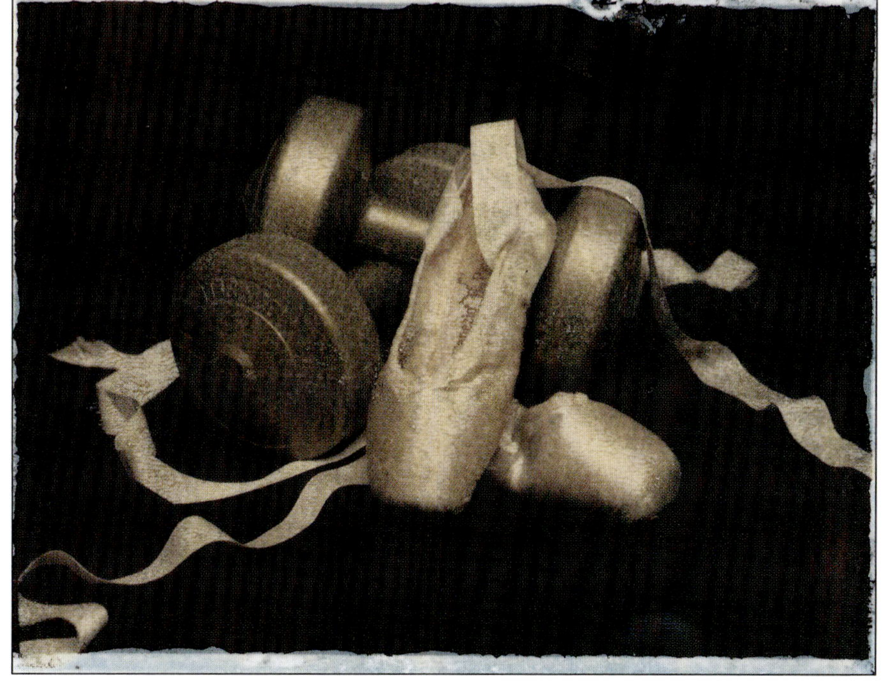

drops of acetic acid. We then blot it dry before attempting to transfer the image. It took us the best part of two boxes (32 sheets) of Type 669, and over half a box (20 sheets) of Type 59, to get the technique more or less right. You are doomed to colour casts, because you peel the negative before all the dyes have fully migrated. You cannot fully correct this, because you will have crossed curves (see page 49), but we found that if you want a white background to stay anything like acceptable, a CC30R filter worked pretty well. Once the image is transferred, you can retouch or enhance it with coloured pencils. We experimented with using it for a cookbook, which is possibly the worst imaginable application of image transfer. (FES)

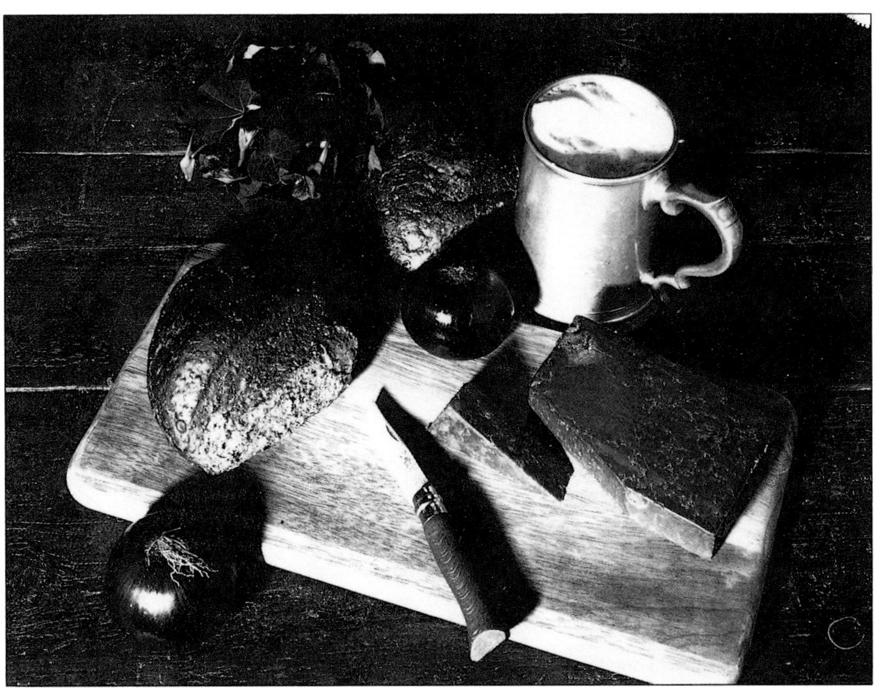

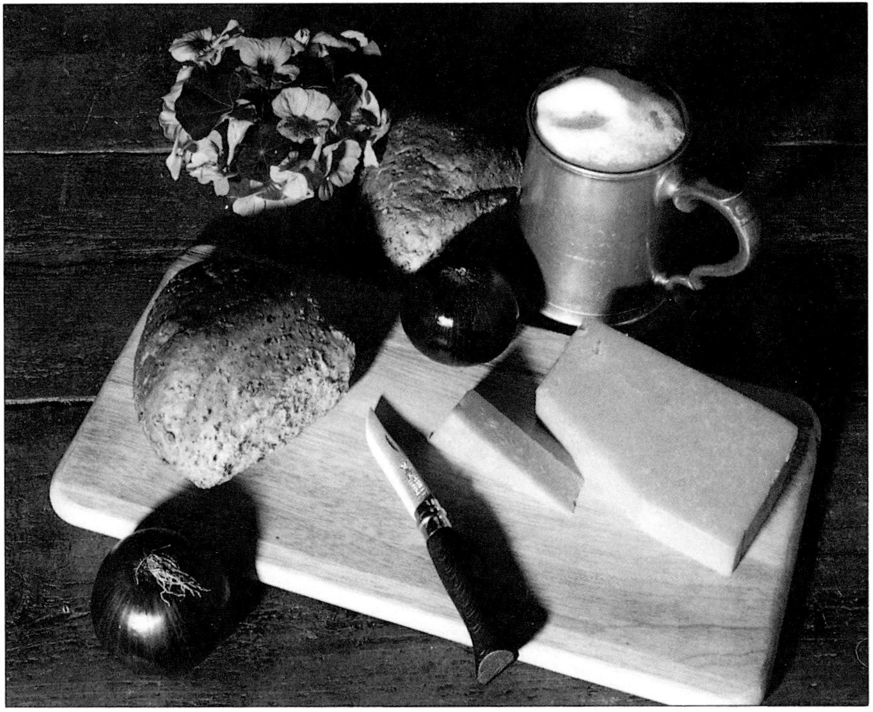

Still life, Polaroid Type 51

Type 51 may no longer be available when you read this – an unspecified 'key component' was apparently no longer available, so production was due to cease – but Polaroid assured us that they were working on a replacement for it. It is a high contrast material, rated at EI 320 to daylight or electronic flash, or EI 125 to tungsten: in other words, it is essentially an 'orthochromatic' or even 'ordinary' film. Exposure is extremely critical: in this picture, an increase of a third of a stop resulted in the edge of the knife disappearing against the cutting board, while a decrease of a third of a stop gave a picture that was so murky as to be all but unusable. For still lifes and for very vintage-style portraits (especially high-key portraits taken with a soft-focus lens) it has all kinds of possibilities, but like so many Polaroid films, the only way to explore the full versatility of it is to use up half a pack or a pack for yourself. (FES/RWH)

Still life, Polaroid Type 54

Polaroid Type 54 (664 in quarter-plate pack form) is an ISO 100 black and white material which is matched to the tonal sensitivity of typical 'chrome films. Some photographers use it as a test material instead of colour Polaroids, and reckon they can get as much information from it as from colour, but we much prefer to use Pro 100 rather than Type 54, because seeing how the colours relate is as important as seeing the tones. On the other hand, we cheerfully use Type 54 for originating 'bromides'. Although printers may initially be unwilling to use it, they can in fact get perfectly good pictures for reproduction from a properly exposed Type 54 film, and sharpness is more than adequate for printing at same size or smaller, or even for 'half up' (150 per cent). We have had some pictures printed at 200 per cent of the print size, though this really is the limit. (FES/RWH)

Bell Inn, St Nicholas at Wade

There is nothing remarkable about this snapshot, except the light level in which it was taken. With an ISO 100 film, the exposure would have been one second at f/1.4. As it was, this was taken at 1/30 second at f/3.5 – the equivalent of 1/200 at f/1.4! It was shot with Polaroid's incredible ISO 20,000 pack film, which is designed for cathode ray trace recording but which can (as witness this picture) be used for normal photography. The more you learn about Polaroid's special films, the more you begin to suspect that it is not so much a matter of what they can do with the peel-apart materials; it is more a question of what they choose to do. Having said that, of course, one has to remember that ISO 20,000 is only (only!) about three stops, or at most 4 stops, faster than the fastest conventional negative materials; indeed, if you accept the wilder claims of some of the marketing men, it is just one stop faster than the fastest pushed conventional materials. Given that a rollfilm lens normally gives away two stops to a 35mm camera lens, the difference is less impressive than it might otherwise be. Even so, this (like a number of Polaroid's other allegedly special-application materials) is a film which cries out for further exploration by the adventurous photographer. With this film, the famously sensitive LunaPro/LunaSix runs out of sensitivity at around 1 second at f/3.5... (RWH)

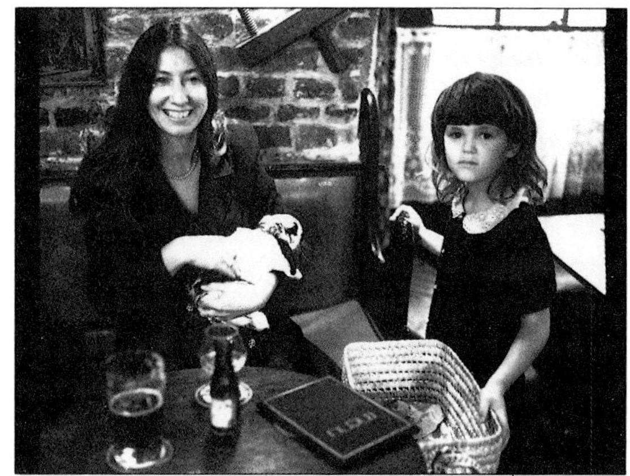

camera originals: this is in the tradition of the artist struggling to master his (or her) materials. Some photographers are however more cautious, and prefer to work with regular 'chrome originals. These are duped onto Polaroid materials using a copy stand or an enlarger or a Vivitar copier which duplicates 35mm slides onto Polaroid. That way, they get more than one bite at each cherry!

INTEGRAL MATERIALS

These are the cameras which whirr and spit the material at you, rather than waiting good-manneredly for you to pull it out. At the time of writing, there were three different formats on offer.

The original was introduced with the SX-70 camera and is reincarnated as the 600 series. The actual image size is 3x3 1/8in (77x79mm) on an overall sheet size of 3 1/2x4 1/4in (89x108mm). A slightly larger and newer version of the same thing is the Image series, with an image size of 2 7/8x3 1/2in (73x90mm) on an overall sheet size of 4in (102mm) square. The smallest version is the Vision, with its 2 1/8x2 7/8in (55x72mm) image size on a sheet size of 2 1/2x4 1/2in.

The image quality from all of them is jewel-like: it is reminiscent of nothing less than the miniature portraits so beloved of medieval monarchs and princes. When the picture comes out, all you can see is a dirty, smeary grey. Then, slowly but magically, the picture begins to materialise in front of your eyes. After about half a minute it is fully recognisable, but the colours will not reach their full richness for several minutes. Indeed, they seem to go on improving for as much as a quarter of an hour or half an hour, maybe even longer.

Unlike the peel-apart materials, which are mostly used in Polaroid backs on other manufacturers' cameras or on a few specialised cameras manufactured by Polaroid themselves, these materials are designed primarily for use in specific cameras. There are a few scientific camera backs, and special emulsions (including black and white) rated from ISO 150 to ISO 3200, but these are normally encountered only in research and development departments, testing labs and the like. Effectively, for normal use, there is only one colour emulsion available for each camera family at any one time.

The main applications of this series of cameras are for snapshots; as tools for recording work in progress, accident damage, or the like; for reference, to remind an artist what a person or a landscape looked like, or to show an interior decorator what sort of effect is wanted; and as selling tools – anywhere where 'a picture is worth a thousand words'. And again, there are

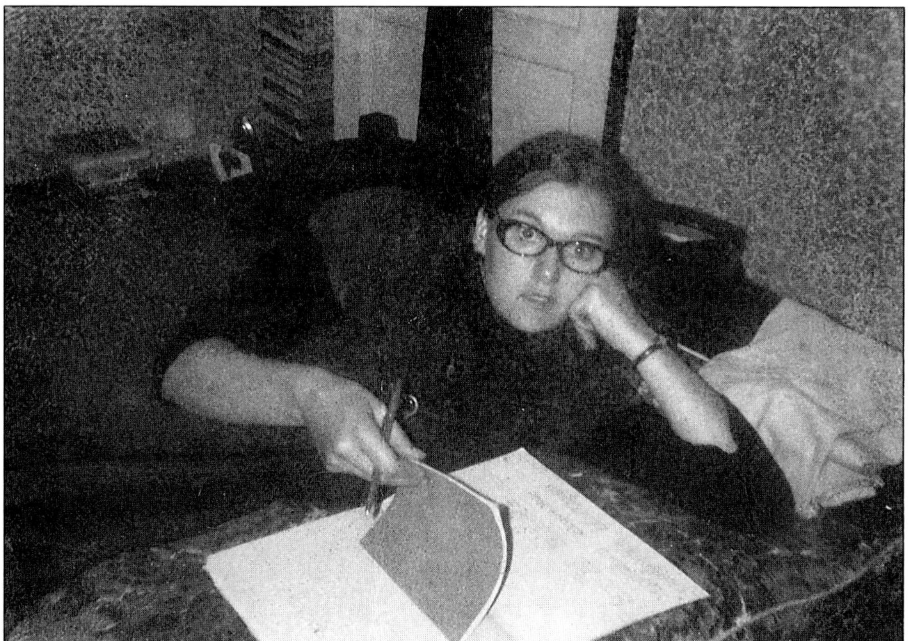

Polaroid Swinger picture

By great good fortune, we came across an old Swinger picture dating from about 1973 when we were working on this book. The young lady in the picture is Miss Linda Le Tissier, now Mrs Trezise: Roger took the picture. He and Linda have known each other since they were in their early 'teens, and this is about the earliest picture that he took of her which has survived. The image has faded and turned sepia, but it is still a very recognisable picture and (somewhat to our surprise) it is almost exactly the same size as the current Vision picture, albeit with a considerably narrower border: the Swinger (which used a peel-apart roll film) is 52x73mm on 64x83mm, while the Vision is 55x73mm on 64x111mm. The image in both cases is roughly 2x3in, or about the same as a contact print from an 8-on-120 box camera. (RWH)

those who use these cameras because of the special image qualities they offer.

For Snapshots

It has to be admitted that as snapshot cameras, Polaroids suffer from four drawbacks. They are expensive to run; the film is bulky to carry; each image is unique, so you cannot easily have extra prints made; and they are about as welcome to environmentalists as a whalers' convention held at a logging camp in the rain forest. In order to get a few pictures, you throw away a tremendous amount of packaging and waste, some of it pretty unpleasant, including the battery which is built into the self-timing film packs and the negatives on peel-apart films. To be fair, though, Polariod has been rated very highly as an 'ethical' company.

They are however enormous fun. You do not really need to worry about having extra pictures made, because you just shoot them at the time, and you can give the pictures to people on the spot: they make wonderful ice-breakers, especially in foreign countries.

If you are reading this book, the chances are that you are a serious photographer who probably disdains Polaroid cameras. Well, so did we – until we were given a Polaroid Vision. It is superb! The relatively tiny image is no real drawback in a snapshot, and in fact the small size almost adds to the appeal: it comes back to what we said a few paragraphs ago, about the jewel-like quality of the pictures. Also, the way that the Vision can stack up the prints in the back of the camera, allowing you to take several in quick succession, is much more convenient that the others where you have to remove each picture in turn and find somewhere to put it.

If you want a Polaroid camera for snapshots, we would have no hesitation

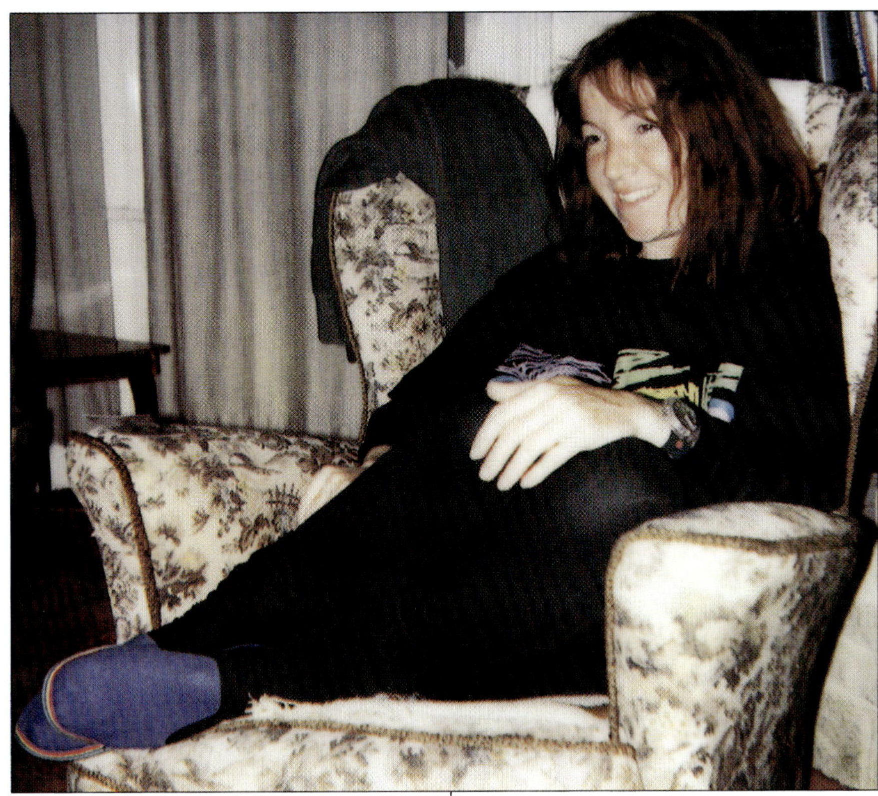

Fran

We all know people who hate having their picture taken, and indeed who seldom seem to come out very well in pictures. The problem is of course a self-reinforcing one. The great advantage of a Polaroid, though, is that you can keep it beside you while you are sitting around talking, and you can keep taking pictures until you get the one you want – assuming you do not mind the price of the film, that is. Roger shot four or five pictures of this charming lady, another Frances, before he finally got one that she liked; but because she could see even the bad ones as soon as they came out (and we have to admit that some of them were pretty bad), the whole thing turned into a sort of joke, and she relaxed. The more she relaxed, the better the pictures got. The picture still does not do justice to her, but at least she can see that she can look good in a photograph. In fact, a Polaroid back can be a useful tool in any portrait session, if you want to show your sitter how he or she looks and how different poses and lighting set-ups look. (RWH)

in recommending the Vision. Still more to the point, if you know someone who wants an easy-to-use snapshot camera, but who is more interested in the image than in photography, the Vision is the camera for them. We asked a friend's four-year-old son to try ours. He photographed his train set, and the very first picture was a success.

You can of course use the larger-format Polaroid integral-film cameras for snapshots, and many people do; but when we were working on this book, we had the choice of both the Vision and the Image (loaned by Polaroid), and we preferred the Vision despite the elegant (indeed classic) design of the Image and the greater versatility of the bigger camera.

Work in Progress

Suppose you are disassembling something very complex. You can make copious notes and sketches, the old-fashioned way – or you can take Polaroids. Or suppose you are supervising or reporting on building or construction work. You can write long reports – or you can take Polaroids. Or suppose you are reporting on accident damage. You can send for a photographer, and have pictures taken and prints made – or you can take Polaroids. Both the 600 series and the Image are highly sophisticated cameras for non-photographers who have to do this sort of thing. They can use them on the spot, and if the picture does not show what they want, they can take it

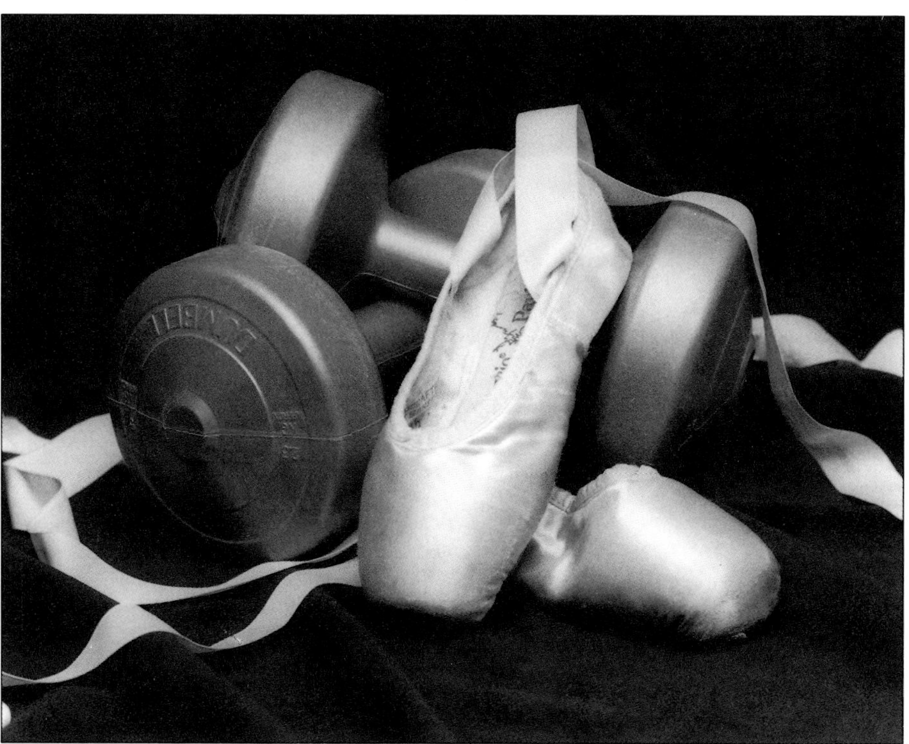

Still life, Polaroid Type 55 P/N
Positive/negative, pos/neg or p/n Polaroid films are another of those Polaroid technologies which are not quite as instant as they seem at first sight: the negative is sticky and damp, and must be washed and dried before it can be used (or, of course, you can wash it and print it wet). If it is to be permanent, it must also be cleared in a solution of sodium sulphite. And to cap it all, although you get both a print and a negative, the optimum exposure for both is only the same at about 75°F (24°C): otherwise, you have to expose for one or the other, and live with the second choice being either too light or too dark. As usual, many people use p/n films because of their unique image characteristics, and there is another use which most people have never discovered. Although the positive is of typically modest resolution, the negative has a very much higher resolution, and can be used for checking sharpness and depth of field. Put it on the light table and examine it with a strong magnifier, and you can see if you have got your sharpness and depth of field right. This is the only Polaroid film, apart from possibly Type 51, where this is feasible. (FES/RWH)

again. Actually, the Vision is pretty good for this sort of thing, too!

Even if you are a skilled photographer, there are still many times when a Polaroid is quicker, easier, and arguably better than a conventional photograph. This is especially true for the kind of assembly/disassembly sequences described above, where you would otherwise have to make a trip to the lab or develop and print the pictures yourself. As so often with Polaroid, you may curse the expense, but you certainly won't complain about the convenience.

Selling Tools

Antique dealers, classic car dealers, and even vintage camera dealers all use Polaroids to help them sell their goods. One man's 'mint' is another man's 'doggy', and how do you describe exactly what a little ivory carving, or an ornate Chinese urn, looks like? For these applications, the larger-image picture is most useful, as it shows the most detail and (because it is larger) also looks more impressive itself. The jewel-like quality of the image also looks more impressive than all but the very best mini-lab prints.

'Refs'

All kinds of people need references or 'refs', and (once again) the integral-film Polaroid cameras are ideal for shooting them. Even a good photographer can sometimes have difficulty in visualising exactly how a picture will look, but with a Polaroid the image is in his hand on the spot: he can look at it and see whether it says what he needs, whether it is about the sweep of a staircase or the shape of a hubcap or the style of shopfront that he wants a scene-builder to recreate.

Fine Art

If you will forgive us using the phrase yet again, the jewel-like quality of integral-film Polaroid cameras appeals to some fine art photographers, and others find that they can manipulate the image during the first few minutes after it has been taken, poking and rubbing it with a blunt-ended rod. Current films are much less amenable to this sort of treatment than the original SX-70 films, but they still respond to some extent.

35MM POLAROIDS

The last group of Polaroid films are once again designed to be used in other people's cameras – in this case, regular 35mm. You have a choice of two black and white transparency films, a blue-and-white transparency film intended principally for making slides of charts, tables, graphs and text, and two-colour

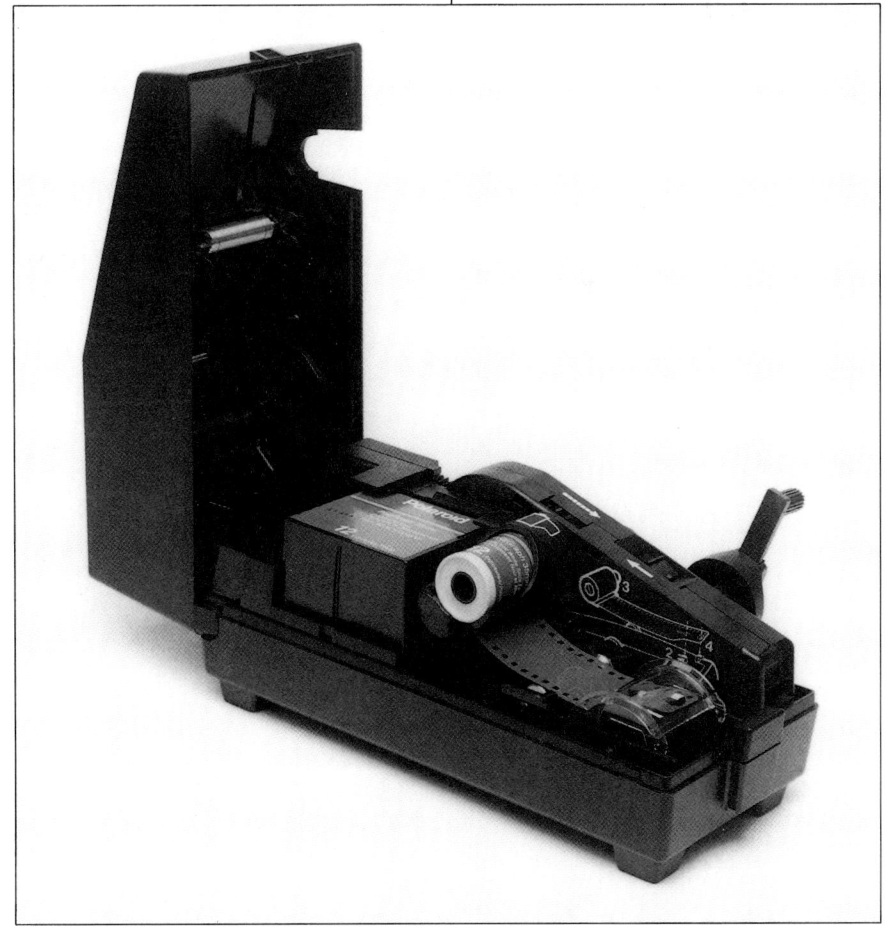

35mm processor

Two versions of the 35mm processor are available, the manual version shown here (which is overwhelmingly the most popular) and an electrically powered version. They are not particularly well-designed or easy to use, and the documentation is frankly poor, but when you get used to them, they are not too bad. Some people use them to produce slides quickly for making presentations and the like, but an increasing number of photographers use them for the unique results which the 35mm Polaroid emulsions can give. They are particularly popular in the fields of advertising and fashion, where 'faults' in the image (the grain of the black and white, or the fragility of the emulsion which is easily marked or scratched) are seen as an essential part of the whole look. If you want to use Polaroids for this sort of work, you would be well advised to shoot two or three or even more identical shots of each subject, in case one of them is marred in some way.

transparency films. It may seem odd that there is no instant negative film, but it is not illogical: a negative film would require a darkroom for printing, and the whole point of Polaroid 35mm films is that they are instant.

The films are inserted in the usual way, though there are some odd and rather irritating quirks: the films are not DX coded, and the ISO speed is not printed in the usual place on the cassette, so it does not line up with the little window that is becoming more and more common on modern cameras.

They are then exposed in the usual way; after that, you put them into a Polaroid processor, and anything from 60 seconds to four minutes later, you have ready-to-use transparencies. There are two processors, manual and electrical, and they are not really very well designed or documented: the first film we tried failed completely. The instructions are of the 'idiot' school: you are told what to do (in several languages), but you are never told why you are doing it or what is going on. Once you are used to them, however, the processors are easy enough to use.

The transparencies can be mounted and projected in the usual way: the easiest way to do this is to use Polaroid's own slide mounter, though the mounts themselves are rather flimsy and the slide mounter is not all that accurate. We preferred to stick with our regular GePe mounts. The transparencies can also be scanned for photomechanical reproduction, though they are not primarily designed for this. It is also worth knowing that the emulsions on all these films are very fragile indeed, so that many people who use them for their unique image qualities will habitually have duplicates made, as soon as possible, on conventional film.

Once again, these films appeal to a number of different users, but because the films are so different from each other we shall revert to discussing films, rather than users.

PolaChrome

There are two PolaChromes, one for normal use and one for high-contrast copying. Both share a somewhat unusual structure, and (at the time of writing) both were rated at a sluggish ISO 40.

In Chapter 2, we saw how a conventional or subtractive integral tripack works. PolaChrome films, however, are additive – rather like a television image. In fact, if you blow the transparency up enough, you will see that the image is made up of lines, rather like a TV screen. You have to magnify it a great deal, 20x or more, and even then you need to examine the projector screen from a few inches away; or, of course, you can use a powerful magnifier on the transparency. These are red, green and blue filter lines. Unlike the sandwich of cyan, magenta and yellow dyes (the subtractive primaries) in a normal slide, these are the additive primaries.

The lines are so incredibly fine that they are no more visible than grain in a conventional film, but the unusual structure means that the PolaChrome image looks rather dark, and it has a curious mirror-like sheen to it: if you reflect the light off it, you will see a rainbow of colours. It looks as if you would need to pump a great deal of light through it for projection, but this is not actually so. You would not necessarily want to mix it with other

Polachrome structure

If you enlarge a Polachrome sufficiently, you can see the ruled lines or reseau which typify an additive colour image. The image is called 'additive' because, like a TV screen, the image is made up by adding red, green and blue together. In effect, only the coloured light which is needed to create an image is allowed to pass through the transparency. Conventional films, which work by filtering out the light which is not needed (a subtle distinction, but an important one) are known as 'subtractive'. This is a sectional blow-up of the picture of the Royal Sea Bathing Hospital in Ramsgate, which appears on page 7. It was duplicated using Kodak SO-366 film in a Nikon F fitted with a 30mm f/4.5 E-Rokkor enlarging lens on a BPM bellows, with a total bellows extension of about 20cm or 8in.

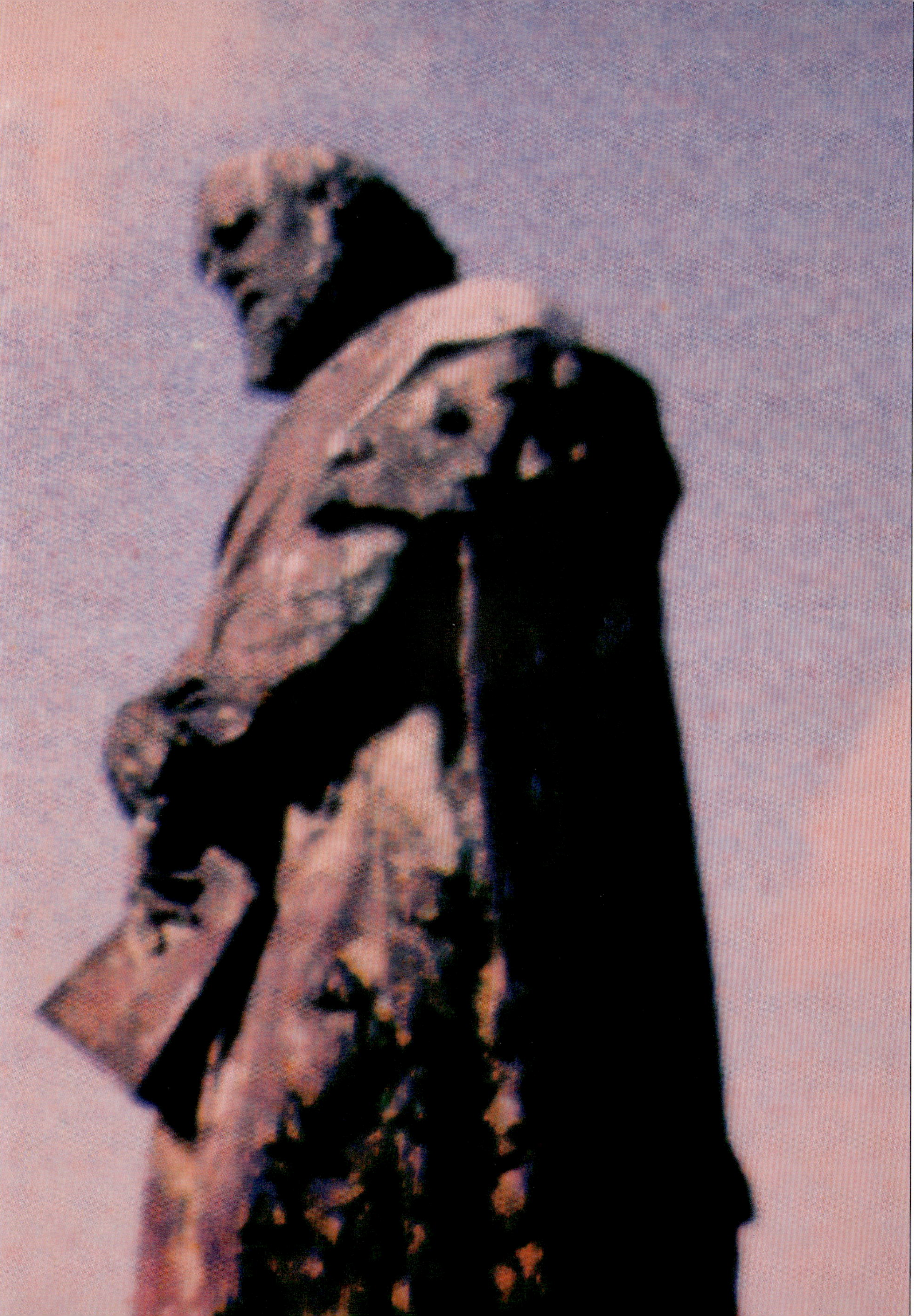

film-stocks, but it projects perfectly well.

The lines also mean that it is possible, if a printer scans the image at just the wrong angle and at just the wrong definition, that it will appear unsuitable for photomechanical reproduction; but a printer who knows his job will soon get round it by varying the angle or the line-count.

The common or garden PolaChrome can be used for almost any application where you would normally use any other slide film. It is obviously very useful for producing presentations in a hurry, or for modifying an existing presentation. You can photograph the new widget-manufacturing machine, show step by step how it manufactures widgets, and photograph a completed widget. You can then have the slides processed and mounted and ready for projection in less than a quarter of an hour.

The high-contrast PolaChrome is used to photograph artwork, charts and the like, and it gives bright, clear colours. It is also ideal for graphic imaging, using electronically generated text and charts; the Polaroid Palette system can do this for you. And once again, it is instant.

Both films have a very distinctive colour 'signature', and they are sometimes employed for general photography, especially fashion and the further reaches of advertising, where a new and different look is required.

PolaPan

Polapan (ISO 125) shares with Agfa's conventional-technology Dia-Direct the distinction of being a direct reversal black and white film for projection. It offers superb tonality in its own right, and it can be used for 'lifting' illustrations out of books or for general photography. One example we have seen was used by a scene-painter: he made a copy of a picture of a room interior in a book, then projected it onto the flats at the rear of the studio to show what he intended to paint. He used the projected image as a guideline for painting, too. Another use was a whole advertising shoot, done on PolaPan and a 1938 Leica with a pre-war lens. It gave results that would have been unobtainable in any other way. Some people make reversal prints from the material, again in the quest for a new 'look'.

PolaGraph

At ISO 400, PolaGraph is a high-contrast panchromatic black and white film designed for line copying of illustrations, which it does very well and with astonishingly fine grain; but (once again) some people use it for general photography. Like every other Polaroid 35mm film, the effect is unique to Polaroid.

PolaBlue

Although this is a deadly slow film, at ISO 8, it is doubly unique: there is nothing else of its kind, quite apart from the fact that it has its own Polaroid look. Used to photograph black-on-white text or graphics, it renders them as white-on-blue: a little monotonous, perhaps, but very easy on the eye, especially when you have to read a lot of text slides. And inevitably, some people use it for general photography...

Polapan portrait

There is something remarkably vintage about the effects obtainable with Polapan: quite large grain, a fairly high degree of contrast, and an overall 1930s sort of tonality. This makes it ideal for fashion photography, especially for the Armani-style fashions which are loosely based on those of the 1930s, or the timeless image of Jaeger. But curiously, although the contrast is high, the tonal range is longer than you might expect – again, a part of the 1930s image. We had never tried it before we wrote this book; but now, it has become a standard tool in our repertory, to be used when it is needed. The biggest single catch is that the emulsion is very soft indeed, so we habitually duplicate it onto colour slide film. Clearly, it is not the fact that it is instant which is the attraction: it is the results we can get from it. (FES)

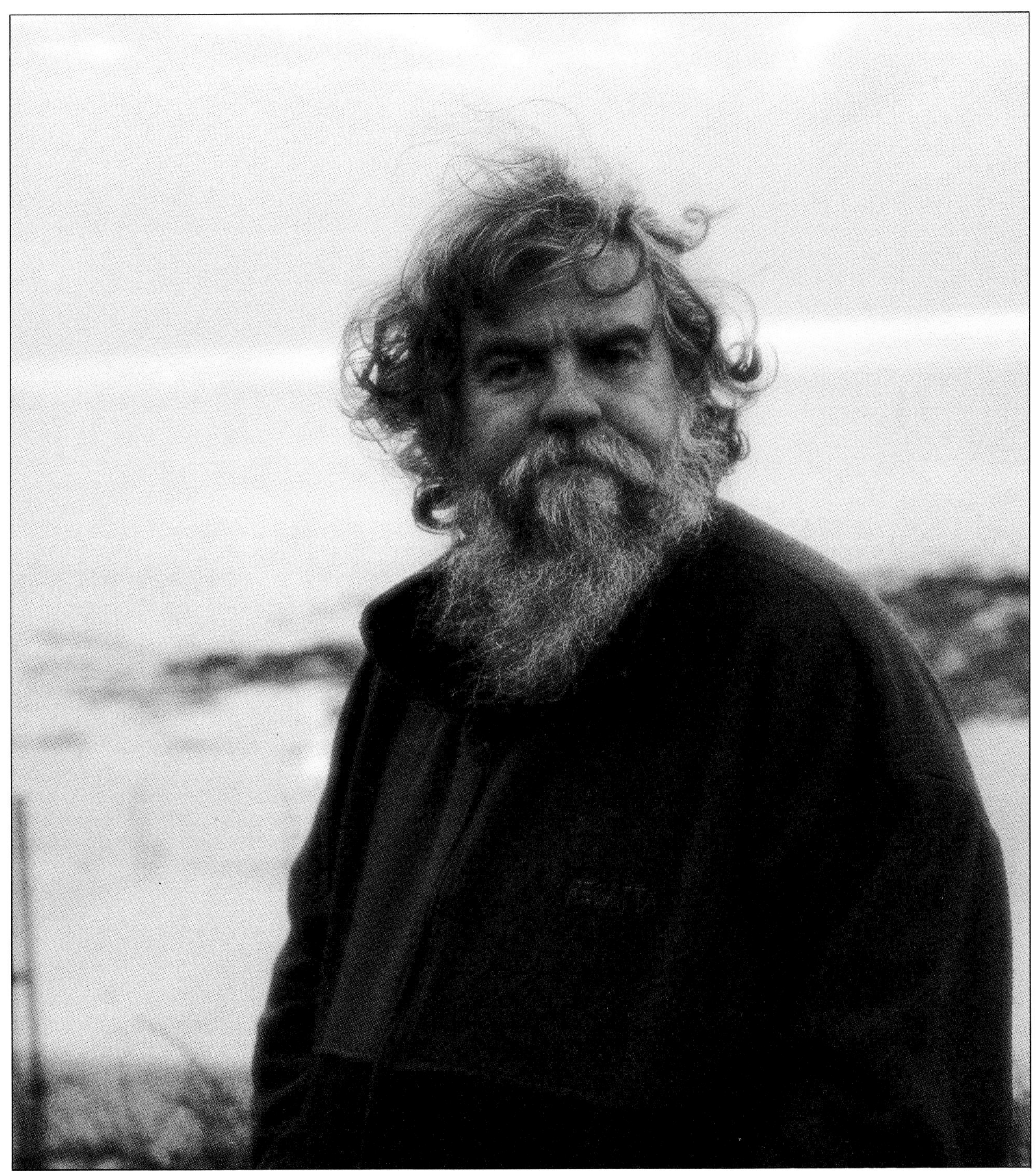

ENVOI

Choosing and using film is very much like life in general. There are all sorts of rules, of which some are made to be broken and others are best followed. Break the right rules, and you grow as a photographer; break the wrong rules, and you will wish you hadn't.

Our aim in this book has been very straightforward: to tell you what the rules are, and which ones can profitably be broken. The rewards, though, are out of all proportion to the penalties. Even if you break the wrong rules, the worst you will usually end up with is a few bad exposures (or maybe a lot). You will be a little out of pocket, but film is not so expensive that you cannot afford to make the occasional mistake.

Get everything right, on the other hand, and you feel like the master of the universe. The raw materials are available to anyone who can afford a camera and some film, and who can photograph the world around him (or of course her). Out of those raw materials, you can make something or nothing. This is a book about making something. We hope we have helped you to do this, and that you will continue to do it in the future.

Boat, Minnis Bay

Polaroid's PolaBlue is designed for making text slides for audio-visual presentations. It is a high-contrast material which creates white-on-blue images from black and white originals, and it is deadly slow with a recommended EI of 8. It says clearly in the instruction sheet that it is not intended for normal, everyday photography. Who, therefore, could resist trying it for precisely that? This is from the first roll Frances shot: we found that the results reminded us of those from the early days of photography. The high contrast means burnt-out highlights, or blocked shadows, or both, and with the ultra-wide lens Frances was using (a Sigma 14mm), $\cos^4$ vignetting meant that the edges of the image disappeared altogether. The white-on-blue rendition suits the sea scene, and destroys our expectations of what constitutes a 'positive' and what constitutes a 'negative'. In the early days of photography, too, the convention of black-on-white was by no means settled: all kinds of other colours were tried, either as a result of technical necessity, or in the interests of aesthetics. The subject is a modern lightweight catamaran, but it looks at first glance more like an ancient picture of a fishing-boat. If you decide to experiment with this ISO 8 film, a one-stop bracket either side of the metered exposure will normally mean that you get at least one picture with a more-or-less correct exposure; and 'more-or-less correct' was the rule in much of the nineteenth century. The exposure was 1/60 at f/5.6 or f/4, hand-held in bright sunlight; the camera was a Nikon F.

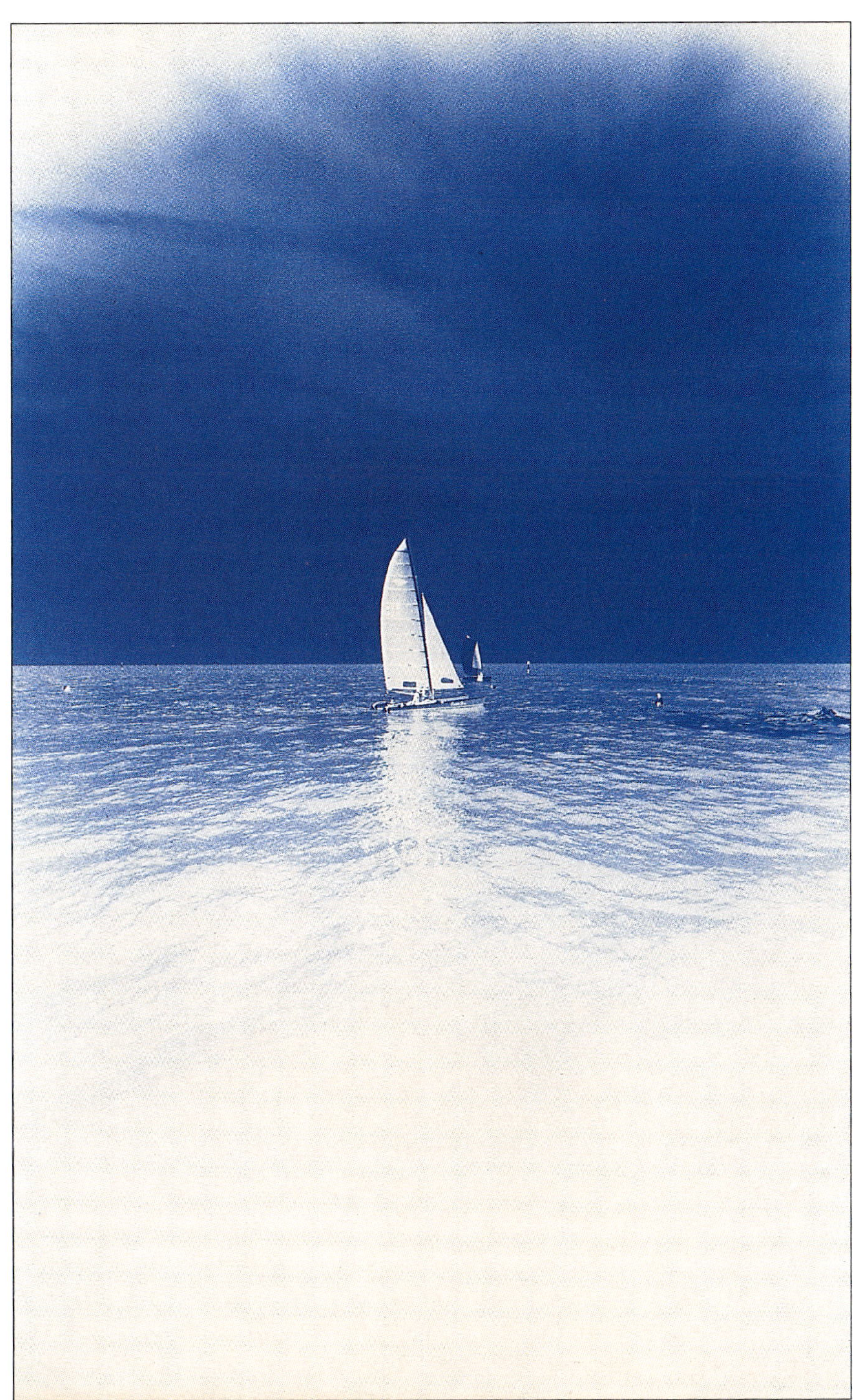

INDEX

Page numbers in *italic* refer to illustrations